EDMUND BURKE AND IRELAND

EDMUND BURKE

AND

IRELAND

Thomas H. D. Mahoney

HARVARD UNIVERSITY PRESS

Cambridge, Massachusetts

1 9 6 0

The publication of this book has been aided by a grant from the Ford Foundation

TO

MY WIFE, PHYLLIS NORTON MAHONEY

whose encouragement and sacrifices made this book possible

Preface

Edmund Burke's connection with the affairs of Ireland is a subject which has failed to receive the attention it merits. Burke's biographers and the legion of those who have assessed his contribution to political thought agree upon the important role his native land and its affairs played in his life. Yet one will search in vain for a satisfactory and comprehensive study of this part of his career.

Interestingly enough at least two very able men have sensed the importance of Ireland to Burke and called attention to it without success. In Germany the historian Heinrich von Sybel published a perceptive sketch, "Edmund Burke und Irland," *Kleine historischen Schriften* (Marburg, 1869), I, 466–510; while in England Matthew Arnold edited a brief collection of previously published material under the title of *Letters, Speeches, and Tracts on Irish Affairs by Edmund Burke* (London, 1881). Many years later the Irish Nationalist William O'Brien in his *Edmund Burke As an Irishman* (2 ed., Dublin, 1926) wrote with much emotion a book which contained far too many errors of omission and commission to fill the need.

Irish problems attracted Burke's attention as early as his student days and continued to hold his interest to his death. Both the first political work of his public career and the last letter written by him and published during his lifetime were on the subject of Ireland.

How then can the long neglect of the role played by Ireland in Burke's life be explained? To answer this involves a number of considerations.

In the first place, despite the fact that no other phase of his career covered such a long period, Burke himself did not consider his labors for the amelioration of his native land his chief claim to fame. On various occasions, he stated that his efforts on behalf of the "undone millions" of India constituted his most important work. More spectacular than his devotion to the cause of Ireland were his defense of English liberties in America and his vehement and unrelenting opposition to the principles of the French Revolution. These matters, along with India, have captured the attention of many students of Burke. By contrast, his more labyrinthine connection with Irish matters has been minimized, neglected, or incompetently investigated.

Perhaps the reason for this failure to grasp the significance of Ireland in Burke's career may be found in Burke's own basic approach to Irish problems which provides a second answer to the question under consideration. It was his firm and unshaken belief that the problems of Ireland required a very cautious approach because their roots lay so deep in the past. The grievances under which Ireland labored had existed for many years. He felt, therefore, that they required a leisurely correction rather than an abrupt one. Such a manner of redress lent itself better to the eradication of prejudice, which might only be further strengthened by precipitate action. Furthermore, this method of proceeding by degrees was calculated, in his opinion, to prevent those who had been long repressed from becoming intoxicated with power once the restrictions binding them had been removed. Burke was fond of saying that nothing has ruined great causes as much as that people have treated the commencement as if it were the conclusion. Consequently, he approached the problems of Ireland gradually, albeit determinedly, through the years.

Thirdly, the incompleteness of one of Burke's most famous Irish pieces, the *Tract*, together with the lack of polish of some of his other writings on Ireland has led to an erroneous feeling in some quarters that Burke did not have the same interest in Ireland which several other subjects inspired in him.

Fourthly, there is the fact that much of what Burke did on Ireland's behalf included efforts that "were not visible." This was inevitable because of his Irish background and connections which combined to make his position on Irish affairs "rather singular, and undoubtedly embarrassing."

Fifthly, both Burke's published and unpublished correspondence are replete with outbursts of disgust over Ireland together with disclaimers of any knowledge of or interest in what was transpiring there. It seems reasonable to assume that these indignant flurries must have thrown more than a few off the track of Burke and Ireland. Actually, the persistency of these vehement remarks indicating how annoyed Burke could get with Ireland, the Irish character, and the whole Irish mess provides this book with one of its major themes — the question of why Burke's disgust and irritation with Ireland never interfered very long or very seriously with his ready concern for the country. This was because his concern for Ireland had deeper roots in his personality than could be accounted for by political theory, practical politics, or indeed any merely rational or practical causes. Like every other responsible and intelligent Irishman with sufficient heart from his day to this, Burke carried Ireland around with him as his personal "old man of the sea," often, certainly, to the detriment of his own interests.

Sixthly, not only has the subject of Burke and the affairs of Ireland been neglected but Burke himself has scarcely received the attention his importance dictates. (The impressive volume of Burke studies published during the past decade bids fair to remedy this long neglect of Burke.) There are numerous reasons to account for this failure. Among them is the fact that much of the recent scholarship on the eighteenth century has been predominantly literary, and, it must be remembered, Burke was not basically a literary man. Although he was a man of letters, he was infinitely more: "He was an orator, a pamphleteer, a political philosopher, an aesthetician, a historian, and a journalist — if we go no farther." The critical study of such a man has been well likened to the classic feat of wrestling with the Hydra.*

Finally, there is the well known fate of Burke's papers which kept them from scholars with very few exceptions for almost a century and a half. Of all the reasons which have precluded serious scholars from a study of the subject of Burke and Ireland, this is perhaps the most cogent. Now, however, this obstacle has been happily removed thanks to the availability of the papers.

* For a fuller account from which this paragraph has been drawn, see the introduction to Thomas W. Copeland, *Our Eminent Friend Edmund Burke* (New Haven, 1949).

PREFACE

The idea of this book grew out of my doctoral dissertation and was brought to fruition by five visits to England and one to Ireland to work in the various collections which have made the volume possible. Approximately half of the material herein presented was delivered as the Lowell Lectures in Boston during January and February 1957. My sincere thanks go to Mr. Ralph Lowell, Trustee, and Dr. Richard Gummere, Curator, of the Lowell Institute for the great privilege of delivering these lectures.

The list of those to whom I am indebted is so great that adequate acknowledgment is difficult. Dean John E. Burchard of the School of Humanities and Social Sciences, M.I.T., and Professor Howard R. Bartlett, Chairman of the Department of Humanities, provided indispensable encouragement and assistance. Dr. Thomas W. Copeland of the University of Massachusetts was unfailingly generous with both his time and advice as was Dr. John V. Kelleher of Harvard.

I am likewise indebted to the following in ways each knows best: Dr. Carl B. Cone, University of Kentucky; Drs. Elmer L. Kayser and Wood Gray, The George Washington University; Dr. William T. Laprade, Duke University; Dr. George H. Guttridge, University of California, Berkeley; and Dr. R. James Hayes, Director of the National Library of Ireland; Mr. Robert E. Burns, University of Notre Dame; Rev. Leonard Mahoney, S.J., Boston College; Mr. J. P. Lamb, formerly City Librarian, Sheffield; and Mrs. William Nesbitt, London. My debt extends also to the late Canon Robert H. Murray, Grove House, Goring-on-Thames, and Professor Dixon Wecter, University of California at Los Angeles. A special expression of gratitude must be given to Miss Ann Orlov who capably saw the book through the final stage of editing and publication.

I should like also to express my appreciation generally for the cooperation I have received from the staffs of the M.I.T. Libraries; the Widener, Houghton, and Baker Libraries of Harvard; the Boston Athenaeum; the Boston Public Library; the Boston College Library; the Massachusetts Historical Society; the New England Deposit Library; the Yale University Library; the New York Public Library; the New York Historical Society; the Pierpont Morgan Library, New York; the Princeton University Library; the

Library of Congress; the Harper Library, University of Chicago; the William L. Clements Library, University of Michigan; the Henry E. Huntington Library and Art Gallery, San Marino, California; the Sheffield City Library; the Bodleian Library, Oxford; the British Museum; the National Maritime Museum, Greenwich; the National Library of Ireland; and the Trinity College Library, Dublin.

For access to and permission to quote from unpublished source material, I am especially grateful to the late Earl Fitzwilliam and his Managers of the Wentworth Woodhouse Estates Co.; the present Earl Fitzwilliam; Mr. P. I. King, Archivist of the Northamptonshire Record Office; Mr. J. H. Hodson, Keeper of the Manuscripts, the University of Nottingham; the Huntington Library; the Morgan Library; and the Harvard, Yale, and Princeton Libraries. My thanks go also to Professor and Mrs. Charles K. Warner, Middlebury College, Vermont, for the use of the Burke letters in their possession.

The arduous task of typing the manuscript was largely done by the secretarial staff of the Department of Humanities, Massachusetts Institute of Technology, especially Mrs. Ruth DuBois, Mrs. Ruth Sullivan, and Mrs. C. Edward Walter. The index was prepared by Mr. Alfred P. Stiernotte.

Finally, a portion of Chapter Two appeared in the *Canadian Historical Review*, XXXVII (June 1956). These passages are reprinted by permission of the *Canadian Historical Review*.

Massachusetts Institute of Technology THOMAS H. D. MAHONEY.
May 1959

CONTENTS

LIST OF ILLUSTRATIONS

Falsely supposed to represent Jesuit-Pad' driven back to his native Potatoes see Romish Common-Wealth   Published August 23d 1782

Burke is here caricatured as a Jesuit. He is eating a potato (an allusion to his Irish birth) and he is seated at a table on which there is a cooking vessel (labeled "Relick No. 1 used by St. Peter") and a crucifix mounted on a small barrel labeled "Whiskey." The "Relick" and the crucifix refer to his supposed Roman Catholicism, while the whiskey is another asperion on his birthplace. Under the table three imps are dancing joyously.

London. Published November 15, 1790 by William Holland, 50 Oxford Street

Burke, caricatured as Don Quixote, emerges from his publisher's shop. He is mounted on a donkey wearing the papal crown. An open copy of his *Reflections* is near the saddle. Burke wears a Jesuit's biretta marked with a skull and crossbones, on top of which is perched a dove of peace. Around his neck is a pendant bearing a bust of Marie Antoinette. He carries a lance in one hand and a shield in the other. The shield is labeled "Shield of Aristocracy and Despotism." The quarters depict practices attributed to the Old Regime. One is a dungeon (probably the Bastille); the second shows two men being burned at the stake; the third a bearded wretch hopelessly shackled; and, finally, a man being broken on a wheel.

The text, which was carefully designed to turn Burke's own words on himself, reads as follows: "It is wonderfully true, though it may seem paradoxical but in general, those who are habitually employed in finding and displaying faults, are unqualified for the work of reformation, because their minds are not only unfurnished with patterns of the fair and good but by habit they come to take no delight in the contemplation of these things. By hating vices too much, they come to love men too little. It is therefore not wonderful that they should be indisposed and unable to serve them. From hence arises the complexional disposition of some guides to pull every thing in pieces. Burke on the French Rev. p. 250."

This is a crude caricature of Burke, who was lampooned along with the other leading members of Pitt's opposition following the fall of the Fox-North coalition. No attempt was made to capture a likeness of Burke but he is recognizable by the label, by the potatoes, and by the dinner bell. This cartoon was published ca. 1784, by which time Burke had acquired a reputation for boring the House of Commons by his long speeches.

These illustrations are all from the Sir Robert Peel Collection, Volume XII, the Pierpont Morgan Library, New York, and are reproduced with the gracious permission of Frederick B. Adams, Jr., Director.

EDMUND BURKE AND IRELAND

CHAPTER I

Early Days in Ireland and England

Edmund Burke was born the son of Richard Burke, an attorney, and his wife, Mary Nagle, on 12 January 1729 in his father's house at Arran Quay, Dublin.[1] He was the second of the fifteen children of this union and one of the few who survived infancy, the others being his eldest brother, Garrett, who followed in the footsteps of his father by becoming an attorney but who died unmarried in 1765, a younger brother named Richard who also died unmarried in 1794, and a sister Juliana, later Mrs. Patrick French, whom Burke also survived.

From his father Burke inherited a mind capable of mastering intricate details — what might be called a legal mind. But Richard Burke, Sr., was also responsible for the hot temper which Edmund so frequently revealed during his public career [2] and which was often the despair of his friends. He later said of his father that he practiced law only in the superior courts and

was for many years not only in the first *rank*, but the very first *man* of his profession in point of practice and credit — until, by giving way to a retired and splenetic humour, he did in a manner voluntarily contract his practice; and yet, after some heavy losses by the banks, and living creditably for nearly forty years (one time pretty expensively), laying out something on Dick's establishment and on my education in the Temple (a thousand pounds or thereabouts for me), he died worth very near six thousand pounds.[3]

From his mother, whom he loved deeply, Burke inherited the finer traits of his character, "the imagination, the elevation of mind and heart, the tenderness for suffering, the capacity for feeling and imparting noble emotions." [4] This lady, whom he reverenced so greatly, was his first teacher, and the lessons he learned from her he did not forget.

Burke was the child of a mixed marriage. His father was a member of the Established Anglican Church, whereas his mother was a Roman Catholic. According to the custom which then prevailed in such cases, the sons were brought up in the religion of the father while the daughters followed that of their mother. Hence, Edmund and his brothers became members of the Established Church and their sister, Juliana became a Catholic. All remained true to their particular religion throughout their lives. In addition to the fact that both his mother and sister were Catholics, Burke had a large number of Catholic relatives among his mother's people, the Nagles of Ballyduff.

Edmund was a delicate child with weak lungs and it became necessary for him to get away from the unhealthy climate of Dublin. When he was six years old, he was sent to his mother's relatives in Ballyduff near Castletown-Roche, County Cork, where he spent some five years of his childhood, years which were as happy as any in the life and which indelibly impressed upon him the inequity of the laws under which the Irish Catholics were forced to live. But it is likely that at this early age the boy was still more impressed by a magnificent region, so lovely that it was the inspiration of Edmund Spenser, who settling there at the expense of the native Irish wrote his *Faërie Queene*. Interestingly enough, Spenser's son, Sylvanus, married a great-aunt of Burke's mother, but Edmund Burke was named after his uncle Edmund Nagle and not the poet.

While in Ballyduff, Burke's formal schooling commenced. His first teacher was an elderly female possessed of a sour disposition in general and a hatred of boys in particular. He soon transferred to a hedge-school conducted in the ruined castle of Monanimy by an old Catholic hedge-master named O'Halloran. Following these idyllic years in Ballyduff, Burke's father brought him home but after a year he and his brothers were sent to a boarding school in Ballitore, County Kildare, run by the kindly Yorkshire Quaker, Abraham Shackleton. These boarding school years like those in Ballyduff were wonderful for young Burke. He now formed a lasting friendship with Shackleton's son, Richard, with whom he afterwards carried on a correspondence remarkable for breadth and toleration.

Mrs. Mary Leadbeater, Abraham Shackleton's grand-daughter, tells us that her grandfather used "to delight in detailing instances of Burke's singular aptitude, and how soon he attained a superior station amongst his schoolfellows, many of whom he readily assisted in their exercises." She also hands on an incident revealing that the generous nature which marked Burke's public and private life developed early: "Burke's heart was tender, too, and my father [Richard Shackleton] was wont to relate a circumstance which proved that in boyhood, as well as in riper years, he felt an invincible hatred to oppression. A poor man having been compelled to pull down his cabin, because the surveyor of roads declared it stood too near the highway, Burke, who saw the reluctant owner perform his melancholy task, observed with great indignation, that if he were in authority such tyranny should never be exercised with impunity over the defenceless; and he urged his schoolfellows to join in rebuilding the cottage. My grandfather, however, would not permit this to be done." [5]

On 14 April 1744, at the age of fifteen, Edmund Burke entered Trinity College, Dublin. At first, he lived at home much to the disgust of his friends who were fond of complaining that he was not allowed out evenings and that he was the victim of his father's violent temper.[6] However, winning a competitive scholarship in June 1746 which required him to reside within the college and provided quarters for him, Burke was enabled at last to get away from the stern parental gaze, although he seems to have done some work while at Trinity in his father's law office from time to time.[7]

A letter to Richard Shackleton shows Burke's spasmodic study habits at this time.

First I was greatly taken with natural Philosophy; which while I should have given my mind to logic, employed me incessantly. This I call my *furor mathematicus*. But this worked off, as soon as I began to read it in the College; as men, by repletion, cast off their stomachs all they have eaten. Then I turned back to logic and metaphysics. Here I remained a good while, and with much pleasure, and this way my *furor logicus*; a disease very common in the days of ignorance, and very uncommon in these enlightened times. Next succeeded the *furor historicus*, which also

3

had its day, but is now no more; being entirely absorbed in the *furor poeticus*, which (as skilful physicians assure me) is as differently cured as a disease very nearly akin to it, namely, the itch.[8]

Another letter to Shackleton [9] reveals both Burke's great love for his mother and an early interest in Ireland. After having described the anguish he had suffered when his mother had become so ill that her life hung in the balance for several days, he said that it was sometime after the crisis had been passed before he could bring himself to do anything. Eventually, he began to spend three hours a day in the public library, "the best way of killing thought." Besides this general reading, he was "deep in metaphysics" and also reading history in order "to get a little into the accounts of this, our poor country."

A study of his career at Trinity reveals the development in Burke of some important ideas. The political ones were destined largely to undergo transformation after he became an Englishman, but the religious ones were merely strengthened with the passage of time.

In debates at college and in his writings Burke supported an Irish tax on English absentees; objected to the poor quality of the English plays which fashionable Dublin was applauding; urged that the Irish encourage their own art and literature, as well as local products, and abhorred the mistreatment of the wretched agrarian poor. His strong religious convictions did not at this time or later lessen his love of tolerance which was to make him a friend to many oppressed people and causes. However, Burke displayed in these early years a pronounced antipathy toward both the irreligious and fanatics whose excesses led to bigotry.

Together with a group of his fellow students, Burke founded the Debating Club from which the Trinity College Historical Society descended.

The numerous speeches which membership in the "Club" enabled him to make were notable for their content rather than for their delivery. Important in the light of the future was the manifestation of Burke's preference for "The *via media* . . . rather than the theoretically perfect." His tendency to be censorious of his fellow members introduces the one unpleasant note which we find from reading of his experiences in the "Club." One of his fellow members told him to his face that he was "damned absolute," and, on another occasion, he was accused of scurrility.[10]

Just before he took his degree, Burke founded a short-lived periodical called *The Reformer* which he produced almost single-handedly. It ran through thirteen issues from January to April 1748, and "excited no interest." [11] While it may have "excited no interest," it was a pretty good piece of work for a student. He tended to emphasize the theatre and literature in this periodical because of his strong conviction of their importance in influencing public taste and morality, but he by no means neglected other subjects. For example, the issue of 18 February 1748 contains an appeal to the nobility and gentry as well as to other men of spirit to reside in Ireland and to give their encouragement to native manufacturers as well as native art and literature.

Burke's early feelings of Irish nationalism declined in later years as he grew enamoured of the British Constitution and Empire, but further illustration of his nationalistic feelings may be gleaned from a speech on Absenteeism which he delivered in the Debating Club a few months earlier on 28 May 1747. Bringing in a mock bill in the Irish parliament to tax the absentees ten per cent of their estates, he said that it was the only means of preserving "some part of the little money in the Kingdome, which appropriated to the Dublin Society might prove of great advantage to it." He also employed "many other arguments" in defense of his position. His opponent in this debate, William Dennis, thought that Burke's bill was a most arbitrary one and that the money that went from Ireland to England could not rightly be said to go away from the country since "the blood which runs from the extream parts of the body to the heart can not be said to be lost to them, because it refunds it much improved" and further that such a tax would be a hindrance to "improvement by travel." [12]

The seventh number of *The Reformer*, 10 March 1748, is devoted to a description of the miserable condition of life among the poor of Ireland and reveals a side of Burke which remained steadfast to the end. He was always to hate the conditions which made such poverty possible and his sympathetic nature led him to do everything in his power to alleviate such conditions by ending both the external and internal misrule of his native land.

5

Another side of Burke's nature, his deep religious feeling, is revealed by the eleventh number of this series, 7 April 1748. He condemned those who while they "allow of morality, cry down revealed religion" and in practice neglect both. The two chief enemies of religion were singled out as infidelity and blind zeal because the former was responsible for the free thinkers and the latter for "our sectaries." [13]

Letters to Richard Shackleton, written during Burke's first year as an undergraduate, foreshadow this deep spiritual sense which was to characterize Burke throughout his life. They give remarkable evidence of the kind of a person Burke was at this youthful stage of his development and they presage his enduring toleration. In one of them, dated 15 October 1744, he declares that he would not exclude from salvation those whose beliefs differed from his own but went on to lament the proliferation of religious sects and said that men ought not to break the unity of the church for any "small matter." [14]

Burke took his A.B. degree in February 1748 but continued to live at Trinity for a time. The earlier opinion that his record there was singularly undistinguished was first challenged by the nineteenth century Whig historian, Lecky who has nothing but praise for his intellectual activity as an undergraduate [15] and then more effectively by Arthur Samuels, although the original interpretation still finds acceptance.[16] Samuels cites the college records and Burke's own letters to demonstrate that he had a distinguished academic record. In addition to earlier officially recognized attainments in Greek, he won a classical scholarship in 1746 which "was then and is now the highest honor that can be obtained in the undergraduate course." [17] Furthermore, Samuels calls attention to Burke's *The Philosophical Inquiry into the origins of our Ideas on the Sublime and Beautiful*, which he wrote as an undergraduate and later polished and refined before publication some years later, and asks "What again would be thought at the present day of the distinction of a boy of nineteen years of age who could produce at Oxford, Cambridge, Dublin or any other university such a work?" [18]

For many years it was the accepted practice among Burke's biographers [19] to claim that he had written a series of pamphlets in 1748–1749 attacking Dr. Charles Lucas, a Dublin apothecary and politician of the "patriot" species of that day in Ireland, who was then a candidate for the Irish Commons from the City of Dublin in a by-election. Since the middle of the last century, however, most students reject this view and even ascribe to Burke a number of pamphlets and several articles which strongly defended Lucas.[20] It is certain at least that the style of these pamphlets bears a resemblance to Burke's. Yet doubt is cast on this claim by a letter which Burke wrote to Charles O'Hara under date of 3 July 1761, in which he remarks: [21]

I own I am somewhat out of humour with patriotism; and can think but meanly of such Publick spirit, as like the fanatical spirit, banishes common sense; I do not understand that spirit, which could raise such hackneyed pretences, and such contemptible Talents as those of Dr. Lucas to so great consideration, not only among the mob, but, as I hear on all hands, among very many of rank and figure. If any of them do it through Policy one may predict witht. rashness, that he will give them room to repent it. I do not know how it is, but I feel myself hurt at this, and the rather as I shall be obliged from decency and other considerations to hold my Tongue. . . . As to the figure he makes in the medical way I do not at all wonder at it; That Profession is the proper sphere of Pretenders; and it is not odd that people should be imposed upon in what they [do] not understand and indeed cannot, when they cannot distinguish Nonesense and absurdity in a common advertisement.

Another letter to O'Hara, one week later,[22] found Burke again referring to Lucas in unflattering terms:

However, I find myself getting forward in strength and spirits; for I ride some miles every day which does me as much service as if I had taken Dr. Hill's five medicines, or Dr. Lucas' one. If the latter Mountebank shd. now descend from his stage, it would be of great service to his Character, which, if he returns to the usual unhealthy soundness of his intellects, will infallibly come to be known by the dullest of his admirers; and thus his medical quackery will cover the Blunders of his political.

These letters which have only recently come to light seem to strengthen the old theory that Burke was anti-Lucas, even if he was not the author of the pamphlets against him.[23]

Whatever his role in the Lucas case, Burke left Ireland shortly afterwards. The reason for his departure was that his father now insisted that his son begin the legal studies which he had agreed to pursue. On 23 April 1747, almost a year before he took his degree at Trinity, Burke's name had been enrolled in London's Middle Temple. At that time, seven years had to elapse between a law student's admission to the Inns of Court and his call to the bar. The study of the law was most unsystematic, and the students learned by frequenting the courts. Burke embarked upon his legal studies by leaving Dublin for London early in 1750 at the age of twenty-one.

Burke took an almost instant liking to London [24] but he was never happy in his legal studies and does not appear to have pursued them with any great industry. In the first few years of his stay in London, he devoted his vacations to visiting other parts of England and thus came to know a great deal about the country. In 1751 he took his M.A. degree at Trinity, although it is likely that he did not go over in person on this occasion to revisit his native land. Writing to Shackleton in the spring of that year, he observed that "my health is tolerable, thank God; my studies too in the same degree, and my situation not disagreeable." [25]

During his first year in London, he made three enduring friendships. The first was with William Burke who had attended Oxford. Whether the Burkes were related is uncertain, but forever afterwards Edmund referred to Will as his "kinsman." [26] They were mutually attracted at their first meeting and became constant friends and traveling companions. Their trips took them about England and may even have brought them to France and their time, whether traveling or otherwise, was largely devoted to reading and writing. So close was their friendship that, even after Edmund married, he and Will shared a common purse to which Edmund's brother, Richard apparently contributed also. And when Edmund acquired Gregories, his home at Beaconsfield, it was a cooperative undertaking, and Will had a home for the rest of his life whenever he was in England.

The other friends Burke made at this time were Dr. Christopher Nugent, an Irish Catholic physician practising in Bath, and his daughter, Jane whom Burke later married. Burke's health was then none too robust and, thus, he became a patient of Nugent's, whose services appear to have been in the nature of a contribution to his

8

new-found friend, since Burke's fortunes were at a rather low ebb at this time. The good doctor not only helped Burke regain his health but even housed him during his visits to Bath.[27]

The possibility exists that Burke's refusal to be called to the bar may have been due to his love for Jane Nugent since the only formality then required of an aspirant to the legal profession was that, when he was due to be called, he had to take an oath in denunciation of the pope. To have done so would have been an affront to both Jane and her father who were Catholics.[28] While there well may be some truth to this, it is a fact that Burke had only consented to study law in the first place to please his irascible father and had never derived any pleasure from it. The result of his refusal to be called was that his father now cut off his allowance, and Burke was faced with the necessity of earning his own livelihood.

He managed to secure occasional work as a secretary to persons in politics but found time to continue with his writing, an occupation with which he was becoming enamored. In 1756 he published anonymously his first book, *A Vindication of Natural Society*, which was an attack upon the rationalistic approach of Bolingbroke to religion. To Burke it was self-evident that religion required something more than reason alone for its foundation. Faith, too, was indispensable, for without it the social order would be unable to withstand the attacks of the rationalists and would be in danger of destruction. The *Vindication*, although an attack on Bolingbroke's theory of natural religion, was written in a perfect imitation of Bolingbroke's style, a fact which caused many, including some leading critics of the day, to think that it was in reality a posthumous work of the famous Tory. By resorting to the weapon of irony Burke showed that the same arguments which Bolingbroke had employed in favor of natural as opposed to revealed religion could be used in behalf of natural as opposed to artificial society. Ironically he made it appear that no political constitution had ever produced freedom and happiness and so appeared to argue for "natural society against politicians." [29]

In writing this book Burke was aware that the French rationalists were already beginning to grow weary of their attacks on religion and were turning increasingly to politics as a vehicle for their speculative assaults.

9

His first literary effort earned Burke something of a reputation when it was discovered that he was the author. His financial condition did not undergo any substantial improvement but he nevertheless decided to get married and the following year was wed to Jane Nugent. Burke's wife was, as already noted, a Catholic, although her mother was a Presbyterian, and one would expect that, in accordance with the custom of the time, Jane would also have been a member of that sect.[30]

The year of his marriage saw the publication of his second book, *A Philosophical Inquiry into the Origin of our Ideas on the Sublime and Beautiful*. This had actually been written while Burke was a student at Trinity, but he had spent considerable time in polishing and refining it. *The Sublime and the Beautiful* went through four editions in England before 1765 and was frequently reissued throughout the rest of the century. The psychological method employed by Burke gave it wide appeal in Germany where both Lessing and Kant became much impressed with it.

Another book, *An Account of the European Settlements in America*, was also published in 1757. Though originally written by Will Burke, it was considerably revised by Edmund. This went into a second edition before the year ended and subsequently went through a number of others. The following year was a most eventful one for Burke. Having given up the idea of emigrating to America [31] which he considered for a short time following his marriage, he and his wife decided to stay in London where her father moved from Bath in order to be near them. The two Burke children of whom we have certain knowledge were both born that year; [32] he began to write his fourth book, a history of England, which the publisher Robert Dodsley contracted for; [33] and he became editor of the *Annual Register*, which was first published for the year 1758. Burke's connection with this review of world affairs was kept secret during his lifetime, but it was widely believed that he was its editor. The *Annual Register* is very important to students of Burke because its volumes constitute a commentary upon affairs which clearly reflect the editor's thinking.[34] The financial reward for such a demanding task was indeed small, but Burke was enriched by his labors in another way — they helped to make him one of the best informed men in England.

Burke was now rising in public opinion and his circle of friends began to widen to include some influential persons, although we find him complaining at this time to one of the number that he had very few friends.[35] In 1759 [36] he was introduced by a noted Irish peer, Lord Charlemont, to William Gerard Hamilton, one of the Commissioners of the Board of Trade and then considered a most promising young man who was expected to go far in politics. His meeting with Hamilton provided Burke with his entry into the sphere of practical politics, a field toward which he was increasingly attracted. Hamilton was quick to recognize Burke's unusual talents and soon determined to avail himself of his services. Just what their financial arrangement was is uncertain, but there is no doubt that Burke was remunerated for whatever help he gave Hamilton. Sometime later, in an *aide memoire* Hamilton noted: "Took Mr. B. up, unknown £2000" and added "Did I ever refuse him money —," [37] Whatever their precise arrangement was, Burke was free during summers to continue his literary pursuits.

Then, in March 1761, Lord Halifax became Lord Lieutenant of Ireland and made his protégé Hamilton his Chief Secretary. Given the opportunity to accompany Hamilton to his native land as the latter's private secretary, Burke accepted and set out in the summer of 1761 to prepare the way for his employer's arrival.[38] In his new capacity, Burke held no official position in the Irish government but secured quarters in Dublin Castle, the viceroy's official residence, for himself and his family.

Burke returned in 1761 to an Ireland where desire for change permeated the atmosphere. Ireland was a land where for centuries past a process of English conquest and colonization had taken place leaving a small minority of English possessed of the vast majority of the land together with its wealth. The mass of the native Irish had been reduced to a position akin to slavery. With the exception of a few landed proprietors who somehow or other had been able to retain small possessions and a few people in business, the Catholics were peasants and their lot one of extreme misery. The Catholic religion was proscribed by the penal laws and Catholics had lost their right to hold seats in the Irish parliament and their franchise as well. Legally, it was impossible for them to secure an education. They were excluded from the profession and practice of the law.

Indeed the list of proscriptions is so long as to be almost incredible. Much has been made of the purported laxity with which the laws were enforced, but the fact is that, whenever it was deemed convenient, they were enforced with frightful consequences to the victims. These unfortunates were also subjected to tithes for the support of an alien religion. So hopeless had their position become that much of the best young Catholic blood preferred to go abroad to serve in the military forces of the Catholic European powers. Those who remained were looked upon by the Anglo-Irish ruling class with a combination of disdain and fear which has been likened to that shown in the United States at various times to the Negro and Indian respectively.

By design the English government had over the years created an English colony in Ireland which was meant to exist for England's sole benefit. Nevertheless, the incidental advantages reaped by the colonists were immense. In return for these manifold privileges they were expected to serve England's interests and to yield when any conflict occurred. As time passed, however, feelings of resentment over their subordinate role began to increase upon the part of these persons of English ancestry and religion. Yet the common bonds shared with the mother country always proved effective enough to produce cohesion in the face of the native Irish and also against the Dissenters of the north of Ireland.

Ever since Tudor days the Irish parliament had been subordinate to the English crown and parliament. Bills which passed the Irish parliament had to be approved by the Privy Council in England, after which the parliament of Ireland could accept or reject the measures but not amend them. By the Declaratory Act of 1719 (the 6 Geo. I, c.5), the British parliament dealt summarily with a claim of the Irish House of Lords, asserting their right to be the final court of appeal for Ireland. This act declared that Ireland was "subordinate unto and dependent upon" the British crown and parliament which had "full power and authority to make laws and statutes of sufficient force and validity to bind the kingdom and the people of Ireland." [39]

The Irish House of Lords was composed of the great territorial magnates together with a number of bishops of the Church of Ireland. The House of Commons consisted of three hundred members who were returned as follows: one hundred and ten boroughs returned two members apiece for a total of two hundred and twenty; thirty-two counties each returned two for a total of sixty-four; seven cities elected a pair of members each for a total of fourteen; and the University of Dublin also returned a pair. Two hundred members or two-thirds of the total membership were chosen by one hundred individuals in rotten boroughs; nearly fifty of these two hundred being elected by a handful of people. Lord Shannon returned sixteen; the Ponsonbys, fourteen; Lord Hillsborough, nine; and the Duke of Leinster, ten. A number of the rotten boroughs had no resident electors at all, and some had only a single elector. Catholics were excluded by law from the parliament whose members were elected for the duration of a reign and who met only every other year for the chief purpose of voting supplies.

The members were largely notorious jobbers and placemen [40] who continued to accept their position of dependence upon the government of Great Britain which exercised the right to legislate for Ireland and to dispose of her revenues. Two-thirds of Ireland's revenue was in perpetuity and hence outside the jurisdiction of her parliament. The Lord Lieutenant or viceroy acted as the executive. With one exception this post had always been filled by a titled Englishman. Prior to 1767 the viceroys restricted their residence in Dublin to a few weeks at the commencement of each biennial session. Affairs of state were conducted during the periods these absentees were away by the Lord Justices who controlled the administration, dispensed patronage, and disposed of the public funds. As a rule, there were three of these officials — the Primate, the Speaker of the House, and the Chancellor.

Local government was no improvement over national. The corporations of the cities and towns were the property of a small group of individuals who, however, were subject to control by Dublin Castle, the executive, although they managed to retain considerable latitude.

Upon his return in 1761, Burke detected grounds for hope that conditions in Ireland could be improved. There seemed to be a new feeling abroad in the land. Even the great families who controlled the electoral system were showing signs of discontent over

England's exploitation of Ireland. These Undertakers, so called because they undertook to manage England's business for her in Ireland, can hardly be considered Irish patriots, of course, since they stood to benefit principally from Ireland's securing a greater role in the conduct of her own affairs.

There was widespread dissatisfaction — especially with the lack of vision which characterized Britain's commercial policy toward Ireland. It was now fervently hoped that Ireland could become sufficiently strong to force Britain to revise her selfish policy. Although Ireland's trade was almost exclusively in non-Catholic hands, it was plain that the desired strength could not be achieved without the aid of the Catholics. This knowledge encouraged Burke who was also pleased that the Catholics had shown their loyalty in 1760 when a French expedition under Thurot had landed at Carrickfergus. The addresses of loyalty which the Catholics had presented at that time had been well received by the government in return.

Pitt had recently achieved some success in quieting the discontented Scots Highlanders by allowing them to enlist in the British Army. The time was now propitious for emulating this success in Ireland. Should such a measure be successful, Burke reasoned that others could then be introduced. What he had in mind first was a plan whereby Irish Catholics would be permitted to form a few regiments of their own under officers of their own religious faith for service in Portugal. There was no question that Britain's forces could stand bolstering. The Seven Years' War was still being fought, and Catholic Portugal, England's historic ally, was in need of assistance against her neighbor Spain. Added to this consideration was the precedent of the Scots Highlanders.

Despite the fact that not a single breach had yet been made, or, for that matter, even attempted, in what Burke called the "ferocious acts of Anne" against the Irish Catholics, Burke managed to convince his employer, Hamilton, to introduce a bill in the Irish Commons so designed.[41] The approval of the Privy Council in England was obtained beforehand. The Hamilton bill provided that six regiments of Irish Catholics under their own officers should be raised for service in Portugal as a defense against Spain. The measure, however, was defeated. Its opponents were unable to oppose it on grounds of economy because this argument had been foreseen by Burke in framing the bill. Portugal was to bear the expense involved. Nevertheless, a combination of selfishness, fear, and prejudice was too strong to be overcome. Despite the fact that the penal laws prohibited Catholics from possessing arms, it was claimed that even to arm them for service abroad would be too dangerous.[42] It is interesting to observe that the rejected bill was a government measure defeated by a parliament which Hamilton had called "the most willing House of Commons that ever sat." The opposition despite its reputation for patriotism very patently drew the line when it came to aiding the Catholics in any way. Such was to be the case almost without exception for the rest of the century, a fact destined to be conveniently overlooked in years to come by many too prone to condemn the government and exalt the "patriots."

Thus, Burke's first effort to bring about some measure of relief for the Catholics of Ireland was a failure although it was a very modest endeavor. It is significant in that it set the pattern for most of his future attempts to help Ireland in that the moment seemed propitious since it coincided with a time when Britain was in distress and hence apt to be generous — a generosity which would initially benefit Ireland but ultimately the British Empire as well would thereby gain.

Meanwhile, Burke was engaged in a thorough study of the various punitive and disabling laws against the Catholics in Ireland.[43] His famous *Tract on the Popery Laws* [44] was probably written during the fall of 1761 but was not published until after Burke's death.[45] All that remains is a fragment, since it is likely that he never actually finished it. But there is enough extant to grasp Burke's feelings on the great injustice of these laws. That it was only a fragment in Burke's last years may be seen from a letter to him from Dr. French Laurence requesting Burke to send "the fragments of the review, which you once made, of the laws against the Irish Catholicks." [46]

In the fragment which remains of this first work on practical politics by Burke in his public career, his plan is intact — envisaging five chapters. A general statement of the penal laws appears in the first chapter. Burke called this legislation a leading cause of

Ireland's "imbecility." The remnants of this chapter found among Burke's papers were imperfect.

The second chapter, however, is virtually complete. Here the laws themselves were dwelt upon.[47] The announced object of the system was, he declared, to render the Irish Catholics a wretched, uneducated, hopeless class stripped both of all property and ambition. This "machine of wise and elaborate contrivance" was devised to divide the nation into two separate classes without any common bond or denominator. The one was to possess all the political power, property, and means of education; the other to be composed solely of hewers of wood and drawers of water. He went on at some length to describe the penal laws,[48] a series of acts which affected the Catholic in his religious worship, family relationships, property, civil rights, and means of earning a livelihood.

Burke said that it was the belief of their persecutors that when the generation of priests who had registered under a mandatory act in 1704 died, they would not be replaced by others due to the numerous obstacles placed in the way of training new priests. However, they had failed to reckon with the spirit and resourcefulness of the Irish, who, despite the great difficulties put against the exercise of their religion, managed to retain their faith.

The third chapter of the *Tract* was designed to embrace Burke's observations on the penal laws. These were to come under three heads: first, was the object of the laws, "a numerous people"; secondly, came the "means — a restraint on property"; and, finally, were "the instruments of execution, — corrupted morals, which affect the national prosperity."

In this chapter is Burke's statement that the penal laws were unlike any system of religious oppression then in existence anywhere in Europe or any which had ever prevailed in any land with which history had made him familiar. He specifically called attention to the revocation of the Edict of Nantes but emphasized that, although it was a very unjust action, it did not begin to match the case of the Irish Catholics. Numerically, the Huguenots were but half the Catholics. Considered in proportion to the total population of their respective countries, he showed that the Huguenots were only five per cent of the people of France whereas the Catholics constituted a majority of the Irish population. Furthermore, he pointed out that the penalties and restrictions suffered by the Huguenots were by no means as serious as those suffered by the Irish Catholics under the penal laws, a system which, he lamented, was everlasting.[49]

Nor was he content to stop there. In convincing fashion, he reasoned that what was attacked as an unjust policy in France, a country governed by an absolute monarch, could not become a fair method of procedure in a country which was ostensibly governed by law. The more so was it the case when this kind of treatment was intensified and increased. Charity began at home he reminded the sympathetic people who expressed their deep solace for the victims of oppression in France. Tartly, he noted that the same ports which were thrown open to receive the foreign victims with warm welcome were the places of exit for the domestic fugitives who were the objects of a much worse system of maltreatment.

The Irish Catholics who suffered under such severe restrictions were not a small group nor an obscure one. They numbered some two million, eight hundred thousand people, at least two-thirds of the nation.[50] He strengthened this point when he declared that the welfare or unhappiness of multitudes can never be a matter of indifference. Laws against the majority of the people are laws against the people themselves. Instead of mistreatment of a mere group they make for general oppression. This in turn results in national misfortune. Moreover, any law which operated against a whole people, even if they themselves were to ratify it, would be against the will of "Him who gave us our nature, and in giving impressed an invariable law upon it," i.e., the natural law. This being so, any such code as the penal laws was void.[51]

Here we see Burke in the very beginning of his long public career as the firm defender of prescription, "the most solid of all titles, not only to property, but, which is to secure property, to government." His argument was based on the high grounds of natural rights,[52] and because of these rights, no body of men could make any laws which pleased them. Legislators could not be frivolous since power was a sacred trust.

Asserting that the sole foundations of law were equity and utility and declaring that the penal laws were based upon neither, he professed to see the Catholics punished because they acted upon a principle which was essential for the preservation of society, namely, a deep assent and an unwavering attachment to the beliefs of their ancestors. Punishment on such grounds was intolerable to Burke who often in the years to come would remind the present generation that it did well to remember its heritage. Change fitted into his scheme of things because there were times when it was needed to preserve something of the precious treasures of the past, but it should never be a sweeping change, rather a gradual one.

If the penal laws represented, as some actually claimed, an improvement of society, Burke said that he should hate to see what the same people called a depravation. Anyway, a little reading of history would show that this legislation was inconsistent. Down to the Reformation, the English kings called upon the Irish for obedience on the grounds that they were vassals and mesne lords between those English rulers and the Papacy. The kings reversed their procedure in Ireland as compared with England itself. In the former nation, they exalted the power of the Papacy. Then came a sudden change. Opinions were now violently attacked which the English had endeavored for four centuries to establish. The old inhabitants of Ireland were confronted with annihilation, and new residents were brought in who adhered to the change. Consider, said Burke, the sad story of Ireland which underwent more suffering for religion than any other country. The ironic fact was that it was harrassed both for Catholicism and Protestantism. And in addition to the demonstrable unnaturalness of the penal laws was the fact that they were contrary to a positive compact. The Treaty of Limerick, which guaranteed the free exercise of their religion to the Catholics of Ireland, had been unilaterally broken.

The fragment concludes with an incomplete fourth chapter which endeavored to demonstrate the ill effects of the system and its instruments upon the national prosperity, peace, and security. The penal laws tended to destroy every contributing factor to what constitutes national prosperity, such items as industry, knowledge or skills, morals, execution of justice, courage, and the national union which directed the other factors to a single point and fixed them all in the common welfare. Since the penal laws destroyed every one of these points, Great Britain did not draw from Ireland

the benefits which could be derived there. Nature had been boun-
tiful in Ireland, but the system imposed upon the majority of the
inhabitants tended to ruin that bounty. Furthermore, the chief contributor to industry was property, and laws against property discouraged industry. The goal of the latter was the acquisition of the
former. The penal laws prevented the vast majority of Ireland's
people from acquiring property for life. Not as yet the gentleman
farmer he was destined to become,[53] Burke was nevertheless well
able to show the ill effects of such a system upon the land.

Of what remains in the fragment, his disposal of the argument
of the supposed danger to the state which would result from the
repeal of the penal laws deserves to be mentioned. It was argued
by their opponents that when the Catholics had land and the influence which its possession brings, peace in Ireland was never
secure. They were guilty of causing dangerous rebellions, the worst
of which were in the periods during which the Catholics were in
enjoyment of maximum benefits and privileges. Such charges Burke
showed to be based on error. He admitted that "those miserable
performances which go about under the names of Histories of Ireland" represented events after that fashion but these were accounts
which attempted to fly in the face of nature by seeking to persuade
men that kindness and decency on the part of the government encouraged the subjects to revolt. This was not what the records revealed to those willing to examine them. These records proved conclusively that the Irish rebellions were caused by persecution, not
by toleration. The records discountenanced the foolish doctrine
that the well-being of any establishment, whether it was religious
or civil, could ever depend upon the unhappiness of those whose lot
it was to live under it. The danger to such establishments did not
come from the peace and prosperity of its people. Instead, it derived
from the continuance of people in a state of repression. This was
what produced rebellions. Keeping alive the spirit of suppression
was responsible for another danger which it would be well to bear
in mind, namely, that the fanaticism of the oppressors might one
day be turned on the very ones who encouraged it.

Although Burke's proofs of the impolicy of the penal laws are
incomplete in this fragment, there is enough left to have shown his
views incontrovertible. The opinions which he expressed thus early

in his life remained unchanged to the end of his days.[54] These were ever the same, but he did alter the basis of his case in pleading the Catholic cause. He changed from the high grounds of natural rights to those of prudence, justice, and expediency. This transformation was dictated by his opposition to the doctrine of the rights of man which the French Revolution espoused. To have continued pleading the Irish Catholic cause on the grounds of natural rights after 1789 was manifestly impossible. Furthermore, the change had come at a time when he was seeking to win political rights for the Catholics, not religious ones.

Writing to Dr. John Curry, the noted Irish Catholic physician and historian, 14 August 1779, Burke declared that his actions in regard to the relief of the Irish Catholics were based upon a uniform principle which regulated his conduct. That fundamental doctrine was a detestation of "all kinds of public injustice and oppression." It was this which made him so thoroughly opposed to the penal laws.[55]

During the years of Burke's return to Ireland in the service of Hamilton, agrarian disturbances were commonplace. These uprisings were chiefly the work of secret societies formed from the ranks of the peasant farmers, and the cause was economic. For one thing, the penal laws made it impossible for Catholics to lease land for more than thirty-one years. Consequently, they lived in dread of the day when the lease would expire and they would be forced to begin all over again, if fortunate enough to secure another farm or bit of land. Added to this enduring source of affliction was the foreign plague on cattle which had broken out around 1750. This blight had tremendously increased the profits to be obtained from the sale of Irish beef and dairy products since the disease had also struck England. Pasturage became more popular, and tillage began to suffer a falling-off which was very marked. With the increase in cattle and sheep raising, the commons were frequently enclosed.[56] The consequence was that the hapless peasantry was faced with imminent starvation in numerous cases. Meanwhile, the system of tithes [57] for the support of the Established Church was not relaxed a whit, and so secret societies offered themselves to the minds of the peasants as the only apparent means of protection. The tithe collectors and proctors, who were in many cases themselves Catholics, were attacked in Munster at the outset of the reign of George III by an organization known as the Whiteboys, so named from their practice of wearing long white shirts over their regular clothing.[58] They filled the nights with terror by burning houses, destroying and crippling livestock, and torturing the tithe-proctors and tithe-farmers. In broad daylight, the authorities visited an indiscriminate vengeance on guilty and innocent with great ferocity.

This violent outbreak upset both the Irish government and upper-class Catholic circles alike. Obvious reasons account for the former's alarm. The latter was frightened over the possibility that the penal laws would be more vigorously enforced despite the fact that it was common knowledge that the Whiteboys were nonsectarian. Furthermore, the Catholic landlords themselves practiced enclosure, a very profitable enterprise.

The cause of the Whiteboy disturbances was laid by the ruling clique in Dublin to a plot engineered, it was claimed, by the French in order to forment an Irish rebellion. The Catholics were accused of having conspired with the French in a "popish" plot, it being tacitly assumed that a common religion automatically created a community of interests. This false and convenient assumption permitted the Irish ruling class to mete out savage chastisement to the unfortunate Catholic small-farmer class. Lord Charlemont, then no friend of the Catholics, ascribed the fierce repression which was visited on their victims to the anger aroused among the Protestant "bashaws" that an attempt should even be made to protest their "established despotism." He likened the punishment dealt out by the government to that which would be accorded to a servile insurrection in another land.[59]

The brutality of the whole episode so touched Burke that he never forgot it, and he frequently recalled the period between 1761 and 1764, during which he spent the winters of 1761–1762 and 1763–1764 in Ireland, as one of unbelievable cruelty.[60] A letter to Charles O'Hara at the time gives testimony of his disgust and revulsion:

Happy & wise are those poor Natives in avoiding yr. great World; that they are unacquainted with the unfeeling Tyranny of a mungril Irish Landlord, or with the Horrors of a Munster Circuit. I have avoided this subject whenever I wrote to you; & I shall now say no more of it;

because it is impossible to preserve ones Temper on the view of so destestable a scene. God save me from the power, (I shall take care to keep myself from the society) of such monsters of Inhumanity. An old acquaintance of mine at the Temple, a man formerly of integrity & good nature, had by living some years in Corke contracted such horrible habits, that I think whilst he talked on these late disturbances, none but hangmen could have had any pleasure in his company – [61]

Acutely aware of the true facts of the situation, Burke managed to have an official investigation conducted into the causes of the disturbances. He well knew that the claim of a foreign plot was simply a good excuse for continuance of the absolute power vested in the hands of a small minority and saw that the peasants, faced with starvation, had been driven to the limit of their endurance by the inhuman tactics of their relentless oppressors. Furthermore, he felt the injustice of ascribing the composition of these bands exclusively to Catholics. Years later in a famous speech at Bristol, 6 September 1780, he declared that crimes are the acts of individuals, not of denominations, and that to classify men by broad descriptions in order to interdict and punish them in the mass was an unfair and succinct method since it prevented much trouble about proof. Nevertheless, it was not law, and it violated both reason and justice and would eventually bring about the ruin of the state which suffered its continuance.[62]

The investigation which Burke inspired was directed by the Irish Chief Justice, Aston. The latter thoroughly probed the matter and made known his findings in a letter to Hamilton, 24 June 1762. This gentleman found that foreign plots were not the cause which was purely domestic, an economic complaint — the price of labor was too cheap, that of food too high, and the conditions of land tenure excessive and oppressive. Aston went on to say that "however industriously the opposite has been promoted, Papist and Protestant were promiscuously concerned" in perpetrating the disorders and stated candidly that there were more Catholics involved simply because they constituted the majority of the nation's inhabitants.[63]

Burke's interest in seeing that justice was accorded his much maligned fellow countrymen was so great that it was difficult for his performance to match his intentions. Hence among his papers there was found an unfinished account of the Whiteboy disturbances which seems to have been composed around 1768 or 1769, certainly early in his career in parliament. This sketch of the White-boy uprising was dictated by the fact that the results of Aston's investigation were not well known among the members of the British parliament.[64] In the argument which he employed in this thin fragment, he used a *reductio ad absurdum*. Despite the patent foolishness of the common charge that the Whiteboy disturbances had been caused by a French conspiracy, he showed that the treat-ment accorded the Catholics had been criminal. He declared that he had taken the pains to make an investigation himself since he was possessed of both the means and the desire to do so. He traced the origin to one Fant, a Protestant attorney living in County Cork, who had become mentally unbalanced. After some petitions of his to restrain neighbors with whom he was at odds had failed, he sought revenge by inciting a group of "the meaner people" of Kilmallock, after "having warmed them with liquor," to tear down the enclosure walls on the town common. This was the beginning of the agrarian disturbances which later spread over much of the adjacent part of the country.[65]

Thus, in the very dawn of his fruitful career, Burke displayed an ability to put his finger on the Irish pulse. He was correct in attributing these agrarian risings to poor domestic conditions, and the harsh punishment visited on the offenders touched his sensitive feelings so deeply that he never ceased to decry the injustice of murderous punishment in consequence of pretended conspiracies on the part of the Irish Catholics with a foreign power.[66]

In the spring of 1762 Burke returned to London since the session of the Irish parliament had concluded. On the whole, it had been a rather satisfactory one for the government. Hamilton, as the Chief Secretary, had adroitly managed the government's business thanks in no small measure to Burke's expert assistance. In addition to the setback received when the attempt was made to raise the Catholic regiments for service in Portugal, the only other rebuff the adminis-tration suffered was in the case of the passage of a septennial act, largely through the efforts of the "patriots" Dr. Lucas and Henry Flood. This act, however, was nullified by the Privy Council in London, a fact which pleased Burke who disliked this legislation.

Back in England once again Burke renewed his correspondence

with Charles O'Hara. These letters reveal that Burke had now distinctly begun to think of himself as an Englishman and there is also unmistakable evidence of his disgust over developments in Ireland. In a letter dated 30 December 1762, Burke informed O'Hara that the Irish military establishment was to be increased and that there was strong evidence that the move was popular in Ireland, a fact which moved him to remark "For my part this same people of Ireland, their notions & their inclinations have always been a riddle to me." He professed it to be incomprehensible to him why "they should abhor a civil & covet a military establishment." Perhaps "the truth is that this military servitude is what they have grown up under; & like all licentious, & wild, but corrupt people, they love a Jobb better than a Salary." He felt that Ireland's funds could not stand this additional burden unless they were increased and thought that a land tax might be a good thing if he did not know that it "would terminate in some measure on the wretched poor whose Burthens are already lamentably heavy." He concluded by telling O'Hara "But I hate to think of Ireland, though my thoughts involuntarily take that turn, & whenever they do only meet objects of grief or indignation." [67]

A change occurred in the post of Lord Lieutenant in the fall of 1763 when Halifax was replaced by Northumberland. Hamilton, however, was retained by the new viceroy. But before the change occurred, Hamilton secured Halifax's approval for a pension of three hundred pounds on the Irish establishment for Burke [68] whose services were so invaluable to Hamilton that he hoped to retain him by thus rewarding him. Burke, however, made it clear that he meant to continue the "little work" which was a "sort of rent-charge" on his thoughts, i.e., the *Annual Register*, and also that he would require some free time to devote to his literary pursuits although he conceded that Hamilton's business must be his principal concern. Otherwise he could not accept the pension.[69]

Burke was pleased that he was to return to Ireland with Hamilton since it meant that he would have a reunion with his Irish friends during the winter of 1763–1764. These were many and included among them were several members of Parliament destined to distinguish themselves in the future, e.g., the able but rapacious John Hely Hutchinson [70] of whom Lord North once said that "if England and Ireland were given to him he would want the Isle of Man for a potato patch," Lord Charlemont,[71] Henry Flood,[72] and Charles O'Hara.

Another consideration which afforded him satisfaction was his feeling that the Earl of Northumberland would make an able viceroy who would be good for Ireland.[73]

Burke's political activities during the winter of 1763–1764 in Ireland remain pretty much of a mystery. It is clear, however, that he and Hamilton incurred the enmity of the powerful Archbishop of Dublin, George Stone,[74] who was backed by Northumberland. The result was that Northumberland dismissed Hamilton in the spring of 1764 at the conclusion of the session, at which time Hamilton and Burke returned to London.

The two winters which Burke spent in Ireland were useful ones as far as his future career was concerned. They enabled him to secure an intimate knowledge of the workings of government and in particular of the manner in which the connection between England and Ireland functioned. He was able, too, to form close and enduring friendships which would be useful to keep him informed on up-to-the-minute developments. Finally, what he saw during that period simply strengthened his determination to help his native land and particularly the Catholics. One of the most broad-minded men of his time, the severity of the treatment given the Catholics shocked him. He was a sympathetic Christian whose toleration reached out to many besides his persecuted fellow-countrymen. Dissenters, Jews, and Negroes were all objects of his Christian justice and charity.[75] So strong were his views on the injustices of the laws against the Catholics that he battled for their complete repeal throughout his entire career.[76]

CHAPTER II

Burke Enters Parliament

$\mathbb{B}$urke had not been back in London long before his friends
Reynolds and Johnson proposed forming a club devoted to good
conversation. The proposal found merit with Burke who became
one of the charter members and who managed to secure the admission of his father-in-law also. The Club met regularly on Monday
evenings at the Turk's Head in Soho. Since politics would have
been too controversial a subject, it was decided that talk should
center on literary subjects. This proved increasingly difficult as
the Club expanded in membership, yet the congeniality and cultivation which were the hallmarks of membership managed to keep
things on an even keel.

Aside from the Club Burke was kept busy with a number of
odds and ends, especially was he active in doing favors for his
friends. Although he was anxious to resume his literary pursuits,
he was an unsuccessful applicant for a colonial agency for Grenada,
where his brother Richard was then serving as receiver-general of
the king's revenue.[1] This bid is a clear indication of the fascination
which politics had for him despite his desire to resume his literary
activities.

Meanwhile, Hamilton began to stress to Burke the necessity
of defining their relationship more clearly. A quarrel ensued which
produced an irrevocable end of their connection and friendship.
The cause of it was Hamilton's desire to bind Burke's services exclusively to himself. Hamilton claimed that Burke's acceptance of
the pension which he had procured for him obligated him to remain in his service permanently, that Burke could not have secured

anywhere else the kind of a beginning in public life which Hamilton had provided, and that Burke was anxious to be released from his service simply because his employer was no longer Irish Chief Secretary. Despite these charges, Hamilton said that he was willing to increase Burke's salary by a considerable sum and would even submit the dispute to an impartial party for arbitration. Burke was seething with indignation and said that it was no matter for anyone else but him and Hamilton. He took issue with the latter's claim that he could not have secured a more advantageous position at the time he entered Hamilton's service. As far as he was concerned, there was no question of his freedom. He was free anytime he so desired, and that time was now. Hence, he resigned his pension to a person chosen by Hamilton. In return it was agreed that they would never meet or correspond again.[2]

Writing to J. Monck Mason, May 1765, Burke declared peremptorily that he would not consider anyone his friend who did not think him "*perfectly* in the right" after hearing his story of the dispute with Hamilton.[3] He told Henry Flood that his reason for resigning his pension was to quit himself forever of Hamilton and never to carry "even a memorial of such a person about me." [4]

Whatever may be said about the merits of the dispute, one thing is abundantly clear. Burke was indebted to Hamilton for having made possible both an invaluable political experience and the formation of some extremely useful contacts.

Burke's withdrawal from Hamilton's service and his resignation of his pension left him in rather desperate financial straits since the only regular remuneration which he now had was the modest sum received for editing the *Annual Register*. Although he told Charles O'Hara, 4 June 1765, a few weeks after the termination of the Hamilton episode, "You see I am little affected by Hamilton," [5] he was worried. His hopes, along with those of Will Burke, now rested upon their being able to make a connection with the Marquis of Rockingham, who was the leader of a group of Whigs possessed of extensive land holdings.

In a letter to O'Hara, begun and ended by Edmund, Will interjected long enough to tell their Irish friend that they wished he were in England to help them:

. . . for want of such a friend as you to forward, to ripen the little budding hopes that arrive, yet birth today and dye tomorrow nothing will be. Lord John Cavendish, possibly from some things dropt by yourself, has mentioned us both as fit men to be employed to Lord Rockingham, who received it well, but what then? We have not a friend in the world to keep the impression alive. Something will I hope however turn up.[6]

Things began to look up a month later, as Edmund revealed to O'Hara.[7] He began by asking his friend to

think a little of those, whose ambitions or necessities oblige them to live in the storm: you have friends high enough to be actuated by the one, & low enough to be impelled by the other; & if the latter are the least considerable, they are the most innocent; &, I am sure, as much therefore, in your thoughts & wishes as the former.

After recounting the names and positions of those proposed for the new cabinet to be headed by Rockingham following the overthrow of the Grenville ministry, Burke then turned from the "ambitious" to "the honest Necessitous" and indicated that:

Will & I are down on their [the "ambitious" ones'] Lists, & I hope & believe will be attended to. Words cannot paint to you the indefatigable, unconquerable zeal & friendship of Fitzherbert to serve us; I shall give you an history of his good or ill success by the next post. In the meantime thank God *the* appearances are tolerable. The young Gentlemen will learn Classical Elegance & Honest Agriculture with you; in both which I envy them; whilst we are tagging at the heels of factions. But they too will be so engaged; but with better abilities; & in more honourable Stations, with better success; but not with more honest intentions.

This is a revealing letter showing that Edmund and Will had probably devoted a good deal of time and effort during the past year to insinuate themselves into the good graces of the Whig faction which was now about to take office. If this is so, and there seems little reason to doubt it, then opportunism rather than principle guided Burke at this particular stage of his political career. His comments in the *Annual Register* for 1765 and in some of his correspondence indicate that he had not as yet become a party man. Rather than a deep and abiding conviction it was to be a combination of custom, association, and affiliation with the Rockingham Whigs which formed Burke into the strong champion of party he was to become.[8]

The likelihood of his making a connection with Rockingham was well received by friends with whom he corresponded. They looked upon it as quite different from the link with Hamilton and were disposed to be optimistic about Burke's future.[9]

Two days after the letter of 9 July to O'Hara, Burke was able to send him definite word that

> I have got an employment of a kind humble enough; but which may be worked into some sort of consideration, or at least advantage; Private Secretary to Lord Rockingham; who has the reputation of a man of honour & integrity; & with whom, they say, it is not difficult to live. Will is strongly talked of for a better thing.[10]

Burke had scarcely begun work in his new capacity before certain unidentified persons tried to ruin him with Rockingham. As Burke put it in a letter to David Garrick, they "made a desperate stroke at my fortune, my liberty, and my reputation." [11] What happened was that the Duke of Newcastle, a member of Rockingham's cabinet, was informed by several sources that the Prime Minister's new secretary was in reality a disguised Jesuit.[12] The greatly alarmed old man hastened to Rockingham to urge that he dismiss Burke at once because of the serious harm which could result politically if it were known that Rockingham's private secretary was a papist. This Rockingham refused to do without giving Burke a hearing. He summoned Burke and told him of the charges. The manner in which Burke conducted himself, easily and convincingly refuting the allegations, made a lasting impression on Rockingham who would not hear of Burke's offer to resign once he had cleared himself to Rockingham's satisfaction.

The incident thus served, as far as Rockingham was concerned, merely to strengthen Burke's place in his esteem. Unfortunately, the rumor that Burke was a disguised papist was destined to endure for the rest of his life.[13] His tormentors never ceased to delight in claiming that he was a former Jesuit and that he had been educated at the Jesuit College of St. Omer, France,[14] charges that persisted even after his death.[15] Burke himself is the authority for the fact that he never even saw St. Omer until 1773.[16] Furthermore, during his entire public life, he had to suffer himself to be called an Irish "adventurer," an experience that had something in common with that of Cicero who was called *civis inquilinus* (lit., a citizen of a place which was not his own) by his Roman enemies because of his birth at Arpinum.[17]

Six months after entering Rockingham's employ, Burke became a member of parliament. What Rockingham's precise role in bringing this about was is not clear, but it would appear that he was not very active in the matter. What we do know is that the pocket borough of Wendover, controlled by Lord Verney, an Irish peer and intimate friend and gambling companion of Will Burke's, provided Edmund with a seat in Commons. Verney had first offered the seat to Will, but the latter with characteristic self-effacement asked that it be given to Edmund instead. He was elected on 23 December 1765, "got very drunk," and the next day had "an heavy cold." [18]

Writing to O'Hara a week later, Burke remarked that through no merits of the Irish their liberties or what passed for them had been saved by developments in America in connection with the Stamp Act and then added another of his critical remarks about Ireland by saying that he did not know how he had come to concern himself about Ireland since he had recently been treated in a most "unhandsome" way there.[19]

However that may be, he took his seat in the House on 14 January 1766 and in the short space of a few days won wide acclaim through the ability displayed in his maiden speech.[20]

Nearly two years later he revealed to Charles O'Hara what his secret feelings were when he entered upon his parliamentary career:

For myself I really have no hopes. Everybody congratulated me on coming into the House of Commons, as being in the certain road of a great & speedy fortune; & when I began to be heard wt. some little attention, every one of my friends was sanguine. But in truth I never was so myself. I came into Parliament not at all as a place of preferment but of refuge; I was pushed into it; & I must have been a Member, & that too with some Eclat, or be a little worse than nothing; Such were the attempts made to ruin me when I first began to meddle in Business. But I considered my situation on the side of fortune as very precarious. I looked on myself, with this New Duty, on me, as on a man devoted; & thinking in this manner, nothing has happened that I did not expect, & was not well prepared for. Therefore, my dear Sir, cheer up; nothing very amiss can happen us, whilst it pleases God that we keep our health, our good humour, & our inward peace; None of wh. is yet gone from us.[21]

Burke had made his debut in the arena of the politics of the British Empire at a time when the dispute with the American colonies was the main business before parliament, and his first speeches there, which gained so much renown for him, had been on American affairs, vigorously favoring the repeal of the Stamp Act. Yet he lost no time in trying to do something for Ireland's amelioration. It is quite conceivable that he had already formed the conviction which was later to be strong with him that Ireland's fortunes were closely linked with developments relating to America. The American question had assumed great proportions during this session of parliament, but the problems of Ireland, which were chronic, could not be completely dismissed.

Somewhat mistakenly as events turned out, Burke informed O'Hara that parliament was preparing for a complete revision of the commercial legislation touching both British and foreign colonies. He wondered "Could not Ireland be somehow hooked into this System?" and asked O'Hara to send him arguments from those who knew most about the importation of West Indian sugar into Ireland.[22]

On the heels of this letter came one showing Burke's willingness to speak out publicly for Ireland. The latter had been "foolishly brought into the Bill for ascertaining the rights of Taxing the Colonies — . . . " Although Burke spoke on the subject "in some degree," he felt that he had been "long & diffused" and that his argument "hurt" him, since the House "was teezed to death & heard no one willingly." [23]

He later conceded to O'Hara that "I wrote in low spirits on what I said about Ireland. I have had since some complement on it, through another, from Lord Hardwicke & others." [24]

In the meantime, O'Hara answered the request for information which Burke might use on behalf of Irish trade. Snatching a few minutes in the House while a witness was being examined, Burke told his friend that some of his suggestions would not do because they would be considered prejudicial to British manufacturers. Others, having to do with such items as sugar and soap, he agreed to push as best he could.[25]

He now found time to indulge himself in a longer letter on the same subject. Characteristically, he argued that the propositions aimed at improving Irish Trade "require time & leisure to make their way by the slow progression of reason into the minds of people here, who just now seem shut against them." Furthermore, since parliament's hands were then "so full of America," he did not see how it was possible to attend to anything else during the session. "The Irish affairs are a System by themselves, & will I hope one day or another undergo a thorough scruting [sic], but in my opinion it would only hurt them to attempt crowding them into the train of an act relating wholly to America." He agreed, however, to make a fight on behalf of proposals for Irish soap.

The interesting and arresting point about Burke's comments here is his conviction that the business of helping Irish trade depended upon "time & leisure to make their way by the slow progression of reason. . . ." This principle became his guide for the remaining long years of effort devoted to the improvement of conditions in Ireland.

Burke was by now becoming so preoccupied with his work in parliament that he confessed to O'Hara that

in general, I find the things which I have most at heart going on very much as I could wish them; I mean the transactions in Parliament, which find my thoughts some employment both in & out of the house, & which I stick to exclusively of everything else, not only as a satisfaction, but as a refuge. There I go on my own imprudent way, speaking my mind without fear or wit, as the old Proverb says; & doing my party what service I can, witht. asking in what light they will consider or attend to it.[26]

Although Burke had been active in calling attention to the plight of Irish trade, the developments in that country where peasant agitators were being ruthlessly dealt with so disgusted him that he complained to O'Hara:

I find you go on in Ireland plotting, alarming, informing, seizing & imprisoning as usual: What surprises me is to find by one or two of your Letters, that you are a little giving way to the ingenious Bon ton of our Country. I see it is impossible totally to avoid it. You seem, to think, that if they do not discover the cause of their distempers by the dissaction [sic] of Sheehy,[27] they will leave off their villainous Theories of Rebellions & Massacres. Sic notus Ulysses? [Thus have you known Ulysses?] I hear they intend to poke in the bowels of a few more for further discoveries. Why had I a connection of feeling or even of knowledge with such a Country! I am not sorry that our schemes for it for the present at least, will not do. On this we will talk more in the summer.[28]

Despite this outburst of revulsion over what was transpiring in Ireland and his expressed satisfaction that nothing was going to be done for her, he went on in the next breath to reveal that he had proposed the previous night in Commons that Ireland be allowed some export concessions for her soap in the West Indies. At least, "a beginning" had been made, and that was encouraging.

This optimism was dispelled, however, as the summer recess of parliament neared. He had made a battle, "strenuous, though unsuccessful" for the Irish soap bill. "The Season was far advanced, the house thin, the proposition (as they said) new & serious. The treasury Bench gave way under me; I debated *alone* for near an hour with some sharp antagonists; I grew warm; . . ." Although he first thought of seeking a division of the House on his proposal, he negatived the idea upon the realization that he lacked support and that a defeat for the measure then might prejudice the future chances of the bill. Instead he retreated as gracefully as possible and resolved to make a motion at the outset of the next session. This experience "mortified" Burke "to the last degree" because he had been so sanguine that he would meet no opposition, but he did not quit on another Irish measure in which he was interested. This was a corn bill. He observed to O'Hara that Ireland's corn system was so badly contrived that "its greatest embarrassments arise from its own confusion." As for some constitutional questions which had arisen, he said that he would leave them to those who best understood them but added that he was sure that the Irish people "ought to eat whether they have Septennial Parliaments or not." [29]

Things, unfortunately, continued in the same sanguinary way in Ireland to Burke's continued disgust as he revealed to O'Hara in this same letter. In fact, the only agreeable news which he received from Ireland was in O'Hara's letters. When his friend came over to visit him in England, Burke would have one less tie with that country and its concerns. Yet as long as O'Hara remained there, Burke would be glad "to hear even of their politics; for in passing through your mind, they will lose something of their original nature; & will soften from Faction into Philosophy."

33

Further on Burke reverted to events in Ireland and was quite pronounced in his condemnation of the actions of the Irish officials who still professed to believe in a "popish" plot and who used this trumped up charge as a reason for indiscriminate punishment of Catholic peasants.

We are all in a Blaze here with your plots, assassinations, massacres, Rebellions, moonlight armies, French officers & French money. Are you not ashamed? You who told me, that if they could get no discovery from Sheehy, they would cool & leave off their detestable plot monging [sic]? You think well of Ireland; but I think rightly of it; & know, that their unmeaning Senseless Malice is insatiable; *cedamus patria!* [Let us withdraw from the country.] I am told, that these miserable wretches whom they have hanged, died with one Voice declaring their innocence but truly for my part, I want no man dying, or risen from the dead, to tell me that lies are lies, & nonsense is nonsense. I wish your absurdity was less mischievous, & less bloody. Are there not a thousand other ways in which fools may make themselves important? I assure you, I look on these things with horror; & cannot talk of such proceedings as the effects of an innocent credulity. If there be an army paid, & armed, & disciplined, & sworn to foreign power in your Country, cannot Government know it by some better means than the evidence of whores & Horsestealers. If these things be so, why is not the publick security provided for by a good body of Troops & a stronger military establishment? If not, why is the publick alarmed by such senseless Tales? But I know not why I reiterate such stuff to you; every company here is tormented with it — adieu. it is late; & I am vexed & ashamed, that the Government we live in, should not know those who endanger it, or who disturb it by false alarms; to furnish the one with knowledge & Vigour; or to silence the other with firmness.

Despite this undisguised feeling of revulsion against the savage treatment accorded the unfortunate victims of supposed "popish" plots in Ireland,[30] Burke had worked hard during his first session in for the betterment of Ireland's trade. For these efforts he won wide recognition in Ireland. He was looked upon in some influential circles there as Ireland's champion in the imperial parliament.[31]

Not long after the letter quoted at length above was written, the Rockingham government fell. The Marquis was dismissed by the king on 30 July 1766, and a new government ostensibly headed by the Duke of Grafton but in reality by Pitt, who had been given a peerage, replaced the outgoing administration.[32]

Burke confided to O'Hara that "As to myself, I hear nothing.

I consider myself as rather ill with Pitt's whole party. The situation & conduct of my own friends is most unfavourable to me. But my way, though unpleasant, is thank God, plain. & nothing is truly miserable but a puzzle. I prepare God willing to set out for you in a very few days." [33]

On 5 August, as he had indicated in the above letter, Burke set out for Ireland with his wife and his brother. Wherever he went he was handsomely received. His return to his native land was in reality in the nature of a triumphal tour. This reception was in marked contrast with his departure from England. Concerning the latter, it is interesting to refer to a letter from Burke to O'Hara under date of 19 August.[34] In it he lamented that the new government had paid him no civility with the exception of Lord Shelburne, Secretary of State for the Southern Department, which had charge of American affairs. According to Will Burke, Shelburne had praised Edmund and "wished of all things to embrace me before I left town." Burke had accordingly hastened to call upon Shelburne only to find him out and what was worse, said Burke, "I had no message to wish me a good Journey or anything." He had also called twice on Conway, Will Burke's friend and a holdover in the new administration from that of Rockingham, and had received no civil message from him either. His treatment at the hands of Shelburne and Conway irritated him and is quite revealing for it shows that Burke was certainly available for a place under the new administration. The decision then would appear to have been in the hands of the government and not, as Burke later believed or professed to believe, his to make.[35]

Another revealing point about this letter is that it shows clearly that Burke still had not become the devoted party man he was destined to be. In a way, of course, this is perhaps not too surprising since attachment to party through thick and thin was yet to make itself very widely felt in English politics. Rockingham himself had no qualms about those of his friends who joined the new ministry and so would not have cared had Burke been made a clear offer and accepted it. In fact, he graciously and generously tried to urge upon Burke the wisdom of joining the new government.

There has long been speculation over the purpose of Burke's visit to Ireland during that summer of 1766. Opinion varies. One

explanation is his supposed desire to be free from the political negotiations going on in England. Another is that it was to look after
some private business. The most recent is the conjecture that since
Rockingham had expected to stay in office and Burke's trip had
been planned well in advance of the government's fall, the major
reason for the trip was to gather information on Irish affairs which
would be of use to the government. When the administration fell,
it still made sense for Burke to secure an up-to-the-minute grasp of
Irish developments since it might assist the Rockingham party in
opposition.[36]

As novel and appealing as this new explanation is, it seems to
me that a combination of business and pleasure is perhaps nearer
the mark. He did have some matters concerning Clogher which
needed his attention and there was also need to look into the situation of his Catholic relatives in places prone to agrarian uprisings.
As for pleasure, the need of a vacation at this time requires no
special pleading and since Burke was going back to Ireland as a
member of the British parliament who had tried to assist his native
land in London the prospects of the vacation being an enjoyable one
were certainly good.

However unpleasant may have been his departure from London,
his experiences wherever he went throughout Ireland more than
compensated for it. Rich and poor alike treated him as a great
celebrity. Yet nowhere did he find greater happiness than with his
family. His mother had gone to be with her only daughter, Juliana,
who was expecting her first child. She was the wife of a prosperous
country gentleman, Pat French of Loughrea. Burke repaired to his
sister's home. Referring later to the visit, after first noting the
arrival of a "foxy" granddaughter, Burke's mother told her niece,
"dear Nelly Hennessy," that "I believe you will think me very vain;
but as you are a mother I hope you will excuse it. I assure you that
it's no honour that is done him that makes me vain of him, but the
goodness of his heart, which I believe no man living has a better;
and sure there can't be a better son, nor can there be a better
daughter-in-law than his wife." [37]

Another touching incident of the Loughrea visit was occasioned by the arrival of a traveling show at a fair. Outside, unable
to afford the modest admission price of one penny, was a host of

ragged urchins whom Burke spotted and at once made every one his guest. His brother-in-law coming upon Burke paying their admission tried vainly to be the host. Burke refused on the grounds that "this must be all my own; for I shall probably never again have the opportunity of making so many human beings happy at so small a cost." [38]

On another occasion, while he was shaving, Burke received a visit from O'Halloran, his old schoolmaster at Ballyduff. Without waiting to finish dressing, he dashed down to see the old man and delighted him with the courtesy with which he received him. After a lengthy reminiscence, he insisted that the poor old teacher take a gift of five guineas which he pressed into his reluctant but needy hand as a remembrance of his affection.[39]

Among the public honors he received during his visit to Ireland were a "Humble and Affectionate Address" from the Linen Manufacturers of Loughrea and the Freedom of Galway.[40] A few months after his return to England, he was also given the Freedom of Dublin. His friend, Dr. Thomas Leland, a Fellow of Trinity College, writing to inform him of this honor, commented on the fact that the freedom was not conveyed in a silver box as was the custom. He remarked that they did not give "freedoms in Silver Boxes here, Except to persons in some public station of the higher kind; they give them only to those who deserve them least." [41] Another friend, George Faulkner, congratulated him warmly — "never did any Man obtain this Freedom with more honour and Unanimity than you have done." [42] Burke graciously acknowledged the honor paid him by Dublin by writing to the lord mayor and declaring that it was impossible to exaggerate his plans for Ireland's welfare.[43] These honors had been awarded Burke in each instance because of the interest he had manifested toward the land of his birth in his first year in parliament.

While still in Ireland, Burke was the recipient of a stroke of good fortune.[44] Writing to tell O'Hara that Burke would be back in London in time for the opening of parliament in November, Will Burke joyously broke the good news. His friend Lord Verney had been speculating in East Indian stock and during the course of it "he considered this an opportunity of making us independent, & actually paid down of his own above £9,000 & engaged for above forty more for me." Already Will estimated his profit at "£12,000 at least." As he put it, the windfall had come at a "critical" season and could be considered "providential." The Burkes must not be vain, however, but rather "endeavour to grow better as we grow richer."

Just before leaving Ireland, Burke and his wife and brother stopped off in Dublin in the hope of seeing O'Hara whom they had missed on their arrival earlier. Once again he was away and as before they were guests at his town house. Writing his host to say how comfortable they were, Burke alluded to the good fortune he and Will shared. It was the kind of news which "is indeed marvellous in the success, marvellous in the Conduct, marvellous in the motives of action." It "certainly leaves one with some freedom of Conduct, but the time holds nothing to guide that freedom. For my part, I see nothing on either side of the Water but thick darkness & utter confusion." [45]

The "freedom of Conduct" to which Burke referred undoubtedly meant that he could decide whether to remain with Rockingham when he returned or to resume his efforts to secure a place in the new administration.

Following a stormy crossing to Holyhead during which all the Burkes were quite ill, they made home safely by easy stages, and Burke attended the opening of parliament. Negotiations looking toward his joining the new government were begun when Conway sent for him. But it was a different Burke than the one who was almost pathetically eager at the beginning of the summer to gain a place. Buoyed up by his triumphal tour of Ireland and feeling secure in his finances, Burke told Conway that he had begun his career with Rockingham and that honor dictated his remaining with that party. He said, however, that he would accept place on one condition, viz., "I must be understood to belong, not to the administration, but to those who were out; & that therefore if ever they should set up a standard, though spread for direct & personal opposition, I must be revocable into their party, & join it." He added that he "wd. act fairly and give due notice." Conway naturally took the position that this reservation "might frustrate the whole," and negotiations were soon terminated.[46]

As he put it to his friend, O'Hara:

As to me, I hope you will always find my little skiff out in the fair open sea — far away from the rocks, shelves & quicksands of politicks. I jumped in first; & plumped over head & ears. You cannot think with what spirit & system our little Corps went on last Tuesday night without the least previous consultation or concert between ourselves or any of the casual auxiliaries. I have broke off all Negotiations with the powers that be. So leave off flattering yourself with reading anything about me in the red book, for some years. I suspect you will soon see Will Burkes name also effaced from that book of Life.[47]

He still maintained a month later that "it would be convenient enough to get into office" and admitted that "opposition never was to me a desirable thing; because I like to see some effect of what I am doing, & this method however pleasant is barren & unproductive, & at best, but preventive of mischief. . . ." By way of compensation for being in opposition "the wear & tear of mind, which is saved by keeping aloof from crooked politicks, is a consideration absolutely inestimable." [48]

Thus, Burke had by the fall of 1766 done a nice bit of rationalization about whether or not he could have joined the government and at the same time had cast his lot with Rockingham for good or ill. He plunged into his work in parliament and distinguished himself in the debates on America and bitterly fought against the imposition of the Townshend Acts. His was a warning voice on American affairs predicting certain disaster for Britain unless she changed her tactics. At this time, too, he was very active in defense of the British East India Company against the interference of the financially hard-pressed government. Here he was on less solid ground since he and Will were then, of course, far from disinterested parties in the success of the company from which they stood to benefit as a result of Will's stock holdings. Burke's arguments for John Company were pitched on a high plane, that of the sanctity and inviolability of contracts together with the sacredness of property rights, but like his pleas for moderation toward the American colonies fell on deaf ears.

When parliament went off on its Christmas recess, Burke went north to visit the Duke of Portland along with the Marquis of Rockingham. He visited Rockingham's magnificent estate in Yorkshire and also stopped with Rockingham at Sir George Savile's estate at Rufford Abbey also in Yorkshire. The significance of these visits is that Burke was now becoming a member of the inner circle of the then nascent Rockingham Whigs. He had in fact become a party man.

As Burke's reputation grew during his second session in parliament, it was not surprising that a group of Lancashire merchants sounded him out about standing for Lancaster in the next election. They were looking for someone to represent them who understood commercial matters and felt that Burke was their man. Although flattered by their offer, Burke at length decided against acceptance.[49] The incident serves, however, to point up the importance Burke had begun to assume throughout England.

During the summer of 1767 political developments made it appear likely that Rockingham was to head a new ministry. Determined to form a government composed of his own party and unwilling to abandon either his friends or his political ideals, Rockingham had to concede to the king that the negotiations he had carried on toward forming a government had failed. There was widespread disappointment among Rockingham's "corps," as Burke often called them, over the fruitless results. Some felt that he ought to have compromised his ideals and taken office on the king's terms, but Burke, although disappointed over the prospect of continuing in opposition and deprived of what seemed a sure prospect of office for himself, was not one of the number. He was proud of Rockingham's steadfastness, and the incident only served to deepen his growing attachment to party.

Immediately following the reconvening of parliament in the fall, Burke rose to the defense of Ireland against some slurs made by Conway, formerly an old friend of the Rockinghams with whom they had now come to the parting of the ways. Conway had proposed that the army in Ireland be augmented. In his remarks he held that the proposed augmentation was necessary "because the Country was, in a great degree R. [oman] Catholick, & therefore a rotten part of the British Dominions." Burke answered him by saying that if Ireland were "rotten," it was due to "the ill policy of Government towards the body of the subjects there," i.e., the Catholics. He went on to recommend to the government that it look into the state of affairs there, especially into "a late Black & detestable proceeding there, which reflected infinitely either on the justice or the policy of the English Govt. in ruining & putting to Death many for carrying on a rebellion at the instigation of France, whilst the throne assured us we were in the most profound peace with that Nation." [50]

This speech is noteworthy in that it marked the first time Burke had taken up the defense of the Catholics in the House, a position once taken he never deserted. It also marked the opening of his long fight in the arena of Commons against the Irish Protestant Ascendancy, another stand to which he held firm.

The army augmentation bill in a different form came up for further consideration later in the session. Burke noted [51] that the proponents of the measure had defended it with references to "the Whiteboys, the Foreign Regimentals, the French money & all that miserable stuff." On the third reading of the bill, Burke spoke for an hour against it. He made fun of the government for allowing the Irish parliament to direct "the military establishment through-out the whole British Empire" and denounced the representations made of the state of the army in Ireland as "very false, glaringly so." Finally, he ridiculed as absurd the stories on which the danger to Ireland had been "presumed" and claimed that it was poor policy on the part of the government to augment Ireland's debt in time of peace. He well knew that this burden would fall mainly on the poor downtrodden Irish people who already bore a heavy enough load.

In the same letter to O'Hara which explained Burke's opposition to the army bill, he denounced both the British and the Irish parliaments for the passage of the Octennial Act.[52] He said that "the madness of the Govt. here" which passed this bill was "equalled only by the Phrenzy of your Country which desired it, & the tame-ness of this Country which bore it." This letter is one of the earliest manifestations of Burke's views on the constitutional arrangement which he felt should obtain between Great Britain and Ireland.

Before entering into any analysis of Burke's constitutional views at this time, it is necessary to digress briefly to a consideration of the motives of the British government in seeking to augment the Irish army (at Ireland's expense) and in permitting a limitation to be placed upon the duration of Irish parliaments.

The necessity of strengthening Britain's control over the sprawl-ing American colonies led in 1767 to the move for augmenting the Irish army. Lord Townshend was sent over to Ireland as Lord Lieutenant with orders to secure the agreement of the Irish parliament to increasing the size of the army from the fixed figure of 12,000 to a little over 15,000 men in order that "some part of the troops should be employed towards the necessary defence of His Majesty's garrisons and plantations abroad." [53] Since Ireland would be expected to bear the financial burden involved in this increase, Townshend was empowered to make it known that the British government would be prepared in return to support a bill designed to limit the duration of the Irish parliament and also to back a measure granting to the Irish judiciary tenure during good behavior rather than during pleasure as was then the custom. Furthermore, so anxious was the administration in London for this increase in the army that it was prepared to concede to Irish requests for a Habeas Corpus Act and for the creation of a militia (to be used at the expense of the majority of the Irish nation). Moreover, the new viceroy was to inaugurate the custom of continuous residence in Dublin during his term of office instead of merely during the sessions of parliament. Ostensibly this was a concession. By way of an added gift to Ireland, he was to promise that the king would henceforth forego the grant of Irish pensions for life or for a period of years, except in extraordinary circumstances. Finally, Townshend's instructions were to promise that, if the army were raised to 15,200 the former number (12,000) would always remain in Ireland except in the case of grave emergency or unless the Irish parliament consented to sending the troops overseas.

The inauguration of the custom of continuous residence by the viceroy had profound implications.[54] Formerly during his prolonged absences, the Lord Justices (usually the Primate, the Chancellor, and the Speaker of the House) managed the crown's business. The prolonged residence of the Lord Lieutenant meant, of course, that the power of these officials was now vastly lessened. In addition, the passage of an Octennial Act meant that the power of the Undertakers as a whole would be considerably reduced since this measure could readily become the first step in making the small number of independent members of the Irish parliament more important. The game of the British government was clearly to make the executive truly supreme and thus to smash the power of the oligarchy which ruled Ireland. The viceroy was to bring this about by securing a dependable majority which would be procured and kept docile by the dispensal of places and other favors within his power.

The army augmentation was ultimately achieved but not until Townshend had first suffered a resounding setback, whereas the Octennial Act had passed earlier. This, for the time being, marked the end of changes. For reasons which need not be entered into here the judiciary bill failed; there was a change of attitude in London toward the Habeas Corpus Act; and no militia materialized.

To return to Burke, he was opposed to the Octennial Bill, although one might have expected him to see that potentially this change could seriously hurt the Ascendancy whose misuse of power he never ceased to decry. His opposition was based upon the fear that one of two alternatives, equally unpalatable to him, would result. Either the triumph of the kind of democratic government which he could never abide or royal domination, a consummation he detested with equal fervor would ensue.[55]

He also feared the unfolding of further unpleasant constitutional developments in the relationship between Britain and Ireland. He believed at this time in the constitutional dependency of Ireland which Poynings' Law [56] and the Declaratory Act of 1719 [57] had ordained. As will be demonstrated later in this study, he came ultimately to favor a political system wherein a reformed Irish parliament, free of the power of the Protestant Ascendancy and numbering Catholics in both branches, would be allowed to legislate for itself in purely domestic matters but on all issues which conceivably related to imperial concerns should be subordinate to the imperial parliament of Great Britain.

At any rate, the session of 1767–1768 came to an end in March, and Burke was content to represent the pocket borough of Wendover in the new parliament which resulted from the general election in the spring of 1768. He intended to make a trip to Italy at that time [58] but gave up the idea when he purchased an estate at Beaconsfield called Gregories through the medium of the common purse of the Burkes (Edmund, Will, and Richard). This attractive estate of six hundred acres in Buckinghamshire was a pretty expensive undertaking as its maintenance costs were considerable.

43

As it was, the purchase price of £20,000 [59] made it something of a luxury for people whose collective income was as pitifully low as that of the Burkes. This "push" to cast a little root in the country [60] was made on the basis of East India stock. Unfortunately for their dreams, a sharp drop in the value of this stock about a year after the purchase of Gregories almost ruined them and necessitated Edmund's mortgaging the "rather superb" [61] estate to the limit to make up for the obligations incurred in buying East Indian stock on margin. Such close friends as David Garrick, the actor, and Lord Rockingham came to Edmund's assistance in this crisis so that it was weathered, although for the rest of his life Burke was destined to be in financial straits which often verged on the desperate. A day or so before the blow fell, he had written to O'Hara "in much security, & in the greatest Tranquility of heart that can be conceived; not at all apprehending the ruin of our Situation in the light I now see & feel it but too distinctly." [62]

Despite the seriousness of the situation, Burke managed to retain his home for the rest of his life and always found there a happiness with his family that was as remarkable as it was enviable. The picture of Burke as a kind and loving husband, doting father, generous host, and gentleman farmer is one that excites admiration.

Following the opening of the new parliament in May 1768, Burke indulged privately in another of his periodic outbursts of indignation over developments in Ireland, and, as was so often the case until that gentleman died, Charles O'Hara was the one to whom he disclosed his feelings: "They have managed their affairs in Ireland gloriously. Here Government is only disgraced; with you it is disgraced & defeated. My sollicitude for Ireland is growning rather less anxious than it was. I endeavour to remove it from my mind as much as I can." [63]

Burke was then engaged in a business in England in which he distinguished himself on the side of the people, as represented by the electors of Middlesex, a most democratic constituency for those times, against the king and his friends. The subject of the struggle was the notorious libertine, Jack Wilkes, whom the electors of Middlesex had four times chosen to represent them in the new parliament only to have the House of Commons set aside the results of the election each time. Although Burke was on the losing side,

44

he had shown himself to good advantage and had conducted himself on the side of liberty with considerable courage and principle.

In 1769, Burke published another book. Entitled *Observations on a Late Publication Intituled "The Present State of the Nation,"* [64] it was a rejoinder to a work of George Grenville's [65] which had attacked, among others, the Rockingham government. Grenville and Knox professed to believe that the economic condition of France was superior to that of Great Britain and recommended extension of the franchise in Britain together with the addition of Americans to the British parliament. Burke, who was rapidly becoming his party's genius, took issue with Grenville and Knox on each of these points. He declared with prophetic insight that France's finances were in such a bad way that he hourly expected "some extraordinary convulsion in that whole system the effect of which on France, and even on all Europe, it is difficult to conjecture." Rather than add to the number of voters, who were already so corrupt, he would reduce their ranks in the hope of making them more consequential and independent. Geography manifestly made impossible the idea of American representation in parliament. In conclusion, he defended Rockingham's American policy, particularly his coupling the repeal of the Stamp Act with the Declaratory Act (which was quite probably Burke's idea in the first place). The Declaratory Act was "reconciled in policy: and politics ought to be adjusted, not to human reasonings, but to human nature; of which the reason is but a part, and by no means the greatest part." [66] The position taken by Burke here is strikingly similar to his Irish policy in that the importance of circumstances is paramount.

From some of his correspondents in Ireland Burke learned of new disorders there, but the combination of his party duties and his financial problems [67] crowded Ireland and her concerns out of his mind.

The *Observations* was followed in 1770 by another piece of writing, a political pamphlet called *Thoughts on the Causes of the Present Discontents,* [68] which was published in April of that year. It contained an attack on the crown which Burke held responsible for the low state of esteem in which politics was being held. The remedy lay in the possession of office by good men, (a commodity with which the Rockingham Whigs were, of course, well stocked): "The laws reach but a very little way. Constitute government how you please, infinitely the greater part of it must depend upon the exercise of powers which are left at large to the prudence and up rightness of ministers of state. Even all the use and potency of the laws depend upon them. Without them, your commonwealth is no better than a scheme upon paper, and not a living, active, effective constitution." [69] Although written as a matter of practical politics, the *Thoughts* is a treasure house of Burke's ideas on politics and human nature. He was rather pleased with its success: ". . . the Pamphlet, which contains our Creed has been received by the publick beyond my expectations. The Courtiers admit it to be a piece of Gentlemanlike Hostility. The fiercest Enemies it has yet met with are in the republican faction." [70] In fact, coupled with his views on American affairs, it served, according to Will Burke, to make him stand "higher than He ever did in his Life. I had almost said the highest of any man in the Country." [71] He distinguished himself at this time by taking the side of liberty in two disputes involving freedom of the press, one of which was to result in the reporting with impunity of the proceedings of parliament.

Before the *Thoughts* was published, an important change in British politics had taken place. Lord North had replaced Grafton as prime minister, although rumors had been erroneously circulated that Rockingham would be the king's choice.[72] Actually, George III had never considered Rockingham once he knew that Grafton was planning to resign. This change served to round out the first decade of the king's reign, and within a short time the administration's majorities began to mount as the opposition had reached the peak of their strength for years to come.

Meanwhile, Burke was criticized in a mild way by an old Irish friend, Dr. Leland, in a letter dated 22 March 1770. Leland's purpose in writing was "to censure & to advise you. — You think too meanly of this place & people. *Without doors* all are, to a man, your favourers & admirers; *within*, you have a great party; If you think an Irish reputation totally immaterial your opponents are more flattering to us," and he went on to plead with Burke to write more frequently so that people like himself, who were his friends, would be correctly informed and thus able to counteract the criticisms of

Burke's enemies in Ireland who took great delight in misrepresentations at Burke's expense.[73] Another letter from Leland on 19 May 1770 was in the same vein, and on 11 June he expressed the wish that Burke would exchange Gregories for a while for Leland's cottage in Burke's "favourite country." [74]

Burke's attention, however, was being continually attracted to the worsening state of affairs between parliament and America. Nevertheless, he did manage to remember the needs of his "favourite country" in a speech on 13 November 1770 when he tried to couple Ireland and America, whose cases, he held, were similar. The support of both these important parts of the empire was needed by the mother country, and to secure their help he recommended that the causes of discontent in each should be removed. If this were done, he predicted that the British Empire would be more closely cemented and its members would act "as if inspired by one soul." [75] If his efforts for Ireland went without recognition, those on behalf of America did not. In December 1770 he was made the London Agent of the Colony New York at an annual salary of five hundred pounds.[76] In one sense his appointment was unfortunate in that it opened him to no little criticism whenever he championed the American cause thereafter and it unquestionably weakened the strength of his arguments.[77] One is here reminded of his past and future battles involving India wherein the knowledge that he had dabbled in East India stock was hurtful. It must be conceded that in the instance of his defense of prescription and the rights of property in the East India Company affair, 1766–1773, Burke's disinterestedness is certainly hard to defend. However, in both his defense of the colonists, wherein a case may be made that he was seeking to protect English liberties, and his subsequent efforts on behalf of the people of India, wherein his enlightened views of empire were violated by flagrant misgovernment of the Company's subjects, it seems to me that his conduct cannot be questioned. He had been fighting for the defense of English liberties in America well in advance of his appointment as New York's London Agent, and the modest compensation which he received could hardly compromise him. Nor is it difficult to believe that anything but the highest of motives fundamentally impelled him to seek the amelioration of India's "undone millions" in the trial of Warren Hastings.

The speech in November 1770 was the only one in which Burke mentioned Ireland for quite a while. Indeed through 1771 Ireland receded further and further from his attention. In his letters to O'Hara, he did allude to his native land but seldom in very complimentary terms. He admitted, 2 April 1771, to his old friend that "As to your proceeding[s] in Ireland, I begin to feel every day less & less, any interest in them; I thank God it is so; for otherwise, I should have uneasiness on what side soever I looked." [78]

As the year was drawing to a close, he had not changed his opinions, although there was something ironical about it:

I read with surprise of the pompous funeral of Dr. Lucas. By the account one would take it for the funeral of a Prince. Was his family in a condition to afford this piece of Vanity — or was it a kind of *Caesar's* funeral made by the opposition to keep alive the Spirits of the *Populace*? What is your Government, if Government at all it be doing? Their scheme seems to me the destruction of the Grants. Never certainly was there more abuse in any practice — but a reformation might, & I think would, unless conducted with care & sobriety greatly retard the improvement of *your* Country — I was going to say *ours* — but I have not much more interest in it, than that it furnishes some matter of reproach agst. me to the Scotch writers in pay of the Ministry, witht. any one in that Country thinking himself concerned in supporting me. It is bad to be loaded with the local prejudices agst. a country witht. getting anything by these in favour of it.[79]

Nor did anything which happened the following year, 1772, inspire him to renew his interest in the land of his birth:

I wish tolerably well to Ireland as to its general Interests. The parties which have, or aim at having the management of them, & indeed the whole Chart of the Country begin to wear out my Memory, & are, I suppose, much changed since I knew them. But I have little desire to renew my acquaintance in that quarter. I see the plan there, is to be of the same Nature with the Scheme here, that of drawing everything from the Natural powers & interests of the Country to private influence and Court Cabal.[80]

The Directors of the East India Company in recognition of the services which he rendered in fighting against parliamentary interference with their chartered rights offered him, in August 1772, the chairmanship of a proposed three-member commission which they were going to send to India to make a thorough study of the entire administration of the Company in the field. The commission was to be empowered to make any changes the members deemed necessary, and Burke's salary for his services was to be a lump sum of ten thousand pounds.[81] He decided to reject this tempting offer in favor of concentrating on helping the Rockingham Party in its role of opposition. He told O'Hara that "If I had leisure to lay open to you the true state of things relatively to the East India Company & to my own situation you would not I think censure me for declining to accept the Offer of the Supervision. The affairs of the Company are at once flourishing, & in the greatest confusion, & the greatest danger; just like the affairs of this Country — . . ." [82]

Earlier that year, Burke had opposed a petition inspired by the Unitarians which called for the repeal of the act which required the clergy and others to subscribe to the Thirty-Nine Articles of the Church of England. His position was that there had to be some standard of faith within the Established Church to make it unique and worthwhile. This, he was fully persuaded, was accomplished by the Articles. The majority of his own party in the House of Commons supported the petition, and thus Burke found himself voting against them. But by so doing he exhibited that independence of judgment and action which was indispensable to him and from which he would never budge if he believed himself in the right.

Early in January 1773, Burke made a trip to France in order to place his son in a French home at Auxerre. He then went to Paris where he was warmly received by the best of French society. The atheism of these circles shocked Burke profoundly as he clearly foresaw what the consequences both for France and the rest of Europe could easily be should rationalist thought come to prevail. This visit of Burke's has been rightly called a milestone in his life. Henceforward, he was to become the spokesman for the old order against the onslaughts of those who sought to overturn the religious and civil bedrocks of Europe.[83]

He had scarcely returned from France when he made a speech in the House on 17 March 1773 in favor of a bill to relieve Dissenters from subscribing to the Thirty-Nine Articles. Contrary to the position he was to adopt in reference to the Dissenters after the outbreak of the French Revolution, Burke now supported the bill on the grounds that there was no question of any standard of conformance since the Dissenters were already outside the Church of England. He denounced the petition of a group who were opposed to the proposed measure in favor of the Dissenters by saying that there was nothing to fear from the Dissenters. Rather it was the atheists who should be feared since "the most horrid and cruel blow that can be offered to civil society is through atheism. . . . The infidels are outlaws of the constitution, not of this country, but of the human race. They are never, never to be supported never to be tolerated. Under the systematic attacks of these people, I see some of the props of good government already begin to fail; I see propagated principles which will not leave to religion even a toleration. I see myself sinking every day under the attacks of these wretched people." [84]

In June of that year, Lord North's Regulating Act was passed, and the British crown now secured some control over the government of India despite Burke's long fight [85] to uphold the charter rights of the East India Company. The first Governor-General was Warren Hastings, a name that was destined to loom large in Burke's future. Now that the business of India was to be settled for over a decade, the stage was clear for the American affairs to come to the front without competition. Before that happened, however, Burke found himself involved in a matter relating to Ireland.

A change had taken place at Dublin Castle. Lord Townshend, who had become so unpopular that he had been forced to resort to an almost prodigal distribution of titles and places to maintain his majority, had been replaced in 1772 by the Earl of Harcourt. Aided by his clever Chief Secretary, Sir John Blaquiere, and no mean politician himself, Harcourt quickly reestablished the hold of the viceroy over the Irish parliament. Looking around for a measure which would both strengthen the treasury and bring popularity to his administration, Harcourt concluded that a bill to tax the rents of absentee proprietors would achieve these results.

Accordingly, in 1773 a proposal was made in the Irish House of Commons that a tax of two shillings per pound be placed upon the net rents of Irish estates, the owners of which did not reside for six months of the year in Ireland. Those who stood to suffer the most, should this proposal become law, were, of course, the great English absentee holders of Irish estates, prominent among whom was the

Marquis of Rockingham. Rockingham became the leader of the opposition in England to the proposed tax, and his town house in Grosvenor Square became the headquarters of this opposition.[86]

Years earlier, when Burke was a Trinity undergraduate, he had proposed a similar tax in one of the sessions of the Debating Club which he had helped to found.[87] Now as a seasoned member of the British parliament, Burke's position on the matter of an absentee tax was just the reverse. His opposition to the measure gives us a first-rate example of Burke's imperialism. In playing the part he did in this instance, Burke was clearly placing himself in opposition to the sentiment prevalent among the majority of his former countrymen. His convictions were so strong that this did not deter him a whit. He was well aware of the popularity of the measure in Ireland,[88] and he knew that its chances of being approved in England were good.

One of the things which disturbed him in connection with the bill was his feeling that its proponents did not foresee that it would drive many absentees to permanent residence in Ireland. The very core of the proposal, as he saw it, was that it would separate Ireland from England to a considerable extent. Furthermore, if the proposal were to be adopted, it would be a case of a most important but nevertheless a subordinate part of the Empire being allowed to legislate for the whole.[89]

Rockingham and four other absentee peers, Devonshire, Bessborough, Milton, and Upper Ossory, all English-born but holders of vast amounts of landed property in Ireland,[90] signed a remonstrance against the suggested tax. Dated 16 October 1773 and addressed to Lord North, the Prime Minister, it was probably written by Burke and has been called one of the best state papers of the entire period.[91] The remonstrance had the desired effect of creating a public agitation against the proposal. In it the signatories claimed the right of free citizens of the Empire to choose their place of residence wherever it might suit them in His Majesty's dominions. They expressed surprise that it should be proposed to stigmatize them for living in the country which was the principal member of the Empire and the residence of its ruler. It was their professed belief that the projected tax would be harmful to both England and Ireland. In the latter country, it would result in a depreciation of the value of landed property. In the former, it would mean that restrictions would result which had no counterpart within the Empire or, for that matter, in the whole civilized world.[92] The protest was widely circulated and most effective.

Nevertheless, there was powerful support for the measure in England. Lord Chatham, for example, felt that there was considerable merit in the idea that the absentees should make a real contribution to Ireland in return for the benefits which they derived there and also was of the opinion that colonial parliaments possessed the sole right of deciding their own taxation. So convincing were his arguments that he won Shelburne over to them, no mean feat in view of the fact that Shelburne was himself an Irish absentee. This Chatham-Shelburne combination was a strong one.[93]

Burke labored vigorously behind the scenes and was assisted by his friend, Joseph Hickey, the attorney. They made Rockingham's town house their headquarters for the campaign against the projected tax. On 16 October, the same day on which the Rockingham remonstrance which was signed by the other four peers made its appearance, Burke wrote a letter to Sir Charles Bingham, Bart., a member of the Irish House of Commons, calling the latter's attention to the writer's conviction that the measure would pass unless those interested in defeating it exerted themselves strenuously. Burke said that the tax would be used to "support Pension lists, useless establishments & every sort of Ministerial Profusion & extravagance" and asked Bingham to intercede with Lord Charlemont. He went on to say that he would oppose the proposal in England and felt that he had "many weighty arguments against it" but could use more and asked Bingham for any which he could suggest.[94]

On 30 October 1773, Burke wrote another letter to Bingham in which he stated his unequivocal opposition to the tax which he said struck a blow both at the power of England and the very unity of the British Empire itself. Bearing in mind his position in the dispute then going on with the American colonies, Burke was careful to make it clear that he did not entertain any odious notions concerning the directing power of the mother country in the Empire and pointed out that, if the Empire were to be preserved as a unit, there had to be an authority capable of maintaining that unity. Such an authority had to reside some place; a place within the Empire which could only be England. No other member of the Empire would approve of any other place of residence unless it be within its own borders. But this was manifestly impossible, hence the seat of that power in the very nature of things was England. This being so, England must have the distinctive privilege of imperial legislation — the law which regulates the policy and economy of the other members as they relate to one another and the whole. Under such an arrangement, the parts could not arrogate to themselves the power of making laws which could upset the order of the Empire.[95]

The proposed tax was equivalent to a declaration that England was a foreign country in the eyes of Ireland, he asserted. Such an implication constituted a real threat to the solidarity of the Empire and was commensurate with the rejection of the principle of "common naturalization" which embraced the whole Empire. He then asked Sir Charles whether he, or any other Irish gentlemen, considered it a mean privilege that the moment he set foot on the soil of England he became to all intents and purposes an Englishman.[96]

Mutual intermarriage and inheritance were likewise discouraged by the tax. This was a bad feature, he observed, because it would mean the loss of factors which bound countries together closer than any laws or constitutions. Another obnoxious feature was the discouragement of travel.[97] As a matter of fact, said Burke, the number of inconveniences which the tax would produce was considerable. He was constrained to admit that, in the nature of things, a large share of the money of each of the members of the Empire would flow to the seat of power, England, but this was unavoidable. Other disadvantages were bound to result for the constituent parts of the Empire, because they were parts, each a member of a larger entity and not a whole themselves. Yet despite these inconveniences, did not the advantages which resulted from the united power of the Empire, considered as an undivided organization, more than make up for them? Burke answered himself affirmatively.[98]

Bingham replied privately to Burke on 7 November and thanked him for the arguments Burke supplied. He suggested to Burke that it would be a good idea for all absentees "who have good estates, to order their agents here to make some Freeholders in the several

Counties where their estates lye, & this before the next general Election — such a step would alarm the Members for those Counties more than you can imagine, & in order to get these Freeholders, they would always vote against any tax that would affect the Absentees — " [99]

In two letters to Rockingham at this time, Burke made mention of his activities to defeat the absentee tax. In the first one, he informed Rockingham that:

I have seen Glynn who has done all that depended on him. My Lord Mayor departed has likewise done all that was to be expected from his character & connections. He cooled by a communication w. Berkeley Square as fast as he heated from the vivacity of his natural temper. The wind that blew from the great house in our quarter quite dulled the Mansion House. No common council has been called; the letters have indeed been communicated to the Irish Society. They have acted properly, & come to a resolution of concurring in an opposition to the proposed tax. Whether it was merely accidental, or the politics of the court or the [?] of Shelburne House, I know not, but a report was universally propagated & credited that the ministry had quite dropped the scheme. This contributed much to the postponing all ideas of calling a common council.[100]

The second letter revealed Burke to be quite sanguine over the prospects of defeating the measure.[101]

In a long communication to Burke, 12 November, Rockingham showed his dependence upon Burke in this business. He spoke of a proposed follow-up to the circular letter of remonstrance dated 16 October and asked Burke to make any changes in it which he desired, assuring him that he would be guided completely by Burke's judgment. In reply, Burke informed his friend and leader that he had heard that Lord North had said that "Nothing could be more popular than an absentee tax in Ireland, if Ministry had not supported it." He went on to advise Rockingham to send out the new circular letter in which he made a few minor changes. In flattering terms he emphasized that the changes were unimportant since Rockingham's letter was such that "Nothing can be more properly conceived or expressed." [102] One alteration which he made was to change the phrase "this Country" to "this Empire" for "reasons very obvious." [103]

As an illustration of the strong feelings of those who would be affected by the tax, there is an amusing letter from Lord Clanricarde, head of the Irish Burkes, who belatedly appealed to Burke "as a Burke" to pass on the word that he was opposed to the tax. His Lordship called the tax "an oppression which Even a Turkish Government would blush [to] Carry into Execution." [104]

Burke himself had grown quite exercised as he revealed to O'Hara:

All the rest of the Kingdom is quite stupified; except a small part which you have awakened by the scheme of an absentee Tax. You know the steps that have been taken in this Business, by the circular Letter & correspondence; which by being sent to all the absentees, have undoubtedly found their way to Ireland through more channels than one. Could any one believe it possible, even among all the drowsy visions of this raving (but not inspired) age we live in, that such a Project should be entertained among the ways & means of English Government? proposed by an English Secretary — to an English Lord Lieutenant, — adopted, — & what is more — avowed by an English first Lord of the Treasury — stante Jove et urbe Roma! I hear the pleasant end of it may be, that it will be smotherd in the filthy slime & mud of that very popularity, to which it owed its equivocal Generation. Sr. Charles Bingham has written me two long & friendly Letters on the Subject. It is amazing with what spirit & activity Ld. Rockingham exerted himself on the occasion. Malagrida [105] disapproved the measure as you may easily judge — but he acted too in the manner you may easily judge.[106]

The opposition which Burke had done so much to raise proved strong enough to defeat the proposed tax. He received word of their victory from Bingham in a letter dated 29 November. Although the initial measure was defeated, a Mr. O'Neil, urged on by Henry Flood, "who was enraged at his disappointment," proposed the same tax in a different form. This time it was "one shilling in the Pound on all remittances arising out of the Lands of Absentees." It, too, was defeated by being withdrawn as the sense of the Irish House of Commons was against it following "a debate very dry & bad, the subject having been exhausted." [107]

In another letter Bingham exulted over their victory and revealed that he "got great applause, thanks to your friendly assistance, for the support I gave against the Tax, and I had the Pleasure to hear from Many Gentlemen, that my arguments had the greatest weight with them, as they came undecided into the House." Bingham remarked that he did not let it be known that he had heard from Burke or that the latter's "Powers" contributed so much "to the throwing out of this infamous attempt of Administration." [108]

Rockingham was also elated but felt that it was no time to rest on their laurels. Rather they should take every precaution and remain vigilantly prepared against a revival of the project. He felt that a parliamentary commendation to the *"Wise & Just* Men in Ireland — would be mustard to L North's nose even in his House of Commons Slumbers." This long letter concluded: "I *am glad* they begin to *abuse me* in the *News Paper — You come in for Your Share* . . . It was a letter in Monday's News Paper signed — Marius." [109]

Burke himself was pleased but was apprehensive that the scheme might be revived:

The Parlt. of Ireland have I think done themselves much Credit. I believe no man rejoiced more who saved ten per Cent on his Estate than the Ministry did here when the Parliament refused to send them that Coal of fire which they could neither know how to cast away or to hold. Most of the Cabinet here was utterly unacquainted with the design. They railed at it open mouthd. If it had come hither there would certainly have been some work; but you saved us the trouble & the Sport. However if I may judge by some conversations, & by the stir the Court hirelings have made in the Newspaper when it was so evident the wish & Interest of most of the ministers to let the matter drop, the attempt will be revived another time. I suspect it came from the Sanctum sanctorum. It must indeed be either very deep design or very consumate folly that first gave rise to it — Possibly a Little of both.[110]

Burke was criticized so often throughout his life for one reason or another and still has so many detractors today that one ought not leave this subject without noting the usual criticisms directed against him for the position he took in this matter of proposed tax. Party feeling, personal friendship, and inconsistency are the customary charges against him. The last may be dismissed rather easily since the fact that he had reversed the position which he had taken as a student ought not to be taken seriously for obvious reasons. The other strictures have considerably more merit. One must admit that there can be no doubt that both of these factors influenced him in this business. Nor is it surprising that he should have been so motivated — most people are when in similar circumstances. But, as is so often the case with Burke, there was something else which was even more important than either of these considerations, as weighty as both of them were with Burke. After all, it must be remembered that Burke had voted against his party before and would do so again and that friendship took second place to his principles on more than one occasion as his famous breaks with Sheridan and Fox demonstrate. That which had for Burke the first order of magnitude in this affair was his reverence for the British Empire and his personal feeling of obligation to it.

The fact that he, an obscure middle-class Irishman, could sit in the British parliament never failed to impress him or to fill him with a truly reverential awe and appreciation for the imperial system which made such a thing possible. In his view of things the benefits of imperial citizenship, as he had learned from personal experience, far out-weighted any disadvantages accruing to it.

The feelings which he had displayed in the absentee tax business remained unaltered for the remainder of his days. In 1797, only five weeks before his death, he wrote to his protégé, Dr. French Laurence, that he sincerely hoped that the Opposition (his friends) in Ireland would desist from the idea of an absentee tax which they were then considering. Such a proposal, he said, even went beyond that of the United Irishmen, then seeking to divide the two countries, in the direction of the separation of England and Ireland, an idea which he would never tolerate.[111]

A couple of months before the above-mentioned letter to Laurence, Burke alluded to the revived idea of an absentee tax in the strongest terms to Fitzwilliam, Rockingham's heir and successor:

The Opposition, your Lordships friends & let me add, my friends, have gone the full length of Jacobinism, & are doing all they can to pull up the land-marks of private property & public safety, & to disunite the two Kingdoms; and that upon the falsest grounds both of fact and principle, which, I might easily prove, if I had heart or strength for such a task. I confess whilst I blame the conduct of the Minority in that Kingdom I know how to excuse it. They, who provoke the passions of men beyond the limits of human prudence, are primarily & much the most heavily responsible for all the excesses into which Men are led by these passions. But the effect on the publick is the same, who ever may be culpable. I am extremely glad that your Lordship had re-solved on the defence of those persons who residing in the seats of their Ancestors, and living in the Country in which they are born;

possess Property in Ireland. I cannot enter into the case of every individual; but of this, I am sure, that several of you have been basely calumniated by the Opposition in Ireland, . . . You are branded by the odious Name of Absentees, as if you were bound to be present in Ireland at every roll call, as if you were Soldiers & the very people, a great part of the power & consideration of whose families has arisen from English Matches, as their Estates have arisen from English grants, have endeavoured to make English intermarriages impracticable, & the inheritance of Irish property by Englishmen odious & precarious. I am glad that your Lordship intends to exert yourself upon this occasion.[112]

The time and energy which Burke put into the fight against the proposed tax in 1773, the forcefulness and pertinency of the arguments which he advanced, and the fact that these convictions remained as strong with him to the end of his life as in 1773 make it difficult to reach any other conclusion than that Burke sincerely believed in the cause which he espoused and was motivated principally not by party feeling or personal friendship but by his belief that such a tax would be a serious blow to the British Empire which could ultimately weaken it dangerously.

The episode is a valuable one since it so clearly reveals Burke's imperial thinking at this time. The position which he took on this Irish business was in perfect consonance with that which he had been holding in reference to America. There he had insisted upon the Declaratory Act because it unequivocally vested in the imperial parliament, to be used whenever needed, the kind of power necessary for upholding imperial unity. Britain, as he saw it, had to be constitutionally supreme over the parts of the empire but in exercising her supremacy must be generous.[113]

CHAPTER III

Member of Parliament for Bristol

ELECTION

With the defeat of the Irish absentee-tax measure and the passage of Lord North's Regulating Act for the government of India, American affairs occupied the attention both of Burke and parliament to a very considerable extent at this time. Occasioned by the dispute over whether Britain had the right to tax the colonies without their being represented in the British parliament, the contest had assumed serious proportions by the end of 1773. Britain's answer to the Boston Tea Party in December 1773 took the form of reprisals which elicited a vigorous reaction upon the part of the colonists.

Through his conduct in the debates on America, Edmund Burke had become one of the best known men in the House of Commons and so had come to the attention of some prominent people in Bristol, then second city in the kingdom. Hard hit by the effective American boycott against British goods, this great trading city was eager for a quick settlement of the differences which had arisen between the mother country and the Americans.

While the summer of 1774 was in general an unhappy one for Burke, he had become involved in negotiations with some people in Bristol with a view toward becoming a candidate for one of Bristol's two seats in the next general election. He had been informed by the Reverend Doctor Thomas Wilson, rector of St. Stephen's, Westminster, on 28 June that he had come to the attention of some residents of Bristol who were men of "Fortune & Character & warm will." These men wished to preserve the "Liberties & Constitution of this *Once* free Nation," and hence Wilson wished to ascertain if Burke would be willing to stand for election in the next contest there should these men prove "strong enough" to secure the necessary support for his candidacy.[1]

Burke responded cautiously to this feeler but revealed that he was interested:

I am desirous of continuing to serve my Country in the situation, upon the principles and with the friends I have have [sic] served it these Eight years past. If I have the honour of a Choice which is upon all accounts so respectable as you propose, I shall be enabled without question to perform my Duty with more satisfaction and greater Authority. If therefore your friends persevere in their intentions and are able to compass what they wish I shall accept the Trust of their Representation with thanks and endeavour to discharge it with Fidelity.

However, he begged them not to take such a step except upon "the most clear and solid Grounds" since a contest in a place like Bristol was a very serious undertaking as Bristol was a "Maritime Town" where "a Court Candidate has great advantages." Furthermore, Burke added that under no circumstances could he help in the expenses of the contest since "The Part I have hitherto acted has not added to my Ability and the part I shall probably act in future does not encourage me to risque any Charge whatsoever."[2]

Wilson expressed his satisfaction with Burke's feelings in the matter and told him that the Bristol people who wished him to stand were "very sensible of the Difficulties" but did not "despair of succeeding."[3]

Despite these negotiations, Burke had grown very dejected and confessed to Rockingham a few days before parliament was dissolved that he was seriously considering retiring from public life. The likelihood that he could win a seat for Westminster, which had apparently been advanced by some of Burke's friends, was not very great as far as he could see. But he was willing to talk it over with those interested in his becoming a candidate there. This he did only to find that his candidacy would be hopeless so the idea was dropped. He could no longer represent Wendover, Lord Verney's pocket borough, since Verney's financial difficulties made it necessary for him to realize whatever he could from the sale of the seat. This coupled with other difficulties drove Burke periodically into fits of melancholy which made him question whether he should continue in "this public station, for which I am so unfit, and have of course been so unfortunate." One thing was certain and that was, if he did continue in parliament, he would be "as much my own master as hitherto I have been, and at liberty to pursue the same course." [4]

He told the Duke of Richmond who had admitted to him that he was growing sick and tired of politics that His Lordship should not give up the fight because his noble birth would not allow him to lead a private life. Comparing their respective situations, Burke declared that "it requires as much struggle and violence to put yourself in private life, as to put me into public. Pardon a slight comparison, but it is as hard to sink a cork, as to buoy up a lump of lead." [5]

This was at the end of September. With the beginning of October, Burke's prospects brightened markedly. Rockingham revealed to him on the second that he felt pretty certain that he could so arrange the disposition of his three seats that Burke could have one of them. He told Burke that he considered it absolutely necessary that Burke continue in the House.[6] Three days later, he was able to inform him that he could have a seat from Malton in Yorkshire [7] although he expressed regret in another letter that Burke had to give up ten guineas "to remove an obstacle in your way to be chose [sic] Member for Malton." [8]

Prior to, and following, his election at Malton, the Bristol contest entered the picture. He had received a letter, dated 1 October, from Richard Champion, the porcelain manufacturer, who was destined to be his closest friend at Bristol although then a complete stranger. Champion gave Burke an account of developments in Bristol where he had been pushing Burke's candidacy by describing him to his friends as "the first literary Character in the Kingdom . . . a perfect Master of its commercial Interests . . . [and the possessor of] a true Knowledge of the Constitution." He assured Burke that they would win a victory which would do honor both to Bristol and Burke.[9]

Burke's name was, with his consent, proposed for nomination at a meeting of the Bristol Whigs on 5 October, but Henry Cruger, Jr., the leading Whig candidate, who had quickly won nomination, and his friends were opposed to Burke.[10] Cruger made it clear that he intended to stand alone. Since the majority of those present upheld him, Joseph Harford, a prominent merchant who had nominated Burke, and Richard Champion, who had seconded him, had to withdraw their candidate. Dejectedly they met Burke at Bath to tell him the bad news. Greatly disappointed, Burke decided to go ahead at Malton which he now knew was open for him. He therefore proceeded there and was elected.

Meanwhile, the Bristol poll had opened on the seventh, when one of the candidates suddenly withdrew leaving Cruger, the Whig, and Matthew Brickdale, the Tory incumbent, alone in the field. Harford and Champion proceeded to put forth Burke's name on the eighth.[11] Brickdale protested on the grounds that the election had already begun, and the Sheriffs of Bristol took the protest under advisement but ruled that the election should continue with Burke entered pending their disposal of the protest. Burke received the consent of the Malton electors to try Bristol and hurried to set out on the evening of 11 October, arriving there almost two sleepless days later. He delivered his first campaign speech that very day, promising to look out for Britain's commercial interests and also to bring about a reconciliation with America.

One argument used against him by the opposition was that he was a "needy Member" of parliament and therefore unreliable.[12] In the light of his sympathies it was somewhat ironical that one of the objections voiced against the Tories in Bristol before Burke's name was entered was that the Tory party had been guilty of "establing [sic] the *Roman Catholic Religion* in Canada on the Ruins of the Protestant Religion of the *Church of England*." [13]

During the contest which ran through 2 November, Burke conducted his canvass quite spiritedly. He told Rockingham near the end of the poll that he was quite sanguine and that his supporters were "noble fellows" who "deserve everything of me I am sure." [14] In addition to all manner of public and private verbal efforts to win votes, Burke wrote quite a few letters asking support at the polls. He maintained that a "civil request by letter is what every Candidate owes to every Elector of Condition." [15] Dignity, however, must always be maintained. He became quite exercised with one man whom he formally asked to grant him leave to withdraw his request for this gentleman's support. He reminded this person that he was not "a common Candidate; nor one who chooses to sneak into Parliament by any means that are low and unworthy. I am not absolutely unknown in the world. . . ." [16]

The night on which the poll closed, "at the confused ending, of all the confusion of the strangest Election we have had since the dissolution of the last Parliament," Burke listed the results for the edification of his friend O'Hara:

Cruger	3565	
Burke	2707	} Majty. for Burke 251
Brickdale	2456	
Clare [17]	283	

He mentioned that "the defeated party threaten a petition; but I do not think they can succeed on the ground they take." [18] He was right on both counts. Brickdale's protest was heard later by a special parliamentary committee which rejected it.[19] Now that his right to the seat had been upheld, the friends of the victorious Whigs in Bristol desired to hold a triumphal celebration. With his usual modesty Burke found it distasteful that he should be expected there for such a purpose. He felt that he could not spare the necessary time away from his parliamentary duties and that it was ungenerous and imprudent to celebrate publicly a victory over a respectable adversary. Moderation and prudence in success helped to make it more acceptable to all classes.[20]

The new parliament met on 30 November 1774, and, as a result of his achievement at Bristol, Burke's prestige was greatly enhanced in this body. Burke's party was still in the minority and so theirs was once again the role of opposition. As the government of Lord North continued its American policy in the same vein as before despite mounting sentiment within Britain for moderation and conciliation, Burke endeavored to lecture them in his famous speech on *Conciliation*, which was delivered on 22 March 1775. Since every schoolboy is familiar with this magnificent speech, there is no need of analyzing it here. All that is necessary is to recall two of its most famous passages, viz., "I do not know the method of drawing up an indictment against an whole people" and "Magnanimity in Politics is not seldom the truest wisdom; and a great empire and little minds go ill together." [21] Both of these passages are reminiscent of his feelings on the subject of Ireland and at the same time foreshadow arguments he would use in the future on behalf of his native land. Within a few weeks after this speech, England had blundered into a fratricidal war with the American colonists,[22] and a short time later in his private correspondence, Burke endeavored to sum up his position in the dispute between Britain and America:

For one I am sure I have labourd as much as any body to procure it [peace]; & upon the only Terms of honour & safety I know of, that is to give them [the colonists] our constitution or what is most substantial in it. How could you imagine that I had in my thoughts anything of the Theoretical separation of a power of Taxing from Legislation. I have no opinion about it. These things depend on conventions real or understood, upon practice, accident, the humour or Genius of those who Govern or are governd, & may be, as they are, modified to infinity. No bounds ever were set to the Parliamentary power over the Colonies; for how could that have been but by *special Convention*. No such convention ever has been; but the reason & nature of things, & the growth of the Colonies ought to have taught Parliament to have set bounds to the exercise of its own power. I never ask what Government may do in *Theory*, except *Theory* be the *Object*; when one talks of *Practice* they must act according to circumstances. If you think it worth yr. while to read that Speech [on Conciliation] over again you will find that principle to be the key of it.[23]

When the session of the Irish parliament opened in 1775, the viceroy Earl Harcourt announced the government's intention to grant various privileges to Irish ships engaged in the Newfoundland fisheries, permission to Ireland to manufacture clothing for Irish troops serving outside the country, and the grant of a small bounty on flaxseed imported into the country. On 11 April Lord North moved in the British House of Commons that the House resolve itself into a Committee of the Whole to consider the fisheries question, he having indicated that his government favored concessions to Irish fishing vessels in the Newfoundland fisheries. Burke expressed his gratitude to North for his willingness to help Ireland in this instance and said that although he was anxious "to promote any scheme for the advantage of Ireland, he would be much better pleased that the benefits thus held out should never be realized, than that Ireland should profit at the expense of a coun-

try [America] which was, if possible, more oppressed than herself."
Burke endeavored unsuccessfully to get North's motion amended to
include trade with fisheries.[24]

Writing to O'Hara to tell him what had transpired, he said: [25]

When Lord North opend the Fishery Business, he expressed himself in an open & Liberal manner: His argument went to a large consideration of the Irish Trade; but when I desired him to have his motion
amended to his argument, & to add the word Trade, he drew himself
immediately into his shell; refused the amendment, & declared that he
only proposed some little matters. In truth the affair I mentiond was
very little indeed, no more than to suffer the Sugars brought from the
West Indies for Irish consumption to be Landed originally in Ireland.
What Connolly proposed in a very supplicatory Tone about the Wool-
lens of Ireland was of greater Magnitude; But he would listen to neither.
I know that some of the Irish here think great matters will be done for
the *Herring* Fishery; but I rather think, that they will go no further
than to put you on a par with America in the *Whale* Fishery; a thing
that I think cannot be of sixpenny worth to you.

As Burke correctly predicted, the British parliament passed an
act which gave bounties to Irish whaling ships as well as their own
and, in addition, permitted Ireland to export clothing and other
items to the Irish troops serving abroad. The Irish were also allowed
to export various fishing implements.

With Lexington and Concord followed by Bunker Hill, this
latter "only a successful sally of a besiegd Garrison," [26] the American War was on in earnest, and Burke turned his thoughts to Ireland in the hope that she might be able to save the threatened disruption of the Empire. He advised the Irish parliament to refrain
from voting all extraordinary grants and supplies as he hoped that
Britain's distresses might now act to the advantage of Ireland by
making it necessary to ameliorate conditions there, a step which
would ultimately be of great advantage to the Empire. One of his
correspondents, a Scots woolen manufacturer named George Glasgow, probably anticipating that Burke would sense that circumstances were now auspicious for such a step, had disingenuously
suggested to him that the time was now ripe in "the Interest of the
British Empire in generale and of the Kingdom of Ireland in particular" to do something for the Irish fisheries. If the Irish were
allowed "the right of fishing Herrings on the Coast of Scotland in

common with the Subjects of Great Britain," it would result in "the addition of 50, 60, or 80 Thousand Sailors to the Kingdom of Ireland employed in the herring fishery and possibly the same number employed to export them to forreign Countrys and to our Collonys & Plantations." This would to a considerable extent put a halt to Ireland's great loss of population due to emigration and by keeping the people thus employed they would in "10, 15, or 20 Years" need "more Wooll" thereby causing a great boom for the woolen manufacturers throughout Great Britain.[27]

At any rate, Burke was thoroughly convinced, as he told the Duke of Richmond, that Ireland's position had not been more advantageous in years and that in her hands lay "the balance of the empire, and perhaps its fate forever." [28] It was his idea that Ireland offer to act as a friendly mediator between Britain and America. She could do more by refusing to vote supplies for troops sent overseas from Ireland. This would force the king's hand, and he would have to capitulate. The fuzziness exhibited by Burke in this letter to Richmond gives ample testimony to his mood at the time.

Meanwhile, the stupidity and intransigence of the North government, which nevertheless had popular support from those who profited from a wartime economy, made it advisable in Burke's opinion for the Rockingham party to make up its mind what role it would play when parliament reopened in the fall. He leaned toward the idea that "the most effectual, and much the most honourable course is, without the obligation of a formal secession, to absent ourselves from Parliament." [29] Otherwise, he added with that indelicacy to which he was so often prone, "what is left for us, but to spin out of our bowels, under the frowns of the court and the hisses of the people, the little slender thread of a peevish and captious opposition, unworthy of our cause and ourselves, and without credit, concurrence, or popularity in the nation!" [30]

It was imperative, he importuned Rockingham, to decide. Perhaps it would be wise for His Lordship to make his town house his headquarters to circularize his friends for a meeting, as he had so successfully done in the defeat of the Irish absentee tax in 1773. The decision was reached to stay away from parliament, and so Burke became very infrequent in his attendance until the shocking news of Burgoyne's defeat at Saratoga in October 1777 served to make clear the general ineptness of North's handling of the war.

In the session which opened on 26 October 1775, Burke did make one last effort to achieve conciliation before it was too late. In a speech on 16 November, he introduced a bill which provided that parliament would tax the colonies only to regulate trade. Customs duties would be disposed of by colonial assemblies. The American Congress would be authorized to legislate for the colonies and to repeal the Intolerable Acts and other obnoxious measures as well as grant amnesties to all who had taken up arms against the mother country. Parliament was left with legislative supremacy, although the door was left open for improving commercial matters.

In making the concessions which he did and thus altering a position of long standing, Burke revealed the importance which he attached to circumstances. He had made concessions, as he would in reference to Ireland, because circumstances dictated them. Although his bill was defeated, the position which he took was to be adopted three years later by a discredited government. For his efforts Burke earned "more approbation" than ever before.[31]

Ireland's failure "to exert her influence" to restore peace continued to upset Burke as his correspondence reveals. He told O'Hara that:

As to your general Politicks in Ireland, they are so sublimely profound, there is such a grandeur of meanness in them, that they pass my expression & indeed my comprehension. Passiveness & servility seem to be natural companions just as Violence & Tyranny. Our conduct to America, though wicked & foolish, yet is natural wickedness & folly; yours is a species of Turpitude not decent to name. Your Conduct has this aggravation in it, that you had a part assigned by Providence to act, that rarely, if ever, happens to a nation, rarely indeed to mankind; you were in the situation, in which you might act as the Guardian Angels of the whole Empire; & without hazard, or danger, or scarcely trouble, have appeared in mediatorial Character of the utmost dignity & Benevolence; & with all certainty, at once have secured your own Liberties & given peace to our general Country. I know, that things have often hung in so even a ballance (& they so hung until very lately) that the least movement on the part of Ireland would have decided in favour of peace. I say I know it; & speak from certain observation, & not loose conjecture. Indeed a refusal on your part to be active in the War or to approve it would have been sufficient. Things are run so near, that witht. the four thousand men, you so handsomely take from defence to lend to oppression, the war, would in all human probability, expire from want of fewel to feed it. What surprises me the most, is the language of your Minority. If Mr. Hussey's speech is rightly represented in the Newspaper, he states himself as in a difficult dilemma — either to do a wrong thing, or offend a Nation too strong for you to contend with. If that be the Case, you never can exercise your own rights without fear of Offence. But the time chosen for this Terrour, is very extraordinary — a time, in my opinion, when the weakness of this Country, in point of power, & of intellect to guide it, is more truly an Object of Pity. I remember that Ireland was capable of making a troublesome, petulant, & obstinate opposition to England, when in the Zenith of her power, & that too for things of doubtful right & certain insignificance; but she is now afraid, not to be active, & to ruin herself in endeavours, fundamentally to destroy everything like Liberty in the dependencies of this Kingdom, in a conjecture wherein our Malice & strength are so totally disproportion[ate] to each other. You will forgive me for speaking so freely of the place where we were born; but I must give myself a little Vent. It is not often that I do it or with so much warmth.[32]

His feelings were still in this vein of "so much warmth" when he lamented to the Earl of Charlemont, one of the few important people in Ireland whom he felt cared "a farthing" for him at this time,[33] that Ireland had lost "the most glorious opportunity ever indulged by heaven to a subordinate state, that of being the safe and certain mediatrix in the quarrels of a great empire" and the thing that made it all the more deplorable was that the war was one which was being fought against "the principle of her own liberties." [34]

The heat which characterized his sentiments in these letters was still burning strongly well over a year later as he expressed his disgust over Ireland to Charles James Fox. Professing to be without any news on the situation there from either the Irish or from London sources, he observed that it was eleven years since he had last been in the country and then after an absence of two years. He admitted that absence for an even shorter period of time could as a rule result in the loss of the "true practical notion of the Country, & what may or may not be done in it." If Ireland were like it used to be, "neither Government nor public opinion can do a great deal; almost the whole is in the hands of a few leading people. . . . On the whole the success of Government usually depended on the bargain made with a very few men." Both the Protestants and the

Catholics were at fault. The former "think in general backward. They are the landed & the monied interests, for the infinitely greater part; & they will not like to pay [for the continued expenses of the American War]. The papists are reduced to beasts of burthen; they will give all they have, their shoulders, readily enough if they are flattered. Surely the state of Ireland ought forever to teach parties moderation in their victories. Those crushed by law have no hopes but from power. If laws are their enemies, they will be enemies to laws; & those who have much to *hope & nothing to lose* will always be dangerous more or less." [35]

Despite his conviction that Ireland had behaved shabbily, Burke realized that the American War was going so badly that it could be used to Ireland's advantage. Accordingly, he forgot his grievances against his native land and in 1778 worked diligently for her betterment. His efforts fell into two categories: one was to aid the Catholics to make a breach in the penal laws, an objective of long-standing with him; and the other was to assist the predominantly Protestant trading elements of Ireland in securing a more generous treatment from Britain. These undertakings on Burke's part will now be considered successively.

THE FIRST CATHOLIC RELIEF ACT

Many Irish Protestants, the Presbyterians in particular, were deeply affected by the American Revolution and the Declaration of Independence and had begun to grow somewhat restive and to commence to manifest a determination to assert their rights. The anomaly of continuing the harsh repression of the Catholics in their country while at the same time they entertained grievances against Britain struck many Protestants forcibly. Particularly was this true of those who looked to the British parliament for improvement of conditions in Ireland. Such people realized that liberty, as well as charity, should begin at home. Moreover, many were well aware that they could hardly hope for the cooperation of their Catholic fellows in a cause which would avail the latter nothing in a country they were scarcely able to call their own.[36] Consequently, there had taken place in Ireland during the half dozen or so years leading up to 1778 a noticeable growth of the spirit of toleration even among the members of the Irish parliament.[37]

69

Burke, despite his disavowal of any knowledge of what was going on in Ireland in the letter to Fox quoted above, knew of this development and reasoned that, in the event that there should be hesitation among these men to afford a real relaxation in the penal laws, it might be well to set them an example by granting some relief to the Catholics of England.[38] However, it behooved him to act with circumspection since he was so active at that time in the cause of improving Irish trade.[39] Furthermore, he had the old bugbear to contend with, viz., that he was too sympathetic toward the Catholics, if, what was indeed worse, he were not secretly one himself. It would be foolish under these circumstances to jeopardize his political career by sponsoring a bill for Catholic relief personally. It could be done just as effectively, if not more so, by entrusting it to the direction of another member of his party and he himself could guide and direct its progress from behind the scenes. He, therefore, induced Sir George Savile, with whom he was very friendly, to sponsor the measure. Savile was of an aristocratic family against whose members no suspicion of "popery" could be raised. Sir George was not averse to introducing the bill owing to personal considerations. He was a large Irish landowner who stood to suffer heavily from the activities of Charles Carroll of Carrollton, an American Catholic signatory of the Declaration of Independence and a member of the American Congress. Carroll had scattered throughout Ireland promises of free land and toleration to every emigrant leaving for America. Should Ireland suffer a depopulation of serious proportions, the great absentee landlords would be given a heavy blow.[40] The fact that Savile had a personal interest in Ireland which led him to sponsor a bill intended to relieve the Catholics of *England* lends substance to the theory that what was to be done in England was really intended as a sensible example for Ireland to follow. Seconding the bill was John Dunning, Recorder of Bristol.[41] Despite Burke's silence on this measure, his known frank and undisguised championship of the Catholic cause managed to a large degree to offset the effect which his silence created. It was virtually universal knowledge in Commons that, although he refrained from appearing to be connected with the proposal, he was its real sponsor.[42]

Despite "the lenient temper and liberal spirit of the times,"[43]

Savile, in introducing the bill, stressed that one of its chief objects was the vindication of Protestantism to which all persecution was alien or at least ought to be.[44] He also emphasized that he was not tampering with the whole mass of the English penal code but sought merely to secure the repeal of certain penalties and disabilities. Brought in on 14 May 1778, the bill passed Commons unanimously and went to Lords where it experienced very little difficulty.

Almost simultaneously another relief bill passed. Introduced by Lord Richard Cavendish, also a friend of Burke's, this measure enabled the Irish parliament to grant to the Irish Catholics the same relief which had been extended to their English coreligionists. Burke later revealed privately that both of these acts of the British parliament were ultimately intended for Ireland.[45]

With the way thus paved, Luke Gardiner (later Lord Mountjoy) introduced a measure for Catholic relief in the Irish House of Commons on 25 May.[46] Gardiner's bill had a much harder time securing passage but it was ultimately adopted by a margin of thirty-eight votes in the House and considerably less in the upper chamber.[47] By its terms, Catholics were now enabled to lease land for a nine hundred and ninety-nine year period and their lands were made subject to the same conditions of sale and inheritance as those of Protestants. No longer was it possible for the eldest son or wife to secure the father's or husband's estate by renouncing Catholicism.[48] Before its final passage in Ireland, it was transmitted to England for approval which was granted,[49] thanks largely to Burke who worked tirelessly.

While the bill was still under consideration, Burke wrote to Edmund Sexton Pery, the Speaker of the Irish House of Commons, to say that "any hints which you may think proper to give relative to the probable advisability of alterations [in the bill], you will be so good either by [the] Chief Justice . . . or by letter from yourself to communicate to Mr. Macnamara who naturally has the conduct of the business before the Council & with the Crown lawyers." [50]

Since there was a good chance that the proposal would not prevail, one of Burke's Irish correspondents, a Mr. O'Halloran, ignorant of the role Burke was playing, asked him to intervene should the bill fail. O'Halloran called Burke the most conspicuous among the "friends & lovers of this once glorious, but now wretched & oppressed Country." [51]

On 11 August Speaker Pery wrote to Burke to tell him the good news that the proposal had successfully passed and to say that "I sincerely congratulate you, being fully persuaded that it is of more real importance to our country, than any law which has passed during my time." Pery was also quite sanguine about the prospects of further steps to help the Catholics.[52]

On the same date, Luke Gardiner, sponsor of the bill, also wrote to Burke to tell him the good news and to lament that the bill "is in itself very imperfect, both as to its extent and operation; and . . . very inadequate to the relief which ought to be granted." He also brought out that the immediate cause of introducing the proposal had been "your liberal procedure with respect to the Roman Catholics in England." [53]

Pery followed up his first letter with another two weeks later in which he said that "only a beginning had been made" in breaching the penal code and then asked Burke a number of detailed questions relating to the Irish Catholics on which he requested information from Burke when the latter had leisure to reply to them.[54]

He had been previously asked some questions about the Irish bill by Alexander Wedderburn (later Lord Loughborough), the Attorney-General, who was well disposed toward it. This was while the bill was awaiting approval in England. Wedderburn told Burke that he would have to break the silence he had meant to keep on the matter and would be forced to write something about the question of the religious tests. He turned to Burke for information because "you can I know, and I hope without much trouble to yourself, refer me to chapter and verse for all that part of ecclesiastical history that regards our tests." He then asked Burke a series of questions on the subject.[55] Burke satisfied Wedderburn's queries both by mail and in person and spared no effort to convince as many of the members of North's government as he could personally contact that they should approve the bill. As an instance of Burke's effective pleading, there is extant a letter of Sir Grey Cooper's, dated 20 July, in which he remarks that everything which Burke said or wrote about the bill deserved respect.[56]

Dr. John Curry, author of the *History of the Civil Wars in Ireland* and other tracts on Irish history, a Catholic and warm friend of Burke's during his stay in Ireland as Hamilton's secretary, sent him a copy of the Catholic Relief Act ("for the relief of his majesty's subjects in Ireland professing the Popish religion") and praised Burke's labors in behalf of the bill for "the procuring of which your firm and unbiassed attachment to the true interests of your country so signally contributed." He then said that Edmund Burke was in reality the author of the bill since he had given Curry a copy of an address and petition for the relief of the Irish Catholics in 1764 which Curry and the other Catholic leaders considered in 1778 so excellent that it formed the basis of the petition they made at that time.[57] Thus, it is literally true that Edmund Burke laid the cornerstone of Ireland's religious freedom, a work taken up by others and finally consummated by the able and resourceful Daniel O'Connell.

So grateful was the Catholic Association of Ireland for the work which Burke had done that the members offered him a gift of five hundred guineas as a token of their appreciation.[58] In refusing the offer, Burke, who sorely needed the money, wrote to Dr. Curry that he could not accept compensation for work done by him on the public account. He explained that his endeavors in this business, in which he admitted that he was "very active and very earnest, both in public and in private," were guided by his detestation of "public injustice and oppression," a fact which had always made him abhor the penal laws. The modest beginning toward correcting them which had just been made was nothing more than a commencement in his estimation. He advised the Catholics to manifest their devotion to the government by showing themselves to be dutiful subjects of the crown but warned against their affection taking on the form of servility. This was a particular piece of advice he never refrained from reiterating time and again in his dealings with the Catholics of Ireland. He disclosed that he knew "more of the secret history, as well as the public, of this business than falls to the share of many." While refusing the gift tendered him by the Catholic Association, he nevertheless commended their collection of a fund and generously suggested that it be applied toward schools for their youth in Ireland when the day came that the parliament would cease "condemning a million and a half of people to ignorance, according to act of parliament." [59]

In returning the draft which they had already sent him, Burke wrote to Anthony Dermott substantially what he had written to Curry adding that he was more than sufficiently rewarded by having been able to assist such a large body of "my Countrymen" whose oppression was not only grievous to themselves but also the state as well.[60]

Edmund Burke revealed himself to have been very happy over the passage of the bill because in addition to the removal of some injustices he thought he saw in it the first step toward the making of Ireland into a real nation which would fit happily into the framework of the British Empire. He told Speaker Pery that "you are now beginning to have a country," [61] and to his cousin, Garret Nagle, he predicted that the relief bill contained a principle "which in time will extend further." [62]

But it is a letter to an unknown person in Ireland which sums up his happy thoughts on the successful termination of this first step for the Catholics. He felt "a sensible Joy on the occasion" for even "if nothing further should be done, a great deal is accomplished. You have, for the first time, got the Government of the country to acknowledge & protect all its Subjects." A real gain had been made, but prudence dictated that it would be foolish to hasten on to the next improvement. Here we have an excellent illustration of Burke's regard for time and circumstances in his efforts to advance the welfare of Ireland. Some time must be permitted to elapse before anything further should be attempted. This being so, he stressed his joy over what had been accomplished and cautiously hoped for better days to come: "You have indeed made Ireland doubly dear to me by your excellent Bill. You have made those who were Countrymen, become fellow Citizens; Before this, they were only the worse Enemies for the accident of a Common birthplace. But they begin to coalesce; & I trust that you will live to see & enjoy the good you have done, in the total extinction of all Spirit of party which has religious opinions for its principle." [63]

As he told Anthony Dermott, he was prepared "whenever things are ripe for any judicial steps to be taken" to help the Catholics because "[my] principles will always lead me to take a very active part in promoting your ease & happiness & not the less active because I can never have any private Interest in it." [64]

Thus, the first step of any consequence had been taken to correct the injustices under which the Catholics labored, and Edmund Burke had played a signal role in the achievement. Much more remained to be done but these things would require careful attention to time and circumstances since such a policy had brought the initial success. The North government had supported the measure because it needed the support of the Catholics who might prove to be potential allies against the Irish Protestants who had been so deeply touched by the American Revolution. Moreover, there had been need of satisfying the majority of the people of Ireland by a concession due to the fear that Ireland might be invaded by the French now that France and America had become allied. Such an invasion could well serve as a signal for a general uprising by a people who were suffering enough grievances to rebel with little compunction. French and American privateers had become increasingly bolder in their attacks with the result that Ireland's coast needed protection sorely enough without the added problem of an uprising by the great majority of the country's inhabitants.

Fully aware of these things, Burke had chosen prudently. England's distress had reacted to Ireland's advantage and, he conceived, in the long run to that of the Empire as well. Unfortunately, he had placed his Bristol seat in jeopardy by his exertions on behalf of Catholic relief and by his efforts aimed at Irish commercial amelioration.

IRISH COMMERCIAL RELIEF

The Catholics were the chief sufferers from the religious restrictions employed in Ireland but the Protestants were the principal, although by no means the exclusive victims of the commercial discriminations practiced toward that country by Britain. This business of the commercial restrictions was characterized by Edmund Burke as one "whose very principle is the concord of the British dominions." [65] His correspondents in Ireland had begun to appeal to him to do something for their trade following the outbreak of the American War, and one of them predicted that Ireland would be deserted by emigration to America once the hostilities concluded if conditions did not improve there.[66]

Ireland felt keenly the burdensome restrictions upon her trade especially after the commencement of the war with the American colonies, and there were those in the British parliament who now felt that she deserved to have the binding restrictions loosened somewhat. Ireland would thereby be in a healthier condition to meet the demands being made upon her economy by Britain in the prosecution of the war. Nothing, however, was done until after the British defeat at Saratoga. In the spring of the following year, Earl Nugent [67] moved on 2 April 1778 that Commons form itself into a Committee of the Whole in order to take into consideration the various acts of parliament relating to the trade and commerce of Ireland. Having thus moved, he lamented England's conduct toward her sister kingdom and remarked that the present grave state of affairs necessitated the revision of Ireland's trade laws.[68] Among those who spoke in favor of Nugent's motion was Burke who saw Ireland now in the position of having become the chief dependency of the British crown, a circumstance which should dictate that the Irish be admitted to the privileges of British citizens.[69]

The business came up, as scheduled meantime, on 7 April, and the first measure introduced was one which would open Britain's possessions directly to the produce or manufacture of Ireland provided that British bottoms were employed in the shipping. Wool, "the sacred fleece," and its manufactures constituted an exception. All of which prompted Burke to protest that other exceptions which Lord North indicated might also be made in the course of the business might well cause the whole thing to end in nothing at all. He declared that the government's policy was a tortuous one as the word of promise had been whispered to Ireland, but death was opposed to her hopes. The general indefiniteness of this policy was unfair so he expressed the wish that Ireland might be told unequivocably what she could expect in this matter.[70]

He then digressed to attack the penal laws against the Irish Catholics. These, he asserted, were odious, oppressive, and impolitic and had effectively destroyed public spirit and industry which had been replaced with abject slavery. True to his professed belief, he held that this code was not aimed against religion but against property and predicted that the barbarous severity of these laws would produce a very heavy emigration to America, a land where he hoped the immigrants would be received with open arms and taken to her free bosom.[71] So impressed was one newspaper by Burke's allusion to the penal laws and the danger they represented that it suggested that the laws be relaxed. The Catholics would then be satisfied through having their property secure, and the Protestants would be happy because they would still retain their political supremacy.[72]

Two bills were then brought in by Nugent after which Burke moved that all sailcloth and cordage manufactured in Ireland be imported into Great Britain free of duty.[73] Opposition to these modest proposals to assist Ireland's trade was both instantaneous and vociferous. Burke knew that such would be the case and hastened to assure his friend Richard Champion in Bristol that the merchants of Bristol had nothing to worry them: "The things intended for Ireland are frivolous; & if they were considerable, they have not capital to carry them on. They are intended to keep Ireland from diverting you with another rebellion. Keep, if you can, our fellow-citizens from exposing themselves upon this subject." [74]

If this private letter of Burke's should be interpreted as duplicity on his part, his subsequent conduct in the affair will effectively clear him of this charge. In writing as he did to Champion, he was merely endeavoring to be practical and prudent. That he was right in anticipating opposition from his constituents may be seen from the fact that only two days after he had written Champion, he received a letter from Samuel Span, Master of the Merchants' Society of Bristol, informing him and Bristol's other member, Cruger, that "the City are greatly alarmed" over the proposed Irish trade improvements and therefore "the interests of your Constituents and of the English Manufacturers call for your Strenuous opposition to this plan." [75] The letters began to pour in and without exception stressed the writers' resentment over their representative's conduct — "so active & decided a part against his Constituents." [76]

On 4 May Burke took occasion to announce in the House that he had been in error on the measure he had introduced and gladly agreed to withdraw it because the privilege had long been on the statute books and, consequently, no further legislation was required. Despite the fact that the privileges he had proposed had long since been granted, he called attention to the fact that his proposal had been assailed as one calculated to bring ruin to Britain. The objectors had not experienced in reality what they pretended to suffer in the mere theory. This being so, were not the other fears they entertained concerning Nugent's bills equally groundless? [77]

Burke was such a thorough master of details that it is inconceivable to think that he had introduced the sailcloth and cordage import privilege without first having studied the background of the matter ("However, I am, perhaps, the only active man in the House, that never did make a motion, without a very good previous knowledge. . . .").[78] Having done so, he would have discovered that such a bill had long been legalized. Could it have been his purpose to lay a trap for the narrow-minded opponents of Irish commercial privilege? His remarks on 4 May certainly make this seem all the more plausible.

Since the opposition to the proposals of Nugent mounted steadily, Burke, "the great and powerful supporter" [79] of the propositions, arose on 5 May to answer the objections raised against the bills. The members of parliament, as was their custom, had sent copies of the measures to their constituents. The great trading cities, including Burke's own constituency, Bristol, had, as we have noted above, raised a great hue and cry against the bills which they professed to believe would bring ruin to Britain at the expense of Ireland. Burke was thus placed in an anomalous position which was "rather singular, and undoubtedly embarrassing." [80] But he did not permit it to sway his judgment, and, although he represented the nation's second city, which owed its preeminence to trade, he supported the Irish bills so strongly opposed by his own constituents.

In his speech he declared that the propositions were merely a restoration of what was rightfully Ireland's because when the Navigation Acts were passed in the twelfth year of the reign of Charles II, they applied to Ireland as well as to England. In the meantime, Ireland had been deprived of these benefits and placed under a very rigorous system of commercial oppression. Yet Ireland had, notwithstanding, done everything in her power to aid

England and to manifest her loyalty. She had given military assistance from which she had derived no return but which cost her dearly in both men and money, and her reward for this costly expenditure had been commercial bondage. In so describing Ireland's situation he said that he hoped to enlist the humanity of Commons in her behalf. However, justice and not mere almsgiving was sought by the Irish, he emphasized, who simply asked that the British display wisdom, not generosity. By being wise, Britain would be providing for her own welfare and securing her own interest.

The argument that Ireland did not deserve this proposed amelioration because she did not bear an equal burden of taxation compared with England was to him an inequitable one. A comparison of the internal opulence and external advantage of the two countries demonstrated that Ireland was taxed four times as heavily as England in proportion. The latter's wealth and trade was forty times that of her sister kingdom, and taxes ought to follow wealth and not precede it. Ireland was taxed without possessing the means of payment. It was true that several excises laid in England did not apply to Ireland. Leather, for example, was taxed in England, but what advantage would there be to such a tax in Ireland, where vast numbers of people were too poor to wear shoes. Candles were likewise taxed in England, but some two hundred thousand homes in Ireland could not afford to burn a single candle.[81]

If the means the Irish parliament had were increased, that body would gladly increase taxes, and the Empire would benefit. It was foolish to think that equality of commercial opportunity or advantage could be established between the two nations, since wealthy England had too great a lead for Ireland ever to obtain a position approaching equality. The Irish, however, could follow at a distance.

The arguments on the cheapness of labor in Ireland were erroneous as far as Burke was concerned. When the price of labor became equal in both countries, England would no longer manufacture the superior products. The price of labor rose with the growth of manufacture and was highest when the manufacture was best. Daily experience had taught that where labor costs were the highest, the manufacturer was able to sell his products at the lowest price. The plenitude of a wealthy country caused trade to circulate much more freely than did the basic requirements of a poor one. Theirs was a peculiar notion of the world's extent who believed that it lacked sufficient space for the free trade of two such islands as Britain and Ireland.

Burke then reverted to the matter of granting Ireland the free exportation of sailcloth, a bill which he had recently introduced and withdrawn. Practically all the petitions which had poured in protesting against the grant of this proposed privilege to Ireland contained predictions of the dire consequences which would attend such a concession. The truth of the matter was that Ireland had long enjoyed this privilege together with the free exportation of iron and steel. Thus it was plain to all that the petitioners had not felt from the reality what they dreaded in the mere idea. This being so, it was fair to assume that the other grounds of apprehension were equally baseless and likewise founded on mere conjectures. But more could be derived from this incident. It was that the British manufacturers possessed so many advantages that it was impossible for the Irish to capitalize on the openings which had been presented to them. So true was this that one had but to consider the case of manufactured iron. England actually exported great amounts of it to Ireland.

He then remarked that it so happened in this one instance of the proposed alleviation of Irish trade that he found himself espousing a cause in opposition to the wishes and views of his constituents. He had always attempted to protect their rights and advance their interests but in this case he had the temerity to act against their desires, since he was firmly persuaded in his own mind that it was not against their interests.[82] While his conduct might well cost him his seat in parliament, since many of his friends and supporters seriously disapproved of his stand, he was satisfied because his suffering would be in the very cause of those who inflicted it. No blame could be attached to Bristol if she deprived him of his seat, because such an event would serve a useful purpose. It would illustrate the case of a "senator inflexibly adhering to his opinion, against interest and even popularity." On the other hand, it would depict an instance of constituents exercising their right to reject their representative because they felt that he had acted in a manner contrary to their judgment and interest.

In conclusion, he accurately predicted that Britain would eventually be compelled to grant Ireland the proposed enlargement of her trade. The state of affairs in the American War would make it absolutely necessary; therefore, it would be prudent to allow the concessions with good grace now rather than to yield later in the face of the inevitable.[83]

In this remarkable speech Burke had exhibited a grasp of economics which was surprisingly far in advance of his time and which would be a credit to contemporary liberal thought in that field today. Despite the strong opposition, his arguments had the desired effect, and, when the question was put, the division was in favor of a second reading.[84] Nevertheless, it was later voted to delay the debate for a period of two months. In the interim, as a result of some compromises between supporters and opponents of the propositions, it was decided to give up for the time being the plans for granting substantial commercial relief to Ireland.[85] Some improvement was granted in the linen trade together with a few new opportunities in the African and West Indian trades.[86]

Due to another alteration in plans, a debate on the subject of Ireland's export privileges was held on 19 May. Burke spoke to the effect that what had been done was nothing but a prelude to what was to come. Ireland would secure a greater freedom of trade than she presently enjoyed. He said that he would not insist on much at present but would wait until the next session of parliament. Since the greatest objection made to the proposition then being considered was the circumstance of the lateness at which it had been introduced, he hoped that no such opposition would be made on that score the following year. Between the present and the opening of parliament the next year there certainly would be ample time to weigh matters carefully. He hoped that parliament would then see its way clear to increasing the advantages given at the present time "to that first and most deserving of the British dependencies." [87]

During this first phase of the fight to alleviate the conditions of Irish trade, Burke had managed his case courageously and had called upon all the arguments which could conceivably make an impression on the opposition. He had stressed the inevitability of the passage of measures aimed to help Irish trade and underscored the wisdom of granting the concessions willingly and not under duress as later would be bound to be the case owing to the American War. Was it not enough that America had come to hate the name of England without adding Ireland to the list? It was the stupidity of Britain's commercial system which had done so much to drive America to revolt. The same stupidity, if insisted upon, could also lose Ireland. The rent in the British Empire which already existed made it imperative that the remaining parts be granted the strength to protect themselves and to cooperate in the defense of the Empire. They would make a united cause if they were happily cultivated. The Carlisle Peace Commission, which the Americans had refused to consider, had demonstrated a willingness upon the part of Lord North's government to concede lavishly to the Americans. Did Ireland also have to be driven to revolt in order to win the advantages denied while she remained peaceful? Scotland offered an excellent illustration of what could happen when England granted favors to her sisters. The world was large enough to contain the trade of both England and Ireland. Furthermore, there could be no trade with a bankrupt country, and it was unfortunate that those who should be fellow workers in a cause were treated as rivals. The greater Ireland's freedom in matters of commerce and industry, the greater must be England's advantage. If she lost in one way, she would gain in twenty.

These then were in substance the arguments which Burke used. The courage which he manifested in advancing them lay, of course, in the fact that his constituents in Bristol were violently opposed to any changes in the restrictions binding Irish trade. Burke was under no illusions as to what the consequences would be if he persisted in his course in the face of this opposition in Bristol. As he told one of his closest supporters there, it meant a great deal to him to represent Bristol, so much so that it was about all that he had to value in an external sense. Should he be spared until the next election and should he wish to remain in parliament at that time, he pledged himself to seek reelection at Bristol. If he did this, he intended to advance his conduct in the Irish business as a point in his favor. But he made it quite clear that it was not his desire to represent Bristol or any other constituency except on terms which were honorable to both his electors and himself. It was his feeling that they who sat in parliament should do so for a single purpose, viz., to promote "the common happiness of all those who are, in any degree, subjected to our legislative authority." This would result in "binding together, in one common tie of civil-interest and constitutional freedom, every denomination of men amongst us." [88]

In other words, Burke eschewed any idea of localism or provincialism. The representative was in reality imperial and not confined to a particular section. His imperial mentality is well brought out in this entire episode since he stressed his conviction throughout the business that the welfare of the British Empire itself required the grant of trade concessions to Ireland at that time. Moreover, this affair is an excellent illustration of Burke's ideas on the relationship which ought to exist between the electors and their representative. The nature of things made it inevitable that a wide gap would often exist between the interests and wishes of a given body, in this instance a body of electors. When such was the case, the representative or senator, as Burke so often styled him, would decide what course to pursue, not the constituents. Burke's position was that he himself should be able to determine when, despite their wishes, the actual interests of the electors would undoubtedly be better served by another course of action than they had indicated.

It was well that the little that was accomplished for Ireland in the session of 1778 was achieved as samples from Burke's correspondence reveal. Speaker Pery wrote him that "tho what has been obtained is far short of what was expected, yet it has already cooled that heat, which otherwise must soon have burst into a devouring flame," [89] and another Irishman informed him of the distressed conditions in Ireland where "the famishing poor wretches are crowding to Dublin fast as they can. I am convinced that not less than six thousand of them were traversing our streets yesterday in several parties — . . ." [90] Still another was happy "to find that even the *Husk is a* little broken, & *that at a future day* We may hope to taste the Kernel." [91]

The debates were resumed in the session of the following year, 1779, when on 15 February Lord Newhaven called the attention of the House to the need which Ireland still had for a free trade import privilege in the West Indian trade. The export bill granted the previous year was of no avail, he said, without the import privilege.[92] There was immediate opposition, and so Edmund Burke arose to answer it with a favorite point of his, viz., that it was this same illiberal policy which had lost America and might one day result in the destruction of the British Empire.[93] He declared that there was much ruin and desolation in Ireland, a state of affairs which called for immediate relief. He again fell back on another favorite argument to the effect that generous concessions had recently been offered to the Americans, a fact which made him blush. As long as England could continue to treat cruelly those whose misfortune it was to be under her sway, it appeared as if she were bent upon proving to the world that hers was a worse government than that of France. She crouched where she was afraid and tyrannized where she could do so with immunity.[94] Although it so happened that he was personally opposed to the particular project under discussion on the grounds that it was "raw and undigested," he supported its principle of "enlargement" because the more often these matters came to be discussed, the more would fears be dispelled and prejudices eradicated.[95]

Once again the opposition of British commercial circles was loudly proclaimed with the result that Newhaven's proposal was killed, but the North government did put forward two minor bills. One was for encouraging the growth of tobacco in Ireland; the other proposed a bounty on hemp exported from that country.[96] Burke objected to both these measures on the grounds that "the cultivation of these weeds (if one of them could be cultivated at all to profit) was adverse to the introduction of a good course of agriculture," and also that encouragement of such bills tended to fix "the mischievous policy of considering Ireland as a country of staple, and a producer of raw materials."[97] Since he had warned the House of the critical and dangerous state of Ireland,[98] it is advisable to sketch the background of affairs in order that this warning might be properly appreciated.

Specifically, Burke was referring to the rise of the Irish Volunteers. During 1778 and 1779, the matter of the protection of the coasts of Ireland became a serious one. The American War and the contest with France and then Spain increased the danger to Ireland and then from her. To carry on the wars, the British were forced to reduce their forces in Ireland greatly. The Royal Navy was sufficiently occupied with its manifold tasks and could not undertake to protect Ireland which lay exposed to attack and possible invasion. There was no militia in the country to fill the void left by the departure of the troops of the Irish Establishment who had been shipped elsewhere, and funds were lacking for the creation and maintenance of a militia. During 1778, enemy privateers became increasingly daring. Belfast, chief city in northern Ireland, was actually endangered by the presence of several of these vessels in sight of its harbor. On 24 April, John Paul Jones, whom the British considered a renegade,[99] in command of the "Ranger," captured HMS "Drake" in an engagement witnessed by many of the citizens of Belfast standing on the shore.[100] This so alarmed the leading citizens there that they formed the first groups out of which grew the Irish Volunteers.

The growth of this body was remarkable. In the counties, the gentry formed companies of their tenants and equipped them, as a general rule, at their own expense. In the towns, the merchants and professional men formed armed bodies and chose their own officers through the device of popular elections. Due to their legal inability to carry arms, the Catholics were initially excluded from the ranks of the Volunteers but they revealed their support of the movement by generously subscribing sums of money for the purchase of arms and other *matériel* by the Volunteers. Gradually, Catholics were permitted to join the Volunteers, the prohibition against their bearing arms being conveniently overlooked. By the summer of 1779, the Volunteers numbered some thirty thousand men and were still growing.[101] By this time, they had become in British eyes something of a menace because their membership was, on the whole, very well disposed toward the Americans whose example in revolting against England's misrule was not lost on them. Almost from the outset, the Irish Volunteers were politically minded, a cause of further worry in England. Their ranks included many able men who were also members of the Irish parliament, such as Henry Grattan, men who had been hopelessly struggling against the corrupt majority in that body.

12 October 1779, Grattan spoke in the Irish House on the poor state of the country and demanded that the attention of the king

be called to it. He was followed by another one of Burke's friends and correspondents, Walter Hussey Burgh, who then introduced a resolution that "it is not by temporary expedients but by a free trade alone, that this nation is now to be saved from impending ruin." An Address to the King was agreed upon and brought to Dublin Castle by the Speaker accompanied by the members of Commons.[102] The reply which they received was evasive but it failed to lessen the enthusiasm then running high. In November, the Irish parliament showed its determination by reducing the term of the customary duties from two years to six months and by denying all supplies for the current services of the executive government.[103]

Faced with this strong spirit on the part of Ireland, it was no wonder that the British House of Commons insisted that Burke speak during the Debate on the Address of Thanks, 25 November 1779. He had considerable difficulty in speaking because of hoarseness and a severe cold. On several occasions, he was compelled to stop and take his seat dramatically, but each time he was entreated to continue. Bitterly, he assailed the Prime Minister's separation of the American War from the serious current situation in Ireland and asserted that the example of the Americans was behind every move in Ireland, where the people were on the edge of revolt. He agreed with the Irish in blaming their poor condition in large measure on Lord North for it was he who had been responsible for the meager economic relief which had been so inadequately accorded to Ireland in 1778. North's cunctative policy no longer had the desired effect since the Irish were now demanding as a right what formerly they would have been happy to receive as a favor. The failure of the government to call the British parliament before the session of the Irish had commenced was a piece of colossal stupidity fraught with dire possibilities. The Irish called into session first were now demanding free trade, and, he concluded, Lord North's failure to heed the warning was inexcusable.[104] A motion to censure the ministry was unsuccessfully introduced by Lord Ossory. The government's chief defender was Lord Beauchamp who was subjected to terrific ridicule by Burke.[105]

On 6 December, the first opportunity which presented itself for Burke to renew his attack on North's Irish policy, he fell back on some of his previous arguments, hoping by reiteration that they would take effect. With the example of America before them and with forty-two thousand men now under arms, Ireland was now in a position to be demanding. She considered herself free and scorned Britain's claim of dominion over her. Taking courage from the example of Boston, a Dublin mob had arisen and nonimportation agreements had resulted. Burke sarcastically asked why the government did not close the port of Dublin, burn Cork, and level Waterford, then prevent freedom of assembly and put an end to all popular elections whatsoever. He continued his argument from analogy by citing more fatal examples upon which the government could draw from its American experience and apply to Ireland. The associations against the purchase and use of British manufactures and for the encouragement of domestic ones which had arisen in Ireland had become quite popular, he added, and those guilty of violating their objects were faced with severe punishment at the hands of the members. (The *Annual Register* later observed that it gave the Irish considerable pleasure to realize that Manchester and Glasgow would suffer as a result of this action, since these cities had been foremost in the ranks of those vigorously opposed to Irish relief.) [106] Ireland, he repeated, had emulated America by arming herself.[107] Her parliament was insisting on free trade with the alternative the severance of political connections with Britain. These were facts that contributed to form an inescapable conclusion. Already parliament had lost the opportunity of taking any credit upon itself, since the grant of commercial relief was now inevitable. He himself could claim the merit of liberality since he had been ready two years ago to grant as much as would now be conceded — redemption from prohibitions which were a shame to the laws of England without in any way being a benefit.[108]

The debates which followed on the subject were, according to the *Annual Register*, "long, various, and interesting." They drew from the opposition all their "wit, ability, and eloquence." Especially was this true of Burke and Charles Fox, "the great leaders and speakers of the opposition in that house [who] took a large share in the debate, and were as usual distinguished." Both men devoted themselves unsparingly and impressively to the task.[109]

At last, the inflammatory temper of Ireland was recognized by the British government, and on 13 December 1779 Lord North brought in three propositions for commercial relief. In exactly ten days, the royal assent was given to the repeal of the restrictions on the export of Irish woolen goods, because "the late great revolutions had rendered every change easy." [110] Repeal of the prohibition on Irish glass was also granted before the Christmas holidays while the other measure had to go over until after the recess, but it then passed handily. This was the grant of free trade with America, the British West Indies, and Africa subject only to such rules as the Irish parliament itself cared to make.

Ireland had scored a considerable victory through the determination of her Volunteers, whose path had been made a great deal easier for them by the arguments and work of Edmund Burke. His part in this victory failed to receive proper credit in Ireland [111] whereas, ironically enough, it was well marked in Bristol and coupled with his championship of the Catholics was to prove too great an obstacle for him to overcome when the next general election occurred. The censure which Burke especially and the other members of his party received from Irish circles was for not having supported Lord North's propositions warmly. The opposition had merely given their approval and let matters rest there. Apparently, what was expected of them from some quarters in Ireland was that they should have waxed eloquent over the relaxation of the commercial strictures. It was impossible for Burke to demonstrate great enthusiasm over the grant of something for which he had fought hard only to see his efforts treated with contempt by the North government. Now that Ireland had demonstrated an armed strength worthy of respect, the ministry had, as Burke predicted would be the case, bestowed freely upon that force what it had denied to respectful petitions from an apparently impotent body. Burke was utterly disgusted by this disedifying spectacle, but such feelings were not understood by those who were stupid enough to have criticized him.

Because he had been so severely criticized in Ireland for his attitude, Burke attempted an *apologia* in a letter to Thomas Burgh, a member of the House there who had written his relative to the opinion prevalent in Ireland about him,[112] in which he vindicated his actions in parliament relative to the matter of commercial re-

lief for Ireland. The letter was dated 1 January 1780, and Burgh
was directed to "communicate it as you please."

The ingratitude manifested in the land of his birth hurt him,
but he claimed that it was not a deep wound.[113] He had acted as he
did from "a strong impulse of right, and from motives in which
popularity" either in England or Ireland had little part. He had enjoyed a "holiday of popularity in Ireland," and his well-wishers
there had not so long ago communicated to him through the Speaker
of the Irish House their desire to erect a statue to him in Dublin
in gratitude for the part he had played in promoting the cause of
Ireland in the British parliament. He had refused on the ground
that such honors should be reserved for the dead and had reminded
his friends that very often the same hands which erect statues pluck
them down. To Burgh, he observed that had he yielded to their
importuning two years ago, the fragments might now be employed
as projectiles to hurl at his defenders.[114]

His bantering mood soon gave way to irony, as he sarcastically
said that he was happy to find Ireland so prosperous that she could
afford to discard her old friends and only wished that it could
have been done with fewer tokens of unpleasantness. It was, of
course, true that no danger could result from insulting men who
were not important enough to hold ministerial posts or to warrant
royal trust or national honors. His bitterness increased and he complained that Ireland paid compliments to North,[115] a man "from
whose imbecility you have extorted what you could never obtain
from his bounty." North at the same time led his opponents "captive
before him." Burke then warned his Irish critics, basking in the security of their Volunteers, that this military force was but temporary,
that it lacked roots, and would be a poor defense against the power
of Britain when the latter, unopposed elsewhere, could be directed
against Ireland. He conceded, however, that the Volunteers comprised an army which, although not sanctioned by it, superseded
law and like faith derived from a higher authority.[116]

He went on to give an account of the part he had personally
played in the easing of the commercial restrictions and said that
his object had been to establish the principle of a free trade in
every part of the British Isles. The principle was founded in justice
and would be beneficial to the whole but principally to England,

the residual center of the power of the Empire. He had been criticized for remaining silent when the victory was ultimately achieved.
Had he thought the concessions too much, he complained that he
would have been accused of an attempt to stir up England. On the
other hand, if he found them too little, he would be charged with
a design of fomenting a rebellion in Ireland. Hence, he had merely
inquired whether the propositions satisfied Ireland. If they did,
they satisfied him. He then concluded with the confession that
the length of the letter showed him that the criticisms of his former
country, in which he still had "a dearness of instict" greater than
he could justify to reason, made a deeper impression on him than
he had realized.[117]

This, of course, was a pretty stiff letter, but there is little reason
to feel that it was unjustified on Burke's part. He admitted to Rockingham that he had been affected by the criticism in Ireland and
as a consequence "wrote in . . . warmth, a letter of no less than
four Sheets upon it." [118] Rockingham told him that he "*suspected*
you would be angry at the gentry on the other side of the Water
— I hope, I shall not find *your Letter* too Warm when I get the
copy of what you have wrote to Ireland." [119] When he did receive
it, he expressed himself as pleasantly surprised even to the extent
that "I admired it, & being a slow reader could have wish'd for
time to have perused it more deliberately —" [120]

The recipient of the original letter, Burgh, professed great
satisfaction with it and maintained that it did a great deal of good
in Ireland. He had had it copied and showed it to many of those
who had been critical of Burke as well as to his friends there but
had refrained from having it published out of deference to Burke's
wishes.[121] Burgh then turned to the subject of the news from Ireland which he thought might be of interest to Burke. This was not
very exciting and "the great objects of speculation in Politicks"
were such things as "some improvements in our constitution, a
revival of the old disputes about Poyning's law, the judicature of
our house of Peers — & the institution of a national bank. . . .
Every thing is quiet throughout the country — no disorders or
irregularities of any kind — a most wonderful & unexpected consequence of 40,000 young Irishmen in arms."

Under the same date as Thomas Burgh's reply to Burke, the latter received a letter from Ireland signed "Nathan," which is a good illustration of the news Burgh sent and at the same time is an example of the kind of abuse which Burke was receiving in his native land. The letter follows: [122]

Permit me to put the following Queries for your consideration. Was Henry 2d justifiable by the law of Nations, or rather, did he not violate the natural Rights of another nation, in his Invasion of Ireland.

Were the People of Ireland bound thenceforth by the success of that Invasion, to unconditional submission to the Legislature of England.

Was not Poyning's Statue a most arbitrary encroachment on the just rights of the Irish Nation.

Have the English such a property in the Laws and Fortunes of the Irish, as to justify them in making the Scots partakers of their assumed Supremacy over Ireland.

Will there probably ever hereafter occur a period so favourable for asserting the Rights of a free State as the present, which cannot be restored but by a solemn renunciation on the part of England of the controlling right of their Legislature; and by a Repeal of Poynings Statue: I do not add *that* since the Union, which I consider as waste paper, as being an Act of the associated power of English and Scots; which every Irishman ought to reprobate. Lastly pardon the seeming rudeness of asking whether you are so naturalized to England as to have renounced all Concern for the *Honour* or Interest of your Native Land; which has notoriously been sold by the most infamous set that ever disgraced the name of Patriots.

Why sleepest thou?

Vale

Nathan

27 January

Aut Nunc aut Nunquam.

Poor Burke had striven hard to bring about commercial relief for Ireland. His efforts had been criticized by those whom he sought to assist while those who had opposed the very idea of reform at every step of the way and who finally only reluctantly consented to it in the face of the Irish Volunteers had praise heaped upon them. Such a performance would have infuriated many a lesser man than Burke, so it is not surprising to find that for the time being he was quite fed up with Ireland. An added irony was the fact that Bristol had marked him for defeat because of these very efforts which Ireland criticized and because of his zeal on behalf of the Catholics. But before considering the loss of his cherished Bristol seat, we shall turn to an event, The Gordon Riots, which grew out of the Catholic episode.

THE GORDON RIOTS

The amelioration of the position of the English Roman Catholics followed so swiftly by a similar improvement of their lot for the members of that faith in Ireland in 1778 suggested that the same should be done in Scotland. Owing to the lateness of the session of parliament when the idea came up, it was decided to postpone action on the Scots Catholics until the following session in 1779. The fierce opposition which immediately flared up in Scotland [123] made it inadvisable, however, and the unfortunate Catholics of that country, who were the victims of an organization called the Protestant Association,[124] requested that nothing be done for them beyond the maintenance of the status quo. The angry mobs in places like Edinburgh and Glasgow had so endangered their lives and property that they were content merely to survive and dropped the idea of seeking improvement of their situation for the time being. But as their lot was far from an enviable one, and as the fury of the first outburst had died, the Catholics decided to draw up a petition seeking redress of their grievances. Knowing Edmund Burke's sympathetic attitude toward their position, they asked him to introduce it, and he agreed. When word of this reached James Boswell, he hastened to warn Burke of the inadvisability of such a step. Boswell professed to be attached to the idea of improving the lot of the Catholics of Scotland but told Burke that, if any measure so designed passed parliament, "there would be as desperate a Rebellion against Government as in the day of Charles the Second." He begged Burke for assurance that there was no present intention of disturbing the status quo in Scotland.[125]

Burke, however, kept his word of promise to the Scots Catholics and on 18 March 1779 brought in their petition for relief, a document characterized for its admirable restraint.[126] Burke condemned the lethargy of the forces of law and order in his speech and expressed the hope that the government was not dead but merely asleep. It so happened that while Burke was reading the petition and delivering his remarks upon it, Lord North had fallen sound asleep on the Treasury Bench. Directing his glance at the slumbering figure of the Prime Minister, Burke could not resist the temptation to remark that "Brother Lazarus is not dead, but sleepeth." [127] We are told that both the government and opposition benches roared with laughter which caused North to awaken and, when "he was sufficiently awake to understand the cause of the joke," join in the general mirth.[128]

The petition of the Scots Catholics which Burke had introduced was ordered laid on the table where it still remained at the conclusion of the session.[129] The upshot of the business was that Burke had added to his reputation for championing the Catholics of the British Isles greatly to the disgust of a number of people.[130] Among them was Lord George Gordon, a fanatical member of Commons who was described by a contemporary paper as a man who made "an everlasting fool of himself on all occasions" [131] and who later proved to be insane. The Protestant Association of England which Lord George headed had originated a short time ago in Scotland and had now branched out to include England and Ireland. In the latter country, Lord Kenmare told Burke that "Ld. G. Gordon's Association makes more Noise here, than probably with you." [132] It was a very simple matter for demagogues like Gordon to stir up mobs of the "meaner sort" of people to a pitch of frenzy by pretending to crusade against the supposed diabolical designs of the "papists." And so on 2 June 1780, Gordon presented a petition of the Protestant Association of England calling for the repeal of the recent Catholic Relief Act. Fourteen reasons were included in the petition to show why the repeal should be enacted,[133] and there were purportedly one hundred and twenty thousand signatures. But great numbers had made their marks, a circumstance which caused Charles Fox to remark wryly upon the incongruity of people who could neither read nor write themselves becoming alarmed because Roman Catholics could do so.[134]

The day on which the petition of the Protestant Association was brought to the House was one unparalleled in the history of parliament. Outside a mob of some sixty thousand people had assembled following a march from St. George's Fields led by Gordon. As the members of parliament passed the mob to enter their respective chambers, they were forced to put blue cockades in their hats and to cry out "No Popery!" Neither age nor position was respected, and many were manhandled. Among the first to suffer physical violence at the hands of the wild mob was the Archbishop of York. The Bishop of Lincoln escaped harm only by clambering over the roofs of nearby houses. The list of the prominent who suffered more than affronts to their dignity is a lengthy one.[135]

From time to time, once the session of parliament began, Lord George would appear at the head of the gallery stairs to keep the mob posted on how the petition was faring. He emphasized the names of members who were opposing it, particularly Burke's. In their impatience the rabble managed at one stage to force their way into the lobby but were cleared out by the military on the latter's promise to retire if the mob would vacate the premises. Having brought in the petition in the House, it was Gordon who moved that it be considered immediately. A division resulted in the overwhelming defeat of this motion, 192 to 7, and it was then resolved to consider it on the sixth of June.[136]

At approximately 8:30 on the night of 2 June, the members of the House of Lords managed to make good their escape from the mob, but Commons was still besieged and its members imprisoned. Finally, with the aid of soldiers, the members of the lower house were able to make their departure around 11 p.m. The mob thereupon turned to rioting with the special objects of their fury at first being Catholic chapels and property. Among the chapels destroyed were those belonging to members of the diplomatic corps accredited to the Court of St. James. The wanton destruction thus commenced continued unabated for days. By this time, the victims included many non-Catholics. On the night of the fifth, a mob was apparently bent on destroying Sir George Savile's town house. Savile was a marked man because he had sponsored the Catholic Relief Act of 1778. Among the friends who gathered to defend Savile's house was Edmund Burke. While preparing for the defense of his friend's property, word reached him that his own house was in danger, so he made haste to save his papers.[137] Finding that the government had thoughtfully sent some troops to protect his residence, Burke immediately returned to Savile's.

He had first made provision for his wife's safety in the home of friends at the earliest opportunity which presented itself. Once she

94

was safely situated in the home of General Burgoyne, his mind was greatly relieved [138] and he had no fear of the mobs which he faced repeatedly without flinching. During the tumults, he was constantly slandered by the crowds, who were spurred on by agitators. The old cry that he was a disguised Jesuit was raised repeatedly.[139] On one occasion, when a mob sought to persuade him to reverse himself on toleration, he drew his sword but did not have to use it.[140] Writing to his old friend, Richard Shackleton, after law and order had been restored, he told him of having ventured among the ranks of the rioters and freely informing them who he was. Some were vicious and fanatical but the majority he found were simply dissolute. He declared that he had even found friends and well-wishers among them. He had refused to leave town when his friends had entreated him because he firmly believed that, if his liberty were once gone, he could not perform his duties.[141]

While his conduct had indeed been "manly," as a friend in Bristol, John Noble, put it,[142] he had run great risks and by his insistence on lecturing and even haranguing these mobs had not perhaps shown great wisdom. An eye-witness on one of these occasions told Burke that

I was present yesterday when you condescended to hear what the people assembled had to say, & to reason in some measure with them on the subject of their Complaint. I thought with you that it had been better if the Guards had not been called out; & that Gentlemen wou'd take the trouble, by *mild* Arguments, to convince the people of their Error — but at the same time I do *not* think, the *barely* telling them that *you are better Judges of the Subject* than they can possibly be; is the sort of Reasoning that is *likely to avail* — It is neither, *Argumentum ad Hominem*, nor *ad rem*.[143]

Burke's brother, Richard, was so overcome with all that had transpired that he began a letter to Richard Champion on 7 June with the heading "in what was London." [144] Burke himself was affected to the extent that the terrible scenes which he had witnessed remained fixed in his mind [145] and like the poet Horace could say with justification, should he so desire, *odi profanum vulgus et arceo* ("I hate the common multitude and keep them at a distance").

When the date set for the hearing of the Protestant Association's petition arrived, 6 June, Burke was said by one paper to have risked his life to enter the House of Commons.[146] When he arose to speak in the debate, he excoriated those responsible for the terrible events of the past few days and allowed his congenital irrascibleness to get the better of him. He was extremely acrid in his denunciations of the supineness of the government.[147] Shortly after he finished speaking, it was voted to adjourn until the nineteenth.[148] In the interim, royal proclamations were issued to provide for the public safety.[149] One of the few who came through this disgraceful affair with honor was the king who manifested real courage and exhibited considerable forcefulness. To him must go credit for the prevention of an irreparable calamity. When his speech was read after parliament reconvened, he promised that those rioters who had been apprehended would be punished but emphasized his intention of preserving the religion of the Established Church, "the first duty of my station, and the chief glory of my reign," a hint which the illiberal elements could not fail to grasp. He concluded with the pledge that the rights and liberties of the people would be perpetuated.[150]

In what must have struck him as the height of irony, the king was openly charged at this time with being at heart a Catholic! He was caricatured in a contemporary print, entitled "A Great Man at his Private Devotions," as kneeling before an altar clad as a monk whose habit bears the words "The holy Roman Catholic faith." A picture of the pope hangs above an open door while one of Martin Luther was falling to pieces on the wall.

Burke had been privately informed by Lord North on the eighteenth that the government would oppose any efforts to repeal the recent Catholic Relief Act but that they had no intention of conducting an inquiry into the facts of the riots or of calling any witnesses. Furthermore, his cabinet would not repeal the penal laws against the Catholics, which Burke might have requested,[151] because of a belief that the people would forceably resent such action.[152] On the day upon which parliament reconvened, North again privately communicated to Burke the intelligence that the government would oppose any alteration in the laws respecting Catholic schools.[153]

In the debates which took place on the nineteenth, Burke con-

tinued to blast those who had been responsible for the recent disturbances together with those who had lent their assistance in one
way or another. Collectively they were nothing but "deluded
fanatics," and the measure which they sought to repeal was one
which would be maintained because it was based upon parliament's
wisdom. Hence, it ought not and would not be repealed "at the
dictatorial requisition of a lawless rabble." [154] Privately, the champion of the Catholics had written Alexander Wedderburn, the
newly-created Baron Loughborough, Lord Chief Justice of the
Common Pleas, suggesting the advisability of the Catholics' appearing before parliament with a petition asserting their rights, renew-
ing their oath of fidelity to the state, and denying the charges of
the Protestant Association. If they failed to do this, they would
be guilty of "that way of skulking, to which, under the idea of a
prudent caution, the Roman Catholics have been advised at other
times, and that has tended in a very great degree to bring that
odium upon them, which men, who conceal their faces and are supposed to entertain secret and concealed dogmas, are always sure to
excite." [155] Actually, he had gone so far himself with this suggestion of his as to draw up a petition for them.[156]

On the twentieth, the House formed itself into a Committee
of the Whole to consider a bill for the securing of the Protestant
religion. This measure was sponsored by Sir George Savile, who
had brought in the proposal for the Catholics which had been the
cause of the recent tumults. In the course of the debate, Mr. Alder-
man Bull, a notorious anti-Catholic, took occasion to condemn the
Act for Catholic Relief and to express the hope that it would be
repealed. Burke followed him and took sharp issue with his remarks.[157] He employed an *ad hominem* in his argument and pictured Bull as an ignorant man, bereft of the slightest semblance of
erudition. Ignorance, falsehood, and fanaticism were the only opposition arrayed against the strong arguments of the wisest men who
had spoken that day, Burke asserted. This caused Sir James Lowther, another of the scant number of Lord George Gordon's supporters and a rather vulgar man who had been engaged in litigation
with Burke's friend, the Duke of Portland, in a case in which Burke
had interested himself to the detriment of Lowther, to call him to
order. Burke became so upset by this that some time elapsed before

he could bring himself to continue. But he recovered and went on to say that the petition of the Protestant Association was in reality an attack upon the Church of England and the crown as well. He reviewed the riots with withering sarcasm and examined the names and marks of the petitioners. Taking his cue from Fox, he scorned those who, unable to read and write themselves, would deny to others an opportunity to secure an education should they so desire. He said that he himself had received his education as a Protestant of the Established Church at the hands of a Dissenter. Then later he had read *all* the theological publications on all sides that were written during the seventeenth and eighteenth centuries and (understandably) reached the conclusion that such studies tended merely to confuse and so he had elected to cling fast to the Church of England. He warmly defended the principle of toleration in his following remarks and then returned to the bill for the securing of the Protestant religion which he characterized as a sop to the Protestant Association. Too many members of parliament had allowed themselves to be frightened by the mob. Finally, he was unalterably opposed to any measure which might hurt the innocent.[158]

26 June, Burke again spoke against the bill to secure the Protestant Religion. In the interim he had been doing some research on the topic of the Catholic schools as a letter to him from a Catholic peer, Lord Petre, indicates. Petre sent him "all the papers relating to the Roman Catholic Schools that has yet been collected." [159] To provide himself with some ammunition should the old charge be gratuitously renewed that the Catholics were bent upon the conversion of any Protestants who found themselves in their employ, he received another letter from Lord Petre which revealed that at present he had eleven Protestants in his service, the greatest number he had ever employed, and all of whom went regularly to their own church. During the space of eighteen years, only two of his non-Catholic servants had ever "been brought over to our Religion," a fact which proves conclusively that "my chaplains have not been unduely busy in making converts." [160]

In his speech on the twenty-sixth against Sir George Savile's bill, whose purpose was to restrain the "Papists, or persons professing the Popish religion, from teaching, or taking upon themselves the education or government of the children of Protestants," Burke was very thorough. He began by regretting the lack of a single Catholic seminary in England which was a serious matter to him because it meant that the Catholics who intended to become ecclesiasts had to seek such education in France, Flanders, or Spain. To Burke, the first of the great English statesmen to become influenced by an enlightened spirit of nationalism,[161] this was a deplorable situation. He then showed that in almost no instances were Catholics engaged in the instruction of Protestants. In the rare cases where this was so, the Protestants were taught the catechism of the Church of England. The story that the Catholics bought or stole children was a myth,[162] he said, but such practices did take place in Ireland only there they were at the expense of the Catholics. There existed in that land what were called charter schools. Money was voted annually by the Irish parliament to sustain them and none but Catholic children were bought. They were then sent to other parts of the country and their names changed. Such proceedings were carried on furtively but it was nevertheless a fact, he declared. He had hesitated before bringing this national disgrace out into the open but circumstances had forced him to do so. He announced that he found himself in full accord with the teachings of Saint Thomas Aquinas that the parents alone had the full right of disposing of the education of their children and concluded on a familiar note by reverting to his dislike of the abstract by demanding to know who the petitioners were in this instance.[163]

His fight in the House of Commons was in a lost cause as the Savile bill passed and then went to the House of Lords. Every energy at his disposal was then enlisted to have the proposal defeated in the upper house. He personally canvassed many of the peers and demonstrated to them the impolicy, cruelty, and absurdity of this measure. In this instance his efforts were successful, and the bill was defeated thus producing a great victory both for Burke and the spirit of toleration.[164]

With peace and order at last restored in London, there remained the question of punishment for the poor wretches apprehended during the rioting. Originally, Burke had been insistent upon the apprehension and punishment of the guilty,[165] but, when the time came, he argued for leniency, thereby manifesting his deep Christian spirit of charity. The number of those executed was only twenty-one, although several hundred lives had been lost in the tumults.[166]

It was not long thereafter before parliament was dissolved in September 1780, because the North government felt that the riots had served to strengthen their position and so they decided to capitalize on this sentiment by holding elections for a new parliament.

We have seen how Burke employed the distresses of England to the advantage of Ireland by putting through Catholic relief in England, knowing full well that its success there would be the signal for a similar relaxation of the penal laws in Ireland. It ought not, I think, be assumed that Burke aimed at favoring Ireland by such action but rather that he saw that the circumstances were advantageous for doing something for Ireland which, in turn, would help to strengthen the Empire. All was managed beautifully until fanaticism broke loose in Scotland and was followed by repercussions in England. In the latter excitement, Burke's very life was placed in danger [167] but his courage saved him. However, his reputation among the public had been besmirched, and the old calumnies against him had been renewed with vigor. In his own constituency of Bristol, his enlightened views on toleration coupled with other causes, chief among which was his championship of Irish commercial relief in the face of the outspoken opposition of the majority of his constituents, proved too much for the voters to accept. Now it was his political life that was at stake, at least in so far as his coveted Bristol seat was concerned.

CHAPTER IV

Severance of the Bristol Connection and its Aftermath

LOSS OF BURKE'S "GREATEST HONOUR"

In the summer of 1780 Edmund Burke's reputation had reached a height previously unsurpassed in his career. The king himself had commented very favorably upon Burke and his approval even extended to his willingness to see Burke come into office. He remarked that Burke would be a "real acquisition." [1] Paradoxically, Burke's hold upon Bristol was very shaky. Long before the dissolution of parliament that summer, the clouds had begun to gather on the horizon of Bristol for Burke. From the very beginning his connection with Bristol had been a rather strange and strained one,[2] since the city was traditionally a Tory stronghold and had elected Burke and Cruger as a protest against the Tory government's bungling of relations with America. Burke, however, professed to feel that the Whig cause was making some headway and he took pride in the "growing strength of the Whiggs in the Bristol Corporation." [3]

The mentality of Burke's constituency was so strongly commercial that there was no community of interests between them and their representative. From the instant of his election, Burke had demonstrated that this gap existed, for in his Speech at the Conclusion of the Poll, 3 November 1774, he had undertaken to lecture the voters on the distinction between a representative and a delegate. And less than a year after his election, he wrote to Rockingham to complain of "the horrid expenses of these expeditions" from London to meet with his Bristol constituents.[4] So distasteful was this practice to him, and so impractical was he, that from August 1776 until the end of August 1780 he failed to pay a single visit to Bristol. He did, of course, seek to make good this deficiency in part by carrying on a voluminous correspondence with Bristol and by doing countless favors in London for his constituents, but this was to prove an unacceptable substitute for his physical presence.

In addition to the differences which had arisen between the representative and his electors over Catholic relief and Irish trade, he had supported a bill for the relief of insolvent debtors which the merchants of Bristol felt was inimical to their interests. On the other hand, some of his constituents had seen fit to make a direct application to the Admiralty for a convoy instead of conducting their business through their representative, and Burke had become very upset over being bypassed. His resentment had further been increased when Samuel Span and some other merchants had failed to show the proper appreciation for a favor which he had performed for them.[5]

Hence by the spring of 1780, Burke had come to the conclusion that it would be up to his friends whether he would stand in the next election or not, the implication being that they would have to do some real work in his behalf. He admitted that "I neither had originally, nor have I now, any thing of what is called a natural Interest in that City. I was called thither merely upon publick ground, & I have no other to stand upon at this moment." Burke told his correspondent that parliament kept him busy most of the year and what free time he had at his disposal he spent at home for the sake of his health and his family affairs. Consequently, he had been unable to cultivate the citizens of Bristol. He then brought up the embarrassing problem of finances which he had been forced to mention when he had been originally approached to represent Bristol. Things had not changed. He simply could not supply any part of the expense for another contest, but if the people of Bristol wished him to stand, he was theirs to command.[6]

10 August, he wrote to Job Watts, another constituent, in reply to the latter's letter informing him that religious bias had put him in ill favor with the people, to deny that he had decided not to

stand for reelection and to say that he had always been a friend to religious toleration. Apart from religious motives, toleration was vital to the state for civil reasons. At no time did he believe in forcing men into hatred of the state through harsh treatment. If he never thought it prudent under any circumstances, how much less did he think it wise when Britain had suffered the loss of "one half of our empire by one idle quarrel not less injudicious and absurd." He declared that no people should be permitted to live in a country who were not given a share in its benefits through "quiet in their goods, their freedom, and their conscience."[7]

The following day he was still exercised over the intolerance of the people mentioned by Watts and so he wrote to John Noble plainly revealing his irritation that the electors should censure his actions. It made him ashamed, he said, that his "conduct relative to the late acts of scanty and imperfect toleration" should cause a "rout."[8]

Although he fully comprehended the difficulties facing him, Burke decided at the dissolution of parliament to seek to retain his Bristol seat. Accordingly, he paid Bristol his first visit in four years at the end of August.[9] On 6 September 1780, he delivered his speech previous to the poll at the Guildhall,[10] an *apologia* which was unquestionably one of the finest speeches he ever made, if not actually the best,[11] and a speech which must be ranked among the greatest of its kind ever delivered.

Burke selected the four charges most commonly made against him in Bristol and devoted himself to refuting them to his own satisfaction if not to that of his audience. These were: (1) failure to visit the city more often; (2) opposition to the wishes of his constituents on the matter of the Irish commercial propositions;[12] (3) action detrimental to the interests of Bristol on the Bill for Imprisonment for Debt; and (4) religious bias for Catholicism. The two charges which are of immediate concern to this study are the second and fourth. Therefore, attention will be focussed upon them.

In the instance of the Irish commercial propositions he stood accused, he said, of having acted as a native Irishman rather than as an English member of parliament. That he had "very warm good wishes for the place of my birth," he readily admitted, but the real object of his duties was his "true country, England." His conduct had always been guided by the interests of his constituents, and of this he was firmly persuaded. What they needed to remember was that Britain was waging a war with America. New policies were taking shape, whether desired or not. So his only thought had been to consider how he could best link closer the ties binding what remained of the Empire to the mother country. In this, he was true to his constant principle that all things which came from Great Britain should emanate as the gifts of a generous donor and not as claims recovered against a protesting litigant.

The first attempt to improve the conditions of Ireland's trade had been emasculated. Then, in the following year, 1779, Lord North crushed the new effort when he saw the opposition to the measures which was provoked in Great Britain. This proved to be unfortunate because all of Ireland arose in protest. The Irish determined to protect themselves against the dual dangers of French invasion and British oppression. Faced with the hard cold reality of Ireland's will, the British parliament had no alternative but to surrender completely in the matter of commercial amelioration for Ireland. Britain yielded the exclusive trade of America, Africa, and the West Indies; all the enumerations of the Acts of Navigation; and all the manufactures. It was done with "no reserve, no exception; no debate, no discussion." This action was a pitiful and disedifying spectacle to his eyes. He had sought to aid Ireland to secure relief under the proper circumstances, and for this he was unpopular in England. When Ireland was then enabled to dictate her own terms, and he felt England's humiliation, he became disliked in Ireland.

He asked his audience to understand that he had been an Irishman in this business in the same sense that he had been an American in the earlier dispute when he had asked Britain to concede to America what she prayed as a concession. Because he foresaw a repetition of the American affair in the case of Ireland, he had opposed the wishes of the Bristol electorate. In so doing, he was in reality obedient to "the instructions of truth and Nature, and maintained your interest, against your opinions, with a constancy that became me."

Turning to the other charge which is pertinent to this study, we

find that the Catholic Act was only a "first faint sketch of toleration." Having made this assertion, he undertook to explain some
of the penal laws against Catholics which had been the subject of
repeal in England and for which he had been so openly castigated
throughout Britain.[13] Despite the conception prevalent in Bristol,
he publicly denied having been either the sponsor or the seconder
of this measure of relief. In fact, the record would show that he
had not even opened his lips on the subject. It had been moved by
Sir George Savile, seconded by Mr. Dunning, the Recorder of
Bristol, and agreed to by the entire membership of parliament, the
king, the clergy of the Established Church, and all the important
Dissenters.

There were good reasons why these unjust laws had been repealed, and the Bristol electors ought to be told what they were
so that they could understand why the bill had been passed.
America and France had become allies, and Britain was threatened
with an invasion. At this critical point, the Catholics of England
had come forward out of the retreats into which they had been
driven and presented a "tottering throne" with an address which
was "one of the most sober, measured, steady, and dutiful addresses
that was ever presented to the crown." It pledged unequivocally
their determination to remain loyal despite the fact that a Catholic
power threatened to invade Protestant Britain. Surely, the state was
obligated to do something in return, he argued. Could Britain refuse
to unite with her Catholic people at a time when "the most Protestant part of this Protestant empire found it for its advantage to
unite with the two principal Popish states," Burke then asked.

This prospect of peace at home, which was then in the offing,
made him happy. Even putting aside thoughts of danger to the
state, he had to support the measure on the grounds of justice, policy, and feeling. It was a wise, albeit imperfect act and was productive of a number of good results, the most important of which
was that it had been reproduced in Ireland, although the Irish
model was likewise imperfect. Britain had obligations toward the
Catholics of Ireland, he reminded his hearers. The Irish Catholics
were certainly grateful for the little which they had received.
Whereas the Catholics of England were not numerous,[14] the members of that faith in Ireland numbered at least "sixteen or seventeen

hundred thousand souls." It was indeed a fortunate matter for England that religion had not been added to the scales in the recent commercial contest with Ireland. Furthermore, the spirit of toleration was practically universal throughout Europe. This being so, should England be a notable exception, he asked.

The legislation which had caused such a furor after it had been enacted should be considered only a beginning and not an end of relief for the Catholics. Still, the process would necessarily have to be slow so that the minds of the people might have an opportunity to become reconciled to the idea. Unfortunately, there had been a terrible consequence to this first demonstration of toleration. Tumults had ensued which were the work of deluded fanatics whose purpose was to force parliament to repeal the Act for Catholic Relief. To have acceded to their demands, he reminded his audience, would have been "an act of national perfidy which has no example." In return for the removal of a handful of the many inequalities under which the Catholics had labored, they were bound by solemn oath to bear true allegiance to the government, to abjure any other temporal power, and to renounce "the doctrines of systematic perfidy" which they were, in Burke's estimation, unjustly charged with holding. The Protestant Association had sought to coerce parliament into breaking its share in that compact without offering any valid reason why it should be done. Such an action on the part of parliament would have made of its members "not only a convention of treacherous tyrants, but a gang of the lowest and dirtiest wretches that ever disgraced humanity."

At this juncture, with the Protestant Association pressing wildly for the repeal of Catholic Relief, Burke, who had been very quiet during the easy passage of the bill, now came forward zealously and employed every faculty he possessed to oppose the petition of the Protestant Association. He confessed that he had worked tirelessly day and night both in and out of parliament.

A circumstance which in itself would completely justify the maintenance of the Catholic Relief Act was the manner in which the Catholics in London conducted themselves during the tumults and persecutions of the Gordon Riots. Burke estimated that there were only four or five thousand Catholics in London and said that their principal districts were the areas in which the mobs committed their worst outrages. These London Catholics were noted for their strength and quickness and had a reputation more for their determination than their foresight. Despite the inducement to rebel which the loss of their homes and chapels offered them, their restraint had been, in his opinion, truly remarkable. To this circumstance he attributed the fact that London still stood. For if the Catholics had fought the mob, its fury would have been unbounded, and London would have been consumed by the flames. Tribute was due also to the Catholic clergy which had restrained the laity and kept them in a state of resignation and quiet that was veritably astonishing. Burke predicted that England would someday be grateful to both the Catholic clergy and laity for their splendid forbearance.

Another thing to remember was that the relief which had been allowed had not been granted too hastily. On the contrary, parliament had been guilty of almost a century of procrastination. The futility of calling the Catholics enemies of the British Constitution should be obvious since they could not be disloyal to something in which they were not given a share.

He then doubled back and remarked that there were some who lamented that the Savile relief measure had been passed because of the lamentable consequences which had attended it. Burke was not one of that number since he professed to believe that what had followed actually made the bill a better one because it gave "clear evidence that there lurked a temper somewhere which ought not to have been fostered by the laws." His own life had not been in vain if, among other things, he had helped to loosen "the foreign holdings of the citizen" and to teach him to look to the laws of his own country for his protection and to the beneficence of his countrymen for his comfort.

Burke then concluded his speech by saying that the charges made against him in Bristol were in reality all of one kind, viz., that he had "pushed the principles of general justice and benevolence too far; further than a cautious policy would warrant; and further than the opinions of many would go along with me." This fact nevertheless would comfort him for the rest of his days no matter what happened.

Except for the charge that he neglected his constituents by his failure to have visited them in four years, Burke was correct in claiming that the opposition to him was based on grounds which were in reality complimentary to him. This conclusion in itself makes the speech one to be remembered. He did not stand accused of dishonesty or incompetence. Instead his opponents could only say that he had been too just and decent in his parliamentary work. Over and above this, he had given his narrow-minded and selfish listeners a lesson in imperial conduct by driving home to them the danger of the American War as it touched Ireland. He had demonstrated that, from both the commercial and religious point of view, it was the part of wisdom to do for Ireland what he had favored and helped to bring into being. He had shown his personal courage by standing firm and defending his conduct in the teeth of a strenuous opposition and had possessed the temerity to tell them unequivocally that he was a better judge of their true interests than they were themselves and openly and unafraid he had rebuked them for their narrowness and greed.

Great as the speech was, there were some features of it wherein Burke let his emotions overcome his better judgment and which must have been received with derisive snorts from not a few of his audience. These were the parts concerned with the English Catholics. For one thing, it was ridiculous to assert seriously that fifty thousand widely scattered Catholics could have made much difference one way or another in the event of an attempted French invasion of England. Secondly, his extravagant praise of the Catholics for their spirit of resignation during the Gordon Riots was not effective reasoning on his part. Four or five thousand people could not have resisted the scores of thousands of rioters bent on destruction as were the London mobs in June 1780.

Despite these flaws, it was a great speech, but sad to say Burke was unable to convince the prejudiced majority of the electorate, although he attracted the support of a large part of the Bristol Corporation and most of the Dissenters. His supporters urged his reelection on the grounds of his "early application, long experience, and enlarged views in trade and manufacture."[15] Seeing that defeat was inevitable, he withdrew his candidacy on 9 September and made a Speech Declining the Poll, which was also one of his best forensic efforts.[16] Prejudice and self-interest had triumphed, and

Burke was deprived of his cherished Bristol seat, a connection which he later described as "the greatest honour of my life." [17]

An honor it was, but perhaps Burke found consolation in thoughts such as those which he once expressed to Sir Joshua Reynolds' niece, thoughts which in no way contradict the fact that to represent Bristol had been something in which he took pride: "They know, it seems, at Calcutta that 'I am declined in popular favour.' That cannot be, for I had never had any to lose, I never conformed myself to the humours of the people. I cannot say that opinion is indifferent to me: but I will take it, if I can, as my companion; never as my Guide." [18]

Or possibly it was the thought that statesmen ought not to look to "the paltry part of the moment, nor to the temporary and transient praise of the vulgar" but rather to the example which they leave to the world [19] which sustained him at this time of rejection.

Despite his defeat he was voted the Thanks of the Bristol Corporation in October, an action which impressed and gratified him to some extent.[20] A reading of the resolution reveals that it was far from perfunctory. But for a time he now contemplated retiring from parliament,[21] a prospect which delighted many, including one vindictive contributor to a contemporary newspaper who told Burke that he had "already sufficiently amused your Fansy with Dreams of Power and Visions of Greatness." He hoped that Rockingham would permit him to remain in private life to make "honourable amends for that waste of Time which you have too long squandered away in visionary Refinements in Politicks, in frothy Declamations, captious Cavils, and groundless Invectives." [22]

On the other hand, Burke's friends were universal in their denunciation of Bristol's action in rejecting Burke. Charles Fox said that "Indeed my dear Burke it requires all your candour & *reverse of selfishness* (for I know no word to express it) to be in patience with that rascally City for so I must call it after the way in which it has behaved to you." [23] General Burgoyne, still home on parole after his defeat at Saratoga, called Bristol "that ungrateful City" and urged Burke not to give up his career but to "yield to the wishes of every honest man in the Nation . . . & accept a seat from those who best know & most respect the value of your services." [24] The Marchioness of Rockingham, writing for her husband, expressed the belief that Burke's "canvass show'd that you . . . was the *real Choice* of the good people, tho not their chosen Representative . . ." and said that "we are vastly hurt at the failure of Bristol, but our good & *wonderful* friend stands in a high & amiable light in that business, & his farewell speech, is really too excellent & too affecting." The Marchioness must have felt the strain of Burke's defeat quite deeply since she concluded the letter in a slightly muddled manner by signing off "Always Dear Admiral your most sincere & obedient servt." [25] And as a final example of these letters, there is one from the Prince of Dashkov who said that Burke's defeat reflected "shame on the country and Bristol in particular." [26]

Rockingham's offer to make available to Burke the pocket borough of Malton in Yorkshire which Burke was to have represented prior to his election at Bristol in 1774 was accepted. As he told Richard Champion on 3 November,[27] he was to be back in parliament whenever he wished and indeed sooner than he desired because he was very busy at this time. Having accepted Malton, Burke continued to represent this constituency for the rest of his long parliamentary career which terminated voluntarily in 1794.[28]

In December 1780, one of the victorious candidates in the recent election died suddenly, and Burke was importuned by his friends in Bristol to stand as a candidate in the by-election necessitated by the death of the incumbent. In his refusal to Champion to consider the request of his friends, Burke stated that he was "not indifferent to the honour" but that it was simply out of the question. Having made his position clear, he proceeded to comment on the suggestion of the friends of Cruger, a defeated Whig candidate who had served as Bristol's other representative with Burke from 1774–1780, that Burke resign his seat for Malton and prevail upon Lord Rockingham to give it to Cruger. In return Cruger's friends would work for him in the Bristol by-election. Burke was somewhat exercised by this strange suggestion and said candidly to Champion that "I must think the proposal of an extraordinary nature indeed." [29]

From the foregoing consideration of the loss of Burke's Bristol seat, it is clear that it was caused in large measure by his attitude toward Catholic relief, both in England and Ireland, and improvement of Irish trade conditions. In both instances, he had acted as he did not only to correct an injustice to an oppressed people but to strengthen the British Empire at a time of crisis. In line with the vital circumstances "the choice of the moment" had been, on the whole, an expeditious one in that the desired objectives were achieved although at the cost of his seat and at great risk to his life in the Gordon Riots.

BURKE'S VIEWS ON PROPOSED CATHOLIC RELIEF, 1782

Now that he was securely seated as the member for Malton, Burke's attention was occupied to a considerable extent by his interest in Indian affairs. His "kinsman," Will Burke had found employment as the London representative of the Rajah of Tanjore, and this potentate was being subjected to what Burke felt was unduly harsh treatment by the authorities in India.[30] Indian affairs grew to be a subject of special interest to Burke which he pursued with great vigor for many years to come. His efforts on behalf of the "undone millions" of India, as he called them, while motivated to some extent by personal considerations soon achieved the proportions of a crusade which was destined to become what he considered the greatest cause of his entire career.

To the growing list of those whom his strong feelings of charity aided, he added at this time the Jewish merchants of the Dutch island of St. Eustatius in the West Indies. These businessmen had been victimized by Admiral Rodney's plunder of the island following the outbreak of war between Britain and The Netherlands in December 1780. Burke in a speech in the House, condemning Rodney's actions, said of the Jews that they were a people whom it was the special object of humanity to protect rather than abuse.[31]

Irish affairs, especially as they related to the Catholics, continued to interest him. Even before his defeat at Bristol, earlier that year he had taken pains to see to it that an Irish Catholic peer, Lord Kenmare, received a copy of an abstract of the penal laws which he had made some years earlier. Kenmare thanked him for his "most Elegant Abstract of our Penal Statutes" and remarked that "Tho' I have lived the Object of them, & had the General Idea of their being the refinement of Legal persecution, I never had before a Conception of their diversity & Extent." [32] The gentleman whom Burke had asked to present Kenmare with this information, Thomas Braughall, reported on his mission and said that it had been carried out. He had waited on Kenmare "and deliver'd the manuscript, mentioning at [the] same time there was not a Copy of it; his Lordship promised to put the Original or [a] Copy into my hands in a short time, but the eagerness of the First men in this Country to peruse it has hitherto prevented him. the Speaker, Mr. Scott, & many persons of equal rank have applied for the perusal; Mr. Perry is now with you [in] his consummate knowledge of the Subject [which] makes him equal to describe its Merits; to him I shall leave it, and confine myself to my humble province of returning the original or a faithful Copy." [33]

He continued to receive information on conditions in Ireland from a variety of correspondents the following year, one of whom, Parkyns MacMahon, told him that his "native country must ever be proud of having given you birth." [34] An optimistic report from the Bishop of Killaloe, a member of the Established Church, informed him that things in Ireland "wear a pleasanter Aspect, and (in spite of all the grievances which our newspapers represent to them,) the People at large seem to be in high good humour. Next session of Parliament we shall probably make some fresh attempts to mend the Constitution: but I believe the majority will be content to leave it as it is for the Present." [35]

As the year wore on, French and Spanish fleets were in the English Channel, and the fear was widespread that an invasion of Ireland was soon to take place. The city of Cork was considered a certain target because the valuable Jamaica fleet had taken refuge in its harbor. In the anticipated fear of the coming of the invaders, virtually all of the specie in the area had gone into hoarding. George Goold, a Catholic merchant of the city, relieved the distress of the British commander there by supplying him with five thousand guineas and even offered him his entire personal fortune should the need arise. Other Catholic gentlemen had cooperated fully with Mr. Goold and for their patriotism and devotion they were warmly praised by the commander. The Lord Lieutenant himself was so impressed that he promised that their loyalty would be brought to the personal attention of the king. Goold, knowing

Burke's public pronouncements on the subject of the loyalty of the Catholics of Ireland, wrote him to inform him of what had transpired. It pleased the merchant to convey the message to Burke that Catholics had helped the government in the latter's hour of need and it proved conclusively that Burke's estimate of their worth had not been mistaken.[36]

A few days later Burke received a letter from another Catholic, this time an Englishman, Lord Petre, which informed him of a proposed edict of toleration to be granted by the Emperor Joseph II of Austria which would grant numerous immunities and privileges to the Jews living within the Hapsburg empire. Petre wished Burke to spread word, with appropriate notes of his own, throughout the press that such an event was to take place in Catholic Austria. It would make, he said, a very effective contrast to the bigotry of Lord George Gordon and the Protestant Association.[37] Burke's reply to this letter showed his pleasure at hearing this news but expressed his sorrow that England was not ready for such generosity yet. In other words, "the choice of the moment" was not propitious. Any such proposal at this particular time would, in his opinion, have to come from the government itself. He expressed the hope that the recent exemplary conduct of the Cork merchants at a critical and dangerous moment would prove to be of service.[38]

The following spring he did do something for Lord Petre which obviously involved furtherance of the Catholic cause, but what it was I have been unable to discover. As the following letter plainly shows, Burke's part in this mysterious business was highly secretive. Charles Butler, also a Catholic, wrote to Burke to say that "I have the Honor to send you, the Copy of the —— —— Memorial left with me this Morning by Lord Petre, and which he desired me to transmit to you, when copied. You may be assured, that no mention shall ever be made of the Part you have so generously and humanely taken, in framing it. I will do myself the honor of calling for it tomorrow morning." [39]

Meanwhile, a bill for additional Catholic relief had been introduced in the Irish House of Commons by Luke Gardiner, sponsor of the previous measure in favor of the Catholics in 1778. While it was still in the projected state, Lord Kenmare, then leader of the Catholic Association of Ireland, wrote Burke about it.[40] Burke's

reply to the letter of Kenmare [41] ranks high among the best things
he has ever written.[42] Professing at first to be "very much in the
dark" concerning the affairs of Ireland, Burke proceeded to air
his views on the proposed legislation. He beheld the bill as one
"grounded at once on contempt and jealousy." Looking at the
bill in the abstract, he bluntly informed Kenmare that "it is neither
more nor less than a renewed act of UNIVERSAL, UNMITIGATED, IN-
DISPENSABLE, EXCEPTIONLESS, DISQUALIFICATION."

In fact, it was so bad, he said, that any man reading it would
never think that he was reading an act of real toleration. The
Catholics were told that they were held to be good, true, loyal
citizens and subjects of the crown, but then followed the universal
exclusion of these worthy people from every office of trust and
profit. They could not vote in any type of election, possess firearms, practice law, etc. Such a list of exclusions was more like an
act of proscription instead of an act of grace. What must the laws
concerning these dutiful citizens have been, he asked, if the present
proposal represented any relaxation of them? Certain of the exclusions were very dangerous in that they placed the Catholics completely at the mercy of juries. He had been in Ireland three times
from 1761 through 1766 and knew from experience to what extremes of cruelty juries in that land could go in order to punish the
Catholics.

The denial of the franchise, it ought to be noted well, was
like the taking away of a shield which the citizen possessed in
order to protect himself against oppression. Herein lay an express
invitation to persecute the Catholics. Since no parliamentary candidate needed to consider them, he could devote his time to winning
favor with those who did possess the franchise. In order to please
this class, it often happened that it would be to the candidate's
advantage to expose the unfortunate Catholics to those various
forms of discrimination which influence possesses.

All of these weaknesses in the position of the Catholics were
dangerous ones, but the worst of them were to be found in the
laws against foreign education. Not only Catholic laymen were
affected by these restrictions, but the matter of a succession to
"about four thousand clergymen" was concerned. He asked if the
authorities could in justice deprive the Catholic clergy of the places

of education which had been made available to them abroad through great sacrifices without providing substitutes in Ireland.

The proposal of Hely Hutchinson, Provost of Trinity College, Dublin, to make available there a few sizarships for the education of Catholic clergymen was assailed by Burke.[43] He showed that when provisions were made for the education of any body of men, careful consideration ought first to be given to the purpose of their education. One had to bear in mind what their duties in life were to be. The religious doctrines of one faith could never be properly taught in the universities of another. A Catholic priest had to be trained in a seminary where such matters as celibacy and confession were respected and not ridiculed. Burke's reasoning in this matter, he sadly observed to Kenmare, would have no effect whatsoever on those whose desire it was to make the Catholic clergy illiterate.

He was likewise opposed to the scheme of Dublin Castle under which the members of the Catholic hierarchy would be selected by the government. His reason was stated plainly — the adherents of one religious belief were never competent to appoint the pastors of another. Even if the present Castle officials were well-disposed toward the Catholics and anxious to see that all the injustices against them were remedied, they might well be followed by another set whose feelings were just the opposite. In short, they were simply not qualified for such a power. This proposed system would be deleterious to the Catholic religion and would result in the discrediting of the clergy which in turn would do harm to the country. Instead of the great good Ireland had long derived from the Catholic clergymen, they would now become the cause of disorders unlike any the country had ever seen.

The proposed act was good as far as it went, he said, but the difficulty with it was patent — it did not go very far. It could be classified as toleration with respect to matters of religion but in the field of civil matters it simply tightened up the old restrictions. Burke thought that it would be better to improve the civic rights of the Catholics first because religious advantages would follow as a matter of course. He said that he did not believe that it was a spirit of religious bigotry that was responsible for the maintenance of the anti-Catholic laws. He would put the blame on pride, arrogance, and a spirit of absolute authority. He could cite instances if he wished of men who oppressed the Catholics in their civil rights but who were very indulgent with them in the matter of religious considerations. There were even cases he could name of men who would become Catholics if it meant that the power of persecution would then be theirs. It was "injustice, and not a mistaken conscience" which accounted for persecution in his opinion.

He concluded the letter in the same vein that he began — he was not well acquainted with the conditions in Ireland at that time since it had been some sixteen years since he had been in that country himself. Moreover, he had heard that he was not considered a friend of Ireland. He knew for a fact that "pains have been taken to lessen the credit I might have had there."

Despite his deep knowledge of Catholicism and the marked influence which Christian principles had on his life and career, Burke was guilty of a misinterpretation of the teachings of Roman Catholicism in this letter to Kenmare. He was too much the statesman to grasp that to the Catholic the free exercise of his religion is of transcendent importance. Catholicism teaches that this life is merely a preparation for the next which is eternal. Therefore, what does it really matter if one cannot vote or hold office so long as he can worship freely and be secure in his family? As Burke said, the religious advantages would follow the civil. Owing to their importance, however, Catholics hold that they must take precedence. Other than this natural enough mistake for one not of that religious persuasion to make, Burke deserved the commendation of all Catholics of spirit in Ireland for his virile attack on the list of proscriptions which would still remain to the Catholics after this act of "toleration" had been passed.

His attitude was in sharp contrast to the manner in which Lord Kenmare and many of the other Catholic leaders habitually conducted themselves.[44] It should have inspired them to act more forcefully but unfortunately it did not. Burke had correctly sensed their timidity and in after years it remained a proper source of annoyance to him. Not only were the lay leaders a very timid lot on the whole, but, even worse, the Catholic hierarchy of Ireland at this time was notorious for its almost grovelling attitude toward a government which was dedicated to their oppression.

Kenmare, the leader of the Catholic Association, was so well known for his lack of determination and his general timidity that Sir Boyle Roche,[45] a member of the Irish Commons whom Burke thoroughly detested, later took advantage of these failings. At a convention of the Irish Volunteers held at Dublin in November 1783, Roche claimed that he had a letter from Kenmare which plainly disavowed any wish on the part of the Irish Catholics to gain the franchise. This was such a flagrant untruth that the Catholic Association, when it heard of this false assertion, emphatically denied it. The damage was done, however, through Kenmare's own failure to come forward with a denial in time. He delayed too long before doing so. A few months after Kenmare tardily repudiated Roche's action, the latter admitted that he had acted on his own authority because he felt that the Catholics should have disowned any hopes they may have had for the franchise.[46] This case is an excellent illustration of the peculiar sense of political honor which existed in Irish governmental circles at this time, and it is very revealing that such a confession of a lack of ethical conduct should have escaped without any punishment whatsoever. The episode is cited here in order to stress the difficulties facing Burke and other honest men in their efforts to correct the misgovernment of the Irish Ascendancy and to call attention to the lack of courage of the Catholic leader at this time, a circumstance which certainly did nothing to make Burke's attempts to help the Catholics any easier.

At any rate, the measure introduced by Luke Gardiner was passed and became law in February 1782. There was plenty of room for criticism of the measure, but at least it was a forward step and as such deserved some respect. Restrictions still remained on the Catholics, some of them petty and annoying and others serious. In the former category, the prohibition placed on steeples for Catholic churches continued in force. In the category of the more serious, Catholics were deemed incapable of intermarrying with Protestants, though either denomination might intermarry with "Mahometans or negroes," as the Irish Chief Secretary, William Eden, remarked to Burke. Eden also pointed out that the bill gave Catholics the power to take and hold property in fee but, at the same time, "anxiously excludes five-sixths of the kingdom from any share in that free legislation which the other sixth, at the same hour, declare and swear to be the indefeasible right of the people of Ireland." [47] The Catholics still had to pay tithes for the support of the Established Church and were, of course, still deprived of the right of voting and of holding seats in parliament. But the restrictions on purchasing, inheriting, and bequeathing land, matters of importance anywhere but especially so in an agricultural country, had been repealed.

That Burke's letter had been productive of good in the Catholic cause may be seen from Kenmare's reply to him. He told Burke that he had shown his letter to such important people as William Eden, Henry Grattan, and Luke Gardiner with the result that "it stop't their proceeding on a Crude & ill digested plan for the Home Education of our Clergy." Kenmare added that Burke was very much misinformed if he still thought that "there is the least division here about your Merits, Talents, & Character; All parties look up to you, as the greatest Ornament of your Country & this Age; we, the dirtiest part of this Community, owe principally to you our Enfranchisement. . . ." [48]

At least one person in Ireland felt this way, as the following letter of a Mr. Poole, writing from Beaumares to Burke, indicates: "Sir! I have with great attention examined the Debates for some years back, and find every argument of yours so pithy and disinterested, that your name shall be revered by me while I live;! In order that the name of *Edmund Burke* shd. never be forgotten in my Family, I will (provided you don't disapprove thereof) call my Infant Son (born 7 days ago) by that much *esteem'd name*. I hope you will forgive this freedom. . . ." [49]

The Irish Chief Secretary, William Eden, told Burke that he had spotted some of the same deficiencies in the Catholic bill which Burke had and had used his influence to have them corrected. He took pride in the fact that this was before he had seen Burke's letter to Lord Kenmare.

As imperfect as the bill was, the fact that it could be passed only four years after the first break in the penal laws had taken place was encouraging and gave promise that better years might lie ahead. One thing was unmistakably clear — a new spirit was beginning to evidence itself in Ireland.

IRISH LEGISLATIVE INDEPENDENCE, 1782

This new spirit was influenced in no small measure by the American Revolution and even before 1782 made it clear that the independence from Britain of Ireland's parliament was its principal objective. Having won what was customarily called "free trade," [50] the Irish were by no means content to rest satisfied with this accomplishment. They comprehended that this concession by the English was the result of the press of circumstances and could, therefore, be once again withdrawn when the conditions responsible for the grant had changed. There was little doubt of the widespread conviction in Ireland that the necessary complement to their recent victory was legislative independence. Nor was there much doubt that the realization of this desirable objective would require extreme care in the management. Preparations had begun with the loss of as little precious time as was necessary. The ranks of the Volunteers were swelled with additional recruits, and Grattan had moved as early as 19 April 1780 in the Irish Commons a resolution that the Irish parliament ought to be independent. Unfortunately for Grattan and the Irish patriots who supported him, the power of Dublin Castle to block such a move was too great and their creatures in the Irish parliament were enabled to secure an indefinite postponement of the proposal. That Edmund Burke did not have much sympathy for such a step as Grattan sought to take was evidenced by his questions — "Will no one speak to this madman? Will no one stop this madman, Grattan?" [51]

That Grattan had strong backing among the privileged element of the Irish nation may be seen from his boast of the support of eighteen of Ireland's thirty-two counties together with various Grand Jury addresses and the resolution of the Irish Volunteers.[52]

Despite the setback dealt to Grattan's first attempt, the strength of the advocates of Irish legislative independence grew rather than waned in that country. Previously, the troops in Ireland had been disciplined by the English Mutiny Bill which included the name of Ireland. The Irish now managed to introduce and pass in the face of stiff governmental opposition an Irish Mutiny Bill, an action which in itself was tantamount to a denial of the right of England to legislate for Ireland. The Irish bill was similar to the English in that it was an annual one to be renewed by the Irish parliament each year. Upon passage it was sent to England where it was approved but altered so as to become a perpetual rather than an annual measure. Despite the strong opposition outside of the Irish parliament, the bill was passed in the now altered form, that is to say, the words limiting the duration of the measure to one year were omitted. Credit for this went to the Lord Lieutenant, Buckinghamshire, who freely resorted to corruption to gain his objective.

In the British parliament when the English Mutiny Bill came up, there was a debate over the omission of the word "Ireland" in it. Speaking on the incident, 21 February 1781, Burke feigned surprise that many members had failed to comprehend that this was a pregnant matter. Now that America, "the brightest ornament" in Britain's "orrery" had been lost, parliament should not be surprised if this great loss should be swiftly followed by that of Ireland as well:

> So star would follow star, and light, light,
> Till all was darkness and eternal night.[53]

Two days later, on the twenty-third, Burke observed during the course of the debate that he felt impelled to give his opinion on the subject of the omission of Ireland from the Mutiny Bill, although it was one on which it might be imagined that his connections would interfere with his duty. But this was a time when a man had to be firm and to consider what remained of the Empire as his first duty. This was as far as he was able to proceed in his remarks as he was interrupted by noise in the House which so irked him that he terminated his speech by saying that it was plain that the House did not wish to hear him and so he would only say that he assented fully to what Mr. Fox had just said.[54]

We might note parenthetically that this was an experience Burke had to suffer many times during his parliamentary career. Closed minds, particularly those of the younger members, could not endure his peculiar eloquence which admittedly was sometimes hard to abide. Lines on Burke in Richard Polwhele's "The English Orator" are appropriate:

> And (if no rival's irritating sneer
> Derange his plan) in regular array

> The series of the harangue proceeds — yet stiff
> Thro' regularity; and not enough
> Savouring of the colloquial — an harangue
> That might beseem the academy or school;
> Like some inaugural oration, rich,
> In classic vein, beneath a pedant's eye.[55]

The matter of the omission of Ireland from the Mutiny Bill rested where it was. That is to say, Ireland retained its own bill as of the preceding year which was in the form of perpetuity thereby putting the regulation of the Irish military forces beyond the power of the Irish parliament.

Burke's actions in this affair are another clear indication of his imperialism. He feared that Ireland sought not merely her legislative independence but her full and complete independence. With such a goal he was entirely unsympathetic. Hence, he endeavored to awaken Commons to what he felt was a real danger. He thought he saw in the Mutiny Bill a clear intention on the part of Ireland to emulate America by seeking independence. Events were to prove that he was incorrect, but at this time it was difficult to determine exactly what Ireland's goal was.

Affairs coursed along in both England and Ireland with no further changes apparent on the surface, yet the patriot party in Ireland headed by Henry Grattan was formulating plans. The Volunteers of Ulster had decided to hold a convention at Dungannon on 15 February 1782. And at this meeting a resolution drawn up by Grattan was adopted which asserted that "a claim of any body of men, other than the King, Lords, and Commons of Ireland, to make laws to bind this kingdom, is unconstitutional, illegal, and a grievance." [56] Then later the Volunteers of Ireland as a whole adopted this resolution.

But before Grattan could carry out his announced intention of tendering the rights of the Irish parliament, the British government of Lord North fell as a result of their blunders in the American War and was replaced on 27 March 1782 by a ministry headed by Burke's friend and benefactor, Lord Rockingham.[57] Burke, despite his intimate connection with Rockingham,[58] failed to achieve ministerial rank. He was, however, made Paymaster-General of the Forces and created a Privy Councillor.

As a result of his reforms while in office, the only perquisites which he obtained were a salary of £4000 and an official residence. The Paymaster's office had formerly been a lucrative plum [59] but thanks to Burke's disinterestedness was purged of the vast sums customarily pocketed by the office-holder. By way of compensation for the generous sacrifice which he thus made, the new government saw to it that his relatives and friends were provided for to his satisfaction. Burke's son, Richard, together with Burke's old Bristol friend, Richard Champion, were made Deputy-Paymasters at salaries of £500 each; Richard Burke, Sr., Edmund's brother, was appointed Secretary of the Treasury at £3000 per annum; Will Burke was made Deputy-Paymaster of the Forces in India with a £5 allowance per diem; and Burke's sister, Juliana (Mrs. Pat French), was given a small pension by the Duke of Portland, the new Lord Lieutenant of Ireland.[60]

Various reasons have been advanced to explain Burke's failure to win cabinet rank. Among them are the following: financial instability, the set by which he was surrounded, a want of taste, impracticality, his vehement temper and frequent violent impulses, and, of course, an invincible aristocratic prejudice which never really recognized him as an equal.[61] Actually, he had given up any idea of ever becoming a minister and, when the negotiations for the formation of the new ministry were taking place, he had presented Rockingham with a memorandum disclaiming any personal ambitions for such rank.[62] When General Conway congratulated him in the House of Commons, 20 March 1782, on his excellent prospects of entering the cabinet, he openly disavowed even remotely dreaming of such a thing.[63]

Thus, before Henry Grattan had been able to act and to place the Irish parliament formally on record in favor of legislative independence, there had come into power in England a government composed of men friendly to Ireland. The question now arose naturally in a good many Irish minds at this crisis in Ireland's history as to what should be done. Grattan felt that no delay should be brooked despite the favorable turn of events in England. Consequently, he determined to adhere to his plan because he was convinced that Ireland's historic hour had come. This view of the resolute Irish leader received the support of his followers. What was the feeling of the new Rockingham administration on the matter?

Theirs was an embarrassing position when it is borne in mind how Burke, and for that matter the others, had plagued North for the loss of the American colonies. While legislative independence for Ireland was not the same thing, it was, nevertheless, an uncomfortable business. As for Burke, he took the position that he did not like to be rushed precipitously into anything so serious and important.[64] However, it so happened that, although he was Rockingham's chief advisor, he was destined to play a very minor role in this business. The government quickly decided upon an initial policy of delay in the hope that a temporary solution could be achieved before the full details of the matter could be satisfactorily arranged. The new Lord Lieutenant of Ireland was the Duke of Portland, and the Chief Secretary was Colonel Richard Fitzpatrick through whose Irish connections there was thought to be some chance of winning a delay.

In an attempt to secure postponement of Grattan's projected declaration, Charles James Fox, now one of the principal Secretaries of State, wrote a letter to Lord Charlemont, the commander of the Irish Volunteers, 4 April. Charlemont had originally brought Grattan into parliament and was known to have great influence with him.[65] Fox asked Charlemont why Ireland should not have a complete change of administration as well as England, and then the old Irish opposition would become the chief support of the new Rockingham government. In this way, a union of Whigs throughout the empire would be begun. They could establish their principles so securely that "no future faction" could ever destroy them. He then went on to request that the Irish parliament be adjourned for a short time so that the new British government could formulate its plans for Ireland.[66]

Meanwhile, Burke was the recipient of intelligence from correspondents in Ireland that the Irish were determined to declare their legislative independence and that it would therefore be the part of wisdom for Burke to advise his party to accept it with good grace.[67]

Lord Rockingham himself also endeavored to secure a postponement of Grattan's proposal and followed Fox's lead in requesting

Charlemont to use his influence for that purpose. In this letter of 9 April, Rockingham used a passage that is so characteristic of Burke that he probably had something to do with the phrasing of it. The Prime Minister declared that he did not think "it would be a good policy in the House of Commons of Ireland, to carry on measures, at this juncture, which should appear as measures to extort." [68]

Having been unsuccessful thus far, the British leaders repeated their proposal that Grattan, Charlemont, and their other friends in Ireland should take office there. Once more they failed, as Grattan and Charlemont felt that to do so would be virtual treason to their country under the circumstances. In the words of Grattan, office in Ireland was a vastly different matter from office in England. The former was merely a situation held for an English government, a body which was often "in collision with" or hostile to Ireland. As far as they were prepared to go, Grattan said, was to be "consulted" but not "considered." [69]

Meantime, in England itself, the Rockingham ministry, still hopeful of a delay, was faced with an attempt to make its embarrassment even greater. Following a recess, the British parliament met on the eighth of April. William Eden, the Irish Chief Secretary under Lord Carlisle, Portland's predecessor as viceroy, appeared in his place in Commons after having left Ireland to bring the resignation of Carlisle. However, the Rockingham government had already removed him and had also deprived him of the Lieutenancy of the East Riding of Yorkshire. In the latter post he was succeeded by Lord Carmathen. Furious over the government's action, Eden was bent upon embarrassing them on the score of Ireland if he could.[70] He arose in the House in response to a prearranged request of another member that he speak on the affairs of Ireland.

Eden began by giving a sketch of Irish history during the last two years. He was lavish in his praise of the Volunteers whom he described as the very personification of the Irish nation. They meant to free their country and were resolute in their determination. They were men deserving of praise on account of their proven devotion and loyalty to England which had been demonstrated by their spontaneous offer to serve the crown when the French and

Spanish fleets had threatened an invasion. Events had so shaped up that they were determined to win their legislative independence, and, therefore, he took the present occasion to move for permission to bring in a bill to repeal that part of the Act of the 6th of George I which asserted a right in the king and parliament of Great Britain to make laws to bind the kingdom and people of Ireland.[71] Eden professed to feel that immediate action was necessary because it was well known that Grattan was going to move a vote for a declaration of the rights of the Irish parliament exactly one week from the following day. He argued the expediency of anticipating the Irish and hoped to be able to take with him to their parliament the news that Great Britain had pledged herself to the fulfilment of Ireland's cherished dream. It so happened that he planned to leave for Ireland that very evening, or at the latest on the following day. Thus, he could find out whether partial repeal of the 6th of George I would satisfy the Irish. If not, he would recommend full repeal. Only if neither partial nor full repeal satisfied them would he suggest that the law as it presently stood be unchanged.[72]

Fox, as leader of the government's forces in the House, spoke for the ministry. He scored Eden's precipitous popping out of his seat without having had any previous consultation with the government on the subject and asserted that Eden's motion amounted to the abandonment of England's supremacy over Ireland and the severing of that nation's connection with England by a single stroke. If the gentleman had not been so rash, he would have discovered upon inquiry that the government was acutely aware of the situation in Ireland. There had been a hesitancy to act only because the ministers were searching for an enduring formula which would prove satisfactory to both kingdoms. Fox then tore into Eden again and severely censured him for his attempt to precipitate action under the guise of a flying trip back to Ireland. After all, Eden had not shown himself so considerate of Ireland's welfare in the past. And after having answered Eden's arguments, he then concluded by moving for the order of the day and expressed the hope that Mr. Eden would withdraw his untimely motion.[73] This worthy demurred and devoted himself to making a defense of his position concluding with the expressed fear that, if his motion were not carried, it would then be too late.[74]

Burke's speech on this occasion was either quite brief,[75] as was probably the case, or else it was inadequately reported because what there is of it is quite terse. His remarks were to the effect that Eden's [76] motion aimed at the destruction, in some measure, of the connection between the sister kingdoms. Notwithstanding the gravity of the matter, the House was asked to act with the greatest possible haste. As for himself, Burke did not care to express his opinion as to whether the act should be repealed. Nevertheless, he saw it as the height of folly to attempt action on such a vital matter without sufficient time for careful deliberation.[77]

Eden was forced to withdraw his motion reluctantly following the debates of the eighth of April. Feverish activity by the government overnight resulted the next day in the presentation by Fox of a message from the king relative to the desirability of consideration of "a final adjustment as may give a mutual satisfaction" in their affairs to both England and Ireland. Fox professed to take great pride in reading the message and claimed that it was only an accident that the message had not been brought down on the previous day since the situation in Ireland had been one of the first matters demanding the attention of the new government. Still the ministers had no intention of precipitate action, he said, since haste would only result in emulating the mistake of their predecessors who had foolishly applied only a temporary remedy. The aim of His Majesty's new servants was a permanent peace for both England and Ireland. The first step was to discover exactly what it was that Ireland wished. This information would be secured by the new Lord Lieutenant, the Duke of Portland. Until this was forthcoming, it would be necessary to pause before any action could be taken.[78]

Ireland's wishes were made clear in exactly one week. On 18 April, the "elastic boy" [79] announced in the Irish Commons that the power of the English Privy Council over Ireland must be abolished; the claim of England to make laws for Ireland must be abrogated; the military forces in Ireland must be dependent upon the parliament of Ireland; and, English courts of law must be excluded from any judicial authority in Ireland. He then successfully moved an Address to the King assuring His Majesty that the people of Ireland were a free people whose crown was an imperial one inseparably annexed to that of Great Britain. He asserted that the interests and happiness of both peoples depended upon that connection, but that the Kingdom of Ireland was a distinct kingdom with its own parliament. This body together with the king was alone competent to legislate for the Irish nation.[80]

The Duke of Portland had meanwhile arrived in Ireland after a rather comical experience which one of Burke's Irish correspondents detailed for him. It seems that, when Portland reached Ireland, his baggage was some distance behind him in a slower boat "so that he had no change of Cloaths but came to the Castle in an old frockcoat, linen waistcoat, plain Shirt, leather Breeches & boots, his one curld Wig with tyburn top completed the figure; when Lord Carlisle had taken his seat in the privy-council, the Duke of Portland proceeded from the presence to the Council Chamber but the door-keeper (one Grant a Scotchman) mistaking him for a Curious Intruder push'd him back telling him he had no business there: his Grace stopt short, this caused a laugh which encreased in the grotesque marks of Confusion which Grant exhibited on finding his mistake." [81]

When the initial confusion had been overcome, Portland went to work to secure a compromise in the openly declared intention of the Irish parliament to achieve immediate legislative independence but his efforts were unavailing. It is interesting to note that when he left for Ireland to take up his new duties, Burke had presented him with an abstract of the penal laws then in operation against the Catholics.[82] As always, he was looking out for their interests.[83]

In a letter written sometime in April to Rockingham, Burke enclosed a copy of part of a letter dated 21 April which he had just received from Portland in Ireland in which the Duke described the situation there as such that concession to the Irish was absolutely necessary.[84] Burke asked Rockingham to inform him whether or not Portland's report was to be accepted, a fact which reveals that, despite Burke's influence with Rockingham, the decision in the Irish business was clearly not to be left to him. Proof that Burke was precluded from even playing a role of any importance in the matter will shortly be seen.

Portland, whose dispatches kept contradicting one another, had finally quite clearly determined what Ireland desired and saw that, if the wishes of the Irish were not granted, the new British government would have to face the consequences — the likelihood of armed rebellion by the Volunteers, who now numbered around 100,000 officers and men. Accordingly, on 17 May, the British House of Commons resolved itself into a Committee of the Whole to debate the question of Ireland. Fox arose to speak for the Treasury Bench and said that, to his way of thinking, there was not much doubt any longer about what Ireland's wishes were. They were four in number: (1) the repeal of the 6th of George I, (2) the restoration of the appellant jurisdiction, (3) the modification of Poynings' Law (the power of the English Privy Council over Ireland's parliamentary bills), and (4) the repeal of the perpetuating clause in the Mutiny Bill. The first and third were the work of the British parliament while the others would be settled by the King and the parliament of Ireland. In due time, provision would have to be made for working out the future connection between the two kingdoms on an enduring basis. That, however, would be the task of the crown and not the problem of parliament at that particular time. He said that he looked forward to the happiness the future would bring and professed to feel not the least bit sad that day because his country was giving up that which she had previously exercised. Ireland would be powerful in the future through freedom of both trade and constitution, and England would benefit through "powerful assistance in seamen to man her fleets, and soldiers to fight her battles." In conclusion he moved for the repeal of the 6th of George I, the statute of imperial authority.[85]

To Burke it was a day on which there was no difference of opinion between England and Ireland, which meant that he did not have to fight the battle of Ireland, a land whose "cause was nearest his heart." He recalled the great satisfaction which a seat in the British parliament had given him since it meant that he was in a position to do something for Ireland, the land of his birth. He was indeed a friend of Ireland's but that automatically made him a friend of England's because "their interests were inseparable." This bond also existed with India, he added.[86]

It was then decided that the simple repeal of the 6th of George I together with permission to the Irish parliament to rescind Poynings' law would be legally sufficient to make Ireland legislatively independent, a victory which was received with great rejoicing in Ireland where the first thing the parliament did to show its gratitude was to vote the sum of £100,000 to raise 20,000 seamen for the Royal Navy.

Thus was accomplished the Irish "Revolution" of 1782 as a result of which the nation was still divided internally into three groups: (1) a proud, over-bearing aristocracy possessed of a parliamentary monopoly by means of pocket and rotten boroughs and the dispensing of lavish emoluments capable of insuring majorities whenever needed, (2) a Protestant reform group anxious to break this power concentrated in the hands of members of the Established Church, and (3) the great mass of the people, the Catholics, who sought to throw off completely the shackles of the penal code and to regain civil rights in their native land.

There are two ways by which to arrive at an estimate of the true significance of Ireland's victory. The first is the traditional one of maintaining that the legislative independence of Ireland was considerably exaggerated at the time and for some years thereafter on both sides of the Irish Sea. Those who hold this view like to call attention to such checks upon Ireland as the following. In the first place, both the Lord Lieutenant and his Chief Secretary were appointed by the king upon the advice of his British ministers and these two officials wielded tremendous power. The Lord Lieutenant was the head of the army, and control of both military and naval forces was British and not Irish. That this was no insignificant matter may be seen from the fact that in time of peace the Irish maintained an army of 15,000 men as compared with the British force of 17,000 or so. This, by the way, was in addition to the substantial manpower contribution of Ireland to the Royal Navy. Secondly, the Irish were still excluded from any role in foreign affairs and diplomacy and were automatically included in any British declaration of war. Thirdly, through his possession of the patronage, the Lord Lieutenant exercised at least a potential control over the Irish parliament. Recourse could always be made by the viceroy to the time-honored practice of sums of money and grants of honor since corruption had long been a successful way of bringing recalcitrant members into line with the wishes of Dublin Castle. Finally, the Irish parliament represented such a small fraction of the nation's population that in the final analysis they were dependent upon the British connection and they knew it.

On the other hand, modern scholarship looks at the matter in a different light. While conceding most of the points in the traditional interpretation, there is a tendency to hold that the ability of the Lord Lieutenant to get his way by bribery and corruption in the years between 1782 (legislative independence) and 1800 (the union between Great Britain and Ireland) has been greatly overestimated. One careful scholar [87] says that if it were true that the Irish legislature could be effectively controlled by the Lord Lieutenant's influence which was strengthened by corruption, then the British ministers during those years would not have had occasion to get alarmed over Ireland. Yet the record shows that they were constantly upset over developments in Ireland during these years. The experiences of such viceroys as Portland and then later Temple who went over to Ireland confident that they could manage the situation there only to be disabused of this notion in short order is a further case in point.

Interestingly enough, this was substantially the position of Burke who consistently held that the Ascendancy really managed the Lord Lieutenant who in turn controlled the British cabinet by his representations. Burke's thoughts on this subject will be abundantly made clear later in this study.

Even more serious than whether Ireland lacked control of the administration of her affairs was the unreformed character of the Irish parliament, a circumstance well known to the corrupt oligarchy in Ireland which unhesitatingly resisted all efforts toward reform.[88]

Returning to Burke's part in the events under review, it was quite minor, as I have already suggested. One of his many Irish correspondents, the Bishop of Killaloe, in a rapturous and completely unrealistic vein thought that he had done a lot to bring it to pass. His Grace congratulated Burke both as a British "Minister and as a Friend to Ireland," (thereby managing to promote Burke to a rank he was never destined to hold), on the happy return of Ireland's old attachment to Great Britain

which I can now venture to say, is Perfect and Entire; . . . But why do I talk of antient attachment? It was hitherto that of a Colony of

English Settlers who sought support from the Mother Country against the Natives. A Party, who crouch'd under the Shadow of Great Britain for Protection against their Injured Fellow Subjects. It is now the gratefull and cordial attachment, of a Numerous, Free and United People. There may perhaps remain a very few Individuals who may endeavour still to obstruct the return of perfect Tranquillity. Men who cannot gratify their own Discontents but by formenting those of the Publick. . . . But even their great abilities, will not enable them to perpetuate the mischief which they plot.[89]

The proof that Burke's part in the granting of Irish legislative independence was unimportant may be seen from a letter which has long escaped notice. It is addressed to Portland and is dated 25 May 1782.[90] In it Burke told Portland that everything Ireland had sought had been given her. He complimented Fox for his manner of handling the whole affair and then said that Portland's post was the most important one in the new government as far as he was concerned. He professed the belief that the Lord Lieutenancy was in very capable hands, a fact which made him "easy, in finding myself more compleatly uninformed about everything that is going on, than I thought it was possible for one that lived in London to be. I heard indeed the most material part, from time to time that your Grace was in perfect health. But that was all I heard about Ireland, or Irish business, directly or indirectly, from the time your Grace left us.[91] From that day I was not able to form the slightest conjecture about what was meant to be done, until the Night before Mr. Fox's motion; when I was, with some other members, invited to the meeting at his house."

Burke went on to say that the Irish affair instead of having been terminated was now only commencing. "The old Link is snapped asunder," and Ireland would now decide what should replace it because she it was who was now enacting the role of decision-maker. It was a good lesson for England, which had abused her power too much in the past. Ireland could become a truly great country if matters were managed carefully. At the moment, she was even better off than England "in all respects," he asserted with characteristic exaggeration. One of the reasons for this was that she had "the full protection of this Country" together with "the full benefits of its remaining dependencies." Ireland was even better off for her previous state of subjection because she had been given compensations on that account. The restraints were now gone, but the compensations remained. This fact, he hoped, would be borne in mind when the time came to make a treaty between the two countries which would permanently clarify their relations.[92]

In Burke's own words, he had not been consulted by the Rockingham government in the matter of legislative independence for Ireland until the night before the decision had been reached to concede to Ireland's demands. Why he was excluded from having an important part in this business is difficult to say. A reasonable explanation is that it was apparently felt that Fox was better able to handle the business by himself without Burke whose feelings on this issue seemingly conflicted with the ministers, as will be made clear below.

A letter to Charlemont, 12 June 1782, declared his happiness over Ireland's success and expressed the hope that mutual affection would result in mutual help and advantage and thus be an improvement over the past when the connection between the two countries was an artificial one. He said that he could not book the thought of any loosening of the true ties which linked them together in the British Empire and hoped that Ireland's newly won legislative independence would in reality strengthen rather than weaken that bond. He fully realized that no "reluctant tie can be a very strong one, and that a natural, cheerful alliance will be a far securer link of connexion than any principle of subordination borne with grudgings and discontent." In conclusion, he expressed the wish that Ireland would be prosperous and would achieve an internal as well as an external union,[93] a direct plea for the improvement of the position of the Irish Catholics which was so necessary if the country were ever to become truly strong and happy.

A few days earlier, he had written to O'Beirne, the future Bishop of Meath, to say "I most sincerely sympathize in the Joy which you feel in Common with an Whole Kingdom . . . Internal quiet union & satisfaction is the great object of our present politicks." [94]

To the end of his days, Burke defended Ireland's right to her legislative independence since it was a *fait accompli*. For example, during a debate in the House of Commons over the affairs of Ireland on 19 December 1782, Burke reiterated the remarks Fox had made the previous day to the effect that the repeal of the 6th of George I was meant by the government which made it to be the permanent surrender of British legislative and judicial supremacy over Ireland, and there were to be no exceptions.[95] Writing to Charlemont, 5 August 1783, he declared that Ireland was to all intents and purposes an independent kingdom, and England could not reclaim "one iota of the concessions made," nor did he think she wished to do so.[96] In other words, Irish legislative independence was an accomplished fact, a reality to be comprehended. Following the founding in Dublin of a Whig Club on 26 June 1789 by a number of influential men whose purpose was the maintenance of Ireland's legislative independence, Burke again wrote to Charlemont to say that he was much in favor and gave his enthusiastic approval.[97]

This episode of the independence of Ireland's parliament presents an opportunity to consider Burke's real views on what Ireland's political status should be. In the first place, his goal for Ireland politically was not independence. When the question of legislative independence had to be faced in 1782, we know what his position was. By his open public acceptance of the government's decision and by the letters quoted above, he appeared to be sympathetic with the development. His real feelings were known to his intimates as the following, from a letter to Lord Fitzwilliam written years later, demonstrates. It is this which might account for the minor role he was given to play in the events of 1782. He wrote:

"*I never liked, as it is well known,* [italics mine] that total independence of Ireland which, without, in my opinion adding any security to its Liberty took it out of the common constitutional protection of the Empire. Besides an Host of other inconveniences, it tends to put their Chief Governour under a subordinate responsibility, or to free him from any responsibility at all. I remember, . . . before this business of total and absolute independence was wholly accomplished in Lord North's time,[98] when a part of the Irish Establishment was thrown on England." [99]

These, then, were his true feelings: inwardly, he was very unhappy over the grant; outwardly, he appeared to accept it gracefully if not overly enthusiastically. It would thus appear that Burke was guilty of hypocrisy in this business, yet this conclusion is too superficial. He was, after all, a party man as even his warmest admirers cannot escape recognizing. And it was his party, the Rockingham Whigs, which had decided to yield to Ireland's wishes. For Burke, the only Irishman in the lot, to have remained silent or to have opposed the measure, would have been the height of impracticality. He was also sufficiently consistent, on the whole, to realize that he had often maintained that a happy connection between England and Ireland was infinitely more desirable than a forced and unnatural one and that a satisfactory tie would add to the strength of the empire as a whole. Furthermore, as we have seen, throughout the remainder of his career in parliament, he defended Ireland's right to her legislative independence so long as it had once been granted.

His dislike was compounded of several factors. For one thing, he was annoyed by the precipitancy of the whole business, a fact which was against his principles, and by the overtones of force which were so clear. He despised extortion, and this struck him as such because in the background loomed the 100,000 officers and men of the Irish Volunteers who were bent upon the independence of Ireland's parliament. The lack of a definite, formal agreement between the two countries was another thing that he decried. But deeper even than any of these considerations was his realization that the vast majority of the Irish people, the Catholics, were left in a state of continued subjugation which could presumably be now exercised with even greater authority by those who had always persecuted them. As he had said, no external privileges could make Ireland into a great and flourishing country so long as four-fifths of the people there were persecuted.[100]

It was this realization which had prompted him to try to help the Catholics as best he could at this time. He had given Portland a copy of the anti-Catholic legislation still in existence in Ireland when the latter set out to become the Irish viceroy, and he had also written to friends in Ireland to tell them that they would be well advised to achieve an internal as well as an external union, in other words to free the Catholics.

While he was opposed to actual independence for Ireland from his earliest to his last days and lacked enthusiasm for even legislative and judicial independence for Ireland, he was also strongly opposed to the idea of a union between the two countries. He once told Fitzwilliam, Rockingham's heir and the Marquis' successor in Burke's affections, that he "always looked upon an union, even under Circumstances infinitely more favourable than any that now exist, as a bold experimental remedy, justified, perhaps called for, in some nearly desperate Crisis of the whole Empire." [101]

If he were not too happy with legislative independence for Ireland and opposed a union, such as that between England and Scotland, what political system did he favor to facilitate relations between England and Ireland? The answer is a reformed Irish parliament rid of the power of the Protestant Ascendancy, and allowed to legislate for itself in purely domestic matters but subordinate to the British parliament on all imperial concerns. An Irish parliamentary reform which broke the power of the Ascendancy would also involve the return of the franchise together with the right to hold seats in both houses of the legislature to the Catholics, long stripped of these privileges and growing restive under the restraints of the penal laws against them. To bind England and a reformed Ireland together, there should be a positive compact drawn up and adhered to by both parties.

He always maintained that a system of mutual help should obtain between the two although certain disadvantages were bound to accrue to the lesser member in the combination simply because she was a part and not the center of a powerful empire. But the advantages which membership in such a strong organization as the British Empire brought far outweighed the disadvantages. The latter certainly existed, as Burke readily admitted. And as far as he was concerned, one of the disadvantages was in the field of trade and commerce. Yet he had not always felt this way, as we have already seen from a study of his efforts to improve Ireland's trade. Why had he changed? To answer this question, which proves to be rather complicated, we now turn to the most disappointing part of the whole record of Burke's performance on behalf of Ireland, his opposition to Pitt's free trade proposals of 1785.

CHAPTER V

Burke's Opposition to Pitt's Plan
for Irish Free Trade

In addition to the "liberation" of the Irish parliament, the brief second Rockingham government put into effect the famous Plan for Economic Reform which Burke had introduced in the House of Commons. Although considerably watered down by the strong opposition aroused, the Plan did strike a rather considerable blow at the power of a government to maintain control of parliament by what amounted to bribery through the dispensation of places and sinecures to members.

Another achievement of this administration was the settlement of a case in which Burke had long interested himself, the lengthy controversy over the efforts of the electors of Middlesex to assert their independence of parliament by the election of the notorious John Wilkes. The Rockingham government secured the formal expunging of all the records of the incapacity of Wilkes to represent Middlesex.

On 1 July 1782, only three months after taking office, Rockingham died. His death was a tremendous loss to Burke. Among other things he was deeply in debt to Rockingham. However, two days after the latter's death, his nephew and heir, Lord Fitzwilliam, informed Burke that Rockingham had cancelled the debt in his will. This, of course, was a great relief to Burke, but his future prospects looked black.

When the king deliberately snubbed the Whigs, who had formally chosen Portland to be their leader, by inviting Shelburne to form a government, Burke, Fox, and several others immediately resigned. Burke's action was labelled that of a "Jesuit-Pad driven back to his native Potatoes" by his loss of place in one of the political cartoons of the day.[1]

Shelburne's government, which recognized American independence in September, had hard sledding, and the ostensible reason for their fall on 24 February 1783 was the generosity of the proposed terms of the American treaty which was attacked by a strange grouping headed by Fox and North and including Burke who went along in this peculiar combination with a man whom both he and Fox had berated with fierce vehemence for years. The king desperately tried to prevent the Fox-North coalition from assuming office but was helpless and finally had to yield. On 2 April, a new government was formed under the nominal leadership of Portland but with Fox and North, the principal Secretaries of State, as the real leaders. Burke resumed his post of Paymaster-General, and his brother and his son also regained their places. Several letters from Portland to Burke at this time kept the latter informed of developments and are of some importance in that they reveal clearly that Burke's role in this strange business was that of a mere follower. The last of this series, 1 April, told him that everything was in readiness for him to be "in possession of the Pay Office" the next day.[2]

Burke's action in making himself a party to this weird grouping injured him badly in the eyes of the public as he was especially vulnerable for a number of reasons, chief of which was the memory of his unrelenting asperity in assailing Lord North over the years of his long administration. A fresh wave of caricatures bears testimony to the delight with which his enemies grasped such an opportunity to attack him.[3] That he had reversed himself is patent, and one cannot find justification for it, although Burke himself took some satisfaction in rationalizing that Shelburne's defeat was necessary if anything were ever to be done about conditions in India, in which he had long interested himself.

There were a few people who thought that it was a good thing that Burke was back in office, as his papers reveal, but their number was small. Among them were Adam Smith[4] and a Scots Roman Catholic vicar apostolic, Dr. George Hay.[5] Burke himself was in poor spirits most of the time[6] due largely to his financial predicament. There can be little doubt that he was none too happy or comfortable in his new found company and that the assiduity of the attacks being made upon him had begun to get under his skin. The "Astonishing Coalition" [7] could not long survive the hostility it had engendered on every side, and the king took great satisfaction in putting an end to it on 17 December 1783.

In June 1783 the Fox-North coalition had appointed Lord Northington as Irish Lord Lieutenant. Northington had not been long at his new post before he concluded that the lack of industrial development was one of the chief causes of the country's backwardness. He, therefore, took it upon himself to endeavor to do something constructive and sent some proposals to the British cabinet for their advice. His suggestions that there be a separate Post Office and Court of Admiralty for Ireland and that annual parliamentary sessions be held there received the consent of his superiors. He was turned down flatly, however, in his efforts to secure preferential duties for Ireland. Some other suggestions to aid Ireland commercially were also negatived. In short, the Fox-North government would have nothing to do with any efforts to improve Ireland's commerce and navigation.[8]

Concerning these Irish matters during the time that Burke was back in office, there is a curious vacuum relating to the role which he played in this business. In the absence of anything definite, I can only surmise that, if indeed his advice were sought at all, he must have been unsympathetic with the Northington proposals. Such a surmise is warranted, I believe, because Burke still smarted under the treatment which Ireland had accorded him in 1780 after his long fight to ameliorate her trade had ended when North had reluctantly made concessions to Irish commerce at which time Burke's earlier enthusiasm faded perceptibly. Then, too, I feel that this guess is justified when one anticipates Burke's reactions to Pitt's proposals for Irish free trade in 1785, a matter which forms the subject of this chapter. Interestingly enough, the Fox-North-Burke opposition to Pitt's efforts to resolve the question of Ireland's trade and commerce and the known opposition of Fox and North, at least, in 1783 proved to be consistent.

The coalition was succeeded by a ministry headed by the youthful William Pitt who quickly solidified his position through the medium of a general election. In the new parliament which convened in May 1784, Burke found himself extremely unpopular. The makeup of Commons had undergone a considerable transformation. There were numerous youthful newcomers who were decidedly hostile toward Burke and who were determined to make things as difficult and unpleasant for him as possible. His part in the discredited coalition was to a large degree responsible for the annoyances which were now visited upon him whenever he attempted to speak. His hecklers took great pleasure in making him lose his temper, and many times when he was speaking, large numbers would get up and walk noisily out of the House. He was becoming known as the "Dinner-Bell" of the House and, as a consequence, his bitterness and sense of disillusionment increased.[9]

He was the subject of numerous rough caricatures at this time. As usual, he was most often represented as a Jesuit. His predilection for verbosity came in for a good share of attention in these prints, and in one of them he was also cartooned as a follower of Satan (Fox). Burke, resentful of the coalition's overwhelming defeat in the election, was pictured trying desperately to rally the beaten forces of his satanic master. A short time later a ballad, addressed to Fox made its appearance in the fall of 1784. In it the several leaders of Pitt's opposition are variously burlesqued. The lines on Burke read:

> For thee, O *beauteous and sublime*!
>   What place of honour shall we find?
> To tempt with money were a crime;
>   Thine are the riches of the mind.
>
> Clad in a matron's cap and robe,
>   Thou shall assist each *wither'd crone*!
> And, as the piercing threat shall probe,
>   Be't thine to lead the choral grone!
>
> Thine to uplift the whiten'd eye,
>   And thine to spread th' uplifted hand!
> Thine to upheave th' expressive sigh,
>   And regulate the *hoary band*!

At almost the same moment at which this ballad made its appearance, a caricature was printed which embraced the same thoughts and which represented Burke in feminine dress and in a devotional position leading the chorus.[10]

Following the settlement of the important question of Irish legislative independence, a demand for parliamentary reform attracted considerable attention in Ireland, and there was fear in England that, if this reform occurred, it would be impossible to prevent a similar move in England where there was considerable sympathy for such a step. One of Burke's Irish correspondents, writing to Burke's brother, Richard, described the picture in Ireland:

> . . . the state of this nation is interesting, convulsed, as it is, through every fibre; for wherever a company of volunteers may be found, & every village has one, there you will find a set of political agitators. The ascendency of the volunteers is universal, & every legal authority stoops to them. . . . & impatient for innovation, they will probably effect some grand revolution in the constitution of this kingdom. . . . Many & these not the least artful are fired with an ambition of imitating their Transatlantic brethren; with whom they have many connecting links. . . . Equal representation is the present acknowledged object, & innumerable, crude theories of it have been engendered — [11]

Fear of the Catholics proved too great an obstacle and resulted in the defeat of the movement for parliamentary reform in Ireland for the time being. The English proponents of the political status quo breathed more easily. Among them was Burke. In a speech two years earlier in opposition to a motion of Pitt's for the reform of parliament, he had expressed the sentiments which he still held:

"I look with filial reverence on the Constitution of my Country, and never will cut it in pieces and put it into the kettle of any magician in order to boil it, with the puddle of their compounds, into youth and vigor. On the contrary, I will drive away such pretenders; I will nurse its venerable age, and with lenient arts extend a parent's breath." [12]

As Lord Northington had rightly grasped during his brief tenure as Lord Lieutenant, a matter which still awaited settlement in the relations between Great Britain and Ireland since the arrangement of 1782 and which had played a part in bringing it to pass was that of a more satisfactory system of commercial intercourse. English newspapers now began to take note of the state of affairs in Ireland with a more lively, and in some instances undoubtedly inspired, interest. One of them commented that the situation in that country was the natural consequence of the manner in which Lord North's administration had prosecuted the American War and said that North's weak conduct had inspired great hopes in Ireland, adding that the aid and comfort given to America by the Rockingham Whigs during that time had galvanized the hopes of the Irish into action. The result was, this paper proclaimed, that Burke would be in "a pitiable predicament" when the affairs of "his country" came to be discussed.[13]

The situation referred to was that of the serious riots which had taken place in Dublin throughout most of 1784 due to a crippling depression. Although the rioting was confined to the capital, there were strong feelings made manifest in other parts of the country as well. Severe agricultural distress worsened the country's industrial plight markedly with the result that poverty in Ireland was described as universal.[14] The need for protection of Irish manufactures against the competition of Great Britain was recognized early in 1784 when an unsuccessful effort was made to impose slight duties on British imports in order to put Irish manufactures on a par in the domestic market. The Irish parliament defeated the measure out of fear of giving offense to Britain. Out of doors, however, there was strong resentment manifested against parliament's action in turning down the measure. Mob spirit prevailed in Dublin for some weeks, and there was considerable looting carried on. Soldiers who chanced to go out alone were marked men, the favorite punishment meted out to these unfortunates being that of hamstringing. Merchants who carried stocks of British goods were also special objects of the brutality of the mobs which sometimes resorted to tarring and feathering their victims.

Parliament did make an effort to improve the agricultural situation through the passage of legislation known as Foster's Corn Laws which granted large bounties on the exportation of corn and imposed heavy duties on its importation. The effect of this measure was delayed, but it has been said that it transformed Ireland from a grazing land and corn-importing country into a country of agriculture and corn-exportation.

Before proceeding, it would be well to take note of the commercial relations between Britain and Ireland at this time. Ireland had previously won the right of direct trade with Britain's American and African possessions — thanks in large measure to the work of Burke — on the same basis as British trade. The Levant was likewise open to her, and her legislative independence gave her the right, exclusive of Britain, to make commercial treaties with any foreign powers. Due to fear of offending England, the Irish parliament moved with maximum circumspection. Owing to the monopoly exercised by the British East India Company, Ireland was excluded from the Asiatic trade. Intercourse between Great Britain and Ireland was regulated by acts of the parliaments of both countries. Ireland admitted all British goods either freely or at a low rate of duty. In either case she gave preference to Britain over the goods of British competitors. Britain, on her part, kept out most manufactured goods of Irish origin through prohibitive duties. Irish woolen yarn, but not woolen manufactures, and Irish linens were duty free, and the latter was even given a modest bounty. Under the Navigation Acts, foreign goods or materials could not be brought into England either by or through Ireland, and this restriction applied also to colonial produce which could not even be sent from England to Ireland. The Irish could send their products to America and Africa and carry back to Britain directly the produce of these regions.

In the spring of 1784 an amended resolution seeking a more liberal arrangement of British-Irish commercial relations passed the Irish parliament unanimously. The Irish Chancellor of the Exchequer, John Foster (of Foster's Corn Laws fame) went over to London to discuss the matter with Pitt and took with him a number of propositions aimed at achieving the objectives of the Irish parliament's resolution. These propositions which Foster brought to Pitt originated with two proposals laid before the Irish Chief Secretary, Thomas Orde, by a Dublin Quaker named Joshua Pim. Orde gave them to Foster who added eight more propositions and then brought them to Pitt as a basis of discussion.[15]

Pitt had devoted considerable study to the subject of commercial relations between the two countries and by October 1784 had reached the conclusion that a commercial union was necessary if Ireland were to be prevented from eventually breaking the bonds linking her with Britain. He decided to grant the Irish the greater concessions in the hope of winning them to his plan. It was his opinion that a system of unrestricted free trade in return for an Irish contribution to the cost of imperial defense which would automatically rise as Ireland grew prosperous would make the countries truly unified and, at the same time, would require no constitutional changes in either country. The result would be a considerable tightening of the empire in its very heart. Such a project one would expect would meet the unqualified approval of Edmund Burke, but such was not to be the case. Instead he spoke with a "parricidal voice" and displayed "a new species of the *amor patriae*." [16]

Despite warnings from his Irish Lord Lieutenant and Chief Secretary, Rutland and Orde, and from Foster that his insistence upon an Irish contribution to imperial defense through the device of the hereditary revenue of Ireland would arouse resentment in Ireland, Pitt persisted and received the backing of his ministers who made it clear that the existing military commitments of Ireland to Great Britain would be unaltered by this new contribution in return for free trade and that Ireland would also be expected in times of war or emergency to make "voluntary" contributions.[17]

Since Pitt had determined upon his plan, the King's Speech on opening the Second Session of the Sixteenth Parliament, 25 January 1785, recommended above all that there be an adjustment made in the system of commercial intercourse between Great Britain and Ireland of such points not yet finally arranged. The aim of this adjustment was the achievement of a system of reciprocal advantage which would unite the two kingdoms as closely as possible.[18]

In the Debate on the Address of Thanks, Pitt sarcastically alluded to Burke's complaint that the throne's brief message had failed to take notice of grievances which were superior to Ireland's i.e., those of India, by saying that Burke was, of all men, best qualified to judge the difference between a very short and a very long speech.[19] Burke, in an extremely lengthy rejoinder,[20] defended himself with regard to his statement about Ireland and accused Pitt of having given it an erroneous shading. What he had said, he asserted, was that Ireland's affairs were trivial in comparison with those of India as matters then stood and he defied the "boldest" member of parliament to claim that he had said more. He emphasized his good wishes for the prosperity of Ireland and declared that they were second to no man's. Indeed the commercial intercourse between Britain and Ireland was of such importance that he thought few things could be proposed more worthy of parliament's attention than its speedy arrangement.[21] Nevertheless, he added, one would have to be an extremely dull or brutal person who held that the present state of Ireland demanded England's attention as urgently as the plight of the "undone millions of India." [22]

Burke had already commenced his efforts on behalf of India which were to be his "monument" and was moved more deeply by this cause than by any other he ever undertook. His attempt to secure the impeachment of Warren Hastings, first Governor-General of British India, became virtually a fetish with him. The speech of 25 January 1785 clearly reveals his passion for the cause of India, and the fact that Indian business now occupied his mind so fully is a partial explanation for the manner in which he conducted himself during this whole episode now under review.

Meanwhile, there had been laid before the Irish parliament a series of proposals to regulate trade relations between Britain and Ireland. These propositions were known as "Orde's Proposals" after the Irish Chief Secretary who introduced them for Pitt. They provided that all foreign goods, together with those of British colonies, were to pass freely between Britain and Ireland. All products or manufactures of either nation could go to the other either duty free or at equal duties for both. Whenever the British import was higher, it would be lowered to the level of the Irish. No bounties were to be granted by either on goods destined for the other, except in the case of foodstuffs, but the advantages already possessed by Irish linen were to be left unmolested. Furthermore, whenever the peacetime revenue of Ireland should go beyond a certain sum, the surplus would automatically be applied to the maintenance of the British navy. The opposition in the Irish parliament to the proposals was based on the proposed automatic contribution demanded of Ireland for imperial defense, i.e., the support of the navy. Orde was forced to accept an amendment making Ireland's contribution contingent upon a peacetime balance between revenue and expenditure at the figure of £656,000. He did this reluctantly but with the knowledge and consent of his chief, the

Duke of Rutland, the Irish viceroy. Following a good deal of debate, the propositions, as now amended, passed the Irish legislature with large majorities. Thus, Rutland and Orde by agreeing to compromise had achieved a victory of no mean proportions. Unfortunately, their action was not so construed in London.

There Pitt was surrounded with hostility to the propositions as they now stood following their passage in Ireland. The king was bitterly opposed to them and remained so. On the opposition side, the Fox-North people were to make political capital out of the situation by representing a supposed threat to British commercial and manufacturing interests. The latter, who were initially confident of their own superiority over Ireland and therefore not prone to oppose the amelioration of Ireland's trade,[23] were to change their tune and to organize themselves into an articulate force arrayed against the propositions. But let us trace the developments as they now unfolded.

On 21 February, Burke in a speech in Commons expressed considerable dissatisfaction that Ireland had been allowed to introduce these commercial propositions before the British parliament had been granted an opportunity to discuss them. He declared that the question was one of great magnitude and therefore required the most mature kind of deliberation,[24] an obvious attempt on his part to stall for time during which the opposition could build up its strength throughout the country for the fight which lay ahead.

Pitt, however, was anxious to get on with the business and on the following day, the 22nd, moved that the House resolve itself into a Committee of the Whole to consider that part of His Majesty's Speech of 25 January which related to the adjustment of commercial relations with Ireland.[25] He pointed out that there were but two methods to be employed by a country situated as England was to Ireland. The first was to make the weaker country subordinate and subservient to the stronger which would use it solely for its own purposes and advancement. England had done just this in its dealings with Ireland in the past, Pitt reminded his audience. The other method was one whereby benefits were mutually shared. Such a manner of doing things had as its goal the strengthening of the empire. Yet such a system of commercial equality imposed joint burdens and responsibilities. His proposals would place a light burden on Ireland in return for the privileges granted since it would be Ireland's obligation to see to it that the surplus of the country's hereditary revenue above its present amount [26] would be appropriated for the support of the British navy. In concluding his remarks, Pitt suggested a delay of one week in order that the members of parliament might acquaint themselves with all the necessary information on the subject. Burke arose to announce that he for one intended to deliberate the matter quite carefully, but that was as far as he could proceed since the clamor that greeted his remarks was so great that he was unable to make himself heard and had to sit down in disgust.[27]

The uproar which ensued from British commercial and manufacturing cities when Pitt's intentions became known was terrific. Under the leadership of Josiah Wedgwood, the manufacturers of Britain formed themselves into a formal organization to make this opposition even more effective. The same arguments flowed in which had greeted Burke in 1778 and 1779 when he had so actively espoused the cause of commercial amelioration for Ireland. This time we are presented with the odd picture of Burke in the ranks of those opposed to the attempt to secure equality for Ireland's trade. Among Burke's strange bedfellows now were his old enemies of the earlier fight to improve Ireland's trade, the merchants and manufacturers of Great Britain whose views he had so ably denounced in the past with a solid grasp of the facts. For the *volte face* of which he was now guilty, he was severely castigated by his enemies among his contemporaries. By way of illustration, there was a cartoon of him entitled "Hibernia in the Character of Charity" in which he was pictured with telling effect as a naked baby bawling out:

> Proceed ye precious Imp! ye politicians good!
> Who first cried that poor Ireland must have cloaths and food!
> Now bawl that Britain's ruin'd with as fair a face
> To get Ministers out and your dear selves in place.[28]

The opposition also made use of caricature as a weapon in their fight against Pitt's propositions. On 20 June there appeared a cartoon entitled "Paddy O'Pitt's Triumphant Exit." In it Pitt is shown riding to Dublin on a very spirited Irish bull in an attempt to escape from an English mob.

In order to popularize their proposals, the Pitt government had distributed gratis a pamphlet written by George Rose which was entitled *The Proposed System of Trade with Ireland Explained*.[29] It was answered by another pamphlet entitled *A Reply to the Treasury Pamphlet Entitled, "The Proposed System of Trade with Ireland Explained."* The authorship of this attack by the opposition to Pitt's proposals was attributed either to Burke or to one Thomas L. O'Beirne, an Irishman and supporter of the Whigs who lived in London. Burke and O'Beirne were friends, a point that makes it possible that he had something to do with the pamphlet. One of Burke's frequently made prophecies is in it, viz., that Ireland's "fall must be involved in that of this country." [30] And in addition it was well written, but whether Burke actually wrote it is still a mystery. If he did, this would help to explain the relatively small yet important part he played in the parliamentary proceedings on this subject. It might be argued that this pamphlet was Burke's chief contribution since he was already so preoccupied with India, a fact which was publicly known.[31] At any rate, the appearance of these two leading pamphlets on both sides of the question touched off a war of pamphlets which was waged by a number of able men in both England and Ireland.[32] Among those who turned pamphleteer on this occasion was James Watt.

Burke did manage to speak briefly in parliament on 18 March on the seriousness of the plight of some eighty thousand Lancashire workers who were against the government's propositions and felt that it demanded the attention of the House immediately. There was nothing more harmful to manufactures and morals, he said, than to have numbers of men idle and supported by public charity who were able to work. Alms only resulted in further idleness which led to crime, the living proof of the destruction of morality.[33]

The opposition to Pitt was so strong throughout Great Britain that he was forced to make several amendments and changes in his original proposals.[34] Ireland was now to be forbidden any trade in the future as well as the present in the regions wherein the British East India Company held its monopoly. Secondly, only colonial, and not foreign, goods might be carried directly from Ireland to England. Thirdly, the Irish parliament would now have to reenact not only all the present English Navigation Acts but also all of those which might become law in the future. This modified version of the original was also received with strong resentment in England when it was first put forward on 12 May. The third point in the above list was productive of the greatest opposition since it was claimed that by it Britain assumed both a present and a future power to bind Ireland by such acts as the former should pass relative to the trade and commerce of both countries. Furthermore, it was quite correctly pointed out that this would be a direct violation of the agreement of 1782 and was in reality the resumption of the right of legislating for Ireland which had been given up at that time.[35]

On 19 May, Burke delivered a speech against the measures in which he claimed to see the situation of England in relation to Ireland as similar to that of the mother country vis-à-vis America in 1774. On both occasions, Burke argued, England was guilty of seeking to extort revenue. This new attempt was once again a case of taxation without representation.[36] This was a reference to the plan to apply the surplus of the hereditary revenue of Ireland to the support of the British navy, a plan which he figured would cost Ireland annually in taxes the sum of at least £323,000, which he called "tribute." [37]

Following a hard battle, Pitt's propositions in their amended form were passed by both houses of the British parliament. In Ireland, however, they had to be withdrawn because of the nationalistic fears which had been aroused as a result of the amendments. Many members of the Irish parliament felt that the measures in their new form meant the death-knell of Irish legislative independence.[38] Actually, permission to introduce the bills had been granted by the Irish Commons following a long debate, but the margin, a majority of only nineteen, was so narrow that Orde, the Irish Chief Secretary, had withdrawn them rather than risk the seeming likelihood of defeat.[39] Grattan's speech in opposition to the amended proposals was described as one of the finest in his career,[40] but in the eyes of the Lord Lieutenant, the Duke of Rutland, it was "seditious," [41] a good indication in itself of the rampant nationalism engendered in Ireland by the change in the proposals. Thus, Ireland retained her "free trade," and the long drawn-out business, which one paper likened to Penelope's web,[42] was ended.

Burke's fading reputation suffered a further blow in England as a result of the role he had played in this affair. Although he had company in his reversal of the position he had taken in 1778 and 1779, his Irish birth and the zeal with which he had worked earlier in the same cause singled him out for special abuse.[43] How does one account for his strange and glaring reversal?

With few exceptions writers on Burke have had remarkably little to say about the curious role he played in this business. Prior holds that a sense of delicacy kept him from much participation in the contest.[44] The conflicting claims of his native land with those of his adopted country reduced him to a minor role — a none too convincing explanation and one which avoids coming to grips with the problem of Burke's inconsistency here. Bisset merely says that Burke opposed Pitt and brought into play the "extent and minuteness of his knowledge" rather than "his oratorical powers or philosophical expansion." [45] This is likewise a most inadequate analysis, but both Murray and Magnus, as well as Burke's most recent biographers,[46] have nothing whatsoever to say on the subject, and O'Brien has likewise omitted the episode. The usually prolix Macknight makes the most sense of any of these writers but is also very terse. He says Burke preferred England to Ireland and moreover was very busy at the time.[47]

Of the few who have much to say on the matter and who are critical of Burke's actions, Lennox [48] and Morley stand out. Since the former seems to have been influenced by the latter to some extent, we can concentrate on Morley's analysis. In fine, he accuses Burke of factiousness but does find explanations for his conduct, although he cannot condone it. In the first place, Burke apparently discovered in Pitt's proposals "the germ of an attempt to extract revenue from Ireland, identical in purpose, principle, and probable effect with the ever-memorable attempt to extract revenue from the American colonies." [49] And secondly, he holds that Burke had not recovered from "what he himself called the delirium of the preceding session, and which had still not subsided." But Burke was blind or he would have seen that Pitt was in reality "taking his first measures for the effective deliverance of Ireland from an unjust and oppressive subordination." But worse than his blindness was his factiousness: "We may almost say that for once he allowed his political integrity to be bewildered." [50]

Unfortunately, nothing in the Burke papers sheds any further light on his behavior in this affair and probably for the reason that there is nothing more to be said. We can add something to Morley's explanation, however, by noting that Burke was already immersed in what he considered the greatest work of his life, the effort to bring the peculators and spoliators of the East India Company to justice, a struggle which conceivably could have crowded everything else to the background. As extreme as this might seem, there could be something to it, for Burke had a habit of throwing himself unreservedly into matters which captured his attention. We might also imagine that if Ireland did secure such trade privileges, either of two extremes, equally unpalatable to Burke, could result. Either complete independence for Ireland might soon follow or else an unrestricted union between the two countries might well ensue.

Whatever way one looks at it, there seems to be no escape from the conclusion that Burke was guilty here of factiousness and as such cannot avoid the charge of inconsistency. In the light of the tragic future of Ireland, Burke was as wrong in helping to defeat Pitt's free trade plans by seizing on the proposal that Pitt had made, when forced to amend his original propositions, which would have required Ireland to contribute to the support of the navy as he was right in just about everything else that related to that country. What he had failed to realize, or even worse blinded himself to, was the likelihood that a goal he had always sought could now be more easily achieved — the breaking of the power of the Irish Ascendancy. Had Ireland secured a free trade, the class which would have profited most was a liberal one and it included Catholics within its ranks, the commercial and mercantile element. Free trade would not have meant nearly as much to the Ascendancy which depended for power upon their control of the government and upon landed interests. Their power would have been vulnerable to a commercial class grown strong and prosperous and backed by the mass of the people to whom more plentiful and more profitable employment would be available. Prosperity, it has been well said, is contagious, and the common people would undoubtedly have enjoyed a higher standard of living. There can be little doubt that Ireland's future would have been vastly different had Pitt's proposals passed. Ironically, Burke who had fought more persistently than any man in England for the amelioration of Ireland and who was still to battle for that objective for more than a decade to come was guilty on this occasion of being opposed to proposals that might have produced what he all along sought.

CHAPTER VI

The Irish Mission of Richard Burke, Jr.

AGENT FOR THE CATHOLIC COMMITTEE OF IRELAND

Although he was kept very busy with preparing the case he intended to make against Warren Hastings, the Governor-General of Bengal and with other matters, Burke found time in the fall of 1786 to make a short trip to his native land with his son Richard in order "to make him a little known there." [1] As events turned out, this was to be the last time that the father ever set foot in Ireland.

Writing from Dublin to an Irish friend in London, 29 September, Burke expressed himself candidly as follows:[2]

> The Affairs of Ireland are somewhat deranged & the public peace somewhat disturbed tho' not at all to the degree to which the Irish in their exaggerating manner, have represented the disorder to have mounted. Whatever they are they are owing to the badness of the Internal frame of that Country, and our Politicians will be tampering with every kind of Quack Medicine for the Cure. Well! things must take their course — I am satisfied there is nothing for us but retreat & to secure our Character relatively to past transactions, I know that the policy with which we set out was directly contrary. It was as much as possible to look forward & to throw every foregone matter to oblivion. But as to the future we shall be little concerned, our opinion will have little or no weight, but our reputation (our all) is deeply concerned in what is past.

A few days later, he wrote to his boyhood friend, Richard Shackleton to express his regret that the shortness of the projected stay in Ireland made it impossible for him to visit Ballitore. As a matter of fact, said Burke, that he and his son had come to Ireland at all was "at that moment a thing almost incomprehensible to me." He felt badly that he would be unable "to renovate myself by the view of our friends, amidst the scenes, of my earliest youth." [3]

Something happened to make Burke change his mind with the result that he visited Ballitore on 23 October. The record of that visit was preserved by Shackleton's daughter, Mary, who said that Burke appeared to great advantage as he remarked on the changes which had taken place since his youth and as he easily and warmly greeted his old acquaintances. One old fellow, who had been a servant of Abraham Shackleton's when his son and Burke were students in Shackleton's school, told Burke that he had a great many friends in Ireland, which pleased Burke who said that he was happy that the old man was one of them. [4]

The distinguished visitor and his son left Ballitore the next morning and were soon back in London. The only ill consequence of their visit was that the son suffered in his health as a result of the trip to "a country little accustomed to the appearance of young Men of fashion'd Manners, extensive information & accomplished Understandings." [5]

Ireland did not seriously occupy Burke's attention for the next couple of years, so engrossed was he with other affairs. Then, in the fall of 1788, George III went insane. The Whigs lost no time in seeking to get the Prince of Wales installed as regent with full power to exercise the prerogatives of the crown. In their haste, however, they embraced the strange doctrine that the prince had an inherent right to the regency, a right which did not depend upon the will of parliament. Recognizing the trap into which they had fallen they tried to straddle by claiming that, while the prince had the right, he lacked actual possession of the royal prerogatives. To secure possession he required parliament's approval. Should they have succeeded, it is probable that Pitt would have been turned out, and power would then have been in the hands of Fox, the real leader of the Whigs. Pitt acted in no uncertain fashion, however, and brought in a Regency Bill designed to have the Prince of Wales appointed regent by act of parliament. His power was circumscribed under the terms of the bill so that he would not be able to do anything which might prove distressing should the king recover his reason.

On the whole, Burke's actions in the debates on the Regency Bill were very wild and his temper worse than ever.[6] On one occasion, when talking about the British constitution, his remarks were in such poor taste that another member recommended a dose of salts for Burke's own constitution and expressed the likelihood that Burke would soon be an inmate of a lunatic asylum. Unlike Burke during the debates, who was frequently called to order and on one occasion forced to apologize, this gentleman apparently spoke the sense of the majority, since he was not censured for his words.[7] Much to the consternation of the Whigs, George III recovered rather quickly and was officially declared fully competent on 10 March 1789.

An aspect of this episode pertinent to this study is the matter of Ireland and the regency. It will be recalled that Burke had not been very happy over Ireland's winning her legislative independence in 1782 but had accepted it as a *fait accompli* and thereafter remained consistent with the position he had then adopted. Thus, he opposed the application to Ireland by the British parliament of the Prince of Wales' claim to the regency. He asked the House on one occasion during the debates if, having become independent, the Irish parliament was bound to receive a regent not appointed by its own members. He pointed out that the unity of the Empire was the factor that kept England and Ireland together despite their separate and independent legislatures. Should that unity be impaired, Ireland would be irrevocably lost, he declared. Such an untoward development would be certain, he predicted, if the idea of forcing Ireland to accept the Prince as regent prevailed. The way to prevent such a calamity was to allow Ireland to vote on the question herself. He expressed himself as certain that her good sense would dictate voting the regency to the Prince of Wales to whom it rightfully belonged.[8]

The fear had been expressed in England that if Ireland were given power to decide for herself, she might vote a different regent. Thus the unifying element between the two nations would be severed. In Ireland it was argued that to permit the British parliament to select a regent for her was a violation of the agreement of 1782. To Burke, the latter was professedly a real fear; the former, an imaginary one. He felt that it was ridiculous to think that the

Irish might pass by the rightful heir so that there could be no harm anticipated from the British Parliament's doing what was right anyway. On the other hand, he maintained that to have deprived the Irish of the right to make their own decision might involve serious imperial consequences.

Two weeks after the king's recovery, Burke received a letter from Lord Charlemont informing him that through Charlemont's efforts the opposition party in Ireland (the Whigs) had passed a resolution that Ireland should have "the full and exclusive Right . . . to appoint her own Regent, and to exercise that Right, whenever occasion should occur, by appointing the Prince of Wales sole Regent for Ireland without Limitation or Restriction." [9] Charlemont was very anxious that Burke inform the Duke of Portland, the nominal leader of the English Whigs, and Fox, the real leader, of what he had accomplished. He also urged that the Prince of Wales be told.

Both Houses of the Irish parliament, supposedly at the instigation of Burke, although this cannot be verified, and certainly at the urging of Grattan, passed resolutions vesting the regency of Ireland in the Prince of Wales without any restrictions. When the Lord Lieutenant refused to have anything to do with this address, the two Houses jointly selected a deputation to wait upon the Prince in London and inform him of their action. His Highness received the delegation with great cordiality but had to inform the members that the king's recovery had now rendered their action unnecessary.

The import of this measure by the Irish parliament is that they had made an unmistakable gesture of independence involving an important constitutional question. If Ireland clearly had such a power, then it was only a step to complete severance of her connection with Britain. Such a move, of course, would be most undesirable from Burke's point of view. Whether he realized this is not certain, but that he acted as if the idea never had crossed his mind is patent. Two persons who recognized that such a step could be next in the order of things were the Attorney General, Fitzgibbon, in Ireland and Pitt in England. There can be little doubt that following upon the defeat of his commercial propositions in 1785, the regency affair convinced Pitt that the only way to keep Ireland safely within the fold of the Empire would be an unrestricted political union.

The king's recovery resulted in a barrage of caricatures at the expense of the Prince and the Whigs. In one of them, drawn by Gillray and published on 29 April, entitled "The Funeral Procession of Miss Regency," Burke preceded the casket and as "Ignatius Loyola" recited the office of the dead.[10]

Exactly what the outcome of this question would have been, one cannot say, since the king's recovery put an end to it. But before he recovered, the Whigs had been very busy making plans for their anticipated return to office. Unknown to Burke, the leaders of the party had made plans which included him. While he would still be excluded from cabinet rank, his future would have been quite bright had these plans materialized. Sir Gilbert Elliot, who was in on the plans, tells us that the Duke of Portland had a "veneration" for Burke and considered "the reward to be given to Burke as a credit and honour to the nation, and he considers the neglect of him and his embarrassed situation as having been long a reproach to the country. The unjust prejudice and clamour which has prevailed against him and his family only determine the Duke the more to do him justice."[11]

What was to be done? In the first place, his brother Richard was to be Secretary of the Treasury, a post paying £3000 a year, until there should be a vacancy in the Customs of a place paying around £1000 a year for life. When such an opening occurred, Richard would resign from the Treasury. Edmund was to return to his old post in the Pay Office at £4000 a year. Since this was, of course, "precarious," the Duke intended that he should be given a grant on the Irish Establishment of a pension of £2000 a year "clear" for his own life, with the reversion of half of it to his son for the latter's life, and the other half to Mrs. Burke for her life. These grants would make Burke "completely happy by leaving his wife and son safe from want after his death."[12]

That Burke was ignorant of these plans may be gleaned from the end of Elliot's account: "You may think it strange that to this moment Burke does not know a word of all this, and his family are indeed, I believe, suffering a little under the apprehension that he may be neglected in the general scramble."[13]

The security which Burke so sorely needed was thus almost within his grasp, but instead of this pleasant prospect he found himself at the end of the regency affair at the very pit of his entire career. He was never more unpopular in the House; he was widely looked upon by the public as mad; his perennially strained financial situation was so desperate that he was on the verge of bankruptcy; the Hastings business looked endless; and he himself reflected his seemingly hopeless situation by growing more and more irritable even with his intimates.[14] To paraphrase Macaulay, he resembled a man who had survived his own wake.

Already he had grown weary of his arduous tasks and had given serious thought to retirement. If it were not for the Hastings case to which he felt bound in point of honor, he told William Windham in a long letter dated 24 January 1789, he would have applied there and then for the Chiltern Hundreds.

Later that very year came the event which rescued Burke from the oblivion to which he seemed destined. The French Revolution brought to him a lofty reputation and new-found importance as a result of his almost single-handed battle to warn England in particular and the rest of the world in general of the dangers to the established order of things which this great upheaval embodied.[15] The reaction to his *Reflections on the Revolution in France*, which was first published in November 1790 was astonishing. The views of Burke on this subject are too well known, and space does not permit our dwelling upon them here. What does concern us, however, is the fact that Burke's faded reputation had been rejuvenated. His finances had also undergone refurbishing thanks to the intervention of such friends as the Duke of Portland and Earl Fitzwilliam.

Once again the great advocate of circumstances found an opportunity "to do something for Ireland." It was the last and greatest of the distresses of England which Burke sought to capitalize upon for the advantage of both Ireland and the Empire itself. Had the wisdom of his views on Ireland prevailed, there can be little doubt that Ireland would have been spared many years of grief and sorrow.

One of the first fruits of Burke's return to a position of honor and respect was his election to the Royal Academy of Ireland as its sole honorary member. Replying to the Earl of Charlemont to express his appreciation, Burke told him that he considered Ireland vital to the safety and tranquillity of England.[16]

To guarantee this Burke felt that the position of the Irish Catholics had to be corrected. These people, the majority of the country's population, were still excluded from all offices and honors. The franchise was likewise denied them, as was the legal profession. The practice of medicine was permitted, but Catholic medical men were refused University teaching positions. Catholics were also prohibited from holding military commissions. With the example of both the Americans and the French before them, it was no wonder that they had already begun to grow restive.

In 1759, there had been formed in Ireland an organization called the Catholic Association.[17] The men who were responsible for its foundation were Dr. Curry, the historian and physician, Charles O'Conor, the historian,[18] and Thomas Wyse. They were members of a class, the old Catholic landlord group, which was rapidly approaching impoverishment as a result of the penal laws. They looked to the aristocracy among their co-religionists for assistance, but these men appeared too willing to allow bad conditions to continue in the hope that they would not grow any worse. Too fearful of further discriminations, these laymen did not differ much from the Catholic clergy of the day in this respect. The latter were, for the most part, exceedingly timid. The vast bulk of the Catholics, the unhappy peasantry, had been ground into a state of virtual impotence by the cruelty and ferocity of their oppressors. The one class to whom the Catholic pioneers could turn for aid was that of the merchants. Trade was one of the few fields open to enterprising Catholics, and a number of them had become quite successful. The first advances to the merchants were quite encouraging in the reception which they met.

It was this combination of Catholic members of the landlord and merchant classes which scored the first successes recorded by the Catholic Association. In 1759, they managed to present an address of loyalty to the then Lord Lieutenant, the Duke of Bedford, on behalf of the Catholic Association.[19] The address bore the signatures of some four hundred men of standing. Unfortunately, this success displeased the Catholic aristocracy of Ireland. In 1760, a new monarch, George III, came to the throne, and the Association drew up an address to him personally. Once more, the aristocrats were annoyed and drew up an address of their own. A compromise between the two Catholic groups was reached, and the founders of the Catholic Association accepted Lord Trimleston as official spokesman for all the country's Catholics.

In 1763, the organization foundered. It was to be ten years before it was revived, this time under the leadership of the timorous Lord Kenmare. The year following its revival, 1774, there took place the passage of the first measure directly in favor of the Catholics. Under it they were allowed to profess their loyalty as citizens upon taking an oath of allegiance. The succeeding years afforded other minor relief. When through the work of the Irish Volunteers, Ireland achieved legislative independence in 1782, amelioration of the lot of the Catholics followed that same year.

After this had been accomplished, the old trepidation of Lord Kenmare and the Catholic aristocrats reappeared. Kenmare willingly complied with a request made by the Irish government that he appeal to Catholics to withdraw from support of the Volunteers. This antagonized the merchants, now stronger than ever within the Catholic Association, and they publicly repudiated Kenmare's action. The opportunity of practicing their religion with greater freedom now served to keep the Catholics quiet and to prevent any serious repercussions until the French Revolution broke out. This operated to set in motion the desires of the Catholics for civil relief. And later when the English Catholics were granted the Catholic Relief Act of 1791 by the British parliament, the more outspoken members of the Catholic Association were disappointed that their parliament had failed to follow England's example.

The new leader of the Catholics was a wealthy Dublin silk mercer, John Keogh,[20] who was ambitious enough to hope that the services of Edmund Burke, long noted as the foremost advocate of the Catholics in Great Britain, might be enlisted at least indirectly through his son, Richard Burke, Jr. So it was decided that the Reverend Doctor Thomas Hussey [21] would bring the application of the Irish Catholics to Burke's son that he become their agent.

Hussey was a native of Ireland who had been educated in Spain. He had come to England as the chaplain of the Spanish Ambassador and had received his appointment from the Spanish monarch personally. When war between Spain and Britain broke out during the American Revolution, Hussey was left in charge of the Spanish Embassy in London.[22] His diplomatic abilities were employed in efforts to secure peace.[23] His reputation was of the very highest, and he was considered by the members of the famous club to which Burke belonged as one of the foremost men of the day.[24]

13 August 1790, Father Hussey wrote to Edmund Burke that he had called that day upon his son in London but had been unable to contact him. Consequently, Hussey took this occasion to ask Burke himself to look over some papers he was enclosing on behalf of the Irish Catholic organization. He took this liberty in the knowledge that Burke humanely interested himself "for the oppressed state of the Roman Catholics of that country." [25] The enclosure was from a relative of Hussey's who was a prominent member of the Catholic group and in it Hussey was requested to retain the professional services of Richard Burke, Jr. in the interests of the Catholic Committee.[26] Young Burke was assured *carte blanche* in drawing up whatever resolutions he deemed necessary. The Committee looked upon their prospective advocate as "a professional man" from whom "they hope for something worthy of the subject." The letter concluded with the compliment that they were well aware of the obligations they owed to Richard's father, the man who had laid the cornerstone of their emancipation.[27]

Richard gladly accepted the invitation, and his father gave his full approval, although he was to write his son later, in 1793, that he wished that it had been possible for the young man to have commenced his career "with an endeavor to render some more moderate and less invidious service to the public." [28]

A letter from Hussey to Richard, 28 August 1790, indicated that he would act temporarily as a middle man between Richard and the Committee and gives Richard a good line of argument on behalf of his clients:

I had forwarded your letter, to Baron Hussey, for instruction of the Committee, I am certain that they will be guided by the excellent principles which you lay down for them. As soon as I get their ideas, I shall take the liberty of transmitting them to you. Should these Kingdoms be involved in a war, a further toleration to the Catholics of

Ireland will become unavoidable; & it is absurd to wait that State necessity should compel, what true Policy ought to offer voluntarily. Hitherto the Catholics of that Country have proceeded with proper deference, & submission to the laws, in their application for redress, notwithstanding the endeavors of *neighbouring* Countries, suggesting to them to wrest by *force*, & violence, what, I hope, they will never mention, but with moderation, & temper. Sublimated, however, as mens minds are by the *french disease* (as it is not improperly called) one cannot foresee, what a continuation of oppressive laws may work upon the minds of people: & those of the Irish Catholics are much altered within my own memory; & they will not in future bear the lash of Tirranny & oppression which I have seen inflicted upon them, without their resisting or even complaining.[29]

A year was to elapse, however, before Richard got down to work for the Catholic Committee. In the interim both he and his father were preoccupied with matters stemming out of the French Revolution. As great as Edmund's success was in many quarters on account of the *Reflections*,[30] his own party, the Whigs, led by Fox, continued to look with favor on the Revolution. He had publicly broken with Fox over their differing interpretations of developments in France and, much to his disgust, found that the majority of the party took the side of Fox. *The Morning Chronicle*, a paper which reflected Fox's views, announced on 12 May 1791 that "the great and firm body of the Whigs of England, true to their principles, have decided on the dispute between Mr. Fox and Mr. Burke; and the former is declared to have maintained the pure doctrines by which they are bound together and upon which they have invariably acted. The consequence is that Mr. Burke retires from Parliament."

This was untrue, since Burke meant to continue until the Hastings business was concluded, but it upset Burke greatly. On 5 June, he wrote to Fitzwilliam to the effect that he no longer saw eye to eye with him and the Whigs and complained bitterly about Fox's conduct. Burke concluded the letter by saying that his seat in parliament would probably be at Fitzwilliam's disposal "early in the next Session." [31]

That summer Burke finished his *Appeal from the New to the Old Whigs*, his reply to Fox, and it was published in August. Burke defended his consistency and asserted that it was he, rather than Fox, who was the real defender of Whig principles. The *Appeal* made a great hit with George III who was very cordial to Burke when they met at court shortly after its publication.

Meanwhile, Richard performed a mission to some important French Royalists in exile at Coblenz. Burke had been approached by an emissary of the king's brothers, the future Louis XVIII and the future Charles X, on the subject of the restoration of the old order in France. Burke discussed the matter with the emissary, and it was agreed that Richard should go with the latter to Coblenz to make known his father's views. Pitt's government would put no official sanction on Richard's mission but did not forbid it. Nothing, however, came of it, but it is interesting to discover that Burke himself was opposed to the return of the old order unless certain reforms were made. He told Richard in a revealing letter that:

Though I make no doubt of preferring the ancient course, or almost any other, to this vile chimera, and sick man's dream of government, yet I could not actively, or with a good heart and clear conscience, go to the re-establishment of a monarchical despotism in the place of this system of anarchy. I should think myself obliged to withdraw wholly from such a competition, and give repose to my age, as I should wish you to give other employment to your youth.[32]

So it was that Richard had already turned to other employment, i.e., to his tasks as agent for the Catholic Committee of Ireland. On 15 September, Edward Byrne, chairman of "the select Committee of the Catholicks of Ireland," informed him how pleased the Catholics were that he had accepted their offer and assured him that they "perfectly coincide with you in your different reflections and in your Sentiments relative to this Business; they are dictated by Wisdom and Experience and are worthy of the Son of our much admired Countryman." John Keogh would call upon him, inform him of the applications made to the Irish government, and bring him up to date on the progress of negotiations. In closing, Byrne made another reference to Richard's father: "The many obligations we are under to the Zeal and brilliant Abilities of the Father inspire us with the strongest reliance on the Son for his most strenuous exertions and able assistance in our behalf." [33]

The selection of young Burke to act as their agent in their efforts to win political emancipation was, at least on the surface, a very wise move on the part of the Irish Catholics. Burke's father was the most articulate opponent of the French Revolution and its principles in the British Empire if not in the world. Choice of his son as their agent belied the charge made by their enemies that the Catholics were actually in league with the forces of the French Revolution.[34] Furthermore, Richard was bound to be advised by his father, and the latter's knowledge of the subject was prodigious.

Actually, as the Committee soon discovered, Richard did not inherit his father's talents. Yet he seems to have had more character and ability than he has generally been credited with possessing. Too many people remember only Wolfe Tone's acid comments about him or Lord Morley's unflattering pen portrait. He was a rather handsome young man given too much to seriousness but often very spirited. Unfortunately, he had inherited from his father, if not his talents, at least his quick temper. Richard had once become involved in a duel with a Mr. Topping whom he had accused of insulting both himself and Lord Fitzwilliam for whom Richard, as a lawyer, did considerable legal work. The altercation actually reached the field of honor and, after shots were fired into the air, Topping gave satisfaction.[35]

His first step in the business which he had now undertaken in earnest following the conclusion of his mission to Coblenz appears to have been to write to Dundas, the Home Secretary, on 5 October, for we have a letter dated the next day from Dundas to Richard. Although not in Dundas' hand, it bears his signature and reads:[36]

The more I think of it, I find it the more impossible for me to write any thing to you on the subject of your communication of yesterday. My Sentiments respecting the situation of the Catholics in this Country, have been so publicly manifested, I have no occasion to say any thing on that Topic. But respecting any objects or plans of Indulgence which the Roman Catholics of Ireland may have in view, I am not now at liberty either to think or act as [an] Individual. I can only act in concert with His Majesty's Confidential Servants, after having received every information which the Government of this Country, or the Government of Ireland shall be able to collect for the final guidance of their Judgement. I rest satisfied that your Candor will readily admit, that I can at present give you no other answer.

Seeking to derive every advantage from his father's newly

found popularity at court, Richard secured an interview with Pitt who informed him, 8 October 1791, that he would be pleased to see him the following morning at 10:30 to discuss the business he had mentioned in his letter.[37] That it was "the Irish business" is clear from a letter to his father which Richard wrote the same day.[38] A later letter from Pitt expressed his appreciation of Richard's letter to him, dated 12 October and containing Richard's "intended answer to Mr. Keogh, which corresponds entirely with what passed when Mr. Pitt had the pleasure of seeing Mr. Burke." Pitt went on to say that he would be happy to have a further conversation with Richard.[39]

It was rumored in London early in November that Richard was slated to receive the first vacant post in the diplomatic corps,[40] but nothing came of it. Meanwhile, his father had irrevocably made up his mind to quit parliament the moment the Hastings business was concluded. He had so informed Fitzwilliam who had then begged him to reconsider. To which he had answered in one of the most revealing letters he ever wrote [41] that he had made his decision and would abide by it. Furthermore, financial help which Burke received from Fitzwilliam was now to be discontinued at the former's request. Fitzwilliam had insisted that it be continued. To his honor, Burke wrote that it would not be "proper or decent" for him "to continue to receive large pecuniary assistance" from Fitzwilliam, although "the fact is known only to my own family, your Lordship & the Duke of Portland."

Following his signature, Burke added this request:

"Of course your Lordship will throw this letter into the fire after you have perused it — except you will first show it to the Duke of Portland from whom I have hitherto concealed nothing, nor ever wish to keep anything secret."

Having taken his position, Burke remained resolute. He could now turn his attention to Richard's business. On 13 December, he began a letter to him on French affairs by saying that "If you are called to Ireland I wish you all success, & that the Season were more favourable." Two days later, he sent along some advice to the effect that the Catholics would be ill-advised to continue to quarrel with the Dissenters as they had lately been doing. Such a split would give the Irish government a splendid chance to play the one group against the other, although the government would be foolish to operate on this divisive principle. "Hitherto all relaxation of penalties proceeded on principles of Union. They relaxed toward Dissenters to unite *Protestants*. They relaxed towards the Catholics to unite *Subjects*. Union was always the idea. . . . Union must still be the word." He concluded that he might "possibly throw out an hint to you on this Subject tomorrow. . . ." [42]

Richard, in addition to his talks with Pitt and Dundas, also had conversations in London with Lord Grenville, the Foreign Secretary, and Major Hobart, the Irish Chief Secretary, who had come over to England on business. Writing his father on 15 December, Richard boasted that he would win the franchise for his clients and declared that it would be a "great event" for him if he could complete the work his father had begun. He mentioned that he had just had a long and satisfactory talk with Hobart and that they would have immediately settled the business if Richard were prepared to drop the idea of the franchise. He reiterated that he had no doubt that he could secure it and said that "the measure of relief is certainly determined, the particular points will therefore be less difficult. They are convinced of the necessity of conciliating & gaining the R.C. [Roman Catholics] to the interests of government." [43]

That Richard was a bit optimistic may be glimpsed from a note written by Grenville to Dundas. Grenville mentioned two conversations he had had with Richard on the subject of the Irish Catholics. The latter's agent seemingly impressed the Foreign Secretary with the importance of the men whom he represented and also stressed the potential danger to England of a union between the Catholics and Dissenters in Ireland. Grenville made it clear that he had taken pains not to be too encouraging to young Burke. He assured Dundas that he confined his remarks to "general assurances of the favourable disposition of Government to do all that should, on consideration, appear to be reasonable and practicable." Grenville did express regret that marks of jealousy toward the Catholics were already being evidenced by the Irish government, i.e., the members of the Ascendancy. [44]

Dundas himself had apparently been initially impressed by Richard. At least he wrote to Grenville that he felt that young

Burke did not lack talent and occasionally showed clear indications of being his brilliant father's son.[45]

On the morning of 24 December, Richard and Dundas held their last talk prior to Richard's departure for Ireland to begin work for his clients in the field. The following day Dundas wrote him that he had "very maturely considered the different particulars which passed in conversation between us yesterday forenoon" and informed him that Hobart was setting out for Ireland immediately with the government's sentiments relative to the Catholics. Westmorland, the viceroy, would "take the proper steps on the subject" and quickly inform the Catholics what the government's position was. He then added significantly that any further communications Richard might wish to hold would have to be with "the government of Ireland." This decision was dictated by no lack of personal respect for Richard but because it seemed the best way "to bring this important question to a happy conclusion." [46]

On the 27th, Hobart set off for Dublin bearing both an official dispatch and a private letter from Dundas to Westmorland, the Lord Lieutenant. The official paper informed the viceroy that it was the government's opinion, based on both justice and wise policy, that the claims of the Catholics be listened to with "a favourable ear." The continuation of the existing system of government in Ireland might be jeopardized by a refusal to take such an attitude, Dundas warned and then tried to deal with the old fear that the Catholics would take over Ireland if the slightest political concession were made to them. He asked Westmorland to consider the alternatives. The continuation of total exclusion could easily lead to a union between the Catholics and the Dissenters who were imbued with French principles. Conversely, the grant of a limited franchise would make more likely moderation on the part of the Catholics. Hope of eventual greater concessions would operate to guarantee their loyalty to the constitution and lessen the likelihood that they might find the Jacobin theories very attractive.

The British government had therefore reached the conclusion that the Protestant interests in Ireland ran a greater risk in continuing the total exclusion of the Catholics from the franchise than they did in admitting them to a limited participation and would be happy if their sentiments found approbation with the Irish government but would only make a recommendation to that effect and not "urge it upon them in the shape of a decision."

Should it be found, however, that the suggestion lacked merit in the eyes of the Irish leaders, the British ministers felt it imperative that the Catholics be convinced that the action was not final but that hope was still held out for them. The Catholics should be given to understand in the light of a failure to grant even a limited suffrage that their best chance of securing an improved status in the future lay in their conducting themselves peaceably. They should also be given to understand that should they resort to force they would face the combined forces of the military power of both Great Britain and Ireland.

Dundas then continued by saying that the cabinet felt that the Irish Catholics ought to enjoy at least as favorable a status as their British co-religionists. The following disabilities should be removed: those which discriminated against their free exercise of any profession, trade, or manufacture; prohibited intermarriage between Catholics and Protestants; restricted education of Catholic children; prevented Catholics from bearing arms; and excluded them from serving on juries.[47]

In the private letter which accompanied the dispatch, Dundas told Westmorland that ordinarily the Ascendancy could count upon the backing of the British but that under the present circumstances both the British public and parliament itself would probably wish to know whether Britain would be justified in interfering. If it were merely to allow one set of Irishmen to dominate another, the chances were slim that such a cause would find support in Britain. Britain was apt to be at war soon, and if this happened the Catholics of Ireland would probably be in a position to demand that their status be improved just as Ireland had resorted to similar threats in 1782 to secure her legislative independence. Hence, it would be better to concede now gracefully what was likely to come about through force later. In putting it this way, Dundas was using one of Burke's favorite arguments, which Richard Burke had unquestionably urged upon him in their recent conversation of two days earlier.

In conclusion, Dundas wrote: "There cannot be a permanency in the frame of the Government and Constitution of Ireland unless the Protestants will lay aside their prejudices, forego their exclusive pre-eminence, and gradually open their arms to the Roman Catholics, and put them on the same footing with every other species of Dissenter." [48]

Thus, it would appear that Richard Burke's mission to Ireland seemed likely to be fruitful since the British government was now disposed to be conciliatory. All that remained, then, was for their sentiments to be appreciated in Ireland.

In a letter written before Richard's departure, his proud father [49] praised him and wished him well. He asked God's blessing on his son's work which he said was in the interest of a just cause. The extravagant estimation which Burke had of Richard's ability is indicated quite plainly in this rather maudlin letter.[50] As Keogh and his friends had foreseen, Burke was very generous with advice to his son because, as he himself said, his mind was very much on Richard and his business.[51]

A FIELD TRIP

Richard set out for Ireland accompanied by Keogh and while waiting passage at Holyhead dashed off a brief note to his father.[52] It seems that at Shrewsbury they had met "a Wild Irishman a (Protestant) friend of Keogh's, who was out of breath with fright at the state of things." While Richard took a more moderate view, he conceded that "there certainly is some ferment, whether it will serve or disserve us is more than I know." He traced the excitement in Dublin "to the one rash step of the Castle, in endeavouring to excite a disavowing party of country gentlemen against the silent neutrality of the Committee." He took pleasure that these timid Catholics had "presented an address signed very respectably, but going full as far in principle tho' with an appearance of officiously [sic] loyalty, as what they call the violent party ever proposed to Lord Kenmare to do." He was sure, he said, that the directions from England were "to treat & deal with *us*, as the R. Catholics."

In the letter he called attention to the fact that one of the names on the address of the moderate Catholic group was that of Dr. Troy, a Catholic bishop,[53] who had signed his name *"in Capitals*

among peers," and wondered what his father thought of this. Richard himself saw it as a good sign, thereby indicating how willing
he was to grasp at any straw which seemed to portend success
for his cause. He interpreted it thus: "But surely this effort of the
Govt (for such they have made) to put in motion the R.C. clergy,
is, if men were conscious of any thing, the most complete humiliation, pennance, amende honorable than any state ever went thro!
. . . After persecuting the Clergy & the People for a century for
the supposed dominion of the former over the latter, in derogation
of the civil authority, that civil authority calls upon *that* clergy
to exercise its influence *in its favour* — & finds it to have none!"

While Richard was in this state just before crossing over to
Dublin, his father was writing him on the same date.[54] He was
happy that Richard found "things in a good train toward success." The father then informed him that the Duke of Portland
had called and that they had talked "with our usual opennes &
ease." Portland was indeed "open" since he made it clear to Burke
that he disliked the pending "Irish business." His dislike stemmed
"from his fear of its being a new subject of discussion and obloquy.
He has an uncertain, undefined, affection about us all, and he is
vexed to find himself in a situation in which one or the other of
us is always doing something of an arduous and disputable nature —
and that we are always going — per praeceps et acuta cacumina."
Portland for once had made a shrewd analysis!

Meanwhile, Richard and Keogh had arrived safely in Dublin,
and in his first letter from there to his father, Richard revealed that
he had been busy from the moment of his arrival and was "in a
great storm, a high sea, & a troubled sky; but I am not confounded.
The difficulties are great but the hopes are something & I propose
staying as long as I can keep . . . steady to the principles you have
instilled . . . by example, reason, affection, taste, duty, & every
principle of the head and heart; and steady in the exertions suitable to such principles."

Richard was coming down to earth. He continued in this more
realistic vein:

The ministers & their friends here have determined *not* to give the
right of franchise, as much as men who from fear & rage have lost the
possession of every human faculty can [be] said to have a determina-

tion. There is indeed hardly one man of any party rightly in his senses, *except* those of the Roman Catholics whom the Castle people call incendiaries. A storm of obloquy & prejudice is raised, of which I have my share; but I am almost sure it is nothing but whistling & noise; In this I may indeed be mistaken; but I must take my chance. I can not desert a post where providence & fortune has placed me, & in which I know to a certainty I may prevent or at least protract evil, & may eventually be of the greatest possible service. The situation is great, however perilous. Expect from me every thing, except the most exact prudence with regard to myself — [.] On that, however necessary, I am not as adept, but I think I shall weather the gale. I have not lost my head & for the present I think I know what is & ought to be done by myself & all others, both those I serve & those I have not the direction of. We shall be able to argue our point of franchise, at least in the Parliament & that probably with the first ability.

In conclusion, he asked his father to send him by the first post either a copy or the original of his letter on the Irish Catholics to Sir Hercules Langrishe.[55]

In an effort to instruct his son on the subject of his clients, Burke wrote Richard a long letter [56] in which he drew upon his vast knowledge of the subject of the Catholics of Ireland and showed him in detail just what the differences were among the people of that faith. He began by saying that the Catholics of any fortune in Ireland belonged to old and respected families but unfortunately they had not recently distinguished themselves. In fact, some of them had never "illustrated their names." There were two classes of aristocratic Irish Catholics; those who were educated abroad and who had wide connections there, and those of the first Catholic families who remained in Ireland. The former were "more proud of their quality of Gentlemen, than many of those could be, who had hopes from anything else." The latter, by remaining in Ireland, were "doomed to an abject servitude, and by the Laws (so far as Laws could operate in that case) were sentenced to beggary."

The distinction between these "old Gentlemen who still retained their religion and Estates, and the Commonalty of that religion and the middle sort, was without all comparison greater than that between people in the same ranks among Protestants." Burke said that to the best of his memory these Catholic aristocrats "perfectly despised their Brethren" and would have been glad, if they could do so in conscience or without its rebounding on themselves, to discriminate against them.

But a new class of Catholics was coming into prominence. Men who had risen "by their industry, their abilities, & their good fortune to considerable opulence, and of course to an independent spirit." The aristocrats were "still less disposed to them (as rivals in consideration and importance) than to the old Catholics who were only poor struggling artizans, Tanners or Tradesmen — They despised these less; but they hated them more."

The arresting thing about this split between the aristocrats and the merchant class was that the former would probably prefer "to remain under their present disqualifications, than partake in the advantages of Freemen, with those they ought to cherish, love, protect, and cooperate in everything rationally proposed for their common benefit."

Burke recommended to Richard that if he should meet any Catholic gentleman "who is in the situation without acquiring the character I have described," he should try to get him to make his colleagues aware of the foolishness of persisting in their mistaken attitude toward their brethren.

By comparing themselves with individuals among their co-religionists, they might indulge in some feeling of pride, but should they compare themselves with the Protestants of Ireland either in landed property, titles, rank, or in "gentility illustrated by great offices and high connexion," let them remember that "they are as *nothing*." They were equalled by many Protestants and even exceeded, Burke said sarcastically, "in the vain matter upon which they despise their Brethren." It will only be "by identifying themselves to the Corps to which they naturally belong" that "their properties will tell tenfold in consideration." Then and only then will they become of real importance. If they but know how to use their situation, they may rank, "as I wish them to do, with any men in the Kingdom."

Burke now turned to the Roman Catholic clergy of Ireland. He began by saying that he was not surprised at their "servility." This was understandable since "the name of a Popish Priest has so long been a matter of reproach, and of a mixed heterogeneous, sensation of fear, abhorrence, and contempt, that there was no charge, however absurd and ridiculous, which would not readily be credited against them."

They were men who "were supposed to be possessed of an influence hardly possible to be obtained by any set of men, but which, in them, had no existence in that degree, or (to my certain knowledge) almost in any degree at all, so that every disorder amongst the common people was attributed either to their direction or connivance."

Furthermore, as Catholic secular clergy without any support whatsoever from the state, it was manifestly impossible that their power could have been considerable.

The very tenets of their religion precluded them from exercising power in Burke's opinion. "Every part of the dogmas of that religion are so known, so fixed, so much in rule, and so unalterable, the Clergy had no scope in the wide field of metaphysical, theological, or critical matters, which from such means of obtaining friends and partizans, and of producing pleasing Novelties to the audience, to exercise those modes of influence which are known to be so very powerful."

He went on: "The Sacraments are in the same frame, the confession which is thought so much of is but a routine, and may be made to any; and the absolution, on conditions of which the Penitent himself must judge, is a thing of course. The Masses are at a fixed rate, and never are or can be refused or delarged — Preaching the most powerful arm of popular Priesthood is sparingly used by them, and what there is of it is mostly in the hands of Friars, who have something more of influence than the Parish Clergy but not much."

In the light of all this, the Catholic clergy would be very unwise to meddle in political matters since they may "disgust their people, they may lose the little consideration they possess, they may lose their flocks, and they will have neither profit or credit in return." On the other hand, "if they either wholly lie by or fall in with their people in their civil pursuits, which the others understand better than the Clergy do, and which they will pursue whether the Clergy like it or not, they will rise every day in the respect and influence which belong to their office. Let them not deceive themselves, they *cannot* possess the sources of influence that are in the hands of dissenters & of other descriptions; but if they do not counteract their own interests, there is a decent field yet open to them."

Having spent so much time on an analysis of the composition of the Catholics, Burke noted that the government's scheme seemed to be to divide the Catholics for what purpose he was not yet sure. However, in dividing them, he was sure that the weakest part would fall to the government. The strength of the Catholics was not in their "dozen or score of old Gentlemen." Rather did it lie in two things: their numbers and their growing property. Should the government abstract the "old Gentlemen" from the natural strength of the Catholic body in Ireland, "they will leave the Gentlemen without credit, and themselves without the service they might derive from their influence with the rest. They will lose the substance and catch a shadow indeed."

Burke then alluded to the address of the aristocrats which Richard had mentioned earlier to him. The father thought that it might require one from the General Committee of Catholics. If this were deemed necessary, it should be an address which was "fully as expressive of zeal and loyalty as theirs — much gratitude for what is passed — the most perfect attachment to his Majesty's Government and to the Constitution of the State, the most perfect acquiescence in that of the Church. With regard to religion to express an inviolable attachment to their own because its principles had to make them good men and good Citizens; not that they are thoroughly satisfied with its present condition — that as they find themselves worthy of the Constitution and know the benefit of its Franchises, they must not dissemble the uneasiness they feel, and the dangers they are continually exposed to from the total want of them, and what they suffer from many other restraints which they are sure they have not deserved; hoping everything from the benignity of Government & of Parliament."

Burke concluded that if the government were in their senses, they would surely give these points to the Catholics even if the latter were not enough in their own senses to desire them.

If the foregoing were not sufficiently indicative that Burke's thoughts were on his son's mission, he sent another letter, dated 8 January 1792, in which he said that he had been seriously reflecting on the subject of the young man's trip to Ireland. It was a matter upon which he was doubly anxious — on its own account, and on account of Richard's connection with it. He hoped Richard would succeed in this undertaking which he "broke off in the middle and 'left half-told — the story of Cambuscan bold.' " Richard was to be the Spenser who would bring the story to a happy conclusion. He observed, however, that Richard would be wise to take a dignified departure from Ireland after thoroughly instructing his clients upon their course of action should it appear that success was not likely to crown his efforts at this time. There was a characteristic note to be found in the words — "as this business may be the work of more sessions than one, and may find more favourable conjunctures." [57]

In the meantime, Richard had written to Hobart, the Irish Chief Secretary, that it was the wish of the Catholic Committee that the Lord Lieutenant (Westmorland) discourage Catholics (meaning, of course, the aristocratic and hierarchal elements) from making addresses of loyalty to the crown and attachments to the constitution. Hobart's reply [58] was rather curt. The Lord Lieutenant would do no such thing, the wishes of Richard and his committee notwithstanding. The opinions of the government toward the Roman Catholics, however, were favorable. In the matter of concessions "whenever they are made they will be the best proof of the disposition of those who make them, and will render nugatory any arguments to the contrary, ingeniously drawn from collateral circumstances."

In his letter of 7 January to which Hobart's was a reply, Richard had unwisely resorted to intimidating language to which Hobart referred: "That part of your letter which relates to the consequences that may arise from the solicitation of addresses, I cannot possibly take further notice of, than to express my concern that it found its way into your letters — Permit me to add, that such notions promulgated abroad wou'd have a tendency the most injurious to your wishes."

Richard then sent Hobart a formal letter [59] which opened by saying that Dundas had told him in London that Hobart had a full communication of the British government's sentiments in the matter of the Roman Catholics of Ireland and that all business on the matter should now be with Hobart. Hence, he would take this opportunity to remind Hobart that the Roman Catholics sought substantially four things: (1) admission to the profession of the law; (2) the exercise of provincial magistracies; (3) the right to serve on grand and petty juries; and (4) a qualified right to vote at elections for Knights of the Shire.

Richard would be happy to receive an answer at Hobart's earliest convenience. Should one not be quickly forthcoming, he could only conclude that the Roman Catholics had failed of success in their representations.

The answer [60] came speedily but it was disappointing. After repeating almost verbatim the contents of Richard's letter of the 11th, Hobart stated:

> The Lord Lieutenant has commanded me to inform you, That it is the present Intention of Government to suggest for the Consideration of Parliament in the ensuing Session, the Expediency of a further Relaxation of the Popery Laws. But it is not in my Power to state specifically what those Relaxations may be, without an opportunity of more particularly ascertaining the opinions of the Friends of the Administration, and the Disposition of Parliament.
>
> His Excellency also commands me to acquaint you, that I have already made a Communication of the same Nature to Lord Kenmare.

This parting shot was a slight, since Richard and his clients had sought to secure recognition for themselves as *the* spokesmen of the Catholics of Ireland. It indicated that the Castle was not at all averse, as Burke himself had guessed, to playing off the aristocratic and conservative element against the more democratic and outspoken middle-class group whose forthright talk was very disconcerting.

While this exchange was taking place in Dublin between Richard and Dublin Castle, Burke sent off two letters in a row to Richard. In the first,[61] dated 12 January 1792, the father recalled that in his last letter he had advised his son to be patient and, if things did not go well, to take a dignified departure since there would be other times to pursue his goals. He now repeated this paternal advice and recommended Richard "not to drink the draught to the dregs, but whenever it was evident that nothing could be done, to return to us, arranging your people for further sober, rational, cool, and unremitting efforts, until the business shall be accomplished, which sooner or later, and indeed but a little sooner or later, will be done."

He concluded with a further note of caution:

I have always had more suspicion of the Dublin Post Office than of any other — I am not quite sure for what reason, but for these five and twenty years at least, I have had myself and known others to have that way of thinking. So whatever you wish to write most secretly, let it be written by safe hands whenever you can find them. I write this as my former, directed to Frank Kiernan at the Custom House.

The following day, Burke wrote a much longer letter to Richard.[62] In this fifth letter extant on Richard's Irish mission, the father told him that he had been comparing various accounts and had found (quite correctly) that the opposition to Richard's clients stemmed chiefly from Dublin Castle itself. The point which they were resolutely determined to refuse was that of "the representation." They would "cheerfully give up the Bar, & would open the Army & Navy." Their reason for being willing to grant occasional commissions in the services was that by doing so they would "completely gain this or that man, & dispose him to dupe, or to disavow his Brethren." Their opposition to the franchise was that "the votes of new opend out men of property might sometimes give them trouble, & never could be of service to them in any Jobb. They would to into the general mass of the feelings & interest of the Country."

The reason why the Castle preferred "the places" to "the representation" is that they felt that "a few Gentlemen, who might, in their families & dependencies, profit of the Jobb, but could get little of any thing which they are used to [in] fact, by the representation."

When Burke discovered that the Castle faction was determined on this and that they spoke "with contempt" of Keogh, who did not represent the "general wishes of the Catholicks," he praised Keogh highly and said that it would be well for the Irish government if they had many men of comparable abilities to serve them.

Burke also found that Hobart did not "at all" like Richard's being connected with the business. It would not surprise him if Hobart did everything he could

underhand, to lessen you in the opinion & confidence of those who employ you, as well as with others. But by this time you are at the bottom
of all this; & you will see whether it is more prudent for your Cause, &
safe for your personal Dignity, (things that ought never be separated)
to continue where you are; or to come hither & sollicit, where you [are]
sure of being heard at least with respect & where [you] may withdraw
to quiet or to remain where you are without proper weight & consideration as you must do where you are, if you do not speedily see something fundamental settled, you must sink into the Character of a mere
common sollicitor. If the Castle do not wish you as a friend & mediator,
they will soon reduce you, for it is compleatly in their power, into the
former situation; & that too with the disadvantage of being an *unsuccessful* solicitor. Let me know whether you have received four letters
from me; all directed to Frank Kiernan.

Finding that his efforts were being blocked in Ireland, Richard
had recourse to writing Dundas in England. Dundas' reply makes
it easy to divine the contents of Richard's letter: [63]

I have received your letter and you guess rightly that the Irish
Government are not more satisfied with you than you are with them.
On that subject I say nothing, but I cannot refrain [from] guarding
you against what I think I perceive too much of in your letter. I mean
an acquiescence in, if not an approbation of the propriety of the
Catholicks having recourse to sentiments and measures of anarchy either
separately or jointly with the Dissenters or any other description of
persons in that part of Ireland where their interest is more prevalent.
For my part I should conceive that there is no given Circumstance in
which such a Conduct would be either Wise or Virtuous. The Utmost
you or any Friend of theirs could say in their favour would be *apolo-
getick*, that they had been drove to it from Passion, seeing no other
Recourse. That is all that could be said in their favour.

Dundas then undertook to instruct Richard on the duty of a
lawyer toward his clients:

If that is the Case, I wish you well to consider the impact of your
Words, *not betraying your Clients*. It is the business of an advocate to
do the utmost he can for the good of the Cause in which he is engaged,
but it is certainly no part either of his Profession or his Duty to engage
with them in every Measure, or in any Measure not justified by Law
or Propriety which the Clients may think proper to adopt in support of
their Claims.

This was all strictly friendly advice that Dundas had given him,
he assured young Burke:

You will observe that in what I say I have not addressed you in any degree as a Minister. My Conduct in that respect must remain to be regulated by what I communicated to you before your departure; I write you merely as a Private person, wishing you sincerely well, and regretting exceedingly if any Zeal for those who employ you, or any confidence in the opinions you have formed should lead you to embark deeper in measures than appear to be justified by your Situation.

Finally came an unmistakable warning:

If the Catholicks should chuse to have recourse to violence of any kind they do it at their own Peril but the first symptom of the kind would, I am persuaded, suggest to your own Understanding the propriety of separating from them and if their Temper and resolution are of the nature you seem to frown at, I do not think you have much to lose in following that Course.

While things were not progressing too smoothly for Richard, his father seemed quite sanguine about the prospects of ultimate victory for his son's clients.[64] He predicted that they would win the franchise. It was in the very nature of things that they would. The one thing that disturbed him was the manner in which the grant would eventually be made. Some courtesy and graciousness toward the Catholics were in order instead of the customary odium and prejudice.

While not published until a few weeks after Sir Hercules Langrishe brought in his bill for Catholic relief on 25 January 1792, Burke's "long dissertation" to him dispelled some of the ignorance on the subject of the Catholics which was prevalent among the Protestants of Ireland. The letter had been written in answer to a request by Langrishe, dated 10 December 1791, that he give him his views on the subject of the Catholics as these ideas might be helpful to him in the Irish Commons when the subject next came up for consideration.

In Burke's reply to Langrishe, published as *A Letter to Sir Hercules Langrishe, Bart., M.P., on the Subject of the Roman Catholics of Ireland and the Propriety of Admitting Them to the Elective Franchise, Consistently with the Principles of the Constitution, as Established at the Revolution,*[65] he was quick to show that historically whenever there was a revolt of the Irish people (a term Burke equated with the Catholics because of their numbers) the authorities always treated it as a conspiracy against the state, no matter what the real cause, and severely punished the rebels.

Burke then demonstrated historically that it was not a basic part of the Glorious Revolution that the state should be Protestant without qualification. In fact, he said that there was so little idea at the time of establishing Protestantism indefinitely that "they did not indefinitely *tolerate* it under that name."

He asserted that the king would not be perjured in so far as his Coronation Oath was concerned, if he were to grant his assent to the enfranchisement of the Roman Catholics. Burke did this by quoting the Oath and then analyzing it. His conclusion was that he could not find one word in the oath to preclude the king "from consenting to any arrangement which Parliament may make with regard to the civil privileges of any part of his subjects." [66]

Furthermore, the disabilities of the people of the Catholic persuasion were in opposition to Magna Charta because the Catholics were deprived of their liberties and "all their free customs." If anything were needed to make the acts against the Irish Catholics worse, it was the fact that they were applied against a people equal in number to the population of the entire kingdoms of Sardinia or Denmark and more numerous than the inhabitants of all the states of Switzerland. To his way of thinking, he could never believe it to be either politic or expedient to proscribe whole nations from the advantages of the government under which they were born.

In England, the Whig Revolution of 1688 had been that of the people against a small group which sought to oppress them. In Ireland, a smaller group was established at the cost of "the civil liberties and properties of the far greater part, and at the expense of the political liberties of the whole." What happened in Ireland was "not a revolution, but a conquest. . . . Time has, by degrees, in all other places and periods, blended and coalited the conquered with the conquerors" except in Ireland.

The Irish government would do well toward its fellow citizens if it emulated the example of the English in respect to Ireland. In 1782, Great Britain had granted legislative independence so unreservedly that the success of the Irish Revolution of 1782 could be likened to that of the Glorious Revolution in England in 1688, said

Burke. He asked if there were any less justice in the claims of the Irish Catholics in 1792 than there had been in those of the Irish Protestants in 1782 simply because the issue was now an intranational one rather than an international one.

If it were fear of the pope that restrained the Irish Protestants from giving their fellow citizens relief, then they could set it aside because His Holiness was merely "a commodious bugbear (who is of infinitely more use to those who pretend to fear than to those who love him)." [67]

The objection that the mass of the Irish was rebellious, disorderly, seditious, and easily duped by unscrupulous men and that, because of this, the conservative and wealthy element among them desired no share, either for themselves or the other Catholics, in the franchise, he now refuted.[68] Naturally, there was a distinction between the upper classes and the masses, he conceded. One should distinguish, however, between those who were "really indigent" and those who were "really intemperate." The Catholic better classes numbered many men of substance and means, nearly all of whom were family men. While such men could be intemperate, fortunately there were two norms of judgment which could be followed in this instance. The first was the worth of the object desired; the second was the means employed to obtain that end. The object sought was a return to the British Constitution. To obtain this desirable objective, they had resorted to the time-honored custom of employing a petition.

While Burke claimed that he did not find evidence that these Catholics of sobriety and judgment accepted the advances of the Dissenters to form a seditious alliance as was charged, it was, nevertheless, a fear of his that they would be tempted to do so. The Dissenters,[69] he observed, did not share the view of the Irish government that the Catholics were unworthy. On the contrary, they courted the Catholics with promises of "every thing." Their attitude was in sharp contrast with treatment accorded to the members of the old faith by "the thousands in Ireland who have never conversed with a Roman Catholic in their whole lives" unless they happened to talk with their workmen, footmen, or other lowly domestics, or to inquire their way if they chanced to be lost while pursuing some sport.

He warned emphatically that a union between the Catholics and Dissenters was quite possible. It should give pause for reflection, since two-thirds of the people of Ireland were Catholics, and the remaining one-third was divided between Dissenters and members of the Established Church. He questioned whether a combination of the Catholics and Dissenters could be successfully resisted.

Suppose that the Catholics were granted the franchise. There was no cause for alarm. One of the features of the constitution was that it looked to property for qualification in a county election, whereas in corporations "a restrained and strict education of seven years in some useful occupation" was requisite. In cases where the principle had been altered downward in practice, the obstacle could be met by increasing somewhat the qualifications of a Catholic voter. Even if they were placed on the same basis as the forty-shilling freeholders, he thought it would not alter a single election due to the condition of Ireland at that time and predicted that it would be a long while before any change would be felt.

Returning to the idea of an increased qualification, Burke saw it as the antithesis of the "great danger of our time, that of setting up numbers against property." On the contrary, this did not mean that the masses were to be neglected, since, in addition to what was due them as human beings, collectively they had great property. Consequently, they were entitled to protection, security, and consideration, but not to domination.

A concluding argument advanced was the reward Britain received in the continued loyalty of Catholic French Canada since the Roman Catholic Church had been established conjointly with the Church of England there. This gratifying spectacle of loyalty confounded the freely made predictions that the pope would reunite Canada with France. Ironically enough, he noted wryly, it had remained instead for all the Protestant colonies to revolt and join with Catholic France. Despite the fine record which they had made, the French Canadian Catholics were neither better men nor better citizens than the Catholic Irish.

The thoughts expressed in this letter were the same as Sir Hercules had known them to be back in 1761 and again as made public in a letter to Lord Kenmare in 1782. Time had served simply to strengthen these convictions of Burke's rather than to alter them, and "the present circumstances fix them deeper in my mind."

The letter to Langrishe was dated 3 January 1792. As late as 29 January, Burke was writing to Richard concerning the Langrishe letter. Caution was recommended on Richard's part with respect to circulating the letter — "omitting such parts as he may choose as applying particularly to himself. If made public it may be more generalised." [70]

In an undated letter in March from Burke to Richard, he points out that it had been published, so it would appear that publication took place sometime in February. Burke told Richard that "Byrne's Dublin publication of my letter to Sir Hercules Langrishe was so blundering as to vex me. He makes me say, and that at a critical point, the direct reverse of my sense. Debret [Burke's London publisher] brought it to me luckily before he printed it, and I corrected the worst parts. I see, in his second edition, he too has chosen to amend it into a blunder; but it is a blunder of not much importance. He printed a large edition of two thousand; what is next I know not. I hear it is well spoken of by the opposition here." [71]

Burke again refers to it in another letter to Richard dated 20 March. He asked Richard if he would like him to write anything else under his own name in the cause of Richard's clients and suggested that, if Richard thought it a good idea, he might write "perhaps a much sharper [letter] than what I wrote to Langrishe, and stronger, might be otherwise addressed. Here, the formless letter I have written to Langrishe has been of a good deal of service." [72] Then, later in the same letter, he blurts out suddenly "O! what a shocking way my letter to Langrishe is printed in! In Debret's edition I have corrected it."

Meanwhile, the Irish parliament was ready to consider the question of the Catholics. But before tracing the progress of the Catholic relief measure introduced on 25 January, a glimpse at what was transpiring behind the scenes in Ireland is indicated. It will be recalled that under date of 26 December 1791, Dundas had sent both an official despatch and a private letter on the subject of the Catholics to Westmorland, the Lord Lieutenant.

Almost immediately following the arrival of Hobart in Dublin with these communications, Westmorland wrote a strong but at times almost incoherent letter to Pitt saying that the dispatch ought to be recalled and claiming that the supporters of British government in Ireland, people like Fitzgibbon, the Chancellor, Beresford, the First Commissioner of Revenue, and others, would be sacrificed on behalf of Grattan and his friends if the recommendations of the British cabinet were to be carried out. In short, the burden of Westmorland's argument was that the Ascendancy was truly representative of Protestant opinion and was dedicated to backing the British government whereas Grattan and his friends could not be relied on and were, in fact, anti-British.[73] This, of course, was misrepresentation but effectively deceived the Pitt government as we shall see.

Westmorland put the proposals of the British cabinet before a meeting of the Irish Privy Council. With considerable reluctance they agreed to remove the restrictions which kept the Catholics from the practice of the law, from marriage with Protestants, and which placed such serious obstacles in the way of their education. But in the matters of a limited franchise and the right to bear arms and serve on juries, they were adamant in their refusal.[74]

In the face of this determined opposition from the Ascendancy, Pitt and Dundas backed down and only insisted that Westmorland refrain from telling the Catholics that the franchise would be permanently denied them. He was told to hold out the hope that concessions might ultimately be forthcoming should the Catholics continue to comport themselves circumspectly.

So the Ascendancy had once again triumphed, and the British government had allowed itself to take dictation from their own subordinate, the Lord Lieutenant, who had been in sympathy with Fitzgibbon, Beresford, and the rest of the enemies of the Catholics.

Against this background, Sir Hercules Langrishe sought permission from the Irish Commons on 25 January to introduce a bill for Catholic relief.[75] It was seconded by Hobart, the Irish Chief Secretary, and proposed granting to the Catholics the profession and practice of the law within prescribed limits; the right to intermarry with Protestants; the repeal of the educational restrictions; and, the removal of some restrictions on apprenticeships in trade.

Although it fell far short of the Catholic demands,[76] when the Langrishe measure was read for the first time in the House, on 4 February, it was strenuously opposed. The opposition to it was directed by Fitzgibbon and his henchmen, and their performance was shocking in the virulence of its anti-Catholic tone.

The Catholics took steps to defend themselves and on 18 February presented a petition to the House. Contrary to the opinion which has hitherto prevailed, it was not composed by young Burke. He later told his father that "it was drawn up not at all on my principles & as it was to be *entirely* submitted to the judgment of others, I interfer'd but little in the construction of it." [77]

The petition merely requested that the House consider whether the removal of some of the civil incapacities under which they labored and restoration to some share in the franchise would not tend to strengthen the Protestant state, improve industry, and bring protection and happiness to the Catholics.[78]

Two days later, following the Sunday recess, a motion that the petition be rejected was carried by the overwhelming vote of 208 to 25 which provoked Burke to write to his son that "since the beginning of time, so outrageous a proceeding . . . has not been heard of . . . monstrous, unheard of, shocking, profligate, and unparliamentary." [79]

Richard described the scene thus to his father:

> On the Monday the ministers rallyed & on la touche's [the Rt. Hon. David La Touche] & during [Sir] Boyle Roche's ridiculous insolence & ribaldry (& when the names to the petition were read), it is impossible to conceive the scoffs & shouts of the house; It was really more like an assembly of Yahoes. Then all the fiery protestants got up & unbottelled their nonesense; when they had exhausted themselves & after two or three just & grave lectures from the other side, they intirely changed their tone; It was at last 'our catholic brethren' & this idea of *perpetual* exclusion from the franchise, was generally exploded; tho' when ever any of them argued the point it was upon principles which go to perpetuity & with increasing strength.[80]

The Catholic Committee was quick to publish disavowals of certain obnoxious tenets ascribed to them by various critics in the House. This new address of the Catholics was backed by quotations from the works of members of the faculties of various foreign universities, such as Paris, Louvain, Salamanca, and Valladolid, in support of the contentions they made. The address categorically denied that the Catholics sought complete civic emancipation.[81] Burke was under the impression that it was Richard's work, but Dr. Hussey had named the men to him who had composed it. Burke liked it, nevertheless, and told Richard that it had made a favorable impression in England. He thought it ought to be circulated widely, and that Richard's clients should bear the expense. On the chance that they would, he went ahead and ordered a reprint in London which he estimated would cost about £10.[82]

The Langrishe bill now had a smoother path. 24 February, it went to Lords where it passed. In its final form, Catholics were allowed to practice law as either barristers or solicitors; they could marry Protestants; were empowered to open schools without the prior consent of the Protestant bishop; and could now send their children abroad to be educated with impunity (something which those who had the means had long been accustomed to doing). In other words, the bill, as it finally passed, coincided exactly with the concessions which the Irish Privy Council had agreed with Westmorland would be made in their meeting of approximately 15 January.

To Burke "this bill of Langrishe's is not only no relief, but it is mischievous and insolent, and ought to be declared against, in some way or other, very publicly, and rejected wholly, with decency, but firmness." [83]

Since the measure was so mild, the Catholics showed little gratitude and their political agitation continued unabated. They now felt more favorably disposed toward the Dissenters of Northern Ireland, a people visibly impressed by the French Revolution. The Belfast United Irishmen, a Protestant body, had gone so far during the debates on the Catholic question as to send in a petition to the Irish parliament recording themselves in favor of the repeal of all anti-Catholic laws. Their petition had received the same unceremonious treatment accorded to that of the Catholics on 20 February. As Richard said, "Our petition has had a companion in its misfortune; the Belfast petn. Dissenters & Caths. are turn'd a drift together — Thus hand in hand; but whether with wandering steps & *slow*, God knows. The marriage however is not yet made tho' every effort is made to couple the two parties." [84]

The London *Times*, in commenting favorably upon the actions of the Irish parliament, reflected the professed fear that, if the Catholics had been granted the franchise (even in the restricted form in which they sought it), the Protestant hierarchy and parliament would have been overturned.[85]

Burke was badly disappointed with the outcome. He had wished that the county franchise at least might have been given to the Catholics because he of all men was deeply aware of the serious state of affairs and was thoroughly convinced that the franchise was necessary to insure Ireland's tranquility at a time when the French menace was apt to grow more serious rather than less.

In addition to his letter to Langrishe, which had been published, he had expressed a willingness to write something "sharper" under his name for public consumption. He had advised Richard unstintingly during his mission, had secured the reprinting of the Catholics' respectful disavowal of the tenets ascribed to them by their enemies, and had done everything in his power in London to help the Catholic cause.

These efforts of his in England included an interview with Dundas to which the Home Secretary had asked him to bring a copy of his letter to Langrishe.[86] This interview, on 13 February, had been most unsatisfactory since Dundas "did not open a word of discourse about Ireland. I introduced it. He preserved a dead silence, and heard me like a man who wished an unpleasant conversation at an end. Nothing could be more completely cold, distant, and even repulsive to me, than the conduct and manner of ministers in this and in every other point." [87]

Some of the Catholic Committee now gave serious consideration to the idea of seeking the franchise on a basis of a £100 qualification. Burke had learned of this through a letter from John Keogh to Dr. Hussey. Despite his preference for property as opposed to numbers, Burke to his credit was shocked by the notion. He told Richard that "the £100 qualification is not a thing to be even whispered, but it would tend to make the world believe, what undoubtedly has no foundation in the mind of the proposer, — that, after all has been said, the committee are like Lord Kenmare and his friends, who look only to the accommodation of a few gentlemen, and leave the common people, who are the heart and strength of the cause of the Catholics, and are the great objects in all popular representation, completely in the lurch." [88]

Although the parliamentary aspects of the business were now

ended for the time being, Richard continued to stay on in Ireland until the end of April.[89] A letter to him from his friend Dr. Walker King, John King's brother, informed him that Dundas had remarked to his brother that his friend Mr. Burke "is playing the Devil in Ireland, I am sorry for it & wish he wd. come back." On other occasions Dundas repeated this sentiment to John King. Walker King also had heard that *at Lambeth House* [the Archbishop of Canterbury's official residence] *& other places letters had been* [received] *from Ireland in wch. you were represented some times as . . . wild & rash . . . at others as a factious & mischievous incendiary.*" Richard's friend doubted, however, if any of these inspired reports from Dublin Castle had been seen by His Majesty himself, but it was possible that some people might have taken the trouble to report these stories to the monarch. He ended on the note of optimism that perhaps he could get his brother to give them some leads on what Richard should do next.[90]

One result of the mildness of the Catholic Relief Act was that the Committee decided to drop Richard as their exclusive agent. At the end of March, John Keogh, as Secretary of the Committee, presented him with the handsome sum of two thousand guineas for his services. While he was not dismissed, he was given to understand that his work would be limited to representing the Catholic Committee in England.

Thus ended the first stage of Richard's work for the Catholics of Ireland. His mission had narrowly escaped a quick and disastrous end shortly after he had arrived in Ireland. He had impetuously dashed from the Visitors' Gallery into the body of the House in open violation of the rules. A cry of "a stranger in the House" and "custody! custody!" was loudly set up, but "by a timely retreat" he escaped arrest.[91] After that he was more careful. As he told his father,[92] "I constantly go to the house of Commons. The very day I seemed to be & in some measure, *was*, treated so roughly, all the people especially of the ministerial side, as they by passed me, for I stood at the door as they all came out, more properly did homage to me, than were civil (more of this) and so it is wherever I meet them. They reserve all their license for the house. — I am tolerably guarded in general. With the ministers I committed no indiscretion whatever more than the necessity of the business required."

There can be no doubt that the Catholic Committee was disappointed in Richard and perhaps would have given him his outright release except for the obligations they owed their best friend, his father. While this is not the place to attempt a judgment on Richard's work, it is clear from the fact of the two petitions' being drawn up without him that his clients felt that he had not lived up to their expectations. It is equally clear that Richard was up against a pretty solid wall of determined opposition to any substantial Catholic relief and that the most powerful elements in Ireland had made up their minds against conceding to the Catholic requests and had been able to make their decision prevail against the better judgment of the British cabinet. It is also patent that this opposition was not averse to using questionable methods to discredit both Richard and his cause. As he himself said, with ample justification, "every word I say is twisted into a thousand shapes & blown about the town. I might have been more cautious, if I had known my own importance. But, as they say, nothing is so easy as lying; so as well without as with facts. They have spit their venom."

CHAPTER VII

Partial Catholic Emancipation

RICHARD'S NEW POST IN ENGLAND

Relieved of his duties as the principal agent of the Catholics in Ireland and made their representative in England, Richard was not completely satisfied with this new arrangement and later made several efforts to regain what he frankly called his "lucrative agency." [1]

Before returning to England from his unsuccessful (although financially rewarding) mission, Richard had written to Dundas seeking an interview with him upon his return. Dundas assured him [2] that he did not feel unfavorably toward him and invited him to call upon his arrival in England.

While Richard was still in Ireland, his father wrote him [3] manifesting his strong feelings on the Catholic question. He said that there were few things he wished more than that the Established Churches of England and Ireland should be continued in positions of strength and security in both countries. "Much nearer" his heart than even this wish, he confessed to his son, was that "the emancipation of that great body of my original countrymen" should be achieved. He claimed that he had never been able to convince himself that there was anything in "our thirty-nine articles" which was worth making "three millions of people slaves, to secure its teachings at public expense." That man must be a strange Christian and a strange Englishman "who would not see Ireland a free, flourishing happy *Catholic* country, though not *one* Protestant existed in it, than an enslaved, beggared, insulted, degraded Catholic country, as it is, with some Protestants here and there scattered through it, for the purpose, not of instructing the people, but of rendering them miserable." Burke had spoken his innermost thoughts. Should this letter have fallen into other hands, there can be no doubt that it would have done incalculable harm to him.

Upon his return to England, Richard attended one of the king's levées at which George III took such "cognizance of my journey to ask me, if I was just come from Ireland." Dundas and Richard also met at the levée, and "we shook hands very cordially & seem to be very good friends. He tells me I am to send my declaration to him; that it ought regularly to have been transmitted thro' the Ld. Lieutenant, but, nevertheless he made no objection to deliver it. This he said on the supposition, before I explained it, of its being a petition." [4]

Richard was here referring to a plan of his that the Catholics should be allowed to lay their representations at the feet of the king without any intermediate channel and then to be allowed free and direct access to the king's English ministers. He reasoned that such a method would be far more satisfactory than to carry on the business of the Catholics by formal memorials transmitted back and forth across the water. Direct negotiations without the intervention of prejudiced middlemen was a method with many advantages to those most concerned, he argued.[5] When Dundas discovered Richard's purpose in wishing to see him, he proceeded to make himself unavailable despite his promise.

News from John Keogh [6] filled gaps in Richard's knowledge of developments since he had left Ireland. "Gog" was quite pessimistic on the whole but was pleased to report that the Kenmare wing of the Catholics was losing ground rapidly. At a recent meeting in Dublin between members of the Catholic Committee and the Kenmare group, the latter promised no further opposition to the efforts of the Committee to win emancipation. The two elements tentatively agreed to a petition to the king which Richard had drawn up prior to his departure, but the idea was subsequently jettisoned for the time being.

As for Richard's mission in England, Keogh said that it was understandable that the British ministers, especially Dundas, might refuse to see Richard as the agent for the Catholic Committee but surely he ought to have access to them as a personal friend and as the son of his "Illustrious Father" whose support the government needed "at this Great & Alarming Crisis." He was glad to perceive that Richard had "hopes in the Ministers" but he had reservations himself which led him to remark that the government "have no objection to have themselves profit up & the State itself Upheld by your Fathers Abilitys — but they do not Wish to render Successful the Sons honourable Agency for so great a Portion of his Majesties Faithful Subjects" or they would have found time to assure Richard that the Irish Catholics "should be Considered & Relieved next Session —."

Richard was then told that meetings had been held in Northern Ireland to raise funds to help the French, but that recent defeats suffered by the latter might disgust "our northerns" who "despise cowards." Keogh felt that there was a grave danger of the Catholics of Ireland revolting against the government and acting in concert with the French since "the wretch condemned for ever to a Dungeon, cannot be expected to be very squeamish about the mean's that would assure him freedom — & not the more so — if his confinement was Unjust."

Keogh returned to the theme of his doubts that much could be hoped from the English ministers particularly if "the wild Theory's of the French are destroyed, & Despotism restored — then the Iron Age may be renewed here." In that event, a Catholic petition would only be treated as in the past, but if Richard could succeed in his applications, the more he would merit. Personally, said Keogh, he felt that they would have to wait the African slave bill and the result of the impending war between Britain and France. Still he ended on a note of optimism by declaring that "Free, the Caths will be, the Seed is Sown, it has taken root — & will produce, abundantly. . . ."

Richard was trying desperately to get to see the ministers but, as Keogh had rightly suspected, it was not proving easy. Dundas told him on 16 May [7] that, for one thing, Richard was very much mistaken if he thought that Dundas was listening to any person who was maligning him. Richard suspected Major Hobart, the Irish Chief Secretary, who had come over to England on business, but Dundas swore that neither Richard nor the Catholics of Ireland had occupied their conversation for as much as five minutes since Hobart came to England.

He then became very blunt and told Richard that "I can further assure you that I am much more minutely informed of the misunderstanding which has taken place between you and the Government of Ireland by your own accounts than by any I have received from any other quarter."

Again he was blunt and to the point:

Having stated this to you so explicitly I am under the Necessity of being equally explicit to acknowledge that I have shown a very great shyness in holding the Conversation with you which you have so earnestly solicited, but my doing so has proceeded from no personal disregard to you. I must continue to do so, otherwise I should be guilty of a flagrant Breach of official Fidelity. It is impossible for me to enter into a separate discussion with you whether the determination of His Majestys Servants is right or wrong, but their firm determination is not to hold communication with any descriptions of Roman Catholicks of Ireland except through the Government of Ireland, and after I have stated this in so direct and explicit a Manner as I have done, you cannot surely wish to press upon me a Conversation in which I cannot possibly take any part. It cannot be an agreeable one to you, and I can assure you with great truth that it would be more unpleasant to me. I wish on every occasion to mark my regard and attention to you, and I feel it rather hard that you should urge me to a Conversation in which it is impossible for me to give you any Proofs of that disposition.

On the same day that Dundas was making himself so painfully clear, Richard got off a letter to his "uncle" Will in India that indicated that he still had hopes.[8] He told Will that "you of course desire to know something of my own history which has indeed begun to be a little more eventful & I am come forward on the stage. Whether it [is] to be only the show & promise of a day, or whether I am to continue a public actor, is even yet problematical. My first on test has been singular enough & very boisterous; I have had a tolerable seasoning; but on the whole, I have given a good impression of me, & closed the first period of my labors with great felicity."

While Richard was thus indulging in self-praise, understatement, and boundless optimism, his "people" in Ireland were growing exercised at his failure to show any tangible results since his return to England. An entry in the diary of Wolfe Tone, his successor as agent for the Catholic Committee, reveals that the

THE RIGHT HON.^{BLE} EDMUND BURKE.

CINCINNATUS in Retirement.

Falsely supposed to represent Jesuit-Pad'driven back to his native Potatoes, on Smugling common Wealth.

Pub.d Aug.st 1782, by W.m Humphrey, S.t James's Street.

Committee was angry with Richard for "never communicating a syllable of information whilst acting as agent in England." [9] Since Tone was quite prejudiced against Richard, this need not be taken too literally. But Mr. Edward Byrne of the Committee wrote him [10] to say that they were "sorry" and "disappointed" at his inability to see either Pitt or Dundas since his return. Furthermore, they were upset that he was unable to give them "some decisive Intelligence how far the English ministry were willing to go in relieving us from our distressed situation, or whether they were willing to go any lengths at all." The Catholics felt that Irish affairs would have been deemed important in England at that particular time and that, as a consequence, the ministers would have eagerly looked forward to discussing them with Richard. If any difficulties had been thrown in Richard's way of meeting with the ministers, Byrne and his associates sincerely hoped that they had been removed. Richard was told finally that it was their "request" that he have an interview with Pitt and Dundas concerning their affairs "without delay." Not only was he to do this but, said Byrne, "I am also directed to request that you will acquaint us as soon as possible with the result of your Interview with the Brittish Ministers."

Byrne's letter, like Keogh's before it, clearly revealed that the Committee had hopes that Richard could discuss their case in "conversation with Mr. Pitt and Mr. Dundas" and convince the ministers of the reasonableness and modesty of their requests. As Byrne put it, "We only ask for a share in the Elective Franchise and an equal participation in the benefits of the Tryal by Jury."

Poor Richard! On the one side, Dundas would not hold any conversations with him because the government had taken the position that all communications on the subject should be with the Irish government; on the other, his Irish clients were convinced that in England lay their only hope of success. They urged upon Richard the necessity of his getting together with Pitt and Dundas to make them conscious of the moderate demands of the Catholics. Once the English were so informed, the Catholics believed, there would be nothing to it since a word from England would force the Irish government to concede the desired grants.

Thus spurred on by the Irish, Richard continued his efforts to hold talks with members of the cabinet. He wrote to the Foreign

Secretary, Lord Grenville, on 2 June [11] of the desirability of direct contact between the king's Irish Catholic subjects and the monarch himself, followed by free and unrestricted conversations between the Irish Catholic representatives and the English ministers without the intervention of the Irish government.

His overtures seemed at last to promise success, because Dundas wrote to him on 20 July [12] to say that he had not forgotten the appointment he had agreed to make with Richard. Before, however, resuming "the conversation which was interrupted" (by some six months), Dundas said that he thought it proper to mention the matter to Pitt. He had not had an opportunity to talk with Pitt for several days but expected to see him the following week and would tell him about the appointment which he was making for Richard.

On the same date as Dundas' note, Richard wrote the Home Secretary an extremely long letter in which he reviewed the history of his agency on behalf of the "People of Ireland" and then requested an immediate interview with the king for a committee of his clients. [13]

While awaiting a reply from Dundas, he heard from Keogh [14] that Belfast was overwhelmingly in favor of immediate admittance of the Catholics to the franchise. There was only one bad spot in Northern Ireland. In the adjoining towns of Castlewellan and Rathfriland the lower element among the Protestants was armed and was killing and mistreating Catholics. Unless these activities stopped, Catholic retaliation was inevitable. Meanwhile, the Catholic Committee was working in conjunction with a number of Protestant gentlemen, including several Presbyterian clergymen, to put an end to the violence. Keogh concluded by reminding Richard that the hopes of the Catholics lay in the petition to the king.

When over a week had passed and no news had come from Dundas, Burke lamented to his son that "our day of any weight with Ministers is completely over." [15]

At last came word from Dundas [16] acknowledging receipt of Richard's formal request of 20 July which had stressed the urgency of an immediate interview with the king. Dundas reneged on the promised appointment and reverted once again to plain talk.

Richard had been told last winter before going to Ireland very explicitly by both Pitt and Dundas that the English ministers would not enter into any discussions with the Catholics of Ireland which did not pass through the Irish government. This was still the case, and Dundas was reduced therefore "to the necessity of declining the honour of an interview with you, on any business, you as Agent to the Catholics of Ireland, are desirous of transacting with me in that capacity."

Dundas was curt in signing off: "Having stated this to you, I shall forbear making any observations on your letter."

Since it was at last plain to Richard that Dundas meant what he said, there was only one alternative left. That was to go back to Ireland. The ostensible reason that he gave out for his trip was his own private affairs. But the London *Times* said that the impression created in London by his trip was that he had gone "to resume his office of Agent for the Roman Catholics of Ireland." [17] His successor as agent for the Catholics, Wolfe Tone, snorted out contemptuously "private fiddlesticks!" The reason was plain. Richard wished to earn "another 2000 guineas." [18]

In a letter to his father written while en route to Ireland,[19] Richard told him that he and Earl Fitzwilliam had talked over the Irish situation a good deal lately and that Fitzwilliam shared his views on the matter. Richard had suggested to His Lordship that he was the ideal man to go to Ireland as Lord Lieutenant, a suggestion toward which Fitzwilliam seemed well disposed.

Richard arrived in Dublin early on the morning of 3 September [20] and was to stop at Frank Kiernan's "during my short stay here." [21] Although he had just arrived, he had sized up the situation or so he told his parents. It looked to him as if the stupidity of the government was pushing the country toward a civil war, which the government was bound to lose.

Richard found conditions had changed during his absence. For one thing, the young Protestant barrister, Wolfe Tone, was handling the work which had formerly been his. Although the Catholics had not known it at the time of his selection, Tone was destined to become as rabid a proponent of the doctrines of the French Revolution as Burke and his son were opponents. Tone's goal was a revolutionary movement in which the Catholics together with the Dissenters would overthrow the Protestant Ascendancy in Ireland. His selection by the Catholics indicated that they were becoming increasingly influenced by bolder thinking and contrasted with their choice of young Burke, which had been partly out of a desire to clear themselves of any suspected connection with either the forces or principles of the French Revolution.

Moreover, the Catholic body had undergone a reorganization. There had been added to the Catholic Committee, as it existed minus the aristocratic Kenmare wing, two men representing each county and borough of Ireland. These men were required to be residents of the districts which elected them and were summoned to Dublin whenever needed. These popularly elected representatives formed the General Committee. The original members of the old Catholic Committee, who were left following the withdrawal of the Kenmare faction, comprised a permanent subcommittee. The democratic system followed in electing the members of the General Committee was ineffectively denounced as illegal by their enemies in Ireland.[22]

Letters of advice from his father began to reach Richard shortly after his arrival. In the first, he asked God's blessing on Richard's efforts and cautioned him to be neither too timid nor too rash.[23] He and his wife had gone to Bath to enable Mrs. Burke to recuperate from an illness.[24]

The theme of Burke's letters to his son was, of course, the Catholics of Ireland. At the outset, Burke pointed out to Richard the futility of the Catholics' blaming England for their plight. It was his considered opinion that the various British governments had ever entertained but one desire relative to Ireland, that "they should hear of it and its concerns as little as possible." [25] The source of Ireland's troubles lay in the country itself. The blame belonged squarely at the feet of "that junto of robbers," the Protestant Ascendancy. This conviction was one which he had held since his early days and never changed. As he later told Richard, the Irish believed that the conduct of the Lord Lieutenant was the result of directions from the British government. He exclaimed sadly that he wished the latter could even be made to think seriously about Ireland. Ever since he could remember, it had been a case of the "junto" in Ireland governing the Lord Lieutenant who, in turn, by his representations governed the British ministers. Thus, "the whole evil has always originated, and still does originate, among ourselves." [26]

Despite Burke's strong opinions to the contrary, the view most generally held by the Irish Catholics at that time and for generations afterwards was that England was chiefly to blame for their plight.[27] I do not think that the observation that the verdict of history has shown Burke to have been right needs to be labored,[28] yet the tragedy of the situation is that the British statesmen unquestionably could have overruled the Ascendency had they so desired. It is in their passivity and willingness to drift that they must assume their share of the blame.

A feeling which he was destined later to modify [29] was expressed by Burke in some of these letters of this period. This was his request that the Irish Catholics refrain from the use of force. He declared that, as a man of "some reflection and much experience," he knew that "the resources of a persevering, litigious, dissatisfied obedience" were greater than those of any force, "even if force they had." [30]

Following his departure from Bath for London on 27 September, Burke wrote to Richard after his arrival.[31] He called for a general cessation of all public and private animosities at this critical juncture of affairs and recommended that the royal family should be reconciled within itself, the opposition with the government, and the Catholics and Protestants of Ireland with one another. The last was indeed the most requisite reconciliation of all.

Things were going so badly that he was convinced that "folly alone cannot wholly ruin an established empire. Cunning must come to its aid." Among the schemes of "this sure and natural ally of absurdity" was the rumor that the Irish government planned to bribe the Catholic clergy by giving them some share "in the establishment of the Church, and letting them into a partnership in the odium attendant upon tithes." As Richard had correctly remarked, this would be "the destruction of all religion whatsoever; and when that is destroyed, nothing can be saved, or is worth saving." Instead of being a piece of "mere substantive ecclesiastical and civil arrangement" whereby "the ecclesiastical estate was put on a more reasonable and durable basis" which would be "wise," this scheme was "a part of the plan of low cunning" whereby the government hoped to divide the clergy from the laity.

But it was doomed because the people would never take this "bribe" to the clergy as a substitute for their just demands. "A clergy known to be creatures of the Castle, and, in a manner avowedly bribed for the purpose of enslaving their flocks, (the bribe, too, taken out of the bowels of their own poor,) this clergy would lose, and that, in the twinkling of an eye, the little remains of influence which they yet retain."

He then remarked that "Gentlemen who call themselves Protestants, (I do not well know what that word means, and nobody would or could inform me,) are dupes of their own calumnious representations, which serve to mislead them, and irritate those against whom they are made." Such men, in order to make the Catholics contemptible, always represented them as incapable of forming any ideas, opinions, or even wishes of their own and claimed that their bodies and souls were "at the entire disposal of their priests."

Not so Burke. He knew the Irish Catholics better than the Ascendancy. Most of them had never conversed with Catholics and were "more ignorant of the real state of their own country than that of Japan." In Burke's considered view, the Catholic clergy never had "a great deal of influence" over their people as long as he could remember. Things were different in ages past when the clergy was composed of the "first and most accredited nobility" of Ireland. Now they have "rather less" influence than any clergy Burke could name.

He then proceeded to repeat almost verbatim what he had had to say to Richard on the subject of the "prescript form to which the Church of Rome binds its clergy" in a letter he had written Richard almost a year ago.[32]

Should the clergy, already thus restricted by the church, be "bribed" by the Irish government, none of the laity would "attend on the ministry of one of these corrupt and silly creatures." With his fondness for puns, he said that the people would call them the "*Castleick* clergy."

The members of the Irish parliament were "poor creatures"

who paradoxically were rendered impotent by their ability, and misled and blinded by their very experience. They were shop-keepers, hucksters, and dealers in retail who were "infinitely expert in the mode of gaining individuals, and at contriving with the greatest waste of the human faculties, to obtain the concurrence of others to make a further waste of them. But, for want of ever dealing in the great, they do not know, that, though multitudes may be deluded, they never can be bribed. Their leaders may be bought once, — perhaps twice, but never more. The third time they will not be worth the bribe."

This is the mistake of the "hucksters of ascendancy." The question is not one of dealing with a credulous mob, as Burke and Richard both knew, "soon inflamed, soon extinguished." Rather did "the igneous fluid" have "its lodgings in a solid mass." Among the Catholics were persons of "deep thought, keen sagacity, and sound understanding; and those not a few." In fact, there was "a succession of them" so that "if one is bought off, twenty will come on."

In conclusion, Burke told Richard that he was impressed in reading the reports of the proceedings of the last meeting of the Catholic General Committee in Dublin. While he did not subscribe to "every word in them, no more than to what I hear in parliamentary debates, where I approve the main matter," he felt constrained to say that in no parliamentary discussion had he ever heard a topic handled better. In fact, he doubted with characteristic exaggeration whether "man's faculties can go beyond it." The Ascendancy was deluded if they thought that "such men can be cheated by their poor little transparent threads."

Richard brought his father up to date on developments in a letter dated only September 1792.[33] He told Burke that he was rather glad on the whole for his latest "excursion" to Ireland because it gave him a better insight into things. He had discovered that "the democratical principles" had been gaining some ground among his Irish Catholic friends and he traced the advance of these ideas to the "extreme irritation of the measures pursuing by government here, & the total deriliction of this country by that of England." The people were growing desperate and saw no hope in anything but "popular causes." Richard was not disturbed, though, since he felt that the "present tendency to speculators & speculation" was only the result of "peevishness." The Catholics, he thought, "might easily be brought back."

One unfortunate development, however, was the tendency of some members of the General Committee to consider Richard "with a little jealousy, as to[o] much attach'd to the cause of that government by which they are so ill treated."

But this was not too serious a thing. Of greater concern was Richard's feeling that the Irish government seemed bent on forcing matters with the Catholics to an issue. "God knows what all this will come to; I much fear it will grow into a strange complication before the English ministers think of any remedy, & when they do, it will probably be some strange patchwork."

Despite his general tone of pessimism, Richard concluded optimistically enough that "the cause looks tolerably well," a theme which his father adopted in a letter of 1 October. Richard's clients were certain to achieve success ultimately if they kept themselves firmly on "the solid ground of the British constitution" [34] and did not allow "any mistaken theorists" to delude them into adopting the principles of the French. If this happened, they would not only fail but would be covered with shame as well.[35]

The elder Burke confided to Fitzwilliam a few days later that he was affected by the state of Ireland yet was "sure that my Ideas on that subject are also right."[36]

While on a visit to Cork, Richard wrote to his father [37] and told him "I heartily approve of all you say relative to our affairs. . . . I cannot help again being agreeably struck & pleased with the similarity of our thoughts on this subject, which goes even to expression & words." He thought that there was time enough "to think more what is to be done" when he returned to Dublin. The situation in Cork was very encouraging, and his stay had been longer than intended so well were things going. "There are engagements & invitations without end. I thought it not amiss, in a little policy, to receive the honors here, partly in your name, partly in my own. . . . I believe I shall have the freedom of the Corporation." (While the latter did not materialize, Cork treated Richard extremely well).

After some further explanation of his actions and ideas, Richard then told his father that "Democracy in this country has made more ground than I should wish; not much, comparatively speaking, among the Catholics; And *more* amongst the *Protestants that oppose them*, than those who are their friends." The people of Belfast have so interested themselves in the Catholic cause that Richard was "sure" that on this account they "might be brought off & wean'd from their extravagances." The more was this likely since, when Richard was in Belfast last year, he "made an evident progress among them, in favour of our opinions & I find in them still a great apparent disposition to listen to me on that subject."

His next stopping off place was Killarney, from which he wrote [38] his father that Lord Kenmare "the great man of this place, I understand after great deliberation, determin'd to shew us no civility. In truth he is a poor little creature, tho as men are mix'd characters, his stile of proceeding in the management & decoration of his estate, is cleaver." The news which Richard had from Dublin in his absence was not inspiring. He feared that "my friends there are playing tricks, tho rather I imagine, by the instigation of the little politicians, than of their own motion. Their revolutionist friends are sticking hard for their own principles against ours, & I much fear they make ground." The "government here, except for the purpose of raising & directing an outcry against the Cath's, has hardly an existence. The royal authority hangs upon a thread; It is in a manner forgot that there is such a thing as a King, all parties laboring might & main, to confine every thing to the little sphere of Irish politics & Irish factions — Alas What trifles I trouble myself with."

Answering Richard's letter of 10 October from Cork, Burke wrote from Bath.[39] Although France occupied most of his attention in the letter, Burke felt glad that their opinions on Ireland coincided, especially in the idea of a royal petition by the Catholics. He longed to talk with Richard face to face about Ireland, but it was better that the son should remain where he was for the time being.

Richard's letter from Killarney, whose water and mountains were as "noble" as their owner, Lord Kenmare, was "shabby," was answered next.[40] Burke expressed the hope that Richard's clients were not "so weak as to imagine that you or I are playing any politic game with regard to them. We have no connexion of interest with either ministry or opposition here; and I think you have shown that you do not mean to pay court to the ministry in Ireland at their expense."

Another letter to Richard [41] suggested that Richard's clients turn their energies toward improving their reputation in England where their enemies were constantly undermining them. Burke had heard reports in England that the Irish Catholics were making large importations of arms. He even met some of the people who were circulating these false tales. He did what he had done on a similar occasion in 1769 and offered to pay a guinea for every piece of serviceable firearms to be found in the province of Munster if the person who was circulating the rumors would pay Burke five hundred guineas if he could not find ten. He had chosen Munster for this purpose, he said, because it was the most Catholic part of Ireland he could recall.

Also while in Bath, he had had three conversations with the Protestant Primate of Ireland, Lord Rokeby, who had told him that everyone he met coming from Ireland said that the Catholics there were universally engaged in arming and preparing for revolution. Burke talked to the primate at length with the freedom he had long enjoyed in his company and spoke "sometimes a little warmly, sometimes ludicrously; sometimes very gravely and temperately." The result was that they "parted in some mutual ill-humour."

Returning to Richard's clients, he urged that they use "a still, discontented, passive obedience. In that mode, I assure them, there is ten thousand times more force than a giddy unsupported resistance." The thing to do was still the same — petition the king!

Writing to Burke from London en route home to Ireland,[42] the Roman Catholic bishop of Cork, Dr. Moylan,[43] whose company Burke had just enjoyed at great length in Bath assured him that on his arrival in Ireland he would attend to what Burke recommended and would try to convince his people that their hopes lay in following moderate advice. Moylan concluded "I trust in God They'll not be induced to deviate from the line of Conduct which so Sincere a friend to their Cause has been pleased to point out for them."

Richard again told his father [44] how happy he was that he continued to write him such full letters, "particularly on our Irish affairs." He said that in the main his father's ideas coincided exactly with his own except that they were "more ample abundant & correct, rather what I wish mine to be than what they are." Nevertheless, it was satisfying to have his father confirm his opinions.

The "new revolutionary principles" of the French Revolution were "the only great evil," and Richard had many battles with his friends on the subject. Some of them, he feared, could not be made to separate their cause from that of the French. If this sort of thing continued, it would end in the ruin of either the Catholic cause or of Ireland itself. "However, the Govt. might bring it all back with a whistle." But for his part he despaired of it. He had exhausted argument with his Catholic friends. He believed he could do anything with the bulk of the Catholics

but if I was to bring these french principles to an issue, It would make a scism, which the adversary would avail himself of; & it would only make a new complication in the politics of the country, which are already more intricate than enough; I should despair of unravelling them, if I had not seen the contexture of the whole from the beginning. Nothing is to be done in the face of a treacherous & hostile government, except to counteract & expose it. In this I think I am safe. In the midst of some vexations, I have moments of singular satisfaction & merriment. I have the pleasure of knowing that the enemy is fretting his guts to fiddle strings, & that he is quite at his wits End.

He then described for his father a conversation between Sir Hercules Langrishe, Major Hobart, and the Catholic Archbishop of Dublin, Dr. Troy. The two former gentlemen bitterly castigated the conduct of Richard whom they supposedly claimed had been sent to Ireland "to throw the country into confusion; to complicate the politics of it & to maltreat the Govt. I have not yet learnt the precise expression; but it was something like 'to whip 'em in.' " They accused him of much "mischief." When Richard's name came up, Sir Hercules interrupted Hobart and attempted to make "a panegyric" on Edmund Burke and to lament that he could not say anything favorable of Richard. This did not annoy Richard in the least as he already knew "our friend to be the greatest rogue in the kingdom."

When Hobart asked Troy what the Catholics meant to do, the prelate replied that they intended to petition the king, a procedure which both Hobart and Langrishe declared was the worst possible thing they could do. They said it would ruin the Catholic cause. Did not Troy know that the British government would receive no communications except through the Lord Lieutenant?

Richard then told his father that the idea of a royal petition "frightens & puzzles" the Ascendancy "beyond measure," and consequently things look better — "In short the tide is on the turn."

Richard next told [45] a friend of his father's, William Cusack Smith, an eminent Irish lawyer and member of the Irish Commons, in what he himself called a "long letter" that he was conscious that the part he was playing in Ireland must appear "ambiguous" and might perhaps actually be so "as is the nature of all arduous duties." He said that he had come into Ireland "to maintain the cause of its established government in Church and State; and have uniformly done so, according to my rooted conviction of their essential interest." But unfortunately he was treated with the greatest hostility by the government and held aloof by the Church whose members were suspicious of him.

Ireland was a strange land where those who erred most strongly on the side of speculation were right in point of practice; and those who, at least in theory, would be expected to battle for the constitution had become "enemies to the application of its most acknowledged principles."

Since Richard had always thought that "the only remedy against the rage of untried speculation was in the ancient principles of our mixed constitution," he was convinced that those who most strongly opposed the "extension and communication" of those principles were its "most dangerous enemies."

On 3 December 1792, the General Committee of the Roman Catholics of Ireland assembled in Dublin and drew up a petition which respectfully asked that they be given a share "in the advantages of the Constitution." [46] Speaking of this petition, which he knew had been previously determined, Dr. Hussey told Burke [47] that his correspondents in Ireland assured him that the Catholics would not resort to force but in his opinion some steps ought to be taken to prevent the threatened union between the Catholics and the Dissenters. He was sure this union would materialize if the Catholic "petition is treated [with] contumelious contempt, which I fear will be their case."

Meanwhile, Richard returned to London early in December. It appears to have been made plain to him by Keogh and the other Catholic leaders that they were satisfied with Wolfe Tone as their agent in Ireland [48] but that it was their desire that Richard continue to represent them in England. From a personal viewpoint, his return trip to Ireland was not without pleasant memories. Perhaps the high point was his reception in Cork at both Protestant and Catholic hands. Among other pleasing memories of Cork was the reception tendered him on 16 October at the Bush Tavern by the leading bankers and merchants who wished to "evince the very high sense they hold of the very great and effectual exertions of the Right Honourable EDMUND BURKE, to serve the Trade of this kingdom."[49]

LIMITED SUCCESS

The meeting of the General Committee was in reality a congress or national assembly of Catholics owing to the representative system which they had adopted. It testified amply both to their determination and that of their Protestant sympathizers to demonstrate unmistakably that they constituted a force with which to reckon. Their vigor and virility contrasted markedly with the habitually timid attitude shown by both the Catholic hierarchy and aristocracy in the past. Largely through the efforts of John Keogh, the Archbishop of Dublin was persuaded to be a delegate, and in consequence many of the old Kenmare faction came into the fold.

The Catholics elected by ballot a five-man committee to present a petition of grievances to the king in person. The viceroy, Westmorland, was greatly piqued by this move which bypassed Dublin Castle. The petition listed their grievances and requested relief in a respectful manner.[50] In resorting to this step, the Catholics had adopted the recommendation of Richard Burke and his father, both of whom had long urged such a move.

An indication that the Catholic convention had made an impression may be found in a letter from a member of the Established Church in Ireland, Sir Robert Staples, to the Earl of Upper Ossory, an English absentee holder of large Irish estates. Upper Ossory considered the letter such a true picture of the state of Ireland that he sent it to Burke on the supposition and in the hope that Pitt's government communicated with him upon the subject of Ireland.[51]

Sir Robert alluded at the outset to the Catholic meeting and said that the delegates had conducted themselves "cooly and moderately," adding that the Irish government had unsuccessfully endeavored to create a division among the Catholics. He then called attention to the fact that in Ireland, as well as in England and Scotland, there was a party of "a levelling disposition." In his opinion the Catholics were not of that "disposition"; if anything they were the reverse. The Catholics merely complained of their grievances, whereas the "levellers who style themselves 'the United Irishmen' " were anxious to throw everything into confusion. If the Catholics could be satisfied, it would then be an easy matter to deal with the United Irishmen. But if reasonable concessions were not made to the Catholics, a union with the "levellers" was inevitable. The result of such a merger would be a general rebellion. Such a prospect frightened Staples whose holdings were small in comparison with Upper Ossory's but nonetheless dear. Necessity and not inclination led Staples to recommend that the grievances of the Catholics be redressed, and he took pains to make it clear that he himself was not "a papist." Staples' letter is indicative of the change of opinion which was taking place among thoughtful people who foresaw the prospect of a sanguinary revolution.

Meanwhile, the Catholic delegation prepared to go to England. Four days before their arrival, Burke delivered a speech on their behalf in the House of Commons, 14 December.[52] He recommended acquiescence in their just demands and maintained that to grant them a share in the franchise was not an innovation, since they had been oppressively deprived of many of their rights at the outset of the last reign.

The Catholic delegation arrived in London on 18 December.[53] While awaiting them and following their arrival, Dundas was bombarded with memorials, statements, and letters from Richard

Burke.[54] If these were not enough to keep Dundas occupied, Edmund himself took up the slack and wrote an essay to the Home Secretary on the state of Ireland.[55] After having told Dundas that the Ascendancy was composed of masters of "the great staple trade, never carried to its full perfection but in Ireland, — the whole art and mystery of jobbing," Burke turned to the Catholics and their desire to secure the franchise, "not as a matter of speculative right, not upon general principles of liberty, or as a conclusion from any given premise, either of natural or even of constitutional right" but as "a protection, and a requisite security" which they lacked for the exercise of legal right. They needed it for the free enjoyment of their property and industry, for a fair dispensation of criminal and civil justice, and to secure to themselves "that just estimation and importance, without which, in human tribunals, they cannot obtain."

Their inability to vote had produced dire consequences daily. They were turned out of good farms; deprived of their maintenance and that of their families; denied honest occupations; and prevented from the exercise of their industry and capital. In many cases they could not even secure leases: under no circumstances could they obtain them "on equal terms." Their exclusion from the franchise operated against their interest "wherever there is room for competition, or room for favour." Where the election spirit ran high, as in Ireland, it touched more or less every transaction of life.

The Catholics were moderate in their demands and had stressed again and again that they sought only " a *small* participation." They insisted that no longer should they be looked upon as dangerous to the government and refused to submit to the idea that they could be considered as objects of suspicion, apprehension, and jealousy on any grounds whatsoever. Such an idea was "the root and baneful cause of their former persecutions, and all their present disqualifications." They were modest in their demands both to show their willingness to make a sacrifice and as "a public-spirited prudence and compliance with the impracticable nature of inveterate evils." The Catholics also believed that it was in the Protestant interest as well as their own that the distinction between Roman Catholic and Protestant should never again be taken up as "the denomination of adverse parties in the state."

Following a historical sketch of persecutions against Catholics in Ireland, Burke reverted to a favorite argument, namely, that the Catholics did not seek an innovation. In fact, he said, they had not only voted for members of parliament in Ireland but also sat as members themselves for a longer period than they had been deprived of these privileges.[56] They even formerly had a majority in both houses but were unable despite it to prevent their "Protestant brethren from dispossessing them of every civil and every political right."

Their restoration to the voting privilege would strengthen the state, since "a greater number of persons will be interested in conservation." In contrast to "the reformers" who ask a "new right of election, and that the whole constitution of representation should be new cast," the Catholics merely desired that the time-honored right should be ratified, confirmed, and extended to a new class of citizens.

Furthermore, "if the experience of mankind is to be credited, a seasonable extension of rights is the best expedient for the conservation of them. Every right, every privilege, every immunity, every distinction known in the world, and which has been preserved throughout the fluctuations of time and circumstance, has been so preserved."

To the legislator it makes all the difference in the world whether it is a new right which is given or merely the capacity to enjoy an old one. The first was "very dangerous"; the latter "extremely safe." In the first instance, "we are all at sea", whereas in the other all the effects, tendencies, and abuses have been long foreseen and, if not provided for, at least could be dealt with since their nature was known.

The wants of the Roman Catholics were real unlike those which grow out of speculation. To satisfy them at this time was especially important because of the threat to the established order of things by those who "embrace the doctrines of the day." It is no secret that other men who embraced these doctrines were anxious to link together with the Catholics. "The Dissenters are roaring it with a thousand mouths."

Moreover, those who know what is going on in Ireland know that things have changed. The old system was not designed to endure forever since "oppression at length exhausts its own re-sources; the miserable pretexts of avarice, bigotry, and party spirit, wear themselves out; the fashion of the time changes; and the great mass of a nation at last recovers something of its natural im-portance. The very reaction of a destructive policy produces a power of resistance."

The "circumstances of the time" strengthen the Catholic in-terest and make it decisive. The Catholics were not responsible for the division which arose among the Protestants and did not seek to take undue advantage of it. But they would be less than human if they did not remind government repeatedly of the changed cir-cumstances in Ireland. The Catholics harbored no seditious or re-bellious designs, and it would be a mistake to think so. The govern-ment would do well to consider what steps should be taken to admit these three million subjects who sought admission to the state.

Make no mistake about their manner of address. It could be understood as contradictory, because they are trying to prove that they are strong enough to be redressed but not powerful enough to be dangerous. This could be interpreted to mean that they are so weak as to be ignored with impunity or, on the other hand, so strong that the least increase whatsoever would enable them to over-run Ireland. As in all things, there is a middle ground here, too. It is entirely possible that they are strong enough to be heeded and yet not strong enough to overthrow the state. Heed their respectful pleas, which they are urging at "one favourable moment to alle-viate the oppressions of a century."

It is important always to remember that whereas the Roman Catholics in England were merely a sect, in Ireland they are a nation. This basic distinction "must affect every reason, and every measure concerning them." They do not claim that the concession of the franchise to them will leave the state unchanged. Of course, what they seek is a change, one which is vital to their situation. But this change will be modest, since the voting share of each indi-vidual Catholic would be "only in the proportion of one to sixty", so heavily weighted is the Protestant franchise. " 'Nine tailors make a man,' " and it will not be thought unreasonable that sixty Catholics should make a Protestant." The grant of the relief sought by the Catholics simply would not bring them a real acquisition of political power.

Since this is so, why do they contend for the franchise? Would they then rest content if they secured it? Burke felt that there was reason to believe that they would, at least for a while. Sometime, of course, they will ask for more since "it would be a mockery, an imposture, on their part, and a mischievous error of government, if they pretended that such a portion was sufficient to answer, to the Roman Catholics, all the just ends of representation, according to the joint relation of their numbers and their property, real and personal. But it is sufficient to satisfy them of the protection of government, of the cessation of the exclusive system, and a security for the continuance and gradual extension of a system of union."

The Catholics are satisfied to keep their request modest because they wish, first of all, to demonstrate that their admission into the political system of their country would not be productive of any danger; secondly, to show that by the temperate use of their franchise they are entitled to a more generous share in the state; and thirdly, to show that the fears of their emancipation are groundless.

But by this manner of proceeding, they will move from point to point until they possess dominion over the whole state. Eventually, there would be "a Popish Church, and Popish State, and then there is the end of it; and thus the basket of rotten eggs becomes a foundation for the subversion of an empire." Admittedly, "benefits may beget ingratitude; friendship, hostility; and freedom, usurpation. True, but this is not the point *now*. The evil with regard to the Roman Catholic interest is, the 'too little,' not the 'too much.' When that is the complaint, we will think of the remedy. By practising the prudence of today, we shall be more likely to practise that of to-morrow. He that knows how to concede with wisdom, may also know how to resist with spirit. But that will never be necessary. It is the fault of government, if the Roman Catholic people and persuasion are not incorporated and lost with the Protestants in one State, and even in one Church."

He concluded by quoting the articles of the Treaty of Limerick [57] by which the Catholics finally submitted to the government of William of Orange. In his conclusion, Burke premised two things: (1) that the Catholics sought to be restored to a *"qualified part of one privilege"*; and (2) that *"all"* the laws of personal disqualification against Catholics and *"all"* the penal statutes against them had been passed since William's reign.

This paper was, on the whole, closely reasoned and impressive with the significant exception of where he attempted to deal with the argument that if the Catholics won the franchise they would eventually control Ireland. Here he was not very convincing, and Dundas, if he took the trouble to read this "requisition", as Burke called it, must have been startled to learn that it would be government's fault if the Catholic people and persuasion "are not incorporated and lost with the Protestants in one State, and even in one Church." This kind of reasoning was not conducive to persuading the opponents of concessions to heed the petitions.

At any rate, Richard Burke, Jr. paved the way for the Catholic delegation to secure an audience with the king. Richard had a private interview with Pitt on Christmas Day,[58] and on 2 January 1793, the Catholics were presented to George III by the Rt. Hon. Henry Dundas, the Home Secretary.[59]

The interviews were crowned by success, and the newspapers carried the information that the British cabinet had decided that the Irish Catholics should be admitted to the franchise without further delay. As *The Times* put it,[60] such a step was "highly expedient", since the Catholics were worthy of every indulgence that could be safely granted. Admittance to parliament, however, was "a measure of very dubious policy", but the grant of a share in the franchise would strengthen England's influence over three million imperial citizens while at the same time weakening the attraction of French ideas for them.

How had this surprising *volte face* occurred? There can be little doubt that the unrelenting campaign waged by the Burkes had finally borne fruit. As early as November 1791, Pitt had informed Westmorland in Ireland that the British would assist the Irish government in resisting any efforts by the Catholics or others to overthrow the government by force but that the British certainly would not aid the Irish Protestants to perpetuate the Catholic exclusion from the franchise. He then went on to say that "I fairly own that in the present state of the world I think such a system cannot ultimately succeed." [61] In the interval between this letter and the Catholic delegation's royal audience, nothing happened to change Pitt's conviction that the Catholics deserved better. His willingness to convince the king of the necessity of receiving the delegates bore ample testimony to this determination.

In February, the Irish parliament began the business of conceding relief to the Catholics which Downing Street had dictated. Burke thereupon proposed to Dundas that a draft of a letter which he had composed on the subject of the Catholics [62] should be forwarded by the Home Secretary to the Irish viceroy, Westmorland. Dundas, however, refused, since the British government did not wish to exacerbate matters vis-à-vis the Ascendancy any further than could be helped.

Burke's letter raised many questions for Westmorland to answer. He asked, for example, if it were fear of a Catholic parliament which kept the Catholics disenfranchised.[63] He also wished to know how the Catholics could be called enemies to the British Constitution, since they merely sought to partake of its benefits.[64]

The reasons for Dundas' refusal to communicate this letter to Westmorland are patent. In each instance, the answer to the question propounded by Burke favored the Catholics and discredited the Irish government. To forward such a damaging and embarrassing letter through the channels of the British cabinet would only exacerbate relations with the Ascendancy.

Burke's feelings toward the Ascendancy have earlier been made clear, nor had they changed as a letter to Richard early in 1793 revealed.[65] This body which controlled Ireland had been named the "Ascendancy" with the result that "honestum nomen imponitur vitio." [67] The sense in which the term had formerly been used was "to signify an influence obtained over the minds of some other persons by love and reverence, or by superior management and dexterity." In its present sense, he found it to be more than "parce detortum." [68] He then defined what he understood by the term ascendancy to which was prefixed the word Protestant.[69] It was:

a liberal distribution of places and pensions, and other graces of government . . . . wide indeed of the significance of the word. New *ascendancy* is the old *mastership*. It is neither more nor less than the resolution of one set of people in Ireland to consider themselves as the sole citizens of the commonwealth, and to keep a dominion over the rest by reducing them to an absolute slavery under a military power, and thus fortified in their power, to divide the public estate . . . as a military booty, solely amongst themselves.

    . . . . I cannot conceive what mode of oppression in civil life, or what mode of religious persecution, may not come within the methods of preserving an *ascendency* . . . it signifies *pride and dominion* on the one part of the relation, and on the other *subserviency and contempt*, and it signifies nothing else.

The fact that the term was qualified by Protestant did not make it any better, because it meant here the name of "a persecuting faction." This persecution was negative, since the persecutors had no positive doctrines of their own. These men could not define what they meant by the word Protestant. All that could be said was that it was not the Christian religion professed by the Roman Catholic Church and those holding communion with it, the majority of Christians. Since this was so, the Irish persecutors were "ten times worse" than any the world had ever seen. The old persecutors, "whether Pagan or Christian, whether Arian or Orthodox, whether Catholics, Anglicans, or Calvinists," were, or at least made a pretense of being, "strong dogmatists."

As proof that the persecution of the Irish Catholics was not on behalf of the Established Church, Burke cited the fact that the Irish statutes did not require conformity as a condition on the part of a Catholic seeking relief. On the contrary, a Catholic who gave up his religion could profess any system of "folly, or impiety, or blasphemy, or atheism" and still enjoy complete civil freedom. Consequently, Burke held that "this Protestant persecution" was one of religion itself not merely the Catholics. He warned that if ever the Established Church and the British Constitution should fall, which would be together and not separately, it would be "the new fanatical religion, now in the heat of its first ferment, of the Rights of Man, which rejects all ecclesiastical, and in truth all civil order, which will triumph in Ireland and in England, as it triumphed in France." Against such a contingency all churches had a common interest, which was to defend themselves.

At the end of his letter, he pointed out that the persecutors of the Irish Catholics professed to see in any protest against the collection of tithes for the support of the Established Church a treasonable conspiracy with foreign powers aimed at the destruction of that institution. The Catholics could not commit any offense without having their enemies attribute it to zeal for their religion. This caused Burke to lament: "Alas! It is not about popes but about potatoes, that the minds of this unhappy people are agitated." [70] He demanded that punishment for offenses should be fitted to the nature of the crime. Two centuries of "experiment" had shown that the government could not make the vast majority of the people Protestants. On the other hand, the people had been demonstrably unable to throw off a Protestant government. This being so, would the reality of the situation be accepted and the best made of it?

Following the visit of the Irish Catholic delegation to England, the British government instructed the Irish Lord Lieutenant to insert a clause which recommended concessions to the Catholics into the Speech from the Throne formally opening the Irish parliament in January 1793. Pitt's government was now keenly aware of the offer made by the new French Republic to aid all oppressed peoples desiring to overthrow their rulers. Moreover, it appeared likely that Britain would soon become involved in the war on the continent. The wisdom of strengthening her position in Ireland by improving the lot of the Catholics, as Burke had so long advocated for this reason among others, was at last abundantly clear.

It is interesting to note that the relief which the British government now insisted must be given the Irish Catholics went far beyond the proposal of the previous year in the matter of the franchise and that the Irish administration had now to concede so much more than they had only so recently prevented. That it was very humiliating and that they bitterly resented being forced may be seen from the language of Fitzgibbon and the other members of the Ascendancy.

In February, the Catholic Relief Bill was introduced in the Irish Commons. It passed both chambers and became law on 9 April as the 33d Geo. III, c.21. The Catholics were given both the parliamentary and municipal franchises, the right to sit on grand juries and to become magistrates, to hold army and navy commissions, and to obtain university degrees. Catholics were still excluded from parliament due to the unfortunate defeat, by a vote of 163–69, of an amendment granting them that privilege,[71] from the higher offices of the Irish government, and from some "20,000 functions or offices of power and emolument." [72] The qualification to carry arms was raised from the proposed figure of £100 to £300.

In return for these privileges a Catholic would be required to take an oath which (a) abjured the principle that a heretic could be murdered or injured (b) declared that wrong is not exonerated by being done for the good of the Church (c) denied it to be an article of faith that the pope was infallible, and (d) promised not to disturb the established religion.

Henry Grattan, leader of the opposition and a friend of Burke's, told Richard that he had "reason to applaud your own conduct and enterprise, and to deride those inhospitable and bigoted attacks which, in the former year [1792], were directed against your cause and your exertions. I don't think England can call Ireland Boeotia, nor yet a land of slaves, while the name of your family exists in the success of its labours, or the fruits of its genius." [73] Grattan also told Burke himself that his son "has had a triumph. He stood the friend of the Catholic in both countries, when it appeared fruitless in the one and formidable in the other." [74]

The delighted Burke expressed his conviction to Grattan that the remaining restrictions on the Catholics would be removed before long and said that he felt Richard was deserving of commendation for the part he had played in aiding the Catholics.[75] In indulging in praise of his son, Burke was to some extent justified. Richard, however, had acted largely throughout his mission as his father's mouthpiece. It was no accident that their opinions had so exactly coincided. It was here that his services were really useful, since he kept persistently hammering home the point that it was wisdom to concede to the Catholics in the face of the dire consequences attending a union of Catholics and Dissenters, which the latter were openly advocating. Then, too, the Burke connections had actually been the means of the Catholic delegation's royal audience. The very idea of petitioning the king, which finally brought success, had been urged all along by the Burkes.

Richard's weaknesses in his role of agent for the Catholics had not been inconsiderable. Among them were his conceit, arrogance, and lack of tact. These combined with his predilection for "long, prancing" letters (as Wolfe Tone called them) had done much to mitigate his effectiveness. Yet it must not be forgotten that the obstacles in his path were formidable. For his perseverance he deserves some praise.[76]

The Act for Catholic Relief was received with great satisfaction on the part of the Catholic lower classes throughout Ireland, and numerous "illuminations" took place all over the country.[77] The upper classes were disappointed over the denial of seats in parliament,[78] even though they had not sought them at this time. It was the defeat of an amendment for this purpose which hurt their feelings. They disliked also their ineligibility for various posts such as Privy Councillors, Staff Generals, University Fellows, and King's Councillors. By granting the franchise to the Catholics everywhere on the same basis with Protestants, the Catholic common man was given an equality with his Protestant counterpart which was denied the Catholic landowners, scholars, barristers, etc. Their exclusion from parliament and from numerous privileges granted to many Protestants whose attainments were inferior to theirs signified, in effect, that they were not yet considered the equals of Protestants. This dissatisfaction was natural enough, but, when one considers the modesty of their requests, it is not so easy to appreciate.

Lord Westmorland, the viceroy, in reporting on the reaction of the Catholics to the measure deliberately misinformed the Pitt government by claiming that the Catholics were satisfied as well as grateful and that Ireland was in a tranquil state. As Grattan rightly pointed out, what gratitude the Catholics did feel was directed to the king whom they considered their benefactor, not the Irish government.

Meanwhile, the French had declared war on Great Britain, and the British had retaliated. The Irish parliament was firm in support of the Pitt government in this crisis, but the feeling outdoors was different. The condition of the country was not at all easy, especially among the Dissenters in northern Ireland.

CHAPTER VIII

The Projected Irish Viceroyship of Fitzwilliam

Later in the year 1793, the Irish authorities began drafting a militia after ordering the Volunteers suppressed in March. The militia draft was so violently resisted throughout the entire country by Catholics and Protestants alike that the government was forced to change the system. Every encouragement was then employed to obtain voluntary enlistments. One device was to provide a degree of security for the families of militiamen. Others were the offer of bounties by the wealthy in the counties and permission to use substitutes in cases where this could be done. Thus, the ranks were filled, but riots and disturbances grew rather than diminished.

3 October, Burke took notice of the situation in a letter to John Coxe Hippisley, an Englishman then residing in Rome.[1] After advocating formal diplomatic relations with the Papal States and praising the character of the reigning pontiff very highly, Burke turned to the subject of Ireland. He said that he was sorry but not surprised to learn that Hippisley had been informed that the Irish Catholics were already in revolt or that they were so disposed. On the contrary, said Burke, he knew of no description of men in either England or Ireland who were more firmly attached to the king's person and authority than these same Irish Catholics who had been falsely represented as either in revolt or on the verge of it.[2] Only persons who were either inconsiderate or malicious would depict the Catholics in such a light.

Burke added that it was likewise unfair to accuse the Catholic hierarchy and clergy of being remiss in their duty through what he called an alleged failure to preach loyalty to the king and obedience to the laws. He himself spoke from knowledge.[3] Far from being deficient in these respects, they had gone beyond their strict duty. The result had been harmful to them because it weakened their influence. Many Catholics accused their clergy of being more concerned over support of the government than they were attentive to the grievances of their people. Not a single clergyman of the Catholic religion had even been charged with encouragement of the militia riots, far less with having participated in them. As a matter of fact, some priests had been injured in their persons and property during the tumults because they sought to exercise a restraining influence. Their places of worship had been closed by the mobs in some parishes.

Burke declared that the militia riots, while greater than anyone would wish them to have been, had been greatly exaggerated out of malevolence. Whatever the extent or violence of the disturbances, the truth of the matter was that these tumults had no connection with either religion or politics. Their origin was traceable to the establishment of the militia in such a way that it bore heavily upon the poor. Parliament had recognized this and had amended the act. One reason for the discontent had been a misconception of the intention of the Irish legislature in forming this body.[4] Burke recalled that the very same thing had happened in England when a militia was formed there. The riots had been just as widespread as those in Ireland. He then observed that, whenever the popular mind is inflamed on any one subject, it is customary to remember all other sources of irritation and to blend them with the original cause of discontent. In Ireland, the complaints were purely of a local and an economic nature.

He reiterated his declaration that the Catholic clergy was entirely innocent of any connection with the affair and added that the less they meddled with it the better anyway. He then decried the attempt on the part of some of Hippisley's Irish correspondents to induce him to bring the matter to the attention of the pope in order that a reprimand might be given to the Catholics of Ireland by the pontiff. Should this be done, the very ones who had suggested it, said Burke, would then attack the Catholic clergy on the grounds of introducing a foreign authority into Ireland. It was nothing but a trap to ensnare the Catholics.

It was true, Burke admitted, that the recent disturbances were caused chiefly by Catholics. This had been the case for the past fifty years. The reason, however, for this was simply that the disorders were the work of the common people. In this class of Ireland's inhabitants, the Catholics outnumbered the Protestants nineteen to one. This disproportion had been produced by the constant but unjust operation of the laws of Ireland aimed against the Catholics for almost two centuries. He told Hippisley that this was a circumstance which was unhappily not generally known in England, thereby giving unscrupulous men an opportunity of "attributing to the religion what belongs to the condition."

In this letter, Burke gave utterance to many of his confirmed convictions on the Catholic situation in Ireland. For one thing, the Catholics, especially the churchmen, were firmly attached to the monarchy. Secondly, there was always an unfair tendency to exaggerate the participation of the Catholics in popular demonstrations without mentioning at the same time that among the lower classes the Catholics formed an overwhelming majority. Thirdly, the tendency to ascribe falsely to the Catholics the motive of zeal for their religion as the cause of their involvement in disorders was abhorrent to him. He always asserted that the motivating force was economic. Fourthly, his propensity for attacking as a palpable falsehood the charge that the Irish Catholics were in league with foreign powers was again evidenced.

Between the fall of 1793 and the summer of 1794, Irish affairs did not occupy Burke's thoughts to much of an extent.[5] In one of his few letters on the subject, he replied to a communication from Sylvester Douglas, who had succeeded Hobart as Irish Chief Secretary when the latter was made Governor of Madras in late 1793. Douglas had written to Burke under date of 30 December 1793, and in his reply [6] Burke undertook to put him on his mettle against the wiles of the Ascendancy.

After having remarked that "the natural taste of my countrymen" was "not bad," Burke went on to say that

But now Ireland is seperated not only in its Legislature, but in its administration, too. England and Ireland, The King, the Lords & the

Commons are absorbed into one Click. . . . All I shall venture to suggest is that you will be a little slow in learning the Ton or rather the Brogue of that Click. Ireland is too considerable now for that kind of Government. Ireland is in danger of being Jacobinized. The Click seem to have but one way of preventing it; that is by doubling every cause of complaint in proportion to the cry well or ill founded of Grievance.

The "Click," to Burke's way of thinking, had a knack for forcing people to rebel by always acting towards them as if they were actually in revolt.

This last part of the System is a trade carried on in Ireland, for six hundred years and of course a long experience has made them very perfect in it. When they continue matters so as to prevent Ireland from doing any thing for the general cause of the Empire, and when it is made evident, that more cannot be done without ruin to that people, they make a merit to themselves, that though of little service, it is at least preserved from rebellion, and in some sort of peaceable connexion, by their endeavours.

They represent themselves as the only men loyal to the crown in order to prevail upon the crown to turn over its powers to them "without a possibility of revocation." Burke's son "who reads things with an eye sufficiently acute" concurred with him in his interpretation.

Such was the country to which Douglas was going, but in other respects he would find it very attractive. He was sure to be well treated by the "Click" who would be very gracious to him. These "Irish politicians [were] chearful, companionable & Hospitable" and "the shrewdest set of people in the world." Douglas would do well, however, not to take it for granted that all who were not "in love" with the Ascendancy were enemies to the cause of "order and government."

Finally, Burke would not be supposed to know how to talk to an Irish minister if he said "nothing of a wish for my friends there. Alas! I have survived most of those whom I loved. There are however two or three whom I wish to be of use to. I shall hereafter give you the trouble of having them presented to you. Dont be frightened. their pretensions will be very moderate, as their situation is; . . ."

Writing to an unknown person early in the new year,[7] Burke revealed that he was then in the grip of despair and was afraid that French principles had already made inroads among the common people of Ireland:

There is still a God, & that is a consolation. Nothing human looks favourable on any side or in any point of View. I am sure we ought to try every resource — though my hopes from the Catholicks of Ireland is faint & dull indeed. There are few Gentlemen amongst them — the expatriated Irish are perfect strangers to them, their names, habits, & ways of thinking; & if they were to *attempt* an influence there (a vain attempt) it would alarm all the Protestants, & they would be instantly expelled — as to the Clergy, I am very sorry to say it, their influence is as nothing or not very much — The common people have no warm zeal for their religion, as you seem to imagine. Nothing would animate them less than the Idea of a Crusade. The enlisting service amongst them is as high as it is amongst any other. The fact is there are in the Naval & Military Service already probably near as many as the spare hands of that Country amounts to. Their number is exceedingly great. However I am sure every thing is to be tried. I am far from certain however that the Catholicks of Ireland are not in many places somewhat Jacobinized. I should write more but from the dejection I am in. But please God I shall recover [from] it.

Although six months were to elapse before there is another extant piece dealing with Ireland, we find that Burke's mood was still pretty much the same:[8]

As to the great scale of Politics in Ireland I cannot think that they have any idea of a change in it; at least of any that is substantial & beneficial. If I understand the matter, the great grievance of the Catholics is that they are treated as a sort of public Enemies; and that persons are supposed to hold their situating upon the principle of their disposition to treat the great body of their Countrymen as such Enemies. As long as that principle is held up it is absolutely impossible that any scheme of equalization in nominal privilege should ever quiet the Country. It seems to me always as if I had a vast deal to talk to you on these subjects.

He then made the first reference to the possibility that Lord Fitzwilliam might go to Ireland as the viceroy that had been made since Richard had discussed the idea with Fitzwilliam himself just before Richard made his initial trip to Ireland in the interests of his Catholic clients in 1792. Burke said that he did not know whether Fitzwilliam would be sent to Ireland but that it was his "clear opinion that Ireland cannot be settled without him." His protracted despair again showed itself as he concluded:

. . . and God knows whether the extravagant courses taken by our friends in Ireland would leave him [Fitzwilliam] Master of his Measures, or these Gentlemen even Masters of their own. Every thing is running to some desperate extremity & Military Govt. & despotism is only to be cured by popular Phrenzy.

What Burke had reference to in the above letter was the critical state in which Ireland continued. The "levelling tendencies" of the French were making such progress that a toast reputedly popular in many circles at the time was: "The British Army, and may the French never overtake them!" [9]

Then, in the summer of 1794, an event took place which was destined to produce most unfortunate consequences in Ireland. Burke's friends among the Whigs, headed by the Duke of Portland, joined Pitt in a coalition government.[10] Burke, the prime sponsor of the move, was present when they kissed the king's hands on 11 July. In the new arrangement, which "faced the Government with Portland stone," [11] the Duke was made Secretary of State for the Home Department in the room of Dundas now Secretary for War and the Colonies; Earl Spencer became Lord Privy Seal; Earl Fitzwilliam took the portfolio of President of the Council; and William Windham was made Secretary at War.[12] It was a union to which the birth of the Conservative Party in England has been traced.[13] The Portland Whigs in uniting with Pitt understood that Ireland was to be left open for changes as soon as possible, one of which was that the position of the Catholics should be improved, but it was agreed that nothing was to be done until Pitt had found a suitable post for Westmorland, the Irish viceroy. Portland himself had manifested interest in returning to Ireland as Lord Lieutenant [14] but yielded to friends who pointed out that the position was subordinate to the Home Secretary. Because he wished the post filled by someone close to him, he endeavored to prevail upon Fitzwilliam to take it. The latter, however, declined owing to domestic reasons but changed his mind a few weeks later and formally accepted in August.

In the meantime, the long parliamentary career of Edmund Burke had drawn to a close. The last day on which he appeared in the House was 20 June at which time the managers of the Hastings case received the Thanks of the House.[15] True to his word, he wrote to Fitzwilliam the following day [16] that he was applying for the Chiltern Hundreds, as he had pledged himself to do the instant the Hastings business was concluded. He told Fitzwilliam that "There cannot be a moment more favourable for my Retreat than the present. At any Rate, a Situation of struggle & contention is not very decorous for one at my time of Life & I ought to get off before the little powers of Mind & body that I possess have quite forsaken me."

Fitzwilliam accepted Burke's decision in a letter of the 24th [17] and wrote again the following day to say that "the House of Commons has now lost not only its brightest ornament, but what is more essential, the source of its greatest wisdom." [18]

He then proceeded to make both Burke and his son ecstatically happy by offering his father's vacated seat at Malton to Richard. In his acceptance,[19] Richard said that "I should be unworthy of your good opinion if I took more time to deliberate on my acceptance than you have in making the offer" and assured him that he "could never differ from your Lordship without sincere sorrow & much diffidence of my own sentiments, And I feel at least as much pleasure in the concurrence of our opinion as in the consequences of that concurrence with regard to myself." He referred to the fact that the difference of opinion, which Richard had stressed earlier in making an unsuccessful application for the Higham Ferrers seat controlled by Fitzwilliam, had now been reconciled. This difference had been over the continued support of Fox by both Fitzwilliam and Portland in disregard of Edmund Burke's insistence that he and not Fox represented true Whiggism.[20]

Burke's own letter of gratitude followed Richard's the next day: [21]

Just as I was proposing to give your Lordship my poor & very inadequate thanks for your great goodness to my Son — (by far the greatest favour which could possibly be conferred on me) I had an accumulation of your kindness to acknowledge upon my part in the handsomest & most friendly letter than ever man received. During the Course of my long service I have had many things to trouble & to mortifye me. But it has pleased God to mingle in my Cup such consolations as no man ever had in the same degree before me. Steady, affectionate, & generous friends — & of such wisdom & Liberality as disposed them to pardon those many faults & imperfections, of which their oblivion ought only to render me the more sensible. I was most deeply affected with the Letter I received this morning. It went much to my heart. How long I shall live to enjoy the satisfaction of that Letter I know not. But it will be a precious record in my family. My son has been too good a Son to be much known in the world. He has devoted himself to his Mother & to me — but we know him for the same reason, that neither his wealth or his Talents are so conspicuous to others: This I can say, & without a Tincture of parental Partiality, that in him you will find your Borough more than supplied for my Loss — & that neither you, nor I, nor the publick will ever have reason to be ashamed of him. God knows, he is coming, under your auspices, into publick Life at a time that calls for all the resources that the human Mind is capable of furnishing, & when nothing of Talents, honour, energy, or influence ought to be suffered to lie idle. In my opinion your Lordship yourself are called upon strongly to come forward — & to come forward into that situation in which the abilities & virtues that God has plentifully bestowed upon you may be the most effectually serviceable.

There was a brief delay in moving for the Writ for Malton which led the *Morning Chronicle* to wonder whether or not it had been determined to give "the author of our war, his *sauf conduit* to Beaconsfield." [22] *The Times*, however, predicted correctly that the son would succeed the father and later verified its forecast.[23]

Burke and Richard went up to Fitzwilliam's magnificent home, Wentworth Woodhouse, for a few days at the beginning of July preparatory to Richard's being presented to the electors of Malton which was duly done. His election was verified, and Burke's cup at this moment was at its fullest. Richard, his pride and joy, had succeeded him in the House of Commons, his friends had at last returned to government, and he himself was to be rewarded with a pension and a peerage for which he had already chosen the name of Lord Beaconsfield. Furthermore, Fitzwilliam had offered to make Richard his Chief Secretary [24] whenever he should go over to Ireland to replace Westmorland as viceroy. The delighted father joyously predicted a distinguished career of great service in Ireland for Richard.

Then tragedy struck and dashed all of Burke's hopes at one blow. Richard had fallen victim to the ravages of consumption, a

London Pub.d Nov.r 15 1790 by Wm Holland No 50 Oxford Street.

It is undoubtedly true, though it may seem paradoxical; but in general, those who are habitually employed in finding and displaying
faults, are unqualified for the work of reformation: because their minds are not only unfurnished with patterns of the fair and good, but
by habit they come to take no delight in the contemplation of those things. By having vices too much, they come to love men too little.
It is therefore not wonderful, that they should be indisposed and unable to serve them. From hence arises the complexional disposition
of some of your guides to pull every thing in pieces. — Burke on the French Revolution. Page 250.

An Irishman.

fact which had been kept from his father's knowledge until one week before his untimely death on 2 August,[25] just ten days after his election to parliament.

Although Burke survived this sad blow for a few years, his grief was almost unendurable [26] and he was never the same man. When the serious danger to his son's life had become known to him, he wrote dejectedly to French Laurence that whether he was to have "any objects" in life depended entirely upon Richard's recovery.[27]

Fitzwilliam wrote him a beautiful letter of condolence on 4 August, and Burke roused himself from the depths of his grief to say that he knew that Fitzwilliam did not expect a reply from him in his present condition but that it was something which he felt he could and knew he ought to do. It is a letter [28] which reveals Burke's deep religious nature, but it is also one which shows him stricken with remorse, as much almost as with grief, for what he felt was his neglect of his son who had devoted himself to trying to keep his father's hopelessly tangled financial affairs from utter chaos and ruin. It was this burdensome task which Burke felt had kept Richard from ever marrying. While it is a very long letter, it deserves to be quoted at some length.

After telling Fitzwilliam that his letter "affects me to the very bottom of my soul," he went on to say:

You have touched the true point of comfort — that, for the little time I live, I ought to wish to resemble him that I have lost, & that I flatter myself might live a long time, & live, under your patronage, an ornament & a benefit to the world. His fortitude was indeed a true & glorious part of his Character — I trust in God he is now in a place where that virtue is useless. If I considered his loss as a mere act of the common providence of God — I think I should instantly profit of your advice, & not suffer my heart to be torn to pieces as it is at present, not by grief but by remorse. I have not husbanded the treasure that was in my hands. I squandered it away in a manner, that when I look back, I can scarcely conceive. I threw him away by every species of neglect & mismanagement — & what did I throw away in this frantick manner? It was not a pious Son, though he carried piety to me & his Mother to a fault — to her — only to what was right — to me — to a species of Idolatry — But it was only in submission & piety he shewed himself a Son — It was a noble, generous, & Heroic friendship he shewed to me: This was among the causes of his being so little known to the world.

But it is known to God; & will by him be rewarded, whilst I am left to the just punishment of a fruitless repentance.

My Dear Lord — you put him, with all the Nobleness & generosity that belongs to you — into the way of turning his wonderful Qualities & dispositions, to the great advantage of this Nation, — perhaps of many nations. He was pleased with his Election. You gave him a glimmering of public hope before his Death. Thank [sic] thank you — thank you — for that one short happy day to us both. . . . As for me, for whom you express much generous sollicitude, I am told by my Wife, that my living is necessary to her existence. I rather think so — & I owe much to a Woman, Whose equal is rarely found, & to the Mother of a Son that never had an equal. I use therefore every art & contrivance I can think of, to bear up against this calamity, & against the sore reproaching feelings of my own Mind. I am told by some wise & good friends — that I ought to endeavour the prolongation of my being here, to suffer firmly whatever providence may have yet to impose for my ultimate good. Otherwise I had & have a serious Doubt, whether it is of good example to the world that I should conquer the just feelings that God & nature have implanted in me, & which indulged, would soon place me in the grave of my dearest Son & impanelled friend. I feel this Doubt — But I give way to the better thoughts of others — who think there may be something in the world, ordained by God, that I should do or suffer — & this I will submit to; & will, I hope, by his Grace, adore his justice for such a space as he pleases to give me, in a life of privacy humiliation, & penitence. Again & again my best thanks for the best & kindest Letter that was ever written. It is of great consolation to me. . . . If any thing could console us, we have great consolation. adieu! & may you be happy — & may I learn to be patiently & submissively miserable. Your unhappy but most faithful, affectionate & grateful friend.

Later in a public pamphlet defending his pension against the attacks of the Duke of Bedford and the Earl of Lauderdale, he told Fitzwilliam that: "The storm has gone over me; and I lie like one of those old oaks which the late hurricane has scattered about me. I am stripped of all my honors, I am torn up by the roots, and lie prostrate on the earth. There, and prostrate there, I most unfeignedly recognize the Divine justice, and in some degree submit to it." [29]

During the three years of life which remained to him, Burke shut himself up almost completely at Beaconsfield, going rarely to Bath, for his health, or to London, when the trip could not be avoided. For the first two years, he and his wife refrained from dining outside of their own home. Of course, there was considerable speculation on his behavior. It was rumored that he was demented and had to stay in the country as a consequence. One story had him walking about Gregories kissing the animals on the grounds. Investigation proved that on one occasion a horse which Richard had loved came up to him and nuzzled him affectionately which caused Burke to throw his arms around the animal and burst into uncontrollable weeping.

If any single thing, other than his grief and remorse and his unrelenting anti-Jacobin crusade, served to occupy Burke's mind for the time of life remaining to him, it was that of final Catholic emancipation in Ireland. In the last letter made public during his lifetime, he told the person to whom it was addressed that it was true that his late son was very much concerned over the conclusion of "a business [Catholic emancipation] which he also had pursued for a long time with infinite zeal, and no small degree of success." Only a half an hour before he expired, Richard had spoken "with considerable earnestness on this very subject." This fact alone, were any inspiration needed, would call forth Burke's greatest energies in an effort to free "the body of my country from the grievances under which they labour." [30]

A letter to his close friend and protégé, French Laurence, was in this same vein. Very few of the objects on his dying son's mind had been left unaccomplished with the exception of "the deliverance of the Job ascendency" from power. This had almost been accomplished but "Providence, for reasons above our wisdom, has suffered this great affair to be snatched out of the hands that alone seemed made for it." [31]

Burke was determined to do everything in his power to accomplish the emancipation of the Catholics from the remaining restrictions binding them. In the light of both the needs of the empire and his own love for the Catholic cause, there can be little doubt that he would have exerted himself on their behalf anyway since it was a cause to which he had devoted so many years, but Richard's death fixed his purpose so resolutely that in time it became almost an obsession with him.

Less than two weeks after his son's passing, Burke wrote Windham denying that he was to become Provost of Trinity

College, Dublin, his alma mater. It was a position that reputedly was worth £10,000 per annum.[32] A persistent rumor, which had originated in Ireland that he planned such a step had come to his ears and had even reached the London press.[33] Denying that he was even remotely interested, he told Windham that it was advisable that the post be given to a clergyman of the Established Church.[34] He followed up this letter two days later with another to Windham which was devoted largely to the same subject.[35] Having shaken off his grief long enough to take cognizance of this rumor, Burke returned to his mood of sorrow, and shortly he was writing to Walker King that he was "really unfit for Business." [36]

His financial prospects were considerably brighter, however, and for this he was thankful. On 31 August he informed Fitzwilliam [37] that he had just heard from Pitt that it was the king's intention to grant him an annuity of £1200 chargeable to the Civil List and that His Majesty further intended to propose a really suitable grant at the next session of parliament. Writing to Walker King on the same day,[38] he mentioned that he had sent Pitt a letter of grateful acknowledgment [39] and then remarked sorrowfully: "Oh! my dear dear friend, how many pangs attend this satisfaction! That he for whom I lived, did not live to see this, & to dispose of money so justly his. Oh pray for my pardon." While waiting for the arrangements to take shape, Burke was forced to borrow £3000 as this letter makes clear.

There now began his letters to Fitzwilliam on the subject of the latter's projected Irish viceroyship. In the first of them,[40] Burke told him that he had his best prayers for success and also assured him that his "best Ideas on that subject are at your Service." Before Fitzwilliam's departure, Burke offered to come into London to hold "half an hours conversation" with him on Ireland. He warned Fitzwilliam that much would depend on those whom he had about him. Fitzwilliam must trust himself because "little of enlargement or manly policy will you find in Ireland; But a narrow subtlity in the greatest plenty & perfection." One of his first difficulties would be the University. Burke then blurted out "For Gods sake suffer the Law & natural succession to be your guides & not the Jobbs acquired by dispensations, for the utter disgrace & destruction of Religion, morals, & Learning. Believe me, your honour in that

Government, & in whatever you undertake, cannot be dearer to your own generous soul, than it is to the afflicted breast of your miserable friend."

This was followed a little later by another letter [41] in which Burke reassured Fitzwilliam that he was right to undertake the post and "yet I feel an anxious awe about it." Everything was at a critical stage, and Ireland was not the least critical part of the empire. Fitzwilliam was going to a "Town terribly provoked by the last Tenants." He hoped that the British government would leave "as much as possible of the open Patronage undisposed of; that you may have some stock in hand at your arrival; & it might not be amiss, that, in some decorous manner, they should be given to understand, that they ought to be cautious in giving promises, as it might not be for the Kings service the successor should think himself bound to fulfil their Engagements. If something of this sort is not done, you may find every thing that is not given away mortgaged." He ended by noting that Grattan was shortly coming over to London, a fact that pleased Burke because Fitzwilliam would find him of the utmost assistance both "in digestion & execution."

Burke next wrote to the Duke of Portland [42] to give him the benefit of his advice on how the two positions held by the recently deceased Hely Hutchinson should be filled. These were the Provostship of the University and the post of Secretary of State. Burke argued that the first should not be considered as patronage but should go rather to someone already at the University and said that there were three or four Senior Fellows who were outstanding men, anyone of whom would do. Grattan agreed with Burke that the Provost should be "a statuteable academical character." [43] The other position was most definitely patronage. As a sinecure, it might be given for life or as long as the government wished, although Burke said that in his opinion "infinite Caution ought to be used in giving any thing in Ireland for Life." He expressed the hope that Portland would not allow Westmorland to "jobb it out of the hands of his Successor." If great care were not exercised, Fitzwilliam would find himself "invested on every side. English Government (if they are suffered to go on there, as they have gone on) will not be left even the miserable shadow of authority which it now seems to possess." He concluded "I am as a dead man; & dead men, in their written opinions, are heard with patience. I have now no one earthly interest of my own."

He was sufficiently revived, however, to send his thoughts at considerable length to Fitzwilliam on two very important questions which had been proposed for the latter's consideration.[44] One was that of a union between Great Britain and Ireland; the other was the desire of the Catholics to be eligible once again to sit in the two branches of the Irish parliament.

Considering the union question first, Burke thought it of some importance to know the exact way in which it had been brought to Fitzwilliam's attention. If it was through his ministerial colleagues, then it was probable that they had formed some plan to carry it into execution. Much would depend upon the efficacy of such a plan. On the other hand, if the idea were merely a loose one "floating in their minds," then Burke thought it ought not to be entertained hastily or even discussed publicly. As matters then stood, it was his opinion that the idea was impracticable. A number of preliminary steps had to be taken to render it effective. He had never been fond of the concept of union between the two kingdoms even when circumstances had been more favorable than they then were. At best, it was to him "a bold experimental remedy, justified, perhaps called for, in some nearly desperate Crisis of the whole Empire."

If the idea were to be advanced now, it would be argued "merely as a speculative question; but not with the coldness which might be expected in a dry speculation." This was owing to the concessions, both constitutional and commercial, which Britain had made to Ireland. These have been so liberal that they have "completely exhausted the fund of compensations" which might be held out as attractive lures to overcome the weight of prejudice in Ireland against union. Burke's assertion that "every thing is already given up. Nothing — literally nothing at all remains on the part of England, as an object of Negotiation" was, to put it mildly, exaggerated.

At any rate, if Fitzwilliam had not found this measure in the cabinet when he joined it, then he should consider whether it may not have been the work of "some Irish politicians." It could be that it is one of the ways in which "the faction there" raises doubts and unrest on the occasion of the commencement of a new viceroyship. It was indeed one of their old tricks. Burke could never recall a new Lord Lieutenant's coming into office that it was not industriously broadcast that he had instructions to raise the question of union. Such a rumor was dangerous to the viceroy in the proportion to which it was believed.

Concluding on the question of a union, Burke said that if the idea "is not seriously proposed, & attended with a regular & well digested plan, whatever its abstract merits may be otherwise, I should humbly conceive that the sooner all discussion on the subject is discountenanced, the better it will be for the peace of England & Ireland; & particularly for the Tranquility of your Lordships Government."

As to the second point, the eligibility of Catholics to sit in parliament, judged as "an independent measure tending upon its intrinsick merits only," he considered it "a matter of little importance indeed." If the Catholics were as eligible for parliament as "Socinians, Independents, & Anabaptists," and more mischief were feared from "the prevalence of Papal Influence" than from the principles of these other sects, who like the Catholics were also more numerous than the members of the Established Church, the fear was groundless. Such was the state of election interests in Ireland that the Catholics would do well to elect "*three* Catholic Members" out of the three hundred members of Commons. Three was "as many as could be rationally calculated." In the richest part of Ireland, it was "morally impossible" that even a single Catholic could get elected. As for Lords, he estimated that only a single Catholic could win one of the two hundred and fourteen or so seats in the upper chamber. And if his single vote should be considered "formidable, government may, & probably will add to the number that is to balance it." As a matter of fact, Burke did not know of more than three or four Catholics who could even be candidates for the House of Lords, and these out of a total of over three million people. Already the Catholics had been restored to the voting right of which they had long been deprived, but such was the weight of the laws against them in the past that they had not yet been restored "to any degree of proportionable importance."

Burke now professed to believe that the franchise was of more significance than the question of eligibility for parliament, which he could neither see as so desirable to the Catholics that they should seek it so strongly nor why their opponents resisted it so stoutly. It probably all boiled down to the desire of the Catholics to have a stigma removed from them and to the mortification of their enemies, such as Fitzgibbon, the Chancellor, if they were to behold the "antient people" of the country as free and equal subjects. That was all that Burke could then see in the question.

There were, however, other matters of infinitely greater importance relating to the great mass of the Irish people which would have to come before Fitzwilliam and upon the manner in which they were settled "a great deal of the weal and woe of the present age & of a long posterity in both Kingdoms" would depend.

Burke was pleased that Fitzwilliam was determined that every matter which could be rationally settled would be resolved before he left for Ireland.[45] On those matters, Fitzwilliam could be assured that Burke would open his mind to him "weakly perhaps but with much freedom."

Concluding, Burke could not refrain from the lament which he would so often utter in those days:

Oh! my dear Lord, what a loss on this, as on all other occasions, have we in the death of my Richard, who knew Ireland to the bottom; & was animated with the same affection to you that warms my unhappy bosom! God bless you. As to the place of our meeting; let your conveniency, & not your opinion of mine, decide it; You have much, very much to arrange. I have nothing at all to do — nothing but your honour to think of — dont consider me at all.

Henry Grattan, long a tower of strength in the ranks of the Irish opposition, had come to London on a visit and wrote Burke[46] that he was in perfect accord with the latter's belief that it was vital that the Catholics clergy be allowed to secure their education in Ireland. Grattan felt that it was a question on which no time should be lost. This was true of Irish education in general. For the latter,

. . . great funds of public royal & private donation have been granted & eaten — there is not one great public school in Ireland & yet the funds are great but sunk in the person of the master who is a species of monster devouring the youth he should educate & the charity he is entrusted to preserve. At the time when government were assuming public ignorance as an argument against Catholic emancipation there lay before them a report of a committee with authentic evidence of the misapplication in which they persisted to connive in common with those false guardians of our youth.

There now developed a crisis in the British cabinet over Fitzwilliam's tactlessness in permitting it to be widely circulated both that he was going to Ireland and that he intended to make changes in the ranks of the holders of office there. On 11 October Fitzwilliam wrote to Windham that he intended to resign his cabinet seat, since, if he were to go to Ireland, he would only be permitted to emulate Westmorland.[47] The Times on 16 October flatly stated that he was not to go to Ireland but did not explain why. This was clarified on both 18 and 28 October when it was said that the reason was that Fitzwilliam's friends there were not in the government.

In the midst of the crisis, Burke also wrote to Windham and urged: "For God's sake let nothing be precipitated." [48] Burke was very worried over this turn for the worse because he feared that it would interfere with his hope of seeing the power of the Ascendancy broken. He had always fought against and despised these monopolists of place and now felt that they had opened "a back door for Jacobinism, to rush in expenses, and take us from the rear." [49] He stressed the advisability of his friends in government remaining on good terms with Pitt and emphasized the power of the Prime Minister's office. He reminded Windham that the Irish viceroyship was "an arangement subservient to the reformation or to the continuance of the abuses reigning in that country, and he who is the real Minister can alone support or destroy them." [50]

There is among the Burke papers at Sheffield a long draft of a letter from Burke to Baron Loughborough [51] which seems to have been composed at this time.[52] It began with Burke's statement that it was true, as he had expected, that Fitzwilliam was not to go to Ireland. The reason for his not going was the very one for which Burke would have wished him to go, namely that "it was apprehended that he might make some changes in Ireland." Burke and Fitzwilliam had seen one another and had talked about Ireland but not at all on the score of "the arrangements of men." Nor had they discussed the "difficult Case which has since occurred, & which it did not seem to me, that Ld. F. had the least suspicion."[53]

Fitzwilliam had wished to talk with Burke "as a man of some knowledge in the affairs of Ireland & of great zeal & earnestness that the King's Business should go on prosperously in that Kingdom," and Burke had given him his "honest opinions (which you know so well as he knows them) on that subject."

Burke concluded:

> But it may be asked, why, when I have for ever quitted Parliament, not only in fact, but in Mind & Inclination, & did so, before Calamity had in a manner buried me alive, I choose to intrude myself into Irish concerns? I will tell you, because tho' I am incapable of all the pleasures of Life, & ever shall be, I am not insensible to its Duties, nor indeed dead to its friendships."

On the 15th of October, Windham informed Burke that Portland and Fitzwilliam were unable to resolve their differences with the government on the matter of Ireland but that they were going to meet that afternoon with Grattan in an effort to do so.[54]

Burke responded to Windham's note with a long letter the following day.[55] He confessed that Fitzwilliam had, in some respects, been guilty of having acted indiscreetly. He then spoke of a conversation he had had with Fitzwilliam in which he had learned that the latter considered without a doubt that the administration of Ireland had been left entirely in his hands "without any reserves than what are supposed in every wise and sober servant of the Crown." Fitzwilliam had hesitated some time before accepting the post but took it in order that he might be of service to the government and to his sovereign. He had then invited various persons to converse with him on the subject of Ireland with complete confidence, although he was not yet actually in office but only "virtually."[56] Because Fitzwilliam had acted as if he were already the Lord Lieutenant, and since Pitt had no idea of permitting any significant change to be made in the Irish administration, the former would have to resign his cabinet post, and Portland would have to follow suit.

Fitzwilliam simply could not go to Ireland with "a direct negative put upon his power." He required the "hearty and effectual support of the Minister here." Without it, he was a "mere pageant," and a man in the pillory was in a place of honor and glory in comparison with such a viceroy. The reason that Westmorland appeared to go along so smoothly in Ireland was that he never had any differences with "the junto who have annihilated English government." This particular Lord Lieutenant did not actually govern any more than "a Basha of Egypt, who is content to let the Beys act as they think proper." Were Fitzwilliam to go to Ireland to emulate such an example, there would be no sense in making a change in viceroys. He would not be troubled by the Irish opposition were he to decide to go. His difficulties would come from those who should be the supporters of the British government. These men had formed themselves into a cabal in order to weaken the king's authority and divide the country as "a spoil" among themselves. Their motto should be "non regnum sed magnum latrocinum." [57] There was happily still a chance to rectify matters, but the attempt had yet to be made.

Ireland's position demanded that these monopolists be ousted. The nation was no longer "an obscure dependency." What took place there affected Europe. Ireland was "known" in France. Contacts had already been established and more would follow. Ireland would be either "a strong digue to keep out Jacobinism, or a broken bank to let it in." Her "little cliques" were to him "as nothing," but the country itself was of tremendous significance. In the crisis of affairs then obtaining, Burke professed to look to Ireland for salvation and in Ireland to Great Britain and in the latter to Europe. The result would be the defeat of the principles of the French Revolution. But to achieve this, Ireland would have to be plucked out of the "unwise and corrupt hands" which were destroying England's position there. He warned Windham that the Ascendancy could never change its ways. Even if the members promised to do so, they were incapable of it. Swearing as a "dying man," Burke declared that Pitt would cause his own ruin and that of Great Britain as well if he were to drop the Portland Whigs in order to satisfy "certain Irish politicians."

Answering Windham's letter of the 18th informing him that the differences between Portland and Fitzwilliam and the government still persisted,[58] Burke again dealt with the ministerial crisis over Ireland.[59] He said that never in his life had he given anything "so thorough a sifting." As a consequence of this soul-searching meditation, he was compelled to reverse himself. He now felt that Fitzwilliam and Portland should not resign. Rather they should wait until they were "turned out." By now advising against resignation, Burke said that he did not mean that they should yield their opinions. In fact, they should reassert them. They held high office for the sole purpose of acting "with rectitude, firmness, and disinterestedness, and particularly to resist *ad internecionem* [60] the corrupt system of Ireland, which goes directly to the ruin of the whole empire." If they were to resign, it would be tantamount to suicide. Let them die fighting for Ireland and the empire rather than take their own political lives, he declared in a flight of rhetoric. If he had changed his opinion, there was no reason why he should be ashamed of himself, since this was one of "the most difficult questions that ever was." He advised the Portland group to resort to the Closet with mildness and firmness. In addition to this manner of stating their case to the king orally, they should do so in writing as well.

Finally, he reminded Windham, two things above all were mandatory — not to resign and not to abandon the ground of dispute. By conducting themselves circumspectly, all might yet be saved. There was to be one exception to their prudent, restrained conduct. This was hostility to "the Irish job system." His friends could defend themselves against this menace only by "open, avowed, unappeasable war."

He told Fitzwilliam [61] that by not resigning he and Portland would put the "Jobbers" into a position where they "will appear to be fighting for their Jobbs, and you will appear what you are, Victims offered at the shrine of Corruption."

On the same day that Burke was writing to Fitzwilliam, the latter sent him an account of the differences which he and Portland were experiencing with Pitt.[62] He said that Burke had never pushed forward their coalition with Pitt in the expectation that it would be broken so quickly and over "the petty score of place & patronage — a jealousy of weight & power — . . ." He and the Duke had not entered administration "to hustle for a place or a title three months afterwards."

Certainly, they had never anticipated that a situation which had always been distinctly held out to them for their management and in a most explicit manner talked of by Portland at all times "as an object he particularly wish'd to have under his care, was to become a subject of dispute, as to the time when, & the terms upon which it was to be transfer'd." It was now claimed that there had been a misunderstanding, "a *great original mistake*." How could there have been, asked Fitzwilliam. Had he not gone to Yorkshire to consult his wife's pleasure about the Lord Lieutenancy? Had it not been offered him? Did he "dream, was it nothing but the child of my fancy"? During his hesitancy to accept the viceroyship, he was pressed to accept the post of Lord President, "*if it were but for a day*, as Mr. P[itt] express'd himself, in order that my name might appear at the opening of the Coalition, was it meant to fix me in that situation without apprizing me of the intention —" No, there could have been no mistake. He knew that Pitt had said that he "must beat about for a situation for Ld Westmorland, adequate to that he had held (the Post Office) previous to his going to Ireland." But if it was to be understood that Westmorland was never to be removed until he could kiss hands for such an office on the day of his return, he might remain in Ireland "in perpetuity."

If again it was to be said in the spirit of the coalition that ancient animosities were to be obliterated and past "delinquencies" forgiven, quite so, and no one understood it otherwise. But were past delinquencies to be "the shield" for existing ones? That the Irish Chancellor, Fitzgibbon, had opposed the Whigs on the Regency question was one thing, but was Fitzwilliam to overlook that in addition just two years ago Fitzgibbon "erected the standard of hostility against ¾ths of the people of Ireland: that he is at this instant in a state of avowed Warfare with them." In these matters and similar ones, there could be no mistake. If he were to undertake the government of Ireland to the end that it be improved, he would have to have the power of appointing "the proper instruments" to secure that objective. In order to do this, he would also need the power of "displacing." He would be wise enough and sufficiently prudent not "to establish a general proscription; far from it." He would achieve his ends better without such an extreme procedure, but it would have to be made clear to one and all that his power was sufficient to do so should he desire. Otherwise he would find himself "deliver'd over to be the sport & instrument of the same gang of Jobbers, that have been robbing & plundering in the most barefaced way for these so [many] years back." He could accommodate in parts if he could but think himself secure upon the whole. Unhappily, he could not see his way clearly in this business because "when Pitt talks about protecting his friend, the Chancellor, he never speaks out, & says, that point conceded, the rest are all settled." Pitt refrains from saying that, this point settled, Lord Westmorland must wait for "his 2000£ a year" or that he will not contend for the Lord Presidency for Westmorland instead of Lord Mansfield, who had clearly agreed to step aside at the time of the coalition so that Fitzwilliam could appear upon the list.

These reservations of Pitt's were suspicious. What was the purpose behind Pitt's conduct? Fitzwilliam thought that his basic object was "to keep the D[uke] of P[ortland] down: not to risk the power authority & credit he would acquire, by a better government in Ireland, & to secure this, he is determin'd even if he yields as to the appointment [of Fitzwilliam], to leave in the government a sufficiency of the old leaven to keep us there in a perpetual state of mischievous fermentation."

Meanwhile, Fitzwilliam and Portland had decided to let the matter rest for a while rather than bring it to a showdown. In the interim, Portland would not allow the Provost's position nor that of the Secretaryship of State in Ireland to be filled by the candidates Westmorland backed. Nor would he permit "a blackguard chaplain" of Westmorland's to be made a bishop. He meant "to stop every thing, but such acts of Government as cannot be stop'd without inconvenience." Now that the subject was before Burke, and his mind "intent upon it," Fitzwilliam would appreciate hearing from him "as any thing occurs."

It seems that what occurred to Burke was that he might play the role of a mediator. Accordingly, he and Henry Grattan paid a visit to Fitzgibbon in London and acted as Fitzwilliam's representatives. In a report to Fitzwilliam,[63] Burke said that they had told Fitzgibbon that Fitzwilliam intended to reform abuses prevailing in the Irish government but that it would be done temperately.

Fitzwilliam was pledged to consider Pitt as the Prime Minister and would do nothing "of weight & moment" without having first consulted him. Neither Fitzwilliam nor Portland had any idea of Ireland as an entity apart from "the general mass of the King's Government."

Fitzgibbon was assured that Fitzwilliam had no intention of introducing "any thing which could be properly called new Systems." However, in return for such restrained and temperate conduct on his part, he expected that Pitt must understand that he would have to support Fitzwilliam's government in Ireland "in efficiency, dignity, & honour" and to consider the representatives of Portland and Fitzwilliam as his own.

Parenthetically, Burke instructed Fitzwilliam that, once the misunderstandings were cleared up, "the best way was to have no sort of retrospect to your former discussions, but to begin the arrangement of Ireland as if it had been but this day thought of."

Returning to the recital of the details of the interview with Fitzgibbon, Burke said that he and Grattan had told the Chancellor that Fitzwilliam would like to see him so that they could have an amicable talk. Then Grattan stressed the opposition which was bound to break out in Ireland if Fitzwilliam should be put aside by Pitt at this stage "particularly when the Reasons & principles on wch it was done, should come to be known."

Burke ended by saying "as for my poor part it is with pain enough I enter into this Business. But, if any thing could tend to make me lay down my sorrowful gray hairs in the Grave with peace; It would be to see an Antijacobin administration, firmly united, & wholly settled; to see my Native Land under the Government of the best & wisest man that either Country possesses."

Thus, Burke had played a part in helping to effect a compromise. Fitzwilliam was able to inform him on 18 November [64] that things were at last settled and that he was to go to Ireland but "not exactly upon the terms I had originally thought of, & I mean particularly in the removal of the Chancellor, who is now to remain, Grattan & the Ponsonbys [65] desire me to accept; I left the decision to them."

While there is one important revelation in this letter, namely, that Fitzgibbon was not to be removed, more was left unsaid. The important amplification of just what the terms were is unfortunately wanting. Whatever these terms were specifically and whatever Fitzwilliam's powers were to be, they were not committed to writing. This failure on Fitzwilliam's part was to prove tragic, as we shall shortly see. The English historian Lecky says that one thing was definite, and that was that Fitzwilliam was instructed to prevent the question of Catholic emancipation from being brought forward unless it were unavoidable. Were the latter to be the case, he was authorised to accept it and give his support to the measure.[66]

Burke answered Fitzwilliam's letter [67] with the reassertion of his longfelt anxiety that nothing should be allowed to break up the coalition and added the revealing statement that he was "nearly as anxious that Ireland should be placed under an upright a wise & a resolute direction." In other words, as great as was his concern over Irish affairs, it played second fiddle to the anti-Jacobin crusade he had long been waging.

Fitzwilliam was reminded that he would be sure to "be forced sometimes from this path [of "publick" principles]: but your Lordship, most assuredly will demonstrate to the world, that you never did so but from a necessary compliance with others." For his part, Burke would not recommend to him "any one person, for any one Object, great or small, Civil military, ecclesiastical, legal, or financial." but he might venture "to sollicit" Fitzwilliam's secretaries [68] "for such triffling things, for such triffling persons, as it may not be worth while to present directly to the chief Gouverneur."

CHAPTER IX

Fitzwilliam's Brief and Tragic Tenure of Office

F itzwilliam reached Dublin in his new capacity of Lord Lieutenant on 4 January 1795. In less than two weeks, he had dismissed several important officeholders, the most influential of whom was the Commissioner of Revenue, John Beresford,[1] head of one of the most powerful families in Ireland.[2] Fitzwilliam wrote to his chief, Portland, on the 15th that the removal of Beresford had been satisfactorily settled.[3] Since Beresford had been twenty-five years in "a Revenue Office," he was to have a pension equal to the amount of his salary.[4] "With this," wrote Fitzwilliam in blissful ignorance of what was to come, "he is satisfied, & himself & family promise support."

These dismissals, however, angered the Ascendancy, whose fury the *Morning Chronicle*, 30 March 1795, likened to that of a swarm of hornets which sought to overwhelm an unwary intruder, and they also upset Pitt, who professed to feel that Fitzwilliam had exceeded his instructions. Nor did the new viceroy add to his popularity as far as the monopolists of place were concerned when he did not permit himself to be seen in the usual company of one in his position. His most frequent companions were the opposition leaders, Grattan and the Ponsonbys.[5] It is quite likely that he also saw a good deal of the Reverend Dr. Hussey, the Irish Catholic priest and confidant of Burke's, although Hussey denied it despite the prevalent rumors to the contrary.[6]

So pleased was Hussey that the prospects of Catholic emancipation were apparently destined for early fulfillment that he told Burke there was nothing to fear from an invasion of Ireland. He asserted that there were not "five Catholics in the kingdom worth ten pounds" who would not shed their blood to resist the French. Hussey added that his opinion was based upon careful investigation. The delighted Burke replied immediately that he was "charmed" with this information. He was all the happier, he said, because such strenuous efforts had been made by their enemies to drive the Catholics into the "phrenzy of that malignant fever," Jacobinism.[7]

Fitzwilliam lost little time in concluding that Catholic emancipation was immediately necessary, if indeed he had not made up his mind before leaving England. Agitation for it had preceded his arrival by some weeks. This was natural enough since Fitzwilliam was known to favor such a step and the fact that he and other persons also considered well disposed to the idea were seemingly in a position to bring it about made the movement spontaneous. He was quick to tell Portland that he would consider himself remiss if he did not say that in his opinion failure to grant emancipation "cheerfully" would not only be impolitic but also dangerous and went on to suggest that it be followed by the creation of a constabulary which would include a large number of Catholics. He concluded unequivocally that unless he received express orders to the contrary, he would acquiesce in the idea of emancipation "with a good grace." It was clear, he said, that the measure was acceptable to the great bulk of the Protestants of Ireland.[8] As a matter of fact, he communicated the intelligence to Portland as early as 8 January that the Catholic question would be brought up in the imminent session of parliament. This letter was acknowledged by Portland on the 13th, but he significantly refrained from any mention whatsoever of the Catholic matter.

When the Irish parliament opened on 22 January, Fitzwilliam refrained in the Speech from the Throne from any mention of the emancipation question. His restraint was dictated by respect for the previous wishes of the government before he left for Ireland and accorded with his understanding of how he was to handle the problem; meaning, of course, that the initiative for it was not to come from him nor was he to oppose it if it came up independently and seemed to express the will of the Irish parliament.

One week after the opening of parliament, he wrote to Portland to inform him that the Catholic business would be carried easily. A conversation with Fitzgibbon [9] that very day had convinced him. The Chancellor had concluded their talk by saying that "if it was my intention to give support to the Catholic petition there was no doubt of its being easily carried." [10]

The information that Catholic emancipation was being officially entertained in Ireland became public in England as early as 16 January when *The Times* reported that a bill granting the Catholics equal rights was very shortly to be introduced. This paper later predicted that only four offices would be denied the Catholics, namely, Lord Lieutenant, Lord Chancellor, Speaker, and Lord Chief Justice.[11]

Burke was asked at this time [12] by a member of the Irish Commons with whom he had previously corresponded, William Cusack Smith, for advice as to "the proper *measure* of concession by the Legislature here of Constitutional Privilege of our Catholick Countrymen." Smith, like Burke himself, was the child of a Catholic mother, and it was this which apparently had first attracted Burke to him. Specifically, he wished to know from Burke, at the time he wrote, the answer to the question "Should the Catholicks sit in Parliament?" He had addressed himself to Burke because he had been his first mentor in politics "& you so taught me to qualify the force of general Principle, by a regard to Times & Circumstances."

Burke's answer,[13] as it appears in his published *Works*, began by once again dismissing the prevalent objection against the Catholics that great danger from the pope would certainly follow from Catholic emancipation in Ireland.[14] The real danger of the times was Jacobinism which aimed at the annihilation of Christianity. What could be more sensible than to have the various divisions of Christianity unite in their common defense? There really was not much of a choice to make — it was unite or perish. Should the Catholic religion be destroyed, no Protestant sect could survive its fall.[15] The three principal churches in the British Isles "in subordination to the legal establishments as they stand in the several countries" should all be recognized. In the case of Ireland, the

Roman Catholic religion represented the most effectual, if not the only, barrier against Jacobinism. The Catholics comprised the vast majority of the lower classes. People from this segment of society were the special objects of the Jacobins, so the choice for "full four fifths of your people" was Catholicism or Jacobinism.

The expressed fear that the Catholics would become powerful if granted the right of parliamentary seats [16] was an empty one to Burke. He displayed, at the end of a parliamentary career of almost thirty years, disillusion over the lack of real power possessed by individual members. He claimed that the chief clerks had more power than nine-tenths of the members. Added to this was the fact that very few Catholics in his opinion would be returned to seats even if they were permitted to stand as candidates. He predicted that the maximum strength which they would be likely to attain would be thirty seats, a mere one-tenth of the total membership of the House of Commons. Even at that, it would be some years before this number was reached. In the House of Lords, only four or five Catholics would probably ever become members.

Meanwhile, matters in Ireland did not stand still. The first ominous note of what was to come, however, had crept into Fitzwilliam's hitherto unbounded optimism. He told Portland [17] that his Chief Secretary recently had a letter from William Windham that Beresford's removal had not been expected by Pitt and that the latter was intending to write him on this matter. Fitzwilliam thought this "very odd, that on the subject of Beresford he forgets, that we had a conversation & that I distinctly told him, that he must be removed, to which he never made the slightest objection: it appeared to me so marked that I made the remark to you." It did not matter, however, whether it was so or not, added Fitzwilliam, since Beresford had no cause to complain as he would retire upon full salary. If he did complain, it was simply because his power had been clipped and not because "his interests are affected." Fitzwilliam intended that his power should be curtailed "& a very popular measure it is."

He had, nevertheless, "other reasons to give besides the above." Specifically, Beresford was guilty of "the extra-ordinary sale of a publick lease" during the last parliamentary session. This was certainly "ground sufficient for common prudence to dictate a suspension of confidence." Beresford was a most fortunate individual that his removal would be attributed to other causes, Fitzwilliam concluded.[18]

At this point things began to happen with breakneck speed. Letters crossed and recrossed one another, and the principal parties involved were often in a state of some excitement. First of all, Portland on 5 February showed the king the despatches he had received from Fitzwilliam which made clear his acquiescence in the idea of Catholic emancipation then being envisaged in Ireland. The king's reaction, as he expressed it to Pitt in a letter of the following day,[19] was one of the "greatest astonishment" that such a step was being projected. He also manifested his hostility as well to the idea of the establishment of "a kind of yeomenry, which in reality would be [a] Roman Catholic police corps, . . . which would keep the Protestant interest under awe." His Majesty concluded by saying that Catholic emancipation was a matter which was "beyond the decision of any Cabinet of Ministers" and that it would be better "even to change the new administration in Ireland, if its continuance depends on the success of this proposal, than to prolong its existence on grounds that must sooner or later ruin one if not both kingdoms."

The next day, the seventh, a cabinet meeting was held wherein it was agreed that Fitzwilliam was to be informed immediately that he was not to commit the government to emancipation. Under date of 8 February,[20] Portland thus belatedly made his long delayed answer to Fitzwilliam's importuning letters asking for instructions. In the letter, Portland said that it had not been until the previous day that he had been able to get the cabinet to consider the very important question of the admission of the Irish Catholics to equality with the members of the Established Church. The cabinet had been unanimous that they needed more information to enable them to form their judgment "of the policy, expediency, safety & necessity of that measure." They were deeply concerned because so much appeared to them "to turn upon the effects it might have upon the present Ecclesiastical Establishment, and the present constitution of the H. of Commons." Portland cautioned Fitzwilliam against committing himself by engagements or even by encouraging language to the proposal. This advice was necessary, said Portland, "seeing as I think I do the inclination of your mind upon this subject." The immediate adoption of a bill for Catholic emancipation, "which by being precipitated may be productive of very unforeseen & dangerous consequences, & which if it could possibly be deferred might afford the means of doing a greater service to the British Empire than it has been capable of receiving since the revolution or at least since the Union."

Fitzwilliam was ordered to bring the Catholics into a feeling of confidence "in the good intentions of Government, and relying upon that to defer urging a measure" which needed time to perfect. Fitzwilliam was here being urged, of course, to do the impossible, since it was already public knowledge that a bill for Catholic relief was shortly to be brought in by Grattan. Anyway he was not in sympathy with further delay and felt that he was justified in his position, since he had assumed that the government, by their policy of silence, had no objections to the consummation of the plan.

Portland then told Fitzwilliam that his "transaction with Beresford has created a very considerable & unpleasant sensation here amongst our own best & most attached friends." As Fitzwilliam knew, Beresford had gone over to England. What he did not know, said Portland, was that Beresford was claiming that he had been forced out of office, that he had refused the pension, and that he and his family were "the reverse of satisfied." Portland concluded that how this was he himself did not know but that he was anxious to be told whether Fitzwilliam had held any conversations with Beresford.

On the ninth, Pitt wrote to Fitzwilliam [21] to say that in his opinion the Lord Lieutenant was mistaken about the extent of Beresford's influence and power. He, too, reported that Beresford claimed to have been dismissed peremptorily. Pitt was disturbed over the whole matter since "no intention was to my recollection ever hinted at even in the most distant manner of proposing his removal from the revenue board, much less of doing so without his consent." Significantly, Pitt made no reference whatsoever in his letter to the Catholic question.

On the same day, Fitzwilliam told Lord Grenville [22] that the only change he intended to make in the Revenue Board was the removal of Beresford. There were to be no sweeping changes despite rumors to the contrary.

Not having as yet received Portland's letter of the eighth forbidding him to encourage Catholic emancipation, Fitzwilliam made a strong case for it in a despatch to Portland on the tenth and asked the latter to convey to the king the reasons why he had taken this position. He was anxious to know His Majesty's pleasure.[23] He followed this up with another despatch two days later [24] saying that the first letter had been sent in the hope of an immediate reply.

On the twelfth, Henry Grattan was given leave by the Irish House of Commons to introduce a bill for emancipation. All over Ireland, the Catholics were in a state of great expectation.[25] They flooded parliament with petitions requesting emancipation. Burke's friend Dr. Hussey claimed that there were over a half-million signatures for this purpose.[26]

Fitzwilliam, having received Pitt's letter of the ninth, undertook to refresh the Prime Minister's memory in a despatch of the twelfth [27] which began by stressing the necessity of Catholic relief and also that Beresford's dismissal must stand. He continued:

Upon that I must endeavour to bring back to your recollection, that in the very first conversation I had the honor of holding with you upon the subject of Irish business, you yourself put the question to me, what was to be done with Mr. B. or what were my intentions with respect to him, or words to that effect — my answer was that I was apprehensive he must be removed — it struck me at the time that you made *no* objection, nor indeed any reply, & never resumed the subject again on any subsequent occasion, it was a matter of indifference to you & which you left to my discretion — on my arrival here the apprehension of his power & influence, which you mention in your letter, that I did express, I discovered to have been too well founded. I found them incompatible with mine, and with that assistance, which I always meant to call in aid of my government I determined therefore to remove him, but in doing this I was anxious not to injure him in his interests, but to remove him from his power: the circumstance of his long service facilitated this by entitling him to the full extent of his Salary, whilst I gave him to understand that not one of his Children, nor any of his extensive family connections should be removed from their innumerable Offices — the question therefore is now brought to the test by his appeal to you: I am glad that it is so, as it is proved that power is his object, for the loss of power only has he a pretext to complain. . . The question therefore now lies with you. I shall send the official document for a new board of Revenue, *without his name*, & after the receipt of this, you will be prepared to decide between Mr. Beresford & me — that the matter is come to this issue is well known *here*. his son is arrived from England, and his friends have taken care that it should be so: from the event therefore Ireland will form its judgment, which of the two possesses the Confidence of the British Cabinet, He or I.

A copy of the above was sent to Portland the same day along with an expression of Fitzwilliam's dissatisfaction over not having heard from Portland relative to his proposals. He then entreated an answer and concluded the same way he had to Pitt, namely, a Lord Lieutenant must be supported or removed.[28]

Portland responded on the sixteenth [29] by saying that the Roman Catholic business was so important that very careful thought must be given to it by the English government and asked Fitzwilliam to send along to the administration the objections raised to it by such people as the Chancellor. He would like also the views of the Protestant hierarchy and "other respectable Clergy of Ireland." In addition, the cabinet wished estimates of the strength it was reckoned that the Roman Catholics would acquire by securing seats in parliament.

Portland then suggested that it might be best to encourage the establishment of seminaries for the education of the Catholic clergy in Ireland. This would both lessen the burden suffered by the Catholics of rank in maintaining the higher clergy and would re- move the state of dependence of the parochial clergy from the lowest orders of the Catholic people, said Portland.

If this were done, he thought, all ideas of further concessions might be put aside and the Catholics might exert every effort "in this momentous crisis, to manifest that they and their protestant brethren were but one people; and that they had but one and the same cause."

Portland was quite serious in thinking that the Catholics could be persuaded to give up their political hopes in return for a promise by the government to educate their clergy for them in Ireland. The proposal was one which both Burke and the Catholics had long favored, but at this moment it would be a poor substitute for a goal now seemingly well within reach. The Catholics of Ireland then enjoyed the relatively free exercise of their religion, so that such a proposal would not have enjoyed the significance it would in the past. Furthermore, it seemed reasonable to assume that this proposed concession in the matter of clerical education in Ireland would come about anyway in the none too distant future once the big step of reopening parliament had been won by the Catholics. Portland's suggestion reveals glaringly the kind of thinking in official places on the subject of Ireland which was characteristic of most English statesmen of that time and contrasts so markedly with Burke's ideas over the years. It corroborates substantially what he had often said about the fuzziness of official English thought on the Catholics of Ireland.

Along with this letter, Portland sent another on the same day marked "Private & confidential." Fitzwilliam was directed to show the first letter to all persons to whom he thought it proper to communicate it. He then went on to say that the numerical superiority of the Roman Catholics would unquestionably place the "present Ecclesiastical Establishment" in jeopardy if the Catholics were given seats in parliament. Portland wished to give the Catholics every right and benefit but not until he was sure that the present church and state were "unquestionably secur'd." But the present system could not survive if the Catholics were to become the armed yeomanry of the country. Portland was referring to a proposal to establish yeoman corps. These, he said, could only be "made up, out of the materials, of which I believe they can only be composed," with the result that "the real power and influence of the Country will be placed in the hands of the Catholics."

There was also the question of tithes to be considered. They had always been criticized by "enemies" of the establishment. There was presently a real danger that the system would be attacked by dissatisfied landholders of both Catholic and Protestant (Dissenters) persuasions. If anything happened to the tithes, "the whole Ecclesiastical Fabrick is but too likely to fall."

For the sake of argument, said Portland, let us concede that the Established Church might give way and in its place the Roman Catholic church be substituted "without any material injury to the morals or Religion of Mankind." What would happen? Well, take away from "its Professors & Teachers the benefits of this provision [establishment], and attempt to substitute what you will in its place," you could be sure that "the Profession of the Gospel" would soon become disreputable, that dissension and confusion would ensue, and that "the same scenes we have shuddered at the relation of, would probably be acted over again in these Kingdoms." Portland had given Fitzwilliam some of "the positive evils" which would result from concessions to the Catholics. In a later letter, he promised to consider "the speculative advantages" which would result from withholding the concessions. These would be "many [and] very important."

Two days later, on the eighteenth,[30] Portland wrote a "most private & *secret*" despatch to the viceroy informing him that the cabinet could not undertake to advise the king on the Catholic question until supplied with "a precise & detailed plan, and without the draft of the Bill which I suppose is prepared, because leave has been given to bring it in; a circumstance at which I can not suppress my astonishment." If it could be postponed until the war with France was concluded, there was no doubt that it would have advantages. At any rate, "it is surely going a little too far to infer from any thing I have said, that this is a task you are desired to undertake." The order to send a draft of the bill was repeated.

Under date of the twentieth, a "private" despatch from Portland [31] bluntly said that as Home Secretary he was "to inform you in the plainest and most direct terms, that we rely upon your Zeal & Influence to take the most effectual means in your power to prevent any further proceeding being held on that bill until His Majesty's pleasure shall be signified to you with respect to your future conduct respecting it."

A "most secret" despatch of the twenty-first [32] brought Fitzwilliam the news that Portland himself had been the first member of the cabinet to hold the opinion that "the true interest, I mean the cause of Government abstractedly considered, requires that you should not continue to administer that of Ireland." Fitzwilliam had clearly fallen too much under the influence of Grattan and the Ponsonbys.

Whatever may be the determination respecting the concessions to the Catholics, the ultimate fate of Mr Beresford & of the Attorney Genl., or the designation of the Office destined for Mr Ponsonby, or any of the questions which might arise out of different constructions, to which the conversation, at Mr Pitts or elsewhere, relative to Ireland, might be to the suggestions and wishes & such an acquiescence in the prejudices of Grattan & the Ponsonbys, that there seems to me no other way of rescuing you & English Government from the annihilation, which is impending over it but by the distressful and affecting measure which I ventured to propose —

Portland then gave a bill of particulars of what the cabinet and he considered inexcusable actions on Fitzwilliam's part. In reference to the Catholic bill, he said:

I can not suppose that leave would have been moved to bring in the Catholic bill on the day before that, on which what is considered by you as the plan of that measure arrived in London; for you will observe that the plan, concerning which I will not add one word to what I have already said, was stated in yours of the 10th inst.: & Grattan moved for leave to bring in the bill on the 12th —

All of these things were bad enough, but Fitzwilliam was in such a condition and "all objects have been presented to you so clouded & discoloured, as to change their shapes and forms." Portland asked forgiveness "if I dwell so much upon the state of your mind; but that is the very subject which has alarmed me, it is that which has created these serious apprehensions in mine, and in the minds of all your friends." The Duke felt badly that he had not warned Fitzwilliam before. The first act which disturbed him had been the removal of the Attorney-General, Wolfe. It was simply unjustifiable but, "distressing" as it was, what came afterwards was worse. In fact, these other steps were so bad that Portland said "I want to get you to some safe & dry spot from whence you may contemplate the flood, which was overwhelming you, & see the inundation subside."

Fitzwilliam had reproached him for not having approved a single measure of his administration, so he thereupon praised a few of them but resumed his attack and told Fitzwilliam:

But ask yourself, can you stop, can you check, can you controll the career that Grattan or Ponsonby chuse to propose? Do you feel that the Government of Ireland is really in your hands? Do you consider that the responsibility for all measures rests solely with you?

The viceroy had unwisely listened to the siren call of popularity and was told to reject it and its allurements. Portland "implored" him to "make it your own desire to come away from Ireland" and left him free to choose the mode and time of resignation. He was sure that it would be in a manner "the least injurious to the welfare and safety of both Kingdoms." So awful was the present moment that "probably the existence of the civilized world is in your power and at your mercy." Portland had told him his own part in the cabinet discussion which unanimously concluded that Fitzwilliam no longer had their confidence and he was now relieved by it but he wrote him "in the agony of my soul impelled by the sense of my friendship and attachment for you & of my duty to the publick."

Portland concluded that he was "almost ashamed to say that I doubt not your adjourning the Parliament if that measure should be necessary" and that he could consider himself at liberty to appoint the usual Lord Justices without waiting for the nomination of another Lord Lieutenant. An official letter for these purposes would follow the next day.

On that same day Pitt had written him from Downing Street [33] to say that he had learned with "pain" of Fitzwilliam's approval of Grattan's Catholic bill. His sentiments on the Catholic question concurred entirely with those of the Duke of Portland who had communicated his thoughts to Fitzwilliam in his despatches. In the arrangement of persons which Fitzwilliam had made, Pitt had been disturbed not only with respect to Beresford but also by "the line of Conduct adopted in so many instances towards the former supporters of Government." Pitt would have to be guided by these sentiments which he had expressed and by a regard to the king's service and his own personal honor, no matter how sincerely he lamented the consequences which arose from the present situation.

In a "most secret & confidential" despatch from Portland to Fitzwilliam, 23 February,[34] the latter was told that it was His Majesty's wish that he would deign to consider accepting a seat in the cabinet upon his return to England. If he bore any grudge, he should take it out on Portland who stood prepared to do whatever he wished. He would retire or make "any expiation or atonement that can satisfy you." Fitzwilliam was the younger of the two, the more active, the more able, and could do more good. "If my absence, if my renunciation of the world will restore you to the publick service, God forbid that I should hesitate a moment or be base enough to deem it a sacrifice."

While Fitzwilliam did not avail himself of this offer on Portland's part, he must have been sorely tempted! Actually, that he was tended a seat in the cabinet was due to Portland who had written the king asking this favor. Since Pitt was willing that it be done, the king agreed. Their motive in consenting to make the offer lay in their mutual belief both that Portland deserved recognition for the part he had played and that Fitzwilliam would reject the offer.

Under date of the twenty-fifth,[35] Fitzwilliam acknowledged receipt of letters from Portland, all of which have been discussed above, and the one from Pitt, dated the twenty-first, which has also been referred to above. Fitzwilliam told Portland that it was pointless to enter into any argument or discussion. He had put the alternatives of supporting him or recalling him to Pitt who had made his decision. Fitzwilliam stood recalled. He would prevent any further proceedings on the Catholic question, get the project for the education of the Catholic clergy under way, and cooperate in all other matters.

In response to Portland's having informed him on the twenty-third that the king would be pleased to have him take a ministerial post, Fitzwilliam said [36] that he would need time to ponder the offer.[37] He requested that Portland give His Majesty the fullest assurances of Fitzwilliam's continued deepest devotion to him and his ready submission to his commands, no matter how painful the latter might be. He wished further that Portland would relay the intelligence to the monarch that Fitzwilliam considered that his had been "a prudent and wise administration" in Ireland and that he trusted in his ability "to set the whole account of it in so clear & irreproachable a light before His Majesty, as to justify myself in his opinion, & to wipe away whatever criminality false and groundless insinuations & unmerited calumnies [that] may have been charged upon me, and have impressed upon his Royal mind when he was induced to withdraw his confidence from me."

During the hectic period of Fitzwilliam's brief tenure of office, there is extant only one letter of Burke's to him prior to his recall.[38] In it Burke mentioned that he had heard good reports of Fitzwilliam's viceroyship from his friend, Dr. Hussey, and from other channels. The purpose of his letter, however, related to one Hylan, a Catholic soldier in a regiment of Irish Light Dragoons. The soldier had attended Protestant church services out of fear of the consequences for not attending. This was a common practice among Catholic soldiers in his regiment and in others. In resorting to the sacrament of confession, Hylan had been advised by the priest to refrain from attending the services of other denominations. As a result, he had refused occasional conformity and had been tried by a court martial. As an example to others, the soldier had been sentenced to two hundred lashes. A hundred or so had actually been inflicted before an order from the War Office intervened to prevent the rest from being administered.

Since a Catholic bishop had asked Burke to secure Hylan's discharge, a small favor, Burke therefore requested that Fitzwilliam attend to the matter. During the American War, Burke had managed to secure several discharges even though he was then "in very marked opposition." The fact that soldiers could be lashed into attendance at services of denominations other than their own was disturbing to Burke. The war which the French were then waging was one which was "against religion." In this state of things, it was most unwise to stir up a civil war between those defending religion against them.

Whilst ever Law or Legislation is acceptable, I have ever recommended (& my dear Son has constantly done the same) to their leading people [the Catholics] to come forward, & to confound their Enemies. But if these leading men have so little sympathy with those, whose heads are thrust into the pillory of a Ladder, & whose bodies are torn with whips in their common cause, they well deserve, what most certainly they will feel, to have their own backs well disciplined with the protestant Cat o' nine tails, in order to make some impression on their unsocial & unfeeling breasts. All the miseries of Ireland have originated, in what has produced all the miseries of India, a servile patience under oppression, by the greatest of all misnomers called prudence. But this is their affair, I only offer my poor insufficient thoughts to you, encouraged by your uniform goodness & condescension on what I conceive to be the true Interest of Government.

Burke concluded in the lachrymose vein which he could not seem to escape:

I ought to make ten thousand apologies for the great Liberty I take in this intrusion. But in the silent gloom of my forlorn situation, I have often asked myself, why it is Gods pleasure, that after having suffered so heavy a punishment, I should continue to drag on a degraded & apparently useless existence? I can discover no reason for it, but that, after having been called by so dreadful an admonission, I might have time for repentance. It is so I have no doubt, & things of this kind are among the works that become repentance or in the old English "are meet for it" (as we are told by authority) & that belong to it. Such at least is my contention. God knows whether right or wrong.

Grattan had written him on the nineteenth [39] to tell him that the Catholic bill was acceptable to the House of Commons and that it would be fatal if the British government should oppose it. The defense of Ireland against the French threat absolutely depended upon the bill's passage. He thereupon asked Burke to press the urgency of the measure upon his friends in the cabinet. Despite his condition, Burke hastened from Beaconsfield into London where he took quarters in a hotel and gave freely of his time and energy in seeking to impress ministers with the necessity of allowing the Catholic bill to pass. [40]

His correspondence with Dr. Hussey was fairly extensive all during this period. It was Hussey who first sent him the news of Fitzwilliam's recall [41] in a letter in which he described Ireland as "now on the brink of a civil war." The information that the Catholic bill would be rejected was also passed on to Burke as well as the news that the project for the education of the Catholic clergy in Ireland would be put through. Hussey was "really terrified by the situation of this country."

In one of his letters to Hussey, [42] Burke mentioned the receipt of a letter from a "Mr. Coppinger, a Catholic prelate." On the seals of this letter were arms and a mitre. Burke advised Hussey to "hint, with all the delicacy which belongs to such a subject, that such exterior remarks should be forborne as much as possible." They were made to order for the enemies of the Catholics, since the arms were of feudal origin and came to the sees in virtue of temporalities. Why remind them of such things? Burke went on to say that he himself wished very much before his death to see "an image of a primitive Christian Church." With "little improvements," he thought the Roman Catholic Church of Ireland "very capable of exhibiting that state of things."

When he had learned of Fitzwilliam's recall, he dashed off a hasty note to the latter in which he reversed his position on "Jobbs" too late: [43]

For Gods sake; for the sake of your friends; for the sake of Country, for your own sake, stay where you are, as long as you are permitted to do so; or till you have accomplished the great matters you are about for the Kings service & the publick settlement, or are, in the face of day, defeated in your attempts. Above all, I conjure you, not to fall, on a question of a Jobb, for or against any man.

And, he added, "My heart is almost broken."

Fitzwilliam acknowledged receipt of this letter,[44] commenting that Burke had recommended patience; but, said Fitzwilliam, firmness was necessary, too. Burke had told him not to fall on account of a job or a man; well

. . . trust me the job and the man that I fall for is the Government of the Country — it is through the person of a man, that it is meant to wrest it out of my hands and to render every measure I had in contemplation absolutely abortive — Mr. Beresford is to be sent back upon me, for the purpose of shewing that my authority is at an end, for the purpose of defeating the Catholick question, as a measure that I countennanced & protected: — His re-instation is the signal for a protestant party to rise up in the House of Commons and to reject the measure; had not so intelligible a standard been raised in the moment that it was, it would have passed without the least difficulty whatsoever: — not a stir in the Country against it; not one address or petition from a single corporation or petty borough was to be got against it; on the contrary, in many of the addresses to me from protestants [there was] direct approbation of the principles expressed —

Fitzwilliam could have achieved all of his goals in Ireland if "I had thrown myself into the hands of the old jobbing, corrupt, & detested Court." Since Burke had counselled patience, he would be patient, but it would avail nothing — "it is not the support of such an old rotten stinking jobber as Beresford that is the question — It is the destruction of my Government."

He was not speaking out of vanity, he said, when he described the situation attendant upon his removal which "has raised such a ferment, [and] has caused such an irritation in every part of the country it has yet reached that it requires but the accidental touch of a match to set the whole in a flame." Conditions were so bad because

the lower orders of the people have had unfortunately jacobinical principles diffused among them: they are ripe for mischief: they are all Catholicks: they want but a cause and a leader, & the Cabinet is furnishing both one & the other — I know they are told they may confide in the army, & in the militia: I believe they might have done so — but have they forgot, that of the latter 3/4ths are Roman Catholicks & the remaining fourth the dissenters of the north, professed democrats, . . .

Fitzwilliam had been "abandoned, deserted and denied by those, to whose earnest sollicitations I yielded my opinion & embarked at their desire in the present government" because, without injury to them, he had gotten rid of "those men, who had been described to me for years back, as the bane of good government in Ireland."

On the sixth of March, in a letter to Windham,[45] Burke added a postscript in which he said that he had been in touch with Dundas and had talked with him for four hours on the Irish situation. He received no hope from that quarter and so told Windham that if Pitt were to make it the principle of his administration not to win the full support of the men who had joined him but, on the contrary, to ruin them, he would wreck his own government.

A letter from Fitzwilliam on the ninth [46] lamented that with three significant exceptions he had not been able to achieve a single arrangement that he had wished to make. He was very bitter but kept insisting to Burke that he had not been "rash & passionate." He turned to a request which Burke had made of Grattan that he go over to England and argue the case of Fitzwilliam and the Catholics. Fitzwilliam had initially been highly in favor of the suggestion but upon reflection had lost his enthusiasm. The idea, after all, was open

to the construction of the wish & anxiety of an Individual, [so] I thought it prudent to be upon my guard, & to be so, for more reasons than one: it was not simply the ridicule to which I should expos'd myself, had I caught at the twig, but it was the infinite mischief, that would have arisen, had a person of Grattan's character & figure been made a dupe & a fool: would the irritation of his own mind been of no consequence: would the irritation of the people of Dublin, & of all Ireland have been of no importance: & yet it would have been an increas'd irritation from the north to the south, from the east to the west, had he return'd neglect'd & scorn'd, as I now know he would have been: we dont want to add fuel to the fire here at this time, believe me, we do not.

Fitzwilliam was clearly upset, and at the end the reason was clear. In the day's post he had received a special mandate from the king to withdraw from Ireland which he proposed to do "in a very few days." The same ship which brought this order had also deposited Beresford in Ireland.

Thus, Fitzwilliam's recall was final, although some forlorn hopes were briefly entertained that it might be rescinded.[47] His recall and the realization that Catholic emancipation was doomed brought the prediction in the House of Commons that Ireland would be faced with "the most awful and alarming crisis she had ever known." [48] The news had produced an "electrical shock," [49] and addresses poured in from many parts of the country praying that the British government reconsider. Fitzwilliam was given many pledges of full support from numerous Protestants, as well as the Catholics, but by the end of February Dublin had become the scene of rioting.[50]

A meeting of the Catholics in Dublin on 27 February was attended by ten thousand persons of whom many were of "the first respectability." [51] A delegation consisting of Baron Hussey, John Keogh, and Edward Byrne was chosen to present an address to the king in which the Catholics expressed regret at the change of viceroys, deprecated the renewal of proscription, and begged His Majesty to prevent the prorogation of parliament until the question of Catholic emancipation could undergo a thorough discussion.

In early March, Burke made one of his infrequent trips into London and took quarters in a hotel. He saw members of the administration to discuss the Fitzwilliam recall and the Catholic question, but all that was achieved was "a great deal of useless discourse." The whole thing had "got above my prudence, and beyond my efforts," he sorrowfully told Hussey.[52] If he were to risk an opinion to Hussey, it would be "to preserve a profound silence." Leave matters to their "own natural operation" since "Nature, in desperate diseases frequently does most when she is left entirely to herself. Whatever I could do here, in the way of poor medical advice, is done." And, he added despairingly, "I can do no more, nor can you, I believe."

He had been unable to see the Duke of Portland [53] that day but expected to contact him later in the evening or on the next day. He promised to write the following day and told Hussey not to "stir till you hear from me." Although the letter has not been found, the subject was probably the projected Catholic seminary in Ireland. Hussey in his next letter [54] told Burke that Portland had just written him urging him to stay in Ireland for the establishment of this college and promising him that a bill for its foundation would be passed during the present parliamentary session. "Knowing the good effect such an intention would produce, towards quieting the present irritated state of the public mind, I made every prudent use of his Grace's letter, and have succeeded," said Hussey indulging in considerable overoptimism.

The Catholic delegation had an interview with Portland in London on 8 March and were received by George III a week later. After a lengthy delay, word was sent to them that His Majesty had communicated his wishes on the subject of the Irish Catholics to Lord Camden, the new Irish Lord Lieutenant. [55] While waiting word from the throne, two of the delegation had written to Burke [56] to deny strenuously that the Catholics had promised in 1793 that, if the relief they then sought were granted they would make no further requests. This denial was necessary because one of the arguments now employed against the Catholics was the false claim that they had made such a pledge in 1793.

Fitzwilliam left Ireland on 25 March. An estimated one hundred thousand people turned out in Dublin to witness his departure. All shops were closed, and many people were in deep mourning. While the populace refrained from disorders at this time, they were "loud in their curses and execrations of the British Cabinet, and the plunderers and peculators whose dark agency procured the recal of so independent and honest a man." In College Green a number of leading gentlemen, all attired in black, unhitched the horses and drew Fitzwilliam's carriage in triumph to the dock. [57]

Burke had instructed Fitzwilliam to have very little to say to his successor and nothing whatsoever to his Chief Secretary.

Above all, he warned against allowing either of them to go with him in his coach to the quay. He should also refrain from receiving any compliments from them or returning any because "The people do not comprehend these Ceremonies in Cases of desperate Hostility. They puzzle their understandings. It makes them of opinion that politicians only differ as Lawyers; & that there is no principle in the world. A sober, cool & manly indignation, is what they think, & in my opinion very properly, to be the just feeling in cases of great & scandalous injury; & that a correspondent demeanour is the most becoming." [58]

The day upon which Fitzwilliam's successor, the Earl of Camden, took the oath of office at Dublin Castle, there was bitter fighting in the capital's streets. Fitzgibbon, the Lord Chancellor, and the nemesis of the Catholics, was badly injured by a paving stone thrown by one of a mob which pursued his carriage. The new viceroy also had a narrow escape from harm.[59] According to custom, upon the arrival of a new Lord Lieutenant the Fellows and Scholars of Trinity College would go to the Castle and present him with an address of welcome. On this occasion, the Scholars upon arriving in the Castle yard gave "three groans" and immediately departed leaving the Fellows alone to make the address.[60]

Before Fitzwilliam's departure, Burke was busily engaged in correspondence which clearly reveals the strain he was then experiencing. There are places where irrationality clearly shows, although Grattan told him at the time [61] that "you would have served them, but they were not to be served. You would have healed wounds, private and public. There is more wisdom in your ardour, than in their cold and overreaching discretion."

That Burke was aflame with "ardour" cannot be doubted, but that it was "wisdom" is open to question. He wrote the Duke of Devonshire [62] calling for full and unqualified support for Fitzwilliam from "us all, from those of your Grace's Rank & Consequence to my insignificance & misery, in what is due, to him, to our King, to our Country & to ourselves. In such company, I do not know how I intrude such a crawling existence on Earth as I am; [63] but having by weak & inconsiderable councils contributed in some degree to involve such a Man as Lord Fitzwilliam & his respectable connexions in the most dreadful perplexity in wch Men of honour can be involved, I feel myself absolutely bound to take my share in all the Results."

Then came the suggestion which indicated Burke's state of mind. As the only way out of "this cursed situation," Fitzwilliam should be prevailed upon to go back to Ireland and "seat from there with the Honour that becomes an honest Servant of the Crown. Crush the betrayers of English Government there; & let those who have refused compensations for their offices, know what it is to feel punishment for their Crimes. Let us hear no more of compromises & compensations, since instead of peace they produced War. Then we, or rather you may hope to see better days."

Burke conceded that "there is some difficulty in what I recommend — True — But difficulties, & far greater difficulties have attended the ruin of the King's Government in the person of your & the Duke of Portland's friend." He ended by saying that "If any one thinks, that the considerable opinions of so low undone & degraded a creature as I am, of any weight, Your Grace may shew them this. Perhaps I may dote — Very likely — But if by accident I should not; then there are the dictates of Age & experience. How can you Aristocrats exist, if you are not true to one another? I am an Aristocrate in Principle. In situation, God knows nothing less — "

Burke was obviously overwrought at this point. The excitement had been too much for him, and he had overextended himself but he had done everything of which he was capable. As he told Fitzwilliam a few days later,[64] "whatever an enfeebled mind in an old & shattered carcass could do, I have done for this fortnight past."

In this last letter to Fitzwilliam while the latter was in Ireland, Burke said that his recommendations to forbearance and patience had been confined to the period when there was still some hope. But "the business is now over," and Fitzwilliam must be "high & illustrious, . . . and true to yourself." His Lordship was now in "more danger than ever you have been. The mode of affectuating your destruction is changed. Formerly you were attacked by violence; now you are to be circumvented by Fraud. Your fame is to be destroyed through your Virtues." To begin with, "a female party is already formed to invest my Lady Fitzwilliam."

All that has gone before was violent and forceful. New methods will now be employed. "The violent storm, which has hitherto blown, has only made you clasp your Cloak, more closely about you; but the sun will very speedily begin to shine upon you — & let us see whether it will persuade you to strip yourself naked." The new tactics will be to soothe. The line adopted will be that of claiming that what happened was a "mere misunderstanding." No disgrace was meant. Fitzwilliam himself had not been condemned. He had not actually been recalled. In fact, nothing would be omitted to make his mind "easy." The public good would also come in for its share. And so it would go.

Turning from a prediction of the treatment awaiting Fitzwilliam in official circles, Burke next expressed his horror that Fitzwilliam should ever think that he would abandon him. Burke had been "responsible to you for the advice I gave you to coalite with their Ministry, & to accept your Late Office of chief Gouverneur of Ireland! I abandon you, who, (if I could suppose myself in your place) would do the very same things, & more of the same kind! I abandon you who would have pulled down much more of that crazy & infected structure that loads my native Country, than you have done; & who have advised the permitting of any part of it to stand only on the pressure of the most rigid & odious necessity!"

Referring to the Catholic delegation, then in London, Burke told Fitzwilliam of retaliations already visited upon them and other Catholic leaders because of their part in seeking to apply to the crown for redress of their grievances, a procedure which had worked successfully two years previously when the Catholics won the franchise. Burke described their interview with Portland and said that they were to see the king on the fifteenth. Portland had asked them to name their enemies, and they had responded with two prime examples, the Marquis of Downshire and Fitzgibbon, the Lord Chancellor, to which Portland made no answer whatsoever. His manner remained icily cool throughout.

Burke thought that the Catholic bill would pass despite all that had happened, if not in the present session then in the next. To maintain consistency, the Ascendancy would have the measure "abused & opposed" but "to save themselves from Ruin they will most certainly pass it." Yet, in the next breath, he was greatly and rightly apprehensive that "the King's mind has been some way or other, poisoned about Ireland; & that he is made to believe, that it is a snug department of his own; & that the people, who in fact have totally deprived him & his ostensibly representatives of their authority, are his particular & attached friends."

He was also disturbed by reports, which had not been contradicted, that the Archbishop of Canterbury, who corresponded widely with "certain Clerical persons in Ireland," had talked with the king and given him "an alarm that if the bill should pass the Church could not exist." This was unwarranted interference by "another Church, wholly without jurisdiction civil or ecclesiastical in the Country to curtail the civil rights of the far greater part of the King's subjects there." The Irish Catholics had come to petition the king, as King of Ireland, for certain civil matters and "they find a foreign prelate privately in the Kings closet interfering to indispose his Mind towards them."

Burke signed off by declaring that "rest has in a manner abandoned me. I am . . . without being able to sleep. But the great sleep will soon come."

Fitzwilliam, who also had been having considerable difficulty in keeping a rein on himself during these hectic days, called Burke's letter [65] "a cordial to my soul" and promised to follow "the line [of] conduct you chalk out."

Answering Grattan's letter of 14 March, Burke told him [66] of the dilemma into which Fitzwilliam's recall had put him owing to the part played in it by his old friend, Portland.

In truth I hardly know where I am. I am, to condemn Lord Fitzwilliam, or to abandon the Duke of Portland. . . . Nothing can convince me, that the D. of Portland is not so essentially good as the Sun is essentially bright . . . . whether I shall live to see him get clear of the Dragons head or the Dragons Tail, it is not certain; but you will see him wade out of it, as surely as the present order of things continues. So beat your brass pots, & Kettles — time will go its pace; & all will be right at last. One thing is good. Grattan & Fitzwilliam are in conjunction.
. . . I agree with you, that this Quarrel cannot be on its ostensible grounds. I have perhaps more reason than you have to think so. If it stood on those grounds I am quite sure, that nothing on earth could more easily have been compromised. But, to the last hour, no sort of

compromise or treaty was listened to. There must be some sort of original Sin. For something or other, Lord Fitzwilliam in a signal & *un-
exampled* punishment, is to be made, at every hazard, a striking *example*.

When Fitzwilliam returned, Burke devoted himself to prepare
a defense of his conduct for him which he could deliver in the
House of Lords. Fitzwilliam was delighted with the news from his
kinsman and former Chief Secretary in Ireland, Lord Milton, that
Burke had "already work'd hard in my cause, & that my memorial
is in great forwardness — why do I call it *my* cause. it is the cause
of the whole people of Ireland, . . ." [67]

Burke was soon able to send him [68] "a specimen for your Judgment & correction." It was Burke's idea that Fitzwilliam should
proceed not so much in the way of answering a direct charge by
his enemies but rather that he should make charges against them
to put them on the defensive. He thought that Fitzwilliam's complaint should be invested with a public character to give it dignity
and that it should remove as much of the narrowness of a private
and personal injury as possible. One of the reasons for such an
approach was to get away from the general position, which Portland had adopted, that Fitzwilliam's basic motivation for his acts
in Ireland had been a desire to exalt the Ponsonbys over the Beres-
fords.

He felt that Portland's letter [69] telling him that it was the unanimous sentiment of the cabinet that his continuing as viceroy would
be "the subversion of the King's Government & of all Government" and desiring him to come away and not await a successor
but to appoint Lord Justices and that a license would be sent him
the next day for that purpose was invaluable to Fitzwilliam's cause.
This letter "alone can render your Conduct justifiable to the World
now, as nothing else could justifye you in running away at the
time, from your friends in Ireland. This Letter is your only clear
& positive recal." Both Lord Grenville and Lord Mansfield were
going around publicly declaring that Fitzwilliam had never been
recalled at all but that it was "among your other rash acts — &
for which, & all its consequences, you are responsible." Burke
thought such actions by their Lordships "profound either in treach-
ery or in folly." Fitzwilliam's only escape from the ruin which

this tactic presaged was "by the production of this very Letter, which alone decisively recals you, . . ."

On the twenty-second of April, Burke advised Fitzwilliam [70] that he had not a minute to lose in getting into town and he recommended that "a short Sketch (nothing more than mere heads) ought to be given in writing to the King the day you go in but reserving the larger & fuller view of your Conduct, for that piece wch. would serve him & the publick together."

Fitzwilliam was received privately by the king who heard from his own lips Fitzwilliam's side of the case. The former Lord Lieutenant followed Burke's advice and left a paper with his interpretation of events in the king's hands for him to study. Fitzwilliam later told Grattan that the king seemed impressed with some of the things he told him and that he was very gracious to him but that he expressed no opinions whatsoever. He merely asked what Fitzwilliam's future intentions were.[71] Privately the king professed to be very much unimpressed with this paper.[72]

Early in May, Fitzwilliam was able to write Burke that things seemed to be going well. In Lords that day he had challenged the ministers to come forward with their charges against him in his presence, but that Lord Grenville, speaking for the Treasury Bench, had declined on the grounds that the king's ministers were not bound to give any account for their reasons for making charges. Fitzwilliam was pleased to inform Burke that Grenville admitted "or at least rais'd no doubt about the recall being a fair recall." Burke was happy with this news and said that, if Fitzwilliam needed him, a short note would fetch him.[73]

A few days later, Burke suggested to Fitzwilliam [74] that he should get the Irish question taken up in Lords when the question of peace was under discussion. He thought that "the whole ability of the House was on your side upon the Catholick Question. Not one man of repute for his Talents [was] on the other." He went on to say how disappointed he was with "the Course they are pursuing in Ireland [which] will Jacobinize all the Frenzies & all the active Talent of that Country. These are very considerable; & the popular mind is more susceptible of any emotion there than it is here. Jacobinism is the Vice of men of Parts; & in this age, it is the Channel in which all discontents will run. It is a vain conceit that property can stand against it, alone & unsupported, under any general popular discontent. Part of the property will be debauched; a part frightened; & the rest subdued. . . ."

Fitzwilliam's efforts to make it clear that he had actually been recalled and to defend the measures which he had taken in his brief term of office dragged on until after Burke was dead.[75] Before that, however, he had given his side of the dispute in two letters to Lord Carlisle both of which found their way into print in the spring of 1795 despite Fitzwilliam's none too convincing disavowals that it was done without either his consent or knowledge. For disclosing confidential information in these letters, Fitzwilliam has long been subject to strong censure by commentators on the history of the Fitzwilliam affair. That he should have done so in the light of the treatment accorded him is not surprising in the least.

It would now appear desirable to summarize the episode and its consequences. One of the latter was a challenge issued by Beresford to Fitzwilliam which grew out of the publication of the letters to Carlisle wherein Fitzwilliam said that he had dismissed Beresford due to "so much imputed malversation." The episode had overtones of opéra bouffe although it actually reached the point of their meeting on the field of honor. Before shots were fired, however, the mysteriously coincidental arrival of the police at precisely the right moment put an end to the affair. These worthies extracted from the parties involved their solemn word as gentlemen that the affair would not be resumed. The business was then terminated to the satisfaction of both parties when Fitzwilliam made an apology.[76]

Fitzwilliam has long been accused of having acted rashly and of having displayed a lack of wisdom in his management of affairs in Ireland,[77] but I am fully persuaded that he did what was in the best interests of both Britain and Ireland. When the post had been offered to him, he had delayed in accepting it although his own natural inclination was probably to undertake the job. Lady Fitzwilliam was a rather emotional person, and it was apparently not easy to convince her that they should go to Ireland. Once her approval was won, he agreed to the assignment with the understanding that he would be supported by the coalition in England. His determination to remove both Fitzgibbon and Beresford was based upon his recognition of the woeful misgovernment of Ireland which could only be corrected by getting rid of those chiefly responsible. This was common sense. He behaved realistically enough in agreeing to what he understood was a compromise in this matter of men: Fitzgibbon was to stay; but Beresford would go. Pitt offered no objection at the time, and Fitzwilliam should not be censured for removing Beresford since he understood that he had carte blanche to do so. Perhaps he should not have acted as swiftly as he did, but this is a matter of conjecture. There is much to be said for his having displayed his authority at this critical time, since a clean break is often more effective than a policy of temporizing. Fitzwilliam knew better than many of his critics that inroads would have to be made in the Ascendancy's ranks if Ireland were to be governed properly. The unfortunate aspect of this business was that his friends, the Ponsonbys, stood to benefit from the removals of their political foes, thus lending to the transaction the coloring of factiousness, but it was perfectly natural that the former Irish opposition would wish power and patronage. Since no one has yet succeeded in proving that Fitzwilliam was motivated by other than honorable intentions, this coloration need not be given much credence. The dismissals may be boiled down to the observation that there was no sense to Fitzwilliam's going to Ireland, holding the opinions he did about the Ascendancy, if he were not to be permitted to make changes.

In the matter of measures, he was also right. It may be argued that he acted precipitously, but I cannot see how this can be taken too seriously. Everything seemed to suggest the immediate completion of emancipation. Both in England and Ireland men known to be favorable to the idea were in office, and there was no opposition to it in Ireland except from the very hard core of the Protestant Ascendancy, notably Fitzgibbon, who even felt himself that it might well pass. The vast majority of the Protestants in parliament were willing to concede the measure under the stress of the French threat and the danger of a civil war so long as they thought that the proposal had the approval of the British government. That this appeared to be the case when Fitzwilliam went to Ireland is abundantly clear. Equally patent is the senselessness of allowing the hopes of the Catholics to be aroused if they were only to be dashed swiftly and unceremoniously. Fitzwilliam certainly put himself clearly on record with Portland as to what his intentions were shortly after his arrival. Yet he had acted with admirable restraint in not mentioning emancipation in his Speech from the Throne on 22 January. The long delay on Portland's part in taking cognizance of Fitzwilliam's intentions naturally led Fitzwilliam to assume that the government had no objections.[78] Added to this was the fact that he had been told by Fitzgibbon that emancipation would pass if he supported it. Not only did Fitzgibbon believe that emancipation would take place, although he was personally bitterly opposed to it and was secretly engaged in trying to block it, but Beresford was also convinced that it was a certainty. The two were related by marriage and in close touch with one another in all important matters. Finally, when Fitzwilliam did give leave to Grattan to introduce his bill for Catholic emancipation, the terms of the measure were carefully kept secret by the Lord Lieutenant from both parliament and the Catholics until the government in London had a chance to form their opinion on it. As late as the time Fitzwilliam was informed by Portland that his administration was unsatisfactory, the terms had still not been disclosed.

Hence, in respect to Fitzwilliam's actions in the matter of both men and measures, a strong case may be made out in defense of his policies in both respects. Why was he removed? He told his friend, Lord Carlisle in a letter which was made public (although Fitzwilliam denied authorizing its publication) that it was not the Catholic question which caused his downfall but rather his dismissal of Beresford,[79] an assertion likewise made openly on the floor of the Irish House of Commons by George Ponsonby.[80] Grattan said cryptically in the House that the government either actually had no object in dismissing Fitzwilliam or one "too despicable or too criminal to be mentioned." [81]

Privately, Fitzwilliam had earlier confided to Burke [82] that he owed his dismissal principally to Pitt who had prevailed upon the viceroy's friends while he was absent in Ireland "to abandon" him. Pitt was "indifferent as to the ground: he decided on my removal with, or without cause." In this privately expressed opinion, he was supported by Grattan who told Burke [83] that it was not Beresford nor the Catholics but Pitt who was responsible for Fitzwilliam's dismissal.

In addition to both the Ascendancy in Ireland and the cabinet in England, there is the factor of the king which needs to be considered. George III was personally strongly opposed to Catholic emancipation and firmly supported the members of the Ascendancy whom he felt upheld the Protestant interest. In his letter to Pitt, 6 February 1795, which is mentioned above, the king had written that the fact that Catholic emancipation had even been attempted then was the strongest proof that the "old servants of the Crown in Ireland" had been right in opposing the concessions granted to the Catholics on former occasions. His Majesty felt that the attempt to secure equality for the Catholics had been dictated by a desire to humiliate the Ascendancy or to pay "implicit obedience to the heated imagination of Mr. Burke." [84]

The king was so disturbed over the Catholic question that he did not allow the matter to rest with his having made known to Pitt his unequivocal opposition. He believed that Catholic emancipation would be a violation of his Coronation Oath which would force him to forfeit the crown. Thus he sought the opinion of various leading lawyers and ecclesiasts. Both the Chief Justice, Lord Kenyon, and the Attorney-General, Sir John Scott, gave negative replies. Lord Loughborough, the Chancellor, gave an ambiguous answer. The Archbishop of Canterbury and the Bishop of London both felt that emancipation would violate the oath. Fitzgibbon, the Irish Chancellor, wrote a memorandum for the king which most convincingly supported His Majesty's position.

Thus, the king would have been so strong an opponent of the measure that Catholic emancipation would probably have failed at this time even if Pitt and the cabinet had given their approval. It was George III's opposition to emancipation which was to cause Pitt's fall from office in 1801 after he had carried the union between Great Britain and Ireland during the previous year.

As for Pitt, he certainly revealed himself susceptible to the warnings of the Ascendancy when he failed to support Fitzwilliam's dismissals and he had a convenient lapse of memory in respect to Fitzwilliam's claim that he had not offered any objections to the latter when he told him that he would dismiss Beresford. Then, too, he was unquestionably influenced by the king's stand. Finally, the unwillingness to make an issue out of the matter by the Portland

Whigs, who failed to stand by Fitzwilliam during the crisis, smoothed his path. It appears that Pitt, following the failure of his commercial propositions for Irish free trade in 1785, had gradually become wedded to the idea of a legislative union between Great Britain and Ireland, which, when once accomplished, would be followed by Catholic emancipation. Thus, he was prepared to risk the immediate consequences in Ireland and take his chances on the future.

The part played by Portland, Spencer, and Windham, Fitzwilliam's friends and fellow Whigs in the coalition, is harder to understand. Even Loughborough who had originally worked hard to get Fitzwilliam to go to Ireland as viceroy must also bear a share of the onus for the failure of Fitzwilliam to find any support in the government. Three possible explanations for their behavior have been offered: [85] their belief that Fitzwilliam had not lived up to the agreements reached before he went to Ireland; their having changed their minds toward further concessions for the Catholics; and their acceptance of the argument that ministerial solidarity was vital at this crucial moment in England's history. Barnes feels that all three influences played a part, although he holds that the first was not decisive in view of Portland's warm backing of Fitzwilliam when the latter returned. I am substantially in agreement with this three-fold explanation but would add the point that Portland was one of the most easily influenced men who ever rose to the high offices which he held, including the Prime Ministership. He was usually influenced by the last person who had his ear. In this instance, Fitzwilliam was away, and Pitt confronted him in person with arguments which His Grace weakly accepted. It is also possible that Portland, too, had become converted to the idea of a union and was likewise willing to accept the immediate consequences.

Whatever the explanation, the mess made of this entire episode by those responsible for the jettisoning of Fitzwilliam, the upholding of the Ascendancy, and the failure of emancipation remains to this day tragic and culpable.

As for Burke, despite his "heated imagination," he saw far more clearly than most what the consequences of a failure to allow Catholic emancipation at the time would be. Even Lord Charlemont, long an opponent of Catholic relief, felt that Fitzwilliam's recall and the stifling of the wishes of the Catholics were "utterly ruinous" and predicted that Ireland would soon be in the hands of the United Irishmen.[86]

The replacement of Fitzwilliam by "the mild administration of fifteen regiments of British Fencibles" [87] was indeed a fateful turning point in the relations between Great Britain and Ireland. It was followed by consuming hatred of England by the majority of the Irish Catholics, renewed religious and class warfare in Ireland, a fierce rebellion in 1798 which was savagely repressed at a cost of some 30,000 lives, and a legislative union which was carried only by resort to wholesale bribery and corruption.

Burke's part in the whole unhappy incident was important. There can be no question as to whom Fitzwilliam meant when he said that he had tried to rid Ireland of those men "who had been described to me for years back, as the bane of good government in Ireland." Burke patently had been Fitzwilliam's mentor here. The desertion of the viceroy by Pitt and the coalition was concrete proof of what Burke had maintained for years in his long fight to overthrow the Ascendancy. His prediction that disastrous consequences would mark failure to grant emancipation were unhappily destined to be fulfilled in the sanguinary uprising of 1798.

His overall approval of Fitzwilliam's conduct in Ireland was governed by the fact that Burke was one of the very few men in England who really understood the true situation in Ireland. Common sense plainly dictated that, since the Catholics had received so much in 1793, they were bound to feel entitled to what had been held back from them at that time.[88] Especially was this true when one took into account the "circumstances" which existed in 1795. Burke exaggerated very little the danger to British control of Ireland which the United Irishmen represented. His estimates of the loyalty and cooperation which the Catholics would demonstrate were shown correct by the patient attitude displayed by the Catholics and by their persistent refusal to join the United Irishmen in any numbers until they were humiliated and insulted by the callous disregard of their dreams and aspirations.

Although Burke was certainly not always consistent in this crisis nor what is sadder to relate always rational, his thoughts and his conduct were, on the whole, fairly sound.

CHAPTER X

The End of a "Great, Just, and Honourable Cause," 1795-1797

During these last years of Edmund Burke's life, his attention was claimed chiefly by Irish affairs. Although downcast by the turn of events, he remained in hope that the errors which had been made in the handling of Ireland could still be remedied before it was too late. Unfortunately, his health deteriorated steadily and he had difficulty in combatting the melancholy which persistently gripped him. Concluding a refusal to accept the offer of Edmund Malone to collaborate with him on a biography of Sir Joshua Reynolds, Burke said that he was sorry to negative the idea but that all his business was "with the deceased." [1] Nevertheless, he managed to retain his interest in Irish matters, although it taxed his powers of concentration greatly.

He had advised Dr. Hussey shortly after the recall of Fitzwilliam that it should be strongly emphasized to the Catholics of Ireland that they should be neither too presuming nor yet too humble in their conduct. Dignity and courage were essential, but arrogance was to be eschewed. On the other hand, it would only serve to court disaster if they became "skulking" in their deportment. They should be quick to protest every transgression of their rights.[2]

Despite his friendship for Fitzwilliam, Hussey had been asked by the Duke of Portland to remain in Ireland following the viceroy's recall so that he might assist in working out the projected plan for the education of the Catholic clergy in Ireland. Burke had long favored such an idea and had advocated that steps be taken in this direction. As recently as September 1794, he had written to Grattan that Catholic clerical education was sorely needed in Ireland as an antidote to Jacobinism.[3]

The Irish government had finally realized the futility of trying to separate the majority of the Irish people from their religion and had reached the conclusion that the wisest course to pursue would be to attempt to exercise control over the Catholic clergy. This could best be accomplished, it was decided, by supervising the education of the priests. Other desirable points from the standpoint of the administration would be to secure some voice in the election of bishops together with a system whereby the state would pay the salaries of secular clergymen. The decision to permit a Catholic seminary had been motivated by a wish to mitigate the consequences of having denied Catholic emancipation. It so happened that the time chosen for the manifestation of this sudden interest in Catholic clerical education was propitious in one sense. The French Revolution, followed by the outbreak of war between Great Britain and France in 1793, had caused the destruction of the Catholic seminaries in France which the Irish attended. This meant that the principal source for the education of the Catholic priests of Ireland had been cut off. On the other hand, the government's timing was not so favorable since a Catholic seminary could hardly be considered a substitute equal to emancipation.

Burke was staunchly opposed to permitting the Irish government any power over the Catholic religion and declared bluntly to Hussey that there must be no "Castle choices" among the Irish bishops.[4] He felt that the Catholics ought to accept gracefully the necessary funds for a seminary but that they should resist any interference whatsoever in the management of the institution. The education of the clergy was too sacred to permit any tampering with its operation, especially by their avowed enemies. He warned Hussey that the grant of money was for no other purpose than mischief. If the ecclesiastical authorities permitted any interference by the government, there would be an end, not only to the Catholic religion, but to "all religion, all morality, all law, and all order, in that unhappy kingdom."

He demonstrated once again his professed hostility for the abstract. Mere theory deserved scorn. The Catholic prelates would do well to avoid men presented to them "in their *abstract*, under the fine, specious, general name of *government*." They should know the men with whom they were to deal "in their *concrete*." It would be wisdom on their part, moreover, to pause and reflect fully before placing their seminary in the power of their enemies, men who "call themselves Protestants." Reflection would show that these men did not manage their own schools very well. He then asked what would happen to the Catholic institution if it fell into such incompetent hands.

He expressed the fear that strenuous efforts would be made to court favor with the Catholic clergy. It recalled to his mind the old trick of the Ascendancy of separating the clergy from the laity and then further dividing the ranks of the latter by playing off the upper classes against the lower. He expressed the hope that the clergy would make common cause with the people and thus avoid the danger of division.

Burke could see no good reason why any innovations in the policy of the Catholic church should be permitted. Such would be the case if the government were granted supervision over the projected seminary, a power which was being sought.[5] The policy of the Catholic church in Ireland had permitted it to weather two and a half centuries of the wildest storms any church had ever been called upon to withstand. It should not be altered now. The "old course, because it is the old course, and because it has been the successful course," should be maintained. Any assistance in keeping things on that path should be welcomed but certainly not the external interference of a diverse religious sect. No elections should be allowed, whether from within or without. They were very dangerous and "very corrupting." [6] Had they been practiced in the past, the Christian religion would never have survived. The contemporary enemies of all religion, the French Jacobins, had cleverly proposed to make the bishops elective, a procedure which was bound to have disastrous results.

As the plans progressed for the Catholic seminary, Burke advised against expending too great a sum for the physical plant itself. The real expense should be incurred for maintenance, clothing, and the instruction of the seminarians.[7]

The measure which resulted in the establishment of the College of St. Patrick at Maynooth, the first Catholic institution for the education of the clergy in Ireland in over a century, became law in April 1795.[8] There was an Irish parliamentary grant of £ 8000 made at the time, but at first the government did not provide any endowment for the education of the students. The cornerstone was laid in May by Lord Camden, the viceroy, and Dr. Hussey was installed as the first president. Control of the seminary was vested in a group of trustees, including the Irish Lord Chancellor and three jurists. In the main, however, it was to be directed by the Catholic bishops. Burke was strongly opposed to the inclusion of the Chancellor and the judges among the trustees, but necessity forced the Catholics to accept this arrangement despite the wishes of their good friend.

While disappointed that Catholic clerical education was not free from the interference of their sworn enemies, people like the Chancellor, Burke hoped that the seminary might help to offset the inroads being made among the Catholics by the principles of the French Revolution. He made a gift of a number of volumes to the library of Maynooth and received the warm thanks of the trustees from the Archbishop of Dublin, John Thomas Troy.[9]

Ever since the recall of Fitzwilliam, Ireland had been in a turbulent state. Some Catholics, previously noteworthy for their perseverance and restraint in the face of many dicouraging setbacks, had openly joined the ranks of the United Irishmen. A new announcement by the government concerning the laws against rebellion served merely to exacerbate matters.[10] On 9 April, a public assembly of the Catholics of Dublin was held in the Francis Street chapel.[11] At the same time, an anti-Catholic assembly took place on College Green, although many "respectable" Protestants, including a delegation from the University, were present at the Catholic meeting to lend their fullest support and sympathy.[12]

The Catholic meeting had been called to hear the report of the delegates who had gone to London to present petitions to the king on the Catholic question and the recall of Fitzwilliam.

Burke wrote to Hussey [13] to express his dislike of the Francis Street meeting because its "tone was wholly Jacobinical." [14] He shuddered at the language which he felt was plainly aimed at a separation of Ireland from Britain. Such a step would be mutually ruinous, but Ireland would suffer first and hardest. He reiterated his old argument that the Irish erred in attributing the source of their grievances to Britain. It would be pure folly for the Catholics to dissolve themselves as a body by throwing their complaints in with those of the Dissenters who formed the United Irishmen and were nothing but Jacobins. By so doing, the Catholics would lose their identity and with that their importance. The possibility that the Catholics would join their grievances to those of the Dissenters irked him because this combination would form an Irish opposition to the imperial connection. Nobody appreciated the grievances of the Catholics better than Burke, but they should keep their complaints separate because

in the name of God, what grievances has Ireland as Ireland, to complain of, with regard to Great Britain; unless the protection of the most powerful country upon earth — giving all her privileges, without exception, in common to Ireland, and reserving to herself only the painful pre-eminence of tenfold burthens — be a matter of complaint? The subject, as a subject, is as free in Ireland as he is in England. As a member of the empire, an Irishman has every privilege of a natural-born Englishman.

Ireland was constitutionally independent, he declared, but she could never be completely independent. France or Britain was the choice she had to make of a protector, since nature had formed her in such a fashion that one or the other must supervise her. The privilege of practicing their religion which the Catholics of Ireland possessed could be traced to Ireland's connection with Britain. A connection with the United Irishmen meant one with France, the avowed enemy of all religions. As matters stood, the Catholics had the support of "all the splendid abilities, and much of the independent property in parliament in their favour, and every Protestant . . . who is really a Christian." The choice before the Catholics was to retain these desirable supporters or to throw in their lot with intemperate, desperate men, who lacked moral principle and religion.

A way out of their difficulties was presented them. They could charge their enemies with defaming them and, at the same time, repudiate the treasonable schemes attributed to them. Then, they should assert themselves in restrained but virile language. Let it be known that they were righteously determined upon redress of their grievances and would not submit to intimidation by "the monopolists of the kingdom." Such a mode of conduct would be bound to gain respect and the removal of bias both in Britain and Ireland. In conclusion, he hoped that the members of the Roman Catholic General Committee who proposed its dissolution [15] and advocated a union with the United Irishmen would be convinced of the advisability of dropping the idea.

The persistent Henry Grattan brought forward the Catholic measure which Fitzwilliam had encouraged and which had been the ostensible reason for his recall. The new viceroy was well prepared in advance to defeat it when the debate took place on 4 May. Although the session lasted until ten o'clock the following morning, the result was a foregone conclusion. Grattan and his supporters were defeated by a vote of 155 to 84.[16]

Saddened by this defeat, Burke wrote a letter to Sir Hercules Langrishe, 26 May 1795,[17] which like the earlier one also found its way into print. In it are the lines so indicative of the policy applied by Burke in his connection with the affairs of Ireland: "What a sad thing it is, that the grand instructor, Time, has not yet been able to teach the grand lesson of his own value, and that, in every question of moral and political prudence, it is the choice of the moment which renders the measure serviceable or useless, noxious or salutary."

He said that in the Catholic question he had been guided by the consideration whether "at the time, and in the circumstances," it was a measure aimed at promoting "the concord of the citizens." He had "no difficulty" in saying that in this recent instance it certainly was such a proposal. It was "a critical season" and demanded the "present concord of the citizens" which could be obtained "by granting a few *capacities*" unlikely to hurt anyone.

Considered from any angle, the recent moment had been a favorable one for introducing and perpetuating concord. Great strength would have resulted from it, strength such as Ireland had never felt in the past. Sorrowfully, Burke confessed:

My sanguine hopes are blasted, and I must consign my feelings on that terrific disappointment to the same patience in which I have been obliged to bury the vexation I suffered on the defeat of the other great, just, and honourable causes in which I have had some share, and which have given more of dignity than of peace and advantage to a long, laborious life. . . . I think I can hardly overrate the malignity of the principles of Protestant ascendency, as they affect Ireland — or of Indianism,[18] as they affect Asia, — or Jacobinism, as they affect all Europe and the state of human society itself. The last is the greatest evil. But it readily combines with the others, and flows from them. Whatever breeds discontent at this time will produce that great master-mischief most infallibly. Whatever tends to persuade the people that the *few*, called by whatever name you please, religious or political, are of [the] opinion that their interest is not compatible with that of the *many*, is a great point gained to Jacobinism.

Burke mentioned his dislike of the Catholic meeting in Francis Street but added that he cared as little for the anti-Catholic assembly held on College Green at the same time. If anything, the Catholics had been provoked into the attitude they displayed. The worst feature of the Catholic flirtation with Jacobinism was that the Protestants of the Ascendancy were guilty of partly leading and partly forcing them into the position they were adopting. The Catholics ought to be "an invisible dike" against the threatened inundation by Jacobinism because of their religion, conservatism, and characteristic discipline. Unfortunately, the Catholics had learned too well at the hands of the Ascendancy as their speeches in the Francis Street meeting demonstrated. The distasteful liberal tenor of those declamations disclosed a spirit imbibed from the Ascendancy.

The ever present fear of the pope once again had to be dismissed by Burke. This time, he exclaimed "*o seri studiorum!*" [19] and expressed confidence that "it will not be difficult to get many called Catholics to laugh at this fundamental part of their religion." In short, the Catholics took their religion from Rome but not their politics.

Besides religion, the other objects of the Jacobin attack were property and "old traditionary constitutions." In regard to the latter, Burke confessed his dislike for parliamentary reform but could not understand how "men can be reconciled to the *practical* merits of a constitution, the theory of which is in litigation, by being *practically* excluded from any of its advantages."

In conclusion, Burke stated that he and Langrishe had talked over the Catholic question more than thirty years ago. Their opinions were the same then as they were at the time he was now writing.

News of this letter to Langrishe caused something of a stir among Catholic circles in Dublin. A prominent Catholic layman, Edward Hay, endeavored unsuccessfully to secure permission from Langrishe to have it published and wrote to Burke to tell him that Langrishe had refused. Hay also communicated to Burke the information that he personally was in accord with Burke's idea that the Catholics ought to reorganize their committee and said that the laity was greatly in favor, inferring that the clergy had opposed the project. Particulars on the sanguinary nature of the disturbances then plaguing Ireland were also sent along by Hay.[20]

Burke replied to Hay immediately [21] and asked that as a favor to him no further attempts be made to get the letter to Langrishe published. He did not think it could be of as much use as he himself had first imagined since his "Sentiments so far as they can be of Weight are already well Known." Burke's earlier letter to Langrishe on the Catholic question was in print. The recent one was "not quite so full or satisfactory."

When he had made a gift of some books to the library of Maynooth, the new Catholic seminary, Burke had given them to Hay and at the same time had suggested to him that it would be a good idea for the Catholics to make "an ennumeration" of their people in Ireland. Since Hay had alluded to this plan in his letter, Burke returned to it by saying that he wished that they would add to their count "the Occupation Trade or Profession of each person whose name and Dwelling you set down whether engaged in Agriculture Manufactures &c &c this would be of great use towards ascertaining the Proportions of the People employed in each Branch."

Hay answered Burke[22] with praise for the idea of adding each person's profession or trade in the Catholic census and then returned to the Langrishe letter and said that his application to Sir Hercules had arisen from Burke's having once expressed regret to Hay that he had not kept a copy of his letter on the rejection of the Catholic bill so that he himself could publish it.

The letter was, as pointed out above, published shortly thereafter but how it came about is not clear. It is probable that someone to whom Langrishe had allowed it to be circulated had made a copy and it found its way into print, which was what happened in the case of the first letter.

In September 1795, the Orange Society, a secret anti-Catholic organization was founded in the County of Armagh. To Burke, the appearance of such a body occasioned no surprise. He later informed Hussey [23] that it was merely the logical conclusion of an unfortunate procedure, namely, the fact that the Catholic clergy had persuaded the Catholic people to yield any arms in their possession to the authorities. Contrary although it was to his principles, Burke was forced to admit that "it is now plain that Catholic *defenderism* [24] is the only restraint upon Protestant ascendency." Nearly a year after having expressed himself thus to Hussey, he wrote to the priest that it was unquestionably right to teach the doctrine of passive obedience but to go beyond it by advocating rebellion was to deceive the people.[25]

By the summer of 1795, Burke's financial embarrassment had become quite acute. Writing to Fitzwilliam,[26] he asked him for the letter which the Duke of Portland had sent him outlining Pitt's intentions toward Burke in the matter of a pension. Burke promised to "make none but a very discreet use of it." He added that "it contains no secret whatever but it is a record & evidence." The simple fact of the matter was that he needed the letter to impress his creditors with his prospects so that he could stave them off for a while.

Fitzwilliam sent the letter as requested but doubted that it was of any value. It could be looked upon "as waste paper." Even so, he asked that the letter be preserved and he begged Burke not to lose it.[27]

In his next letter to Fitzwilliam,[28] Burke was able to report that his financial picture was brighter. One of the proposed grants he was to receive was "meant to be vendible, for the discharge of my Debts." Unfortunately, he discovered that he had failed to give them in to Pitt at their full amount and that it was now too late to change it. Philosophically, he remarked that "even as it is, I ought to be thankful to Providence for what is done. It produces a serious change for the better in my circumstances." His one regret remained — Richard was gone and so: "The decorations [the proposed peerage] indeed are gone; but then every thing is gone, which could give me a wish for them, or any thing else, beyond what smooths the way to the Grave with some degree of repose, & enables me to go out of the world without making others suffer materially by their confidence in me."

This mood was still upon him several days later when he told Fitzwilliam[29] that "I think your Lordship feels, in the settlement of my affair, more pleasure than I am capable of feeling for any thing."

Some delay ensued, however, in the arrangements since Dundas wrote to Burke that he "had not a conception that your business had not been all arranged" and promised to attend to it the moment Pitt returned to London, which he expected would be the next day.[30] It was not until the 23d or 24th of December, however, that Burke actually received the sums granted him [31] and even then it was not in the manner in which he had originally expected. There was too much opposition to a parliamentary grant so in its place Burke was given two annuities on the West Indian 4½ per cent fund. This meant that the three grants which combined to form Burke's pension were all from the crown, a circumstance which hurt Burke's pride but one which necessity compelled him to accept. On 15 November 1795, the Duke of Bedford and the Earl of Lauderdale accused him in the House of Lords of having been bought by the very crown whose power and patronage he had so often attacked in the past. Burke was stung to the quick by the charge that he had become a paid creature of the crown. His enemies joyfully seized upon the subject of the pension, and the old calumny that he was a disguised Jesuit reappeared. He was variously described as "Old Honesty the Jesuit" [32] and "St. Edmund." [33] Considerable doggerel and a number of witty epigrams were written in an effort to ruin him finally in the public eye.[34]

Burke defended himself ably. First, he sent a news item for publication to Mr. Beauchamp, the official gazeteer. Dated 8 March 1796, it read as follows:[35]

Mr. Burke's Pension

That Mr. Burke may not be, either
erroneously or invidiously described
as receiving more from the royal
bounty than he actually does, it cannot
prove improper to insert the following
statement.

A pension for his own and that of
   his wife on the civil list 12,00
Another on three lives out of 4½ per
        cent fund 13,50
Another on three lives, out of the same for . . 11,50 [sic]

                  [£] 3,700

In addition, he wrote a pamphlet entitled *A Letter to a Noble Lord*, which was addressed to Fitzwilliam and published in 1796. It has been deservedly called one of the most brilliant and successful political pamphlets ever written.[36] In a passage which reviewed his life, Burke wrote:

I was not, like his Grace of Bedford, swaddled and rocked and dandled into a legislator: *"Nitor in adversum"* [37] is the motto for a man like me. I possessed not one of the qualities nor cultivated one of the arts that recommend men to the favor and protection of the great. I was not made for a minion or a tool. As little did I follow the trade of winning the hearts by imposing on the understandings of the people. At every step of my progress in life, (for in every step was I traversed and opposed,) and at every turnpike I met, I was obliged to show my passport, and again and again to prove my sole title to the honor of being useful to my country, by a proof that I was not wholly unacquainted with its laws and the whole system of its interests both abroad and at home. Otherwise, no rank, no toleration even, for me. I had no arts but manly arts. On them I have stood, and, please God, in spite of the Duke of Bedford and the Earl of Lauderdale, to the last gasp will I stand.

The remarkable and most revealing thing about this pamphlet is that it demonstrates quite conclusively that Burke was still very much in possession of his faculties. This *apologia pro sua vita* was as closely reasoned and well written as anything he could have done in his prime and shows that his sustained interest in Ireland during these last years of his life was rational and clear. It is ad-

mittedly true that he suffered fits of depression, that his health
was failing rapidly, and that some of his letters were rather woolly,
but the fact remains that his mind was still sound.

In the fall of 1795, he had written another excellent piece of
work in which he showed his very real grasp of economics and
especially of the theories of Adam Smith. Called *Thoughts and
Details on Scarcity*,[38] it was prompted by the poor crops of that
fall. In addition to showing his knowledge of economics, it revealed once again Burke's humaneness. Burke opposed a proposal
to put an end to the distilling of gin, which beverage he defended
as invigorating the stomach for the digestion of the inadequate
diet of the poor. Gin, he said, is not food but it greatly makes
up for the want of it. He also called it "medicine for the mind"
and considered it a physical aid to the moral consolation of the
poor.

His correspondence now became more and more dominated by
the affairs of Ireland. Disturbances in Armagh [39] at the expense of
the Catholics particularly upset him as he made clear to both
Fitzwilliam [40] and Hussey [41] in letters a few days apart. He concluded that the indignities and injuries being inflicted upon the
Catholics of that county were the result of the impractical advice
of the clergy to the laity to give up their arms to the authorities.

Burke derived some pleasure from a communication of Hussey's
which informed him that he had had a letter from George III in
which His Majesty expressed his approbation of the thanksgiving
prayer of the Catholics of Ireland upon his recent escape from
harm.[42] The king called the Catholic prayer "a handsome, & acceptable mark of duty, from the heads of the R Catholic Clergy of
Ireland." As was so often the case, Hussey expressed his great
apprehensions about his mail in Ireland, a feeling which Burke
shared, and asked Burke to write him henceforward at his London
address from whence the letters would go to him by the "first safe
hands." [43]

There followed a gap of several months in Burke's correspondence on the subject of Ireland, but by the fall of 1796 it grew
heavy once again. Burke had been busy in the interim seeing to the
implementation of his plan for a school at Penn, three miles from
Beaconsfield, for the children of French refugees. Many of the

boys' fathers were serving in the British forces. He managed to get Pitt to provide a suitable building for the school together with an endowment, and Burke and a number of his friends composed the board of trustees.

Another reason which accounts for the temporary paucity of correspondence on Ireland in the period of some months before November 1796, was Burke's fear that Britain might make peace with a victorious France which had temporarily subdued the continent. He wrote his *Letters Addressed to A Member of the Present Parliament on the Proposals for Peace with the Regicide Directory of France*, of which there were ultimately several.[44] Despite Burke's public plea in these pamphlets [45] against such a step, Pitt sent Lord Malmesbury to Paris to negotiate a peace if one could be obtained on honorable terms. Malmesbury was ordered out of France on 19 December and given forty-eight hours to make good his departure. The French were confident that they could reduce Britain by arms.

While the unsuccessful Malmesbury mission was a topic of discussion, Burke received a letter from Thomas Townshend, bearing a Dublin dateline,[46] which sarcastically observed "should the piratical legislators of France, who doom mankind to pillage & murder vouchsafe to accede to our abject solicitations for the offals of their barbarous mercy, the situation of Ireland will then become eminently critical. . . . In this state should a peace qualify the visits of a few French missionaries from the Parisian synod of anarchy, it would not be difficult to predict the abhorred issue."

The real reason for the Malmesbury mission, Fitzwilliam told Burke, was Ireland.[47] Pitt was afraid that a French expedition would slip over to that country, then seething with unrest, and provoke a rebellion. Pitt was "determined not to make friends with the Irish, and he doubts dragooning them into a submission during war." For this reason, Burke's labors in the first Regicide Peace pamphlet were "in vain, though they have produced effect in the country beyond expectation."

To his credit, Burke could not accept this explanation and told Fitzwilliam [48] that Irish politics were the main ingredients "in the scandalous & mischievous sollicitation for peace at Paris: But I do not think they were the sole motives to that contemptible measure." Instead of clarifying what these other motives were, Burke launched into a discourse on the state of Ireland.

The ministry was "less sollicitous about preserving that Country from the Invasion with which it is threatened,[49] than for the support of the miserable & corrupt faction which is the Cause of all its Evils. They venture all upon the bottom of that Faction." The Catholics were being irritated into the dilemma of submitting to "a disgraceful Yoke" or of seeking "for redress from that Jacobinism which must bring on universal confusion." They will take refuge in the end in an alliance with the United Irishmen, "the protestant republicans who have been made by Government one of the instruments of their persecution." The defense of Ireland will then rest upon "the narrow faction of Tyrants & peculators, & of those, whom fear, & fear alone, of greater Evils will arm for their support."

The new army commander in Ireland, Luttrell, was "a man universally odious without any pretence of greater military capacity, knowledge, skill, or experience [than his predecessor, Cunningham], but only known in every stage of his Life, for a desperate defiance of publick opinion & the good will of mankind & lately for the most outrageous acts against poor people in open violation of all pretence & colour of law." The appointment of a man of this calibre left no doubt as to what the government's intentions in Ireland were.

In such a state of affairs, what part should Fitzwilliam and his colleagues play? One thing was clear. They could take no "rational step" unless in concert with Fitzwilliam's Irish friends. What the latter had in mind, Burke said, he could not divine.

Burke then alluded to the idea of a political union between Britain and Ireland, an idea which he had never liked and which has already been discussed in this book.

Next he mentioned Fox and said that he acted in so far as he did anything in these matters "in concert with & on the principles of the Jacobins in England & Ireland, & has no managements whatever." He then said that he knew that a prominent Irishman named O'Connor [50] had lived in close connection with Fox and his friends while he stayed in London. This was followed by a startling tergiversation on John Keogh by Burke who said: "I am far from sure, that Keogh is not at this instant in the same Cabal. I enclose to you two Letters,[51] one of them dated very lately, which I had from him. I have reason to believe, that he is no more a Catholick than Buonoparte is — further than it serves his purposes. He is a man of very great natural parts; but a franc Jacobin, crafty, ambitious, full of dark & perplexed intrigue, & of very suspicious connexions. I send you the answer I made to him,[52] which, by my having nothing in reply, I suppose was not much to his liking. I do not know whether he is here merely on his own account or in consequence of some delegation."

Fitzwilliam replied to Burke's letter a week later [53] and agreed that it would be wise to make his conduct in Lords coincide with the sentiments of his Irish friends and, in fact, "to take just as much or as little part as they think most advantageous for our general cause." He was greatly disturbed over the growing crisis in Ireland and said that he made no pretense of knowing what "the treasonable intentions of the diggers of potatoes (en masse)" might be; perhaps they were treasonable and the government was therefore justified in checking them, but he did know that "Govt never can be justified in surrounding a field by the military, making the whole mob prisoners, picking out the stout & the strong, & without trial, without pretence of Law, without even an enquiry on the Drum's head, sending these last on board a tender; of course to be dispos'd of, as any naval Bashaw may think fit." There were two laws and two constitutions in Ireland, one set for the rich, and the other for the poor. He wished that the cause of the mistreated majority, the Irish poor, could be taken up in their own parliament, but this was manifestly impossible as matters stood. He would, however, try to fortify Grattan and the Ponsonbys "in making a shew of exertion" on behalf of the afflicted. The place to do this was in parliament and not in "the popular Societies", e.g., the Whig Club in Dublin.[54]

Fitzwilliam concluded by saying that he was "almost sorry" that Burke had not seen Keogh. Burke's letter had not been a refusal, but it certainly was not "a warm invitation." By talking with him, Burke might have learned some news that "might lead to a guess of what is the actual state of things in I[reland] — at present it is all surmize, at least for us."

Burke admitted [55] that his letter to Keogh "was too repulsive. But I wrote in bad health & in ill humour." He said that he had since heard from Keogh [56] despite "the forbidding manner" in which he had written and that this time his reply to Keogh was in a different vein. He had invited Keogh to visit him or if his asthma made it inconvenient for him to come to Beaconsfield Burke suggested that he see his protégé, Dr. French Laurence in town.[57] This change of heart on Burke's part pleased Fitzwilliam who felt that no harm could come from hearing what Keogh had to say and perhaps some positive good might result.[58] Burke was soon able to report that Keogh had seen Laurence [59] and that he showed a disposition to visit Burke. The latter, however, doubted that he would come owing to the weather and the condition of the roads. And any way, he added showing that his feelings toward Keogh had reverted to the earlier stage of "ill humour," he was sure that Keogh's influence among the Catholics was no longer very great and that he was in London "without any deputation, real or understood, from that body." Whether Keogh did actually visit Burke is problematical. The whole episode is trivial except for two things. It points up clearly the frame of mind in which Burke was at the time when he could say what he did about a gentleman whom he had long held in esteem and had often praised lavishly. It also shows how desperate Fitzwilliam was for information on what was going on in Ireland.

That something was going on among his friends there which he did not like was manifested to Burke in a letter of 5 December from Fitzwilliam wherein he said that he lamented the fact that Grattan and the Ponsonbys were taking up the consideration of the representation of Ireland. He disliked this the more because they were doing it at the Whig Club. It was not that the existing system of representation was not a grievance since it was a "most crying one" and to a considerable extent the reason for "the misery of the lower orders." These people were left without any protection because the system was so aristocratic. This should teach "what tyrants we aristocrats can be, when there is no check whatever on the selfish bent of the human mind. — Happy the country where there is such an alloy of democracy, as brings the overbearing inclination of the great to a fellow-feeling with the low; as makes it necessary that the one should court the other." Even so, he trembled when he saw "ancient arrangements meddled with" for there was no ascertaining once the dyke was cut how far the waters would flow. He disliked this "meddling" the more when it occurred "not in a *constituted*, but in a *self-created* authority — it savors of Jacobinism." Hence, Fitzwilliam had lately thrown out "a loose hint upon the subject" by strongly urging that "our friends there" stand firm in their proper station, the Irish House of Commons. His fear of Arthur O'Connor, who had risen to the top ranks of the United Irishmen although he had only recently gone over to them, would have deterred Fitzwilliam above all other things from bringing a constitutional question before a club.[60]

Burke was "perfectly sensible of the mischief that must arise from the Success of the Scheme, or even from the Struggle" in the part Grattan and the Ponsonbys were taking about a reform of the Irish parliament. But what could be done? How could anyone expect to restrain them when they had run "every risk & made every sacrifice? to serve not only English government which they approved but also that which "they detested & abhorred" and for a reward had not only been "discountenanced & suppressed but even persecuted." Neither Fitzwilliam nor any man could assure them that the grievances of which they complain could be redressed in any other way. So he would advise Fitzwilliam to restrain his advice to their friends and furthermore he would be "shy of interfering" because the ministry "keep this very door to popularity, which is to be shut to these Gentlemen, open to themselves." Pitt was "a declared Zealot (whether in earnest or not does not signify sixpence) for these Parliamentary reforms; & those too to be carried on by Clubbs & associations." What would come of it all, God alone knew. The only man Burke knew who could straighten things out had been "fairly, or rather foully, abandond by all men & all parties. The Providence of God can only bring into order this Chaos of confusion." [61]

In a letter of 9 December, Fitzwilliam had said that only a complete change of men in Ireland would do any good. Burke agreed [62] but added that this could not be achieved without an equally complete change of men, principles, and opinions in England. As long as Pitt's government continued, Burke was as sure as he was of his own existence that "the sinking of that Island to the bottom of the Sea would be sooner risqued, than the change, not only of the whole of that Knot of low Jobbers, but even of one of the meanest amongst them. We do not hold them up for the sake of the Government of Ireland; but we keep the Govt of Ireland to accommodate them. The Rats are not tolerated, because it is hard to keep rats out of Ships, but the Ship is kept up for the Benefit of the Rats."

In the correspondence between Burke and Fitzwilliam at this time, considerable attention was devoted to the subject of Dr. Hussey's return to Ireland at the express wish of the Duke of Portland, who was acting on a request of Lord Camden, the Irish viceroy. Hussey then held two positions there, for neither of which was there any emolument. He continued as President of Maynooth, the new Catholic seminary, and in addition had become Chaplain General to the Irish Brigade, "a sort of superintendent to the Regimental Chaplains," as Burke called it.

Under date of 30 November 1796, Hussey had written his first letter to Burke since his return to Ireland.[63] He revealed that he had accepted the mission with some apprehensiveness since he knew the state of the country. He had scarcely settled at Maynooth than he received letters complaining of the violence used upon Catholic soldiers, who had enlisted either with the explicit promise or at least the expectation that their service would not be contrary to their religion in any way, to force them to attend the services of the Established Church. Hussey's representations went unheeded by the Lord Lieutenant and the Chief Secretary, but the matter itself had become notorious as Catholic noblemen and gentlemen who held commissions in the army were also complaining.

A proposed pastoral letter on the subject was sent by Hussey to Pelham, the Chief Secretary, so that the Castle might know of it in advance. Although over two months had elapsed, no word had been sent to Hussey. What disturbed him even more, however, was that the soldiers themselves, he had been informed, had taken to forming "associations in the camps to redress themselves; and, in a country not remarkable for military discipline, where this evil will end, Heaven only knows."

Hussey lamented that the king little knew that those upon whom he heaped both honor and power in Ireland were really his worst enemies, and by their actions were "jacobinizing" the country. French revolutionary ideas were being widely circulated by the United Irishmen who were swearing in thousands of recruits secretly each week. Hussey was "terrified" at what he foresaw for his native land. The United Irishmen were "wretches" whose plan was to bypass the Irish parliament and break the connection with Great Britain forcibly. They failed to consider that their grievances did not stem from England but from "a junto of their own countrymen." The British viceroy and his assistants were "as completely junto-ridden as my former patron, the king of Spain, is convention-ridden", said Hussey. He concluded by declaring that he was completely shut off from any conversation with Dublin Castle and asked Burke's advice in his "hour of need."

This letter touched off the series between Burke and Fitzwilliam which follows. Burke sent Hussey's letter to Fitzwilliam,[64] saying that he knew what he felt but swearing that he did not know how to advise the priest. He was working on his letter to Hussey and hoped to finish it that night or the next day in time for the post. The main difficulty was that "it costs me a good deal to fix my attention to any kind of Business." He felt that his advice to Hussey, at least until he had heard from Fitzwilliam, would be for him to stay close to Maynooth and to forget for a while that he had gone to Ireland at the express wish of the government. Burke said that he had intended to send Hussey's letter together with his own answer to Portland but had thought better of it. Still he was not sure but that Hussey should send Portland an account of what had happened to his mission.

Fitzwilliam found Hussey's letter [65] very interesting but most alarming. It was his feeling that "insignificant as certainly the D[uke] of P[ortland] is, in the state in which he suffers himself to be; Let him be rouz'd to decision & energy, it still may be in his power to avert the greater evils, circumstanc'd as he is with respect to Office, He has the means of *forcing* a total change of System: Half measures will not be the cure, nor even a palliative for the rancour of the disease."

He grew warmer and when he finished he had decided that

his recommendation was to inform Portland by all means, since it was not certain that he had any sources of truth about Ireland. Had he represented conditions to the king? Did His Majesty know "how that crown totters on his brow"? Realizing that he had generated a good deal of heat in the letter, Fitzwilliam said at the end that his feelings of what was necessary to be done were "for the consideration of your sober judgment", i.e., not to be circulated.

Since Fitzwilliam had allowed himself the luxury of some strong expressions in his letter, Burke apparently felt disposed to go him a few better in his reply. He first sailed into the Ascendancy, "rats" and "low Jobbers" that they were, and then expressed surprise that Fitzwilliam thought any good could come of Burke's communicating Hussey's sentiments to Portland. If Portland could treat Fitzwilliam, an equal in all respects and a friend, as badly as he had, what would he not permit to be done to Hussey?

Then came a furious onslaught on the Duke which Burke himself felt was "so improper to get into other hands that I wish it burnt." Among other things, Burke said:

Of this I am certain, that he has not one man about him, no not one about him, subordinately in office, or connected by confidence, that is better than a rag on a Dunghill. I have also good reason to think that he never in a Case of difficulty consults any person whatsoever — & trusting very little to himself, he trusts full as little, in any other person. So that those who are masters in the first digestion of measures necessarily become his Masters. He takes all his statement of Facts, implicitly from Pelham; officially as secretary, confidentially as a friend — & how can he form a reasoning, or state a remonstrance in the Cabinet directly in the Teeth of all his information both official & private? Unluckily too, we cannot conceal from ourselves, his well known nullity in that Cabinet — that he rarely opens his Mouth in it — & that from some natural impediment or rather from evil habits, he cannot get out three perfect sentences in a regular sequel. The defect, of which he is abundantly sensible, disables him from making any sort of struggle with those who take the lead — at the same time, that a feeling of pride rather inclines him to adopt Measures as his own, which he finds himself unable to resist, than to confess himself in that odd situation, of not yielding to the reasons of others, & not being able to enforce his own. I do not mention all this as laying Load on one that I have always loved & valued & always shall, — but to give you my Reasons, why I think all my interference with him, directly or indirectly, to be a thing quite improper & quite disparate — but I have no Objection at all that Hussey should do it himself, though I am far from sure, it will not rather bring him into some scrape than be of use to the Business he was sent on: But I know that personal risques are nothing to his Courage.

Fitzwilliam's hopes of any good coming from a communication to Portland of the information sent by Hussey on the alarming situation of Ireland had been based merely on his readiness "to snatch at every twig", so desperate was the state of affairs. He had just received another communication detailing the terrible conditions in Ireland from another source which predicted that the news that the French had made a landing would instantly be followed by "Rebellion, Assasination & Rapine." After quoting from this letter for Burke's information, he reverted to the Hussey mission and now seemed to feel that the mere fact that he had been sent to Ireland by Portland offered a shadow of hope. Hussey, either directly or through Burke, must communicate with Portland, although Fitzwilliam repeated his slender expectation of Portland's acting "consistently, & pursuing the late dictates of his own feelings, when it comes to the point, & when he is to act upon them in the face of his Master —. . ." At any rate, Portland should have "fair play, & Ireland the miserable chance of his firmness, for wretched as it is, it is its only chance of salvation —" [66]

Since Fitzwilliam was so insistent, Burke reluctantly went into London, although he was far from well, "finding myself more ill at Ease in mind than in body to make an application to the D. of P." The first thing he found upon his arrival was that certain inconsequential persons had just reported to Portland that "the five troubled Counties (which by the way made two Counties more than I had any Notion of being troubled) were perfectly composed & pacified." This news gave great satisfaction to the government, so Burke thought "it would be blowing against the North Wind to employ a puny Breeze in opposition to this Storm" and consequently dropped his project of telling Portland about the lack of success which attended Hussey's mission. However, as Lord John Cavendish, a relative of Fitzwilliam's, had called upon him that morning, Burke had showed him Hussey's letter and those of Fitzwilliam's on the subject. His Lordship was of the opinion that communicating Hussey's intelligence to Portland would "not only be fruitless but possibly in some degree mischievous." [67]

Upon further reflection it occurred to Burke, quite belatedly one must say, that the whole Hussey affair had "never been properly explained" to Fitzwilliam. He thereupon undertook to set him right. In the first place, Hussey had not seen Portland in a very long time although he had often called upon him only to be denied admittance. It had been Lord Camden, the viceroy, who had asked Portland to send Hussey over as Chaplain General for the purpose of making him "an instrument in quieting the Catholicks under the cruel Treatment which they had received, & the further oppressions they were to look for — and even to make him active in obtaining addresses of satisfaction in that Government, from whence they had experienced the most bitter hostility." Hussey had told Portland his determination not to be a part of any such design, and Portland had heard him patiently as usual "& with what is near as usual to him without any observation one way or another, at least that I can recollect to have heard." Hussey had then seen Pelham, who happened to be in London, and found that Camden had taken the step of sending for Hussey without Pelham's knowledge. The latter coldly professed to be pleased, although he had not been previously consulted, and expressed the wish that Hussey would obey Camden's request.

No salary was offered to Hussey nor had he asked for any. Burke had told him that this was a serious mistake as his expenses would be considerable and promised to write to John King, who was then one of Portland's Under-Secretaries of State, about it, which he did. King's answer was that no salary had ever been intended nor would there be any. It was the kind of employment which was distinctly an honor. Burke was provoked by this and told Walker King, John's brother and one of Burke's closest friends, that it was a disgraceful thing. Certainly, neither Pitt, Portland, nor John King served merely for the honor attached to their services.

Burke said that he could not find by any inquiries he had made that Portland was other than satisfied with the proceedings of government in Ireland or with his own situation in England. In despair, he asked what could be done. It was clear to him what was intended when General Cunningham had been replaced as the head of the army in Ireland by General Luttrell,[68] an arrangement which had not passed through Portland's office and yet which must have been made with his full knowledge. Burke had never heard that Portland had made the slightest objection to it. "For what qualities & for what previous services was the whole military defense, & whole military police, put into the hands of this General? I go no further." [69]

French Laurence had sent Burke a letter of Grattan's to Fitzwilliam which plainly showed how "truly melancholy" Ireland's condition was. War had been declared there between "property & no property — between the high & the Low, the rich & the poor, . . . between Wealth & Want." The oppressed could no nothing at all but aggravate the tyranny by provoking it. Only with the help of "a foreign Jacobin force" could they be victorious over their oppressors, but such a victory would be "the utter subversion of human Society itself, of all religion, all Law, all order, all humanity, as well as of all property." [70]

The plan of informing Portland of what was really transpiring in Ireland came to nothing but it occasioned a lengthy exchange of letters between Burke and Fitzwilliam and inconvenienced Burke to the extent of making a trip into London.

In his reply [71] to Hussey's letter of 30 November which had touched off this reaction, Burke said that he vigorously condemned the practice of whipping Catholic soldiers into attendance at the Sunday services of the Established Church. Sarcastically, he wrote that those churches lacked a voluntary congregation and "an army of well scourged Papists" was needed to fill the void. This was an imitation of the methods which one would expect to find in France, the "empire of pure and perfect Protestantism." What was happening in Ireland was only another part of the war against Catholicism which the French had commenced. Ireland was merely "a little busy meddling province of servile imitators." Far more effective blows against Catholicism were being struck by Bonaparte, "the illustrious champion of the Protestant world." [72] Lord Malmesbury's peace mission to Paris [73] was for the purpose of balancing the account — "defeat and dishonour abroad; oppression at home.

We sneak to the regicides, but we boldly trample on our poor fellow-citizens. But all is for the Protestant cause."

As usual, Burke found that all of Ireland's ills originated in that country itself. The United Irishmen were incorrect in blaming England, which, admittedly, was painfully callous and indifferent to Ireland. The English were guilty of having turned Ireland over unreservedly to "the little narrow faction that domineers there." The Ascendancy was England's sole source of information on what transpired in Ireland. Since parliamentary independence had been granted to Ireland in 1782, it was virtually a breach of order to mention Ireland in the British parliament. While a large part of the natives of Ireland were being "annihilated," the British parliament was "no better than an instrument in the hands of an Irish faction. This is Ascendancy with a witness!"

The Protestant Ascendancy in Ireland was every bit as much of a Directory as that functioning in France. It was impossible to find fault with what the French did and, at the same time, remain quiet over what transpired in Ireland. Burke and Hussey hated Jacobinism as they hated "the gates of Hell" because it was a system of oppression. So, too, was the "directory of Ireland."

The letter concluded with a plea that Hussey use his influence to persuade the Catholics to be more indifferent for the time being in the matter of the political objects which they sought. In other words, they ought not to allow themselves to become "heated" and to do anything rash. To obtain the desired emancipation, they must "follow opportunities and not attempt to force anything." They would do well to work among themselves, i.e., to avoid the United Irishmen, and by all means they should shun any imitation of the methods of the Ascendancy. Above all, they should refrain from intrigues and factious practices. He declared that, if he had his "youth and strength," he would go over to Ireland "to work on that plan." He was certain that the welfare of the entire country, as well as their own, depended upon "a reformation amongst the Catholics."

In the next to last letter from Hussey to be published in Burke's correspondence,[74] Hussey revealed that he still had not had any correspondence with Dublin Castle since he had made his representations against the whipping of Catholic soldiers some five months earlier. Hussey had since become Bishop of Waterford and when he convened his clergy recently he had made it a charge upon them to employ "all their *spiritual* power" to resist the practice. He detailed instances of further floggings, one of which was fatal. Although he had now become a bishop, he promised Burke that he would continue to serve as President of Maynooth and as Chaplain General, although he still received no emolument for either of these posts.

The threatened invasion of Ireland by the French, which Burke had so often predicted, was attempted late in December. Headed by the able young General Lazare Hoche, a French fleet attempted to invade Bantry Bay in the southwestern part of Ireland. The expedition failed due to a combination of adverse weather and poor seamanship.

Burke received several letters from Ireland, including one from Cork from Patrick O'Conor,[75] chairman of a committee of the inhabitants of Cork "selected for general public business in this alarming Crisis," detailing the attempted invasion. Burke sent these letters to Fitzwilliam to read and in his accompanying letter [76] was very critical of the manner in which the defense against the French had been planned. He asserted that the very people on whom the authorities had been dependent for the protection of the country in this crisis were "those descriptions of people in the Country & in the army which they had done every thing to irritate, & to alienate in every possible way." He added that he was not sure whether "the Conduct of that unfortunate people has more of good or of evil example. But let these things go as they will." Burke's point was that the Catholics had been willing to save the country had it been necessary and that by so doing they were proving their loyalty but depriving themselves of an improvement of their status since their actions could be construed to indicate that they were not dissatisfied with their condition.

Burke's protégé, French Laurence, was then at work on a projected remonstrance to the king to call His Majesty's attention to the urgency of alleviating the Catholic grievances. While preparing it, he wrote to Burke [77] to request the fragment of the *Tract Relative to the Laws Against Popery in Ireland* so that he might make use of it in his proposed paper. Burke called Laurence's attention to the fact that the worst parts of the code had been repealed.[78] The remaining grievances were chiefly incapacities relative to civil and military matters which constituted a stigma on the majority of the country's inhabitants. The Irish Catholics were a people who could not justly be accused of factiousness or perverseness in the opinions which they held, he said. They gave at least as good proofs of their loyalty as any other set of people in Ireland. They had subscribed to tests which were contrived to clear them from any suspicion of holding political principles supposedly connected with their religion. On the contrary, the persons "called Protestants, which Protestantism, as things stand now, is no description of a religion at all, or of any principle, religious, moral, or political, but is a mere negation" were not required to take any tests whatsoever. Not even the clergy of the Established Church were asked to sign the thirty-nine articles of their faith. The people who were being persecuted were the only ones in the country "who make an positive profession of the Christian faith." They were treated as enemies and as long as they were under any restrictions their persecutors were armed with a legal excuse for punishing them and "they never fail to make use of it." If the incapacities were removed, and the Catholics judged by their conduct like their fellow citizens, Ireland would soon be blessed with quiet. The fear that the Catholics would control parliament if they were allowed to hold seats was a mere excuse known to be false by the very ones who gave rise to it. The Catholics at the time could not win over three seats out of the three hundred in the House of Commons. In all probability, they would never win more than one-tenth of the seats even in the years to come because property was too firmly fixed in the hands of the Protestants. At that moment, however, the worst opposition which the Catholics faced in Ireland was the abuse of executive government, "which may more effectually harass an obnoxious people, than even adverse laws themselves."

Laurence continued with his plan, and there is in the *Burke-Laurence Correspondence* a fragment of a letter of his to Burke which is marked "most secret." [79] It was on the subject of the projected representation to the king on the affairs of Ireland. Laurence and some unnamed person had written it, and it was signed by various persons, including a number of prominent British peers who held properties in Ireland. The remonstrance called the attention of the monarch to the seriousness of the situation and said that the crisis called for immediate amelioration of conditions. The disturbances then taking place were cited, and attention was directed to the fact of the preponderant Catholic majority in the troubled country. This majority was "obedient to the laws, and friends to monarchy from opinions, habits, and prejudices." The petitioners conceded that the majority of the Catholics were not directly interested in the restriction which prevented Catholics from being elected to parliament, but it was asserted that they would unite with those Catholics who were interested in the matter. The latter were their "natural protectors in the state," and the restriction operated to place a "brand on their religion."

The old argument that the Catholics were to be feared on account of their supposed status as "a political party in connection with a foreign power supported by France" was now clearly invalid. The Dissenters of northern Ireland, on the other hand, were actually and not merely supposedly intriguing with France. At the same time, these same Presbyterians (the United Irishmen) were trying to win over their Catholic fellow countrymen by offering them "every thing." Thus far, the Catholics had resisted these enticing overtures because they preferred a small share in the present constitution to the entire power in a state shaped along the lines of the new republican theories. Despite their resistance up to that time, it was stated that the danger was still present of a union in great force between the Catholics and the Dissenters. If such a junction took place, the "party of the Established Church — who formed not *one tenth* of the population" and who, while wealthy, were "an obnoxious and comparatively helpless class" scattered throughout the entire island — would be in a desperate position.

The remedy suggested by the petitioners, who clearly had drawn the substance of all their arguments from Burke, was that of granting the Catholic demands in a gracious manner. It ought to be done, if possible, in such a way as to indicate that it was a personal act of the king. Moreover, a change in the administration of Ireland was requisite. Those place-holders who lacked the confidence of the public ought to be dropped.

Burke's reply [80] began by saying that he doubted the petition's chances of success under the circumstances. He thought that the signatures were unlikely to prove of sufficient influence. He pointed out, moreover, that the objection was bound to be raised that the king could not act "on the sense of individuals, however respectable," if the parliaments of both kingdoms thought differently. He could find no way in which an answer to this objection could be "legally and constitutionally" made. It was, in addition, a proposal likely to arouse hostile feelings in both England and Ireland. How the Irish opposition would receive it, he professed himself unable to guess. These people, who numbered many of his old friends, he described as "running the full length of Jacobinism" and aiming at the disruption of the union between the two kingdoms. He felt that they might well use the situation to make the absentees unpopular and he was certain that this would be pleasing to the king.

It was not that Burke did not wish to see the Catholics emancipated and the monopolists ousted that he threw cold water on the plan. It was simply a disagreement with the means projected to secure the desired end. The "circumstances" were not to his liking. The particular problem about which he was concerned at this point was his old dislike of an Irish absentee tax, and he had touched upon this in his letter to Laurence expressing his disapproval of the latter's planned petition.

In 1773 when the project of an absentee tax had been earlier broached, Burke had performed yeoman service in its defeat. This time the opposition in Ireland, which included Burke's and Fitzwilliam's friends, was again toying with the idea. Writing to Fitzwilliam, [81] Burke expressed himself in the same vein as he had to Laurence — the opposition was now going "the full length of Jacobinism, & are doing all they can to pull up the landmarks of private property & public safety, & to disunite the two Kingdoms; and that upon the fullest grounds both of fact and principle, which, I might easily prove, if I had heart or strength for such a task." He conceded that the government's conduct had provoked "the passions of men beyond the limits of human prudence." The effect upon the public was nevertheless the same. Burke then remarked that he was glad that Fitzwilliam had resolved himself to defend "those persons who residing in the seats of their Ancestors, and living in the Country in which they are born, possess Property in Ireland." These men, and they included Fitzwilliam among the foremost, were "branded by the odious Name of Absentees, as if you were bound to be present in Ireland at every roll call, as if you were Soldiers & the very people, a great part of the power & consideration of whose families has arisen from English Matches, as their Estates have arisen from English grants, have endeavoured to make English intermarriages impracticable, & the inheritance of Irish property by Englishmen odious & precarious."

Nothing came of the proposal, but the interesting thing about it is that it provoked Burke as strongly as before and revealed how thoroughly English in his thinking he had become and showed that any question between England and Ireland which offered him a choice of sides without doing violence to his conscience would always be resolved in favor of England. In the matter of the absentee tax, Burke was in the wrong as it was patently an equitable proposition which would have beneficial results in Ireland in the long run.

A couple of weeks after this letter to Fitzwilliam, Burke wrote to Windham [82] to say that he was still convinced that Catholic emancipation meant the salvation of Ireland. His weariness led him to add that he himself was now done with the subject, perhaps forever, although he continued to receive many requests from the friends of the Catholics seeking his intercession with the Pitt government.

Burke was at this time in Bath where he had gone in February for his rapidly failing health. For some time, evidence of his ill health had crept into his correspondence. As early as 30 October 1795, he had written Lord Auckland that he could "sail no longer." In fact, he added, his "vessel cannot be said to be even in port. She is wholly condemned and broken up." [83] In a letter to Edward Jerningham, he had to employ an amanuensis because he was so ill. There were few hours in the twenty-four which he was not compelled to pass in bed or on a couch.[84] He told Windham [85] that "everything I eat and drink turns to tough phlegm, and storms of wind." He was suffering from a stomach cancer and to secure relief found it advisable by February 1797 to resort to taking laudanum. His friend, Lord Frederick Cavendish described his own success with the opiate and recommended it to Burke. When the latter consulted his physician, Dr. Brocklesby, he received his approval. At first, it made Burke violently ill but eventually it began to help him. Cavendish told Burke of his own experiences in typical eighteenth century fashion:[86]

I have for about 20 year been subject to a very turbulent and flatulent Stomach, wind roaring up & down till it finds its' way to my shoulder, my side or my foot with the most acute pain. (I have endured a fair tryal for the gout without effect) and I have been oblig'd to take 80 & 100 Drops of Laudanum at a dose.

I have longer been under the necessity of using Purgatives, but if they do too much wind seems to take possession of the Vacant space & mischief follows, from thence it was suggested to me, Why not take habitually a small quantity of Laudanum, My Doctor agreeing, I have for near two year taken 8 or ten drops every day, midway between breakfast & dinner; from that & a pretty steady attention to my diet I have found great Benefit, my Stomach seems to go about its business quietly, for I take much less purgative than I us'd, & I have not found a necessity of encreasing the Opiate, on the contrary, & am seldom, without indiscretion required to take it in large quantities; One bad effect it has, it makes me most extremely indolent.

Before the Bath trip, Burke had attended to two important matters. The first concerned the office of Receiver Generalship of Land Revenues, which Richard Burke, Jr. had shared with Walker King. 13 January 1797, he made the necessary disposal of this business by signing a deed along with his wife and King.[87] The second task was that of drawing up a will. This was officially taken care of 30 January 1797. No act of Burke's is more indicative of his deep religious nature.[88]

In April, Burke underwent a slight turn for the better and his state of health appeared improved to the extent that it was publicly noted in *The Times* of 4 April. It was the kind of a temporary improvement, however, which often characterizes dying persons. As he told Fitzwilliam at the end of the month,[89] "though the muscles & flesh be wasted & indeed almost wholly gone, Some Strength is recovered & on the whole, the radical malady (not to be conquered at my time of Life) excepted, I feel better." Mrs. Burke was able to write a friend that the doctor had given them considerable encouragement that Burke's symptoms were expected to become "lighter and lighter every day." Furthermore, "every symptom about him is better than it was." [90]

His brief improvement led him to renew his interest in Irish affairs, but his feelings had become even more pessimistic.[91] The actions of the opposition disturbed him, and "as to the little Blackguard Click, that has long domineered there, (& in Truth even here,) the ill state of their Country, they have always considered, as a means of perpetuating their power." Parliament and the people of property in general have given "a blind support to the existing junto" simply because of its existence but "without affection or attachment to it, but entirely from their dread of that Jacobinism, which so openly attacks their property, & perhaps their Lives." But now they have found that the government is unable to protect itself or them and so they are ready, "many, very many of them, to fly for refuge to that very discontented body, the apprehension of which has hitherto made them cling to the Castle."

Things were so bad that Burke refused to rely upon Catholic emancipation to save the day because such a grant now would be "a late ungracious & forced concession." Two months earlier emancipation or even "a civil temporary refusal" would have cemented the Catholics in the interests of the crown and of both the kingdoms. Now even in Dublin "the discontents of the Protestants & Catholicks run into one common channel." This was unfortunate since "all these discontents, without management or disguise, unite in French Jacobinism."

In conclusion, Burke recommended to Fitzwilliam that, if he were still getting rents in Ireland, he have his steward put him down for a contribution in the subscription then being raised in Dublin for unemployed tradesmen. "At this moment all attentions of the kind are politick."

In another letter to Fitzwilliam,[92] Burke criticized the proposed sending of Lord Cornwallis to Ireland as viceroy, although, according to the report Burke had received, His Lordship would bring concessions to the Catholics, because in all other respects the "abominable junto system" was to be preserved. With whatever views Cornwallis were to go, the Irish were certain to consider his mission a more militaristic step than ever and one which would probably be "the tocsin of instant insurrection — the fatal issue of such an event is too certain —"

He noted to Windham [93] that more troops were being sent to Ireland to assist "a Military Government there under the auspices of that Junto to which both Kingdoms are sacrificed." Criticism levelled at Bishop Hussey for his pastoral letter condemning the whipping of Catholic soldiers into attendance at Established Church services angered Burke. He ended despairingly by saying that the peace and property of Ireland were at an end.

In a postscript he revealed that, despite his statement to Windham in the letter of 30 March that he was through with Ireland perhaps forever, he was still trying to help the Catholics. He mentioned the pleasure he had derived from having opened his mind fully on Irish affairs to Dundas in two conversations which lasted for four hours apiece. Burke went into the "minutest details concerning Ireland" in order to make Dundas "sensible of what was then doing." Unfortunately, neither Burke's "laborious remonstrance" nor Dundas' "indulgent hearing" resulted in anything favorable to Burke's purpose, which he had "so much at Heart." His goals were "the Peace of Ireland, its consolidation with this Kingdom, and a direction of our common force against our common Enemy."

The fact that it was necessary for Burke to explain to a member of the British cabinet what was really going on in Ireland bears out his oft-repeated statement that the source of Ireland's troubles lay in that country itself.

Two days after this letter to Windham, he wrote at great length to French Laurence.[94] His letter was concerned entirely with Irish affairs except for the first paragraph, which was devoted to a recent mutiny in the navy. This combined with the parlous situation in Ireland to produce times "so deplorable" that he confessed inability to know how to write about them.

That very day he had been asked if, in his opinion, a concession to the Irish Catholics would bring peace there. He told Laurence that he had not been able to answer because he felt "utterly incapable of giving any, the least distinct." Three months ago, possibly even two, he could have said with confidence that, despite the source whence it might have come, it would have prevented Ireland's discontented forces from uniting. So desirous were the Catholics of gaining emancipation that he thought they would not revolt even if the concession had been "decently evaded" so long as they felt certain that it would be granted in the near future. The authorities unhappily had not done this but had resorted to every measure that could hurt and annoy the Catholics.

He then commented upon a recent speech in the British House of Commons on the subject of the Irish Catholics. As he had so often in the past, Burke declared that it placed the Catholics in a practical dilemma. If they were turbulent, nothing should be done for them because of their nefarious actions; if they remained loyal, obedient, and restrained, there was no point in doing anything for them because their conduct indicated their complete satisfaction with the status quo.

Burke enclosed extracts from two letters written him from Cork by "intelligent and well informed people." Both emphasized the alarming change that was taking place among the Catholics due to the failure of the authorities to treat them decently.

He then manifested his feelings on what he considered would be the results in Ireland "under the existing circumstances" if Catholic emancipation were granted by the Irish parliament. He declared that it would necessarily have to be "a fundamental part in any plan for quieting that country and reconciling it to this." The manner in which it was done was of vast importance. Equally significant were the persons connected with the grant. As long as "the present junto continue to govern in Ireland, such a measure never can produce the effects proposed by it."

He did not feel that the dismissal of the "junto" followed by Catholic emancipation could be accomplished in the Irish parliament because "strong ferment would be excited in the church partty [sic], who though but few in numbers, have in their hands most of the ultimate and superior property of the kingdom."

Should such formidable obstacles be finally removed, the opposition leaders ought to replace the "junto" in the positions of power and be made repositories of the confidence of the English government. The difficulty with this, as he saw it, was that the leaders of the opposition were pledged to parliamentary reform over and above Catholic emancipation. If they were suffered to put their plan of reform into effect, he was afraid that the same thing would inevitably result in England. He had always held since attaining the use of reason that to take such a step in England would be the preliminary to "utter ruin." An even better solution for "settling" England and Ireland was a "great change in the superior Government *here*." He would replace Pitt's government by a coalition headed by Fox and Sheridan!

The reasoning displayed here is clearly indicative of the strain of Burke's illness coupled with his despair over conditions in both the land of his birth and of his adoption. After having told Laurence at the outset that he was unable to give any distinct reply to the question of whether or not Catholic emancipation could then save Ireland, he immediately proceeded to advocate that it be done. It was, in fact, an absolute necessity. Furthermore, the Ascendancy must be smashed and its leaders removed from office and replaced by the principal members of the Irish opposition. Yet this was a somewhat dangerous step because the latter were pledged to parliamentary reform in addition to that which emancipation would effect. This gave reason for pause. The ideal solution came as an afterthought — drop Pitt's government and replace it with a Fox-Sheridan coalition. How he imagined that Fox would then be converted from the position which he and the Foxite Whigs continued to hold on the French Revolution was not made clear. Perhaps some *deus ex machina* could contrive this transformation.

This was generally a pretty muddled performance on Burke's part, although two things were eminently sensible — the Catholics must win their emancipation and the power of the Ascendancy must be broken forever if Ireland were to know peace and Britain were to benefit.

To his friend Mrs. Crewe he wrote rationally enough to complain about the deplorable state of both England and Ireland. Sorrowfully but indignantly, he attacked the stupid denials being made in England that there were then any disorders in Ireland. The riots and tumults there had achieved such proportions that no force appeared adequate to overcome them under the circumstances.[95]

On the same day,[96] he revealed to Fitzwilliam that he knew that he was dying and that it was deemed wise, while he still had the strength, to return to Beaconsfield by easy stages from Bath and "there to finish my career along with that of the civil & moral world." He was convinced that no serious intention existed to make any changes in the government either in personnel or "things." [97]

He arrived home, as *The Times*, 30 May, said in "a feeble state of health" and either just before or shortly thereafter his last published letter on public affairs during his lifetime made its appearance. Appropriately enough, it was on the subject of Ireland. Thus both his first and last published essays on public affairs were concerned with his native land. The person to whom this letter was addressed is unknown.[98]

It commenced by noting that Burke and his dying son had discussed the grievances of Ireland only half an hour before Richard's death. This circumstance alone would have been sufficient to induce Burke to try to win emancipation for the Catholics, but he had additional reasons.

He had unsuccessfully attempted to prevent the removal of Lord Fitzwilliam by personally interceding with several members of the government. To them he had represented "the true state of Ireland, and the mischief which sooner or later must arise from subjecting the mass of the people to the capricious and interested domination of an exceedingly small faction and its dependencies." His fruitless efforts marked practically the last time he ever saw the ministers.

Ireland's cause was hopeless as long as the Ascendancy continued to possess the power to make out a case that the majority of the Catholics were not to be trusted. The continued ability to do this successfully left the monopolists possessed of an unshaken hold over the country.

The Catholics through their principles and the unflagging zeal of their clergy had, in general, refrained from Jacobinism. Unhappily, whenever they came into contact with Irish Protestants who espoused that hated system, the Catholics became tainted.

The kindliest and best intended set of laws could do nothing, if the minds of the governing class were opposed to those whom the laws sought to help.

The war waged by the Irish "junto" against "the person whom they call the Pope, and against all his adherents" was a professed source of astonishment to Burke on account of the times. The "Protestant" Directory of France, considered as statesmen, and the "Protestant hero," Napoleon as a general, had done more to destroy the pope and his followers than the Irish "junto" had ever been able to accomplish. If that "true Protestant," General Lazare Hoche, with an army untainted in the least by "Popery", had been able to make good his attempted invasion of Ireland,[99] he would have saved the Ascendancy the considerable trouble which they took to keep the Catholics "obnoxious" on account of their religion. Had Hoche been successful, Catholicism would not have enjoyed "a month's existence." Unfortunately, the authorities in both England and Ireland appeared to act as if they sought to promote an alliance with this atheistic force. Their blindness to the great danger from the French that was mounting and from the spread of their revolutionary principles in the British Isles was appalling. This inability to sense the ever increasing perils seemed to rest content on the assumption that "all is well, provided we are safe from Popery."

Once again Burke demonstrated his spirit of religious toleration. Every man should be "as pious as he pleases, and in the way that pleases." It was not in keeping with piety to grant all civil advantages and privileges to "a negative religion", such as Protestantism, while at the same time denying these very benefits to the Catholics whose doctrines possessed the "whole" of that which was positive in the teachings of the Anglican Church. The only difference between the Roman and the Anglican churches was that the latter denied certain tenets of the former.

Burke then advanced two of his favorite arguments. The first was that anyone who renounced the Catholic religion in Ireland was accorded great freedom. Such a one could join any of the various churches among the Dissenters or found a church of his own. Were he to choose the latter course, the church he founded could be based upon the "most anti-christian principles" if he so desired. The Catholic who gave up his faith was not circumscribed by any civil incapacity.

The second point which he had so often raised in the past was that of the case of the Catholics who did unite with a vast majority of "factious Protestants." Because some did so, the entire Catholic body was unjustly accused of harboring traitorous designs. On the contrary, where the Catholics formed the greater part of the people and were everywhere loyal, they were depicted as satisfied. Cruelty, however, was the reward for their loyalty. Hence the turbulence of the few and the peacefulness of the many were equally given as reasons for not raising the Catholics to equality with the Protestants.[100]

The Catholic clergy was likewise embarrassed. If they exerted themselves to maintain quiet, they risked the loss of the "little credit they possess." [101] The people considered them government tools who acted against the civil interests of their congregations. Conversely, if they made no attempts to check discontent, the authorities charged them with sedition.

The letter concluded with the assertion that Burke did not wish to have it concealed that he was of the same opinion about the grievances of Ireland to his dying breath as he had been when his faculties were at their zenith. He was proud of the fact that he had done everything in his power to convince the ministers of his sentiments "on this melancholy subject, so long as I had means of access to persons of their consideration."

Two of his last three extant letters on Ireland are in the same vein. In both [102] of them he said that he was convinced that there was nothing to any reports of a change in the government's attitude toward Ireland except a determination to make Ireland's government a military one by the appointment of Lord Cornwallis as viceroy.

In the final letter,[103] Burke wrote a strong endorsement of Bishop Hussey to Fitzwilliam, whose opinion of him was already high, in the hope that the latter would recommend Hussey to the Duke of Devonshire and that the Duke would then call the attention of his principal agents and managers in Waterford to Hussey. The Bishop was doing fine work "in point of religion & morals" in his diocese and could improve the material conditions of his flock by "giving a direction to the industry & pursuits of the Inhabitants."

Edmund Burke died at Beaconsfield on 9 July 1797,[104] convinced that there was "nothing like a fixed intention of making a real change of system in Ireland." On the contrary, the Irish authorities were daily growing "more and more difficult." The incapacities of the Irish "jobbers" were becoming more and more apparent, but as long as they could continue drawing upon England for "indefinite aids of men and sums of money, they will go on with more resolution than ever in their jobbing system." [105] He felt at his death a sense of discouragement over Ireland and was thoroughly convinced that another of his "great, just, and honourable causes" had culminated in failure.

CHAPTER XI

Retrospect

This study of Burke's connection with Ireland reveals that his interest in his native land was motivated by several factors. His great devotion to the British Empire, his sympathy for and understanding of the Roman Catholic religion and its Irish communicants, and his hatred of oppression stand out clearly. Pervading these are two other considerations: a "dearness of instinct," which was greater than Burke could ever justify to reason;[1] and a deep sense of responsibility which made him always conscious of his duties.[2]

Among the fields to which he devoted his talents, Ireland enjoys the unique distinction of having occupied him over the period of his entire life. Significantly, both the first political work of his public career and the last letter on public affairs written by Burke and published during his lifetime were on the subject of Ireland. The former was the *Tract Relative to the Laws Against Popery in Ireland*; the latter was published as *A Letter on the Affairs of Ireland*.

One thing which emerges markedly from an analysis of the role the affairs of Ireland played in his life is that Burke was a statesman of principles.[3] Yet a vital qualification must be added, namely, that he considered time and circumstances to be all important in determining when principles should be applied. He held that these factors should govern the conduct of public affairs at all times. They were the elements that determined whether or not a measure would be useful or serviceable.[4]

A devoted lover of principle, Burke expressed a hatred for theory on countless occasions throughout his life beginning with his college days. He realized that the difference between a principle and a theory might appear slight to some and, accordingly, made clear the distinction as he saw it. He declared that no rational man ever governed himself by abstractions and universals but claimed that he did not leave abstract ideas entirely out of a question because to do so would mean that he was omitting principles. Without the latter, it would be impossible to acquire the habit of political reasoning. Yet a statesman differs from a university professor in the matter of principles. The latter is guided merely by a general view of society; the former, always bearing in mind his principles, is guided by circumstances because if he were to make a judgment unmindful of the exigencies of the moment, he might ruin his country. Sound principles were requisite for reaching careful conclusions which should then be applied only after cautious consideration of the circumstances.[5] These gave vitality to what would otherwise be mere theories.[6] Despite his numerous protestations to the contrary, Burke was, of course, by no means innocent of indulging in the practice of theorizing.[7]

Since circumstances were so important to his way of thinking, he was quick to recognize that the distresses of England could frequently be turned to the immediate advantage of Ireland and to the ultimate advantage of the empire itself. In this manner he was satisfied that he was serving both his adopted country and that of his birth. He frequently proclaimed the belief that their interests were inseparable, and it was his prayer that disputes between the two would be rare. If any did take place, he would endeavor first to reconcile the disputants because he believed that it was his special mission to help settle the differences. Should he fail to adjust the difficulty which arose, it was with England that he would side because she was the more important, and his debt to her was even greater than to Ireland. When England was patently in the wrong, he would do his utmost to correct her error.

It was his firm belief that the problems of Ireland required a very cautious approach because their roots lay so deep in the past.[8] The grievances under which Ireland labored had existed for many years. He felt, therefore, that they called for a leisurely correction rather than an abrupt one. Such a manner of redress lent itself better to the eradication of prejudice, which might only be strengthened by precipitate action. Moreover, this method of proceeding by degrees would prevent those who had long been repressed from becoming intoxicated with power once the restrictions binding them had been removed.[9] He was fond of saying that nothing ruined great causes so much as that people treated the commencement of them as if it were the conclusion. Consequently, Burke approached the problems of Ireland gradually but determinedly through the years.

When Edmund Burke entered the British House of Commons, his background severely handicapped him. His Irish birth and training, the suspicion that he was secretly a Roman Catholic and perhaps even a former Jesuit, his rich brogue, and his numerous Irish relatives and connections seemed to point to his becoming a virtual Irish lobbyist. Those who felt that such would be the case were soon destined to learn that parliament possessed no member who was more devoted to the British Empire than this "Irish adventurer." Far ahead of his time in his imperial thought, Burke enjoys to this day the reputation of one of the most advanced imperialists in British history.

There can be little doubt that the most important motivating force behind Burke's work for Ireland was the great attachment which he had formed for the British Empire. His concern for the Catholics and his hatred of oppression were both intimately connected with this prime factor. During his entire political career, he strove to preserve his beloved empire which he maintained functioned under a constitution made "for the happiness of man."[10] The parts of which the empire was constituted had to be strong and content, if the whole were to be powerful. Therefore, he battled zealously against those who abused the power vested in them for conducting in any way the management of the affairs of the empire's constituent parts. He fought equally hard against the infiltration of radical ideas which might have a divisive or disruptive influence. It always grieved him to see the strength of the empire diminished by the loss of any of its parts, and he often cited the case of America as an example which Ireland might well emulate if misgovernment there did not cease.

He saw England in relation to the other parts of the empire not as a shepherd to his sheep whom he can feed, shear, or slaughter as he so desires, but rather as the oldest brother who guards the family possessions for a number of younger brothers on whose help he, too, depends. They, on their side, find an indispensable support in his strength and resources. It is the empire, composed of mother country and the parts, which should benefit wherever possible, not just England alone.[11] It was a system of mutual help, as he once called it in the *Annual Register*, and it was to the interest of the whole to see to it that all parts of the empire were fairly treated.[12]

Apart from all other considerations, Ireland's geographical location so close to the heart of the empire would have made the welfare of that country tremendously important to him. He looked upon his native land as a woman ordained by nature to be protected. That protection, in the very nature of things, could only come from England or France, as he saw it, and he was determined that it should be England. The manner in which it was to be done, however, was most important to Burke who ruled out force, which was only temporary, and advocated the application to Ireland of a spirit of magnanimity. Ireland should be made happy and contented since her happiness would strengthen the empire, which could only be as strong and prosperous an entity as its parts were. Burke never wearied of saying this and of trying to make it a reality. He was firmly convinced that no reluctant tie could ever be a strong one and advocated a natural, cheerful alliance which would be infinitely superior to the one which existed when he began his public career.

His goal for Ireland politically was not independence. Contrary to the opinion which has long prevailed, Irish legislative independence never found much favor with him. His true position has long remained obscured probably because of his public acceptance of Ireland's nominal legislative independence in 1782. His real role in the attainment of that independence was something quite different from what it has hitherto been thought. But once this independence had been achieved, Burke defended it throughout the remainder of his life. Since it had become an accomplished fact, he felt that greater harm would ensue were it to be taken away again.

His dislike of the matter stemmed from its precipitancy, a thing which did violence to his principles, and from the overtones of force. He abhorred extortion and professed to see the Irish Volunteers as having resorted to it both by their language and bearing. Even deeper, however, was his realization that Ireland remained a badly divided nation, whose Catholic majority was still left in subjection to their oppressors, the Protestant Ascendancy. The latter could conceivably, as a consequence of Irish legislative independence, oppress their victims even more stringently than previously.

Once Ireland had its legislative independence along with that of its judiciary as well, Burke's view was that there was nothing further which she could rightfully expect from England. While he certainly lacked enthusiasm for the grant of legislative independence, he had even less interest in the idea of a union between Britain and Ireland. Whenever the proposition was discussed, he gave it his opposition. The political system which he favored was that a reformed Irish parliament, rid of the power of the Protestant Ascendancy and numbering Catholic members in both branches of the legislature, should be allowed to legislate for itself in purely domestic matters but on all things which conceivably related to imperial concerns should be subordinate to the British parliament.

He always maintained that a system of mutual help should obtain between the two countries. Certain disadvantages were bound to accrue to the lesser member in such a combination simply because it was a part and not the center of a powerful empire, but the advantages of membership in such a strong organization as the British Empire outweighed the disadvantages. The latter certainly existed, and as far as Burke came to be concerned one of them had to be in the field of trade and commerce.

But he had not always felt this way since, during the first fourteen years in his parliamentary career, he had done more than anyone else to remove these disadvantages. Indeed, coupled with his work on behalf of the Catholics in 1778, his efforts to improve Ireland's trade cost him his seat at Bristol. Even though he knew that this was likely to happen, he refused to swerve from the course he had charted and stuck resolutely to it. Ironically, considering what the cost to him was to be, his efforts had not been appreciated in Ireland, a fact which naturally enough irked him a good deal.

After having played such a signal role in 1778–1779 in the

amelioration of Ireland's trade, Burke's *volte face* in 1785, when he opposed Pitt's propositions for Irish free trade, was as shocking as it was inexcusable. Burke was as wrong in opposing Pitt's proposals as he was right in almost everything else relating to Ireland and its problems.

If his position on the political connection which should obtain between Great Britain and Ireland requires some labor to clarify, and if his views on the commercial relations between the two were patently colored by an indefensible factiousness, his stand on the Irish Catholics is a jewel of consistency and shows him to his best advantage. He was far more liberal in his approach to Irish questions than his contemporaries, and this is especially true of the Catholic problem, because he understood Ireland as no other Englishman of his generation did. He sought, guided by his own lights in the matter, to do two things for Ireland. One was to end external misrule; the other was to terminate internal misgovernment.

As far as he was concerned, the first was accomplished through the grants of commercial relief from 1778 to 1780 and by the award of legislative independence in 1782. Internal misrule was quite another matter and involved two steps if it was to be corrected. The first of these was the improvement of the position of the Roman Catholics; the second was to remove forever the power of the monopolists of place, the Ascendancy.

From the outset, Burke had a personal motive for improving the lot of the Irish Catholics. His mother and sister were lifelong Catholics as were a large number of his relatives. Even his own wife had been a Catholic at the time of their marriage, although she conformed to the Church of England and remained one of its communicants for the rest of her life. The restrictions placed upon those so near and dear to him and his intimate connection with others of the Roman Catholic faith made him warmly attached to that religion and produced in him an understanding of it which was a mixture of respect and admiration. The warmth of his affection for Catholicism caused his contemporary, the Earl of Charlemont, to observe that Burke's mind had acquired "an almost constitutional bent toward the Popish party." [13] As we have noted, his Catholic connections and his favorable attitude toward the Catholics caused him to be caricatured relentlessly as a "Papist."

Burke was deeply religious as a youth, and the passing years merely served to strengthen his religiosity. In his early years he was fond of carrying on theological discussions with his friend, Richard Shackleton, in their correspondence. Later, as a member of parliament, he said that he had read all the theological publications on all sides which had been written during the seventeenth and eighteenth centuries,[14] a task of rather awesome proportions. His conclusion was that these studies only tended to confuse (a somewhat understandable deduction) so he had elected to remain in the Church of England, which was the best church for the English nation. England's attachment to a national religious establishment struck him very forcibly. He expressed inability to see how in a Christian country the church and state could be anything but complementary parts of one and the same whole.[15] Despite his adherence to Anglicanism, he exhibited a striking similarity to Catholicism in much of his system of thought and action and was patently profoundly influenced by the doctrines of the old faith. Its dogmas always commanded his respect, although there were points which did not receive his approval. Yet his knowledge of the religion was exceptionally thorough. This coupled with his sincerity enabled him to argue so intelligently for the Catholics throughout his life.

Possessed of a mind which instinctively loved and fully appreciated truth, he felt strongly both the injustice and the inexpediency of the treatment accorded the Irish Catholics. He bitterly condemned their proscription as the wretched invention of a lust for power by those who stood to profit by keeping the Catholics weak. To correct these abuses he relied in large measure upon a policy of expediency, which was by no means opportunism.[16] To him expediency meant that which was good for the entire community, collectively and individually.[17] To realize the expedient required diligent search through the long slow process of social organization. There one could find those principles of both civil and religious freedom whereby the good of the Irish community could be achieved.

Among those principles were toleration, justice, and charity. Burke tolerated in the true sense of the word, that is to say, he respected justice. He found much good in many religions with which he was not necessarily in agreement, and this caused him to respect these faiths and their adherents.[18]

An exception to his tolerance were the atheists. Atheism he always denounced as contrary to reason because "man is by his constitution a religious animal." [19] He had an abiding dread that atheism would cause the ruin of the state. In addition to the atheists, he condemned and despised those "miserable bigots" whose hatred of religions other than their own was greater than their love of the substance of religion." [20] For this "substance" Burke had a permanent affection which convinced him that religion is the foundation of civil society; the origin of all good and all solace.[21]

Bigotry, then, had no place in his scheme of things, yet he did not base his opposition to the Irish monopolists who persecuted the Catholics of that land on grounds of religious bigotry on their part. Instead he always argued that they were motivated simply by an inordinate lust for power. This did violence to his deep religious convictions and made him condemn those whom he felt were guilty of a consuming ambition for power. He detested such men because they failed to appreciate that all who act as administrators of the powers of government were responsible to God and should, therefore, have a high estimate of both their operation of those powers and their own ultimate destination when their stewardship in this life ended. The mere fact that they had in their hands any portion of power should fill them with awe and respect for its source, he maintained. They should comprehend that they acted only as trustees who one day would have to face an accounting.[22] In brief, the exercise of authority is "a holy function," [23] a fact which the holders of office in Ireland almost universally disregarded and so drew the fire of Burke's attack for their irreverence.

He argued that religion is the basis of civil society, which, in turn, is made for the advantage of man. All the benefits which civil society can bestow are man's right. He is entitled to justice; to the acquisitions of his parents; to the protection and improvement of his children and their education, as well as his own; to consolation at death; to the possession of that which he can acquire without trespassing upon the rights of others; and, lastly, to an equitable portion of that which society, with its great dexterity and power, can do for him.[24]

Under the penal laws operating against them in Ireland the Catholics were largely deprived of these rights. Feeling keenly the patent injustice of this proscription and realizing its deleterious effects, Burke was early moved to act in the interests of these oppressed people. In his work of helping these special objects of his affections among the Irish people, his mentality exhibited so many striking similarities to Catholic thought and teaching that he was so often accused of secretly being a Catholic.

Despite his familiarity with Roman Catholicism and its obvious influence over him, it is well to reiterate that Burke was not a Catholic. He declared many times that he preferred Protestantism as exemplified by the Church of England to any other religion. His strong feelings of nationalism played an important part here. But he came to feel that without Roman Catholicism no Protestant sect could survive. He unhesitatingly asserted this both publicly and privately.[25] He held that the church of his choice was possessed of the major part of the doctrines of the Roman Catholic religion and he derived consolation from this belief together with the knowledge that it had once been in communion with Rome. The split, he said, had come over some of the doctrines of the Roman church and against its authority. He himself remained well disposed toward the old church and its interests and to many of its clergy and laity personally. With the clergy in particular he had several close ties, chief among whom was Bishop Hussey. Burke's home at Beaconsfield became a mecca for émigré clerics after the French Revolution. He hospitably entertained and aided these visitors in generous fashion.[26] Indeed he has been accused of a bias for sacerdotalism [27] but his liking was induced by a reverent respect and fell far short of bias.

He was positive in his assertions that England had nothing to fear from the pope and made light of those who charged that the Catholics owed a temporal allegiance to the pontiff which took precedence over that to their own rulers. For the person of Pope Pius VI, who was the spiritual leader of the world's Catholics from 1775 to 1799, he had great reverence.[28] He was signally honored with an autograph letter from His Holiness, at that time a rare distinction for a non-Catholic, praising his work on behalf of the Catholics of England and Ireland and for his kindness to the refugee French clergy. In 1793, Burke advocated establishment of formal diplomatic relations between Great Britain and the Papal States. Failure to do so would be bigotry on the part of Britain, he wrote and predicted that much good and no harm could result from such relations.[29]

In his last years, Burke came to liken the Catholic church of Ireland to the original apostolic model, although he thought some improvements were needed to make the analogy more perfect.[30] Its constitution, discipline, lack of wealth, and its doctrines possessed an appeal for him which he did not seek to hide.[31] His own deference to authority, tradition, and prescription helped to make the cause of the Irish Catholics dear to his heart.[32] On the sound basis of his intimate knowledge of the Roman Catholic religion together with his respect and admiration for so much of it, Burke was well qualified to undertake the task of the amelioration of the position of the Catholics of Ireland.

In both 1778 and 1782, Burke worked both "in public and in private" to secure Catholic relief. He never wavered from the conviction that the empire needed Ireland, and the crisis of the French Revolution merely strengthened this feeling. To insure Ireland's loyalty, it was clear to him that the position of the Catholics would have to be improved. Time and circumstances were propitious as far as he was concerned so from 1790 on to his death seven years later he worked ceaselessly for emancipation both because it had long enjoyed his support and because he was firmly persuaded that the Catholics would ultimately determine whether Ireland remained loyal to the empire.

He permitted his son to become the agent of the General Committee of the Irish Catholics and freely advised him and his clients in the pursuit of their objectives. That the Catholics won the franchise in 1793 together with the removal of many of the remaining penal laws was due in no small measure to Burke. The completion of Catholic emancipation occupied him in the last years of his life more fully than his crusade against the French Revolution. However, the latter was even more important to him than the former. As we have observed, in the Fitzwilliam episode Burke extended himself almost to the limits of his being. Despite what George III called his "heated imagination," he saw far more clearly than most what the consequences of failure to grant emancipation at that time would be. This stupid blunder together with the removal of Fitzwilliam was, as Burke accurately predicted, a crucial turning point in the relations between Britain and Ireland.

Personal factors may have been responsible for attracting Burke to the work of helping the Catholics, as we have noted, but there was much more to it. Burke's mind was one which worked upon concrete objects, and the Irish Catholics were a numerous people who were, he once observed, equal in numbers to those of the entire kingdoms of Sardinia or Denmark and more numerous than those of Switzerland. Experience had taught Burke the impolicy and inexpediency of proscribing whole nations from the constitutions under which they were born. To him the laws against the Irish Catholics were unlike any system of religious oppression then in existence or with which history had made him familiar, and their mistreatment was not in accord with the principles of the Glorious Revolution, as he professed to understand them.

He recognized that men cannot be argued into slavery and understood that a government which flew in the face of the basic impulses of mankind could only invite disaster in the end. How could such a government find security by openly defying the wishes of the overwhelming majority of the subjects and why should the Irish Catholic have less justice for his share than the French Canadian Catholic or the Indian Moslem or Hindu were two questions which he endlessly posed.[33]

The ultimate solution of the Catholic problem, as he came to see it, was to restore the Catholics to the franchise and then later to return them their former privilege of holding seats in the Irish parliament. This involved him in an apparent inconsistency. He was a vigorous opponent throughout his career of reformation of the British parliament through extension of the suffrage. To favor the franchise for the Irish Catholics was tantamount to advocating reform of the Irish parliament while at the same time opposing it in Britain. Burke thus laid himself open to charges of inconsistency. The truth is that he felt that the Irish Catholics, the majority of the Irish nation, were unrepresented in their legislature whereas the situation was such in England that rather than add to the number of voters, it would be better to reduce it. This would minimize the corruption then existent in England. It goes without saying that Burke's stand in the matter of the reform of the British parliament left much to be desired. By contrast Pitt's position on this matter was more intelligent.

I would say that Burke is open to criticism also in his opposition to the idea of a reform of the Irish parliament apart from the admission of the Catholics. This body was one of the most corrupt and rotten that the world has ever seen, and Burke's blindness to concede that parliamentary reform would correct this is open to criticism. His reluctance is understandable for, were he to advocate such a reform, he would then in the interests of consistency have to favor a similar step in England. His realization of this probably accounts for his stubborn refusal. He seems to have contented himself with championing the defeat of the Ascendancy in other ways, notably that of the opposition taking office in Ireland whenever their British counterparts were in power. Yet at the very end of his life he gently chided his friend Fitzwilliam when the latter became exercised over the espousal of Irish parliamentary reform by Grattan and the Ponsonbys and other leading Irish Whigs. He told Fitzwilliam on this occasion that no one could expect to restrain their friends when they had run "every risk & made every sacrifice" to serve not only English government which they approved but that which they "detested & abhorred" and for a reward had not only been "discountenanced & suppressed but even persecuted." Neither Fitzwilliam nor any man could assure them that the grievances of which they complained could be redressed in any other way. Hence he advised Fitzwilliam to restrain his advice to their friends and furthermore he would be "shy of interfering" because the ministry "keep this very door to popularity, which is to be shut to these Gentlemen, open to themselves." Pitt was "a declared Zealot . . . for these Parliamentary reforms; . . ." [34] But that this admission was but a temporary departure from his lifelong stand may be seen from a letter to French Laurence five months later wherein he expressed his old fear that parliamentary reform in Ireland would result in the same thing in England, a step which he had asserted since he had attained the use of reason would be preliminary to "utter ruin." [35]

Despite his pessimistic feeling at his death that he had failed in his work for Ireland, fortunately he was wrong. His efforts to make Ireland a free, happy country within the British Empire and a land where Protestant and Catholic would be fellow-citizens had borne some fruit during his lifetime, and many of his arguments were destined to be employed effectively in the long years to come. The lot of the Roman Catholics, while still leaving much to be desired, had been greatly improved by the battle Burke had waged for them, but there can be no doubt that the future of Ireland would have been vastly different if Burke had been heeded.

He had tried desperately to show that Catholic Emancipation was quite consistent with the retention of Ireland within the empire and that both justice and expediency made emancipation mandatory. Persistently, he had demonstrated that the Catholics were not bent upon rebellion, that they were loyal subjects whose clergy preached obedience to the government, and that whenever the Catholics took up arms they had been motivated by economic and not religious forces. As he once told his son: "It is not about Popes but about potatoes that the minds of this unhappy people are agitated. It is not from the spirit of zeal, but the spirit of whiskey that these wretches [the common people] act." [36]

Because of his refusal to recommend rebellion in Ireland, Burke has been accused of inconsistency. The argument runs that he did not dare to advise this extreme course of action, even though he was a staunch defender of the Glorious Revolution and certainly made it quite obvious that his sympathies were publicly with the Americans in their Revolutionary War, because to do so would have ruined him in England. As Burke made abundantly clear, he knew that the Irish would have been overwhelmingly defeated should they take up arms against England. Especially was this true of the Catholics, but he also demonstrated that an England, free of the American War, would have made short work of the predominantly Protestant Volunteers. Thus, he always refrained from recommending or even approving recourse to rebellion in Ireland for reasons of expediency and, of course, because he did not wish Ireland to break away from the empire. He did reluctantly conclude that "Catholic *defenderism* is the only restraint upon Protestant ascendancy" but beyond that he would not go. He told Dr. Hussey at the end of 1796 that it was unquestionably right to teach a species of passive obedience but that to advocate rebellion was to deceive the people. In other words, what he advocated long in advance of its acceptance by peoples desirous of their independence was passive resistance: "The resources of a persevering, dissatisfied obedience, are much greater than those of almost any force." [37] As Harold Laski pointed out, Burke was an "apostle of order" and "had too much the sense of a Divine Providence taking thought for the welfare of men to interfere with violence in his handiwork. The tinge of caution is never absent, even from his most liberal moments; and he was willing to endure great evil if it seemed dangerous to estimate the cost of change." [38]

Burke's analysis of what was wrong in Ireland placed the onus at the doorstep of the Ascendancy. Ireland, as such, and the Roman Catholics of Ireland, had no grievances against England. Get rid of the Ascendancy, and Ireland's woes would be cured since they originated there and not in England. This was the solution, as he never grew tired of saying.

The political system which he advocated for Ireland was, in effect, home rule, a goal most Irishmen were prepared to accept as late as World War I. Independence for Ireland was simply out of the question in Burke's day even if he had believed in it. He was also opposed to the alternative of an unrestricted union between Britain and Ireland. This was never a happy solution as time was destined to show. The forces which made for the success of the union between England and Scotland simply did not exist so that an English-Irish union was impractical from the start. Irish Home Rule would unquestionably have worked, especially if it had been based on Catholic emancipation and the elimination of the power of the Ascendancy. In the political and religious spheres, we can only conclude that Burke was right in the program which he espoused.

The tragedy of Burke's selfless advocacy of the cause of Ireland was twofold. Had he been heeded and the blueprint which he had drawn up for the solution of Ireland's problems, particularly those of the Catholics, been followed, it seems patent that Ireland's long and dreary history in the nineteenth and much of the twentieth centuries need not have occurred. For this Burke is not to be blamed, but he must be censured for having failed to grasp an excellent opportunity to try to bring to fruition his dreams for Ireland. When Pitt brought forward his commercial propositions to free the trade of Ireland, proposals which bore the advanced thinking of Adam Smith, Ireland stood at the threshold of equal participation in the commercial advantages enjoyed by England and Scotland. For Burke to have failed to realize this and to have seized upon Pitt's stipulation, that in return for free trade the Irish would have to contribute to common imperial expenses, such as the support of the navy, and to have branded it as an attempt to enslave Ireland was not only ridiculous but inexcusable. What free trade could have meant for Ireland has already been suggested above. That few men in public life had a better comprehension of economics than Burke is well known.

In criticizing the part played by Burke in the defeat of Pitt's proposals, there is no intention to suggest that had he supported them, they would have succeeded. Certainly, their chances might have been somewhat improved, but the important thing is that Burke would have been consistent. Following this sorry performance, his remaining years were spent in large measure in a sincere and praiseworthy attempt to help the bulk of Ireland's people, the Catholics. But as good an opportunity as that of 1785, when he had been so blind and inconsistent, never again presented itself.

In concluding this study of Burke's connection with Irish affairs, it can be noted that essentially, he was most consistent; accidentally, he was inconsistent. The persistency with which he hammered away over the years on such points as the following was as admirable as it was true: (1) the Catholics of Ireland were firmly attached to the monarchy; (2) there had always been an inequitable tendency to exaggerate Catholic participation in popular disturbances while neglecting at the same time mention of the fact that among the lower classes the Catholics formed an overwhelming majority; (3) the tendency to ascribe falsely to the Catholics the motive of zeal for their religion as the cause of their involvement in disorders rather than the true motivating force which was economic; (4) the palpable falsity of the charge that the Catholics were in league with foreign powers; (5) the baselessness of fear of the pope should the Catholics receive their emancipation; and (6) the responsibility of the Ascendancy for the plight of the Catholics.

APPENDIXES

Appendix I — The Penal Law of 1704 (excerpts)

An act to prevent the further growth of popery (2 Anne, c.3)

I. Whereas divers emissaries of the church of Rome, popish priests, and other persons of that persuasion, taking advantage of the weakness and ignorance of some of her majesty's subjects, or of the extreme sickness and decay of their reason and senses, in the absence of friends and spiritual guides, do daily endeavor to persuade and pervert them from the protestant religion, to the great dishonour of Almighty God, the weakening of the true religion, by His blessing so happily established in this realm, to the disquieting the peace and settlement, and discomfort of many particular families thereof; and in further manifestation of their hatred and aversion to the said true religion, many of the said persons so professing the popish religion in this kingdom, have refused to make provision for their own children for no other reason but their being of the protestant religion; and also by cunning devices and contrivances found out ways to avoid and elude the intents of an act of parliament, made in the ninth year of the reign of the late King William the Third for preventing protestants intermarrying with papists, and of several other laws made for the security of the protestant religion; and whereas many persons so professing the popish religion have it in their power to raise division among protestants, by voting in elections for members of parliament, and also have it in their power to use other ways and means tending to the destruction of the protestant interest in this kingdom; for remedy of which great mischiefs, and to prevent the like evil practices for the future be it enacted . . . that if any person or persons from and after the twenty-fourth day of March, in this present year of our Lord 1703, shall seduce, persuade or pervert any person or persons professing, or that shall profess, the protestant religion, to renounce, forsake, or adjure the same, and to profess the popish religion, or reconcile him or them to the church of Rome, then and in such case every such person or persons so seducing, as also every such protestant or protestants who shall be so seduced, perverted, and reconciled to popery, shall for the said offences, being thereof lawfully convicted, incur the danger and penalty of praemunire, mentioned in the statute of praemunire made in England in the sixteenth year of the reign of King Richard the Second; and if any person or persons professing the popish religion, shall from and after the said twenty-fourth day of March send, or cause, or willingly suffer, to be sent or conveyed any child under the age of one and twenty years, except sailors, ship-boys, or the apprentice or factor of some merchant in trade of merchandise, into France or any other parts beyond the seas, out of her majesty's dominions, without the special licence of her majesty, her heirs or successors or of her or their chief governor or governors of this kingdom . . . he, she or they shall incur the pains, penalties and forfeitures mentioned in act made in the seventh year of his late majesty King William, entitled, *An act to restrain foreign education.*

III. And to the end that no child or children of popish parent or parents who have professed or embraced the protestant religion, or who shall profess and embrace, or are or shall be desirous or willing to be instructed and educated therein, may in the life time of such popish parent or parents, for fear of being cast off or disinherited by them, or for want of fitting maintenance or further provision, be compelled and necessitated to embrace the popish religion, be it further enacted . . . that from and after the twenty-fourth day of March 1703, upon complaint in the high court of chancery . . . it shall and may be lawful for the said court to make such order for the maintenance of every such protestant child, not maintained by such popish parent, suitable to the degree and ability of such parent, and to the age of such child, and also for the portion of every such protestant child, to be paid at the decrease of such popish parent, as the court shall adjudge fit, suitable to the degree and ability of such parent; and in case the eldest son and heir of such popish parent shall be a protestant, that then from the time of enrollment in the high court of chancery of a certificate of the bishop of the diocese, in which he shall inhabit, testifying his being a protestant, and conforming himself to the church of Ireland as by law established, such popish parent shall become, and shall be, only tenant for life of all the real estate, whereof such popish parent shall then be seized in fee-tail or fee-simple, and the reversion in fee shall be vested in such eldest son being a protestant; subject nevertheless to all such debts and real encumbrances at the time of the enrollment of such certificate charging such estate, and subject also to such maintenances and portions for the other children, as well protestants as papists of such popish parents then born, or after to be born, as the said court of chancery in manner aforesaid shall order. . . .

IV. And that care may be taken for the education of children in the communion of the church of Ireland as by law established, be it enacted . . . that no person of the popish religion shall, or may be guardian unto, or have the tuition or custody of, any orphan child or children, under the age of twenty-one years; but that the same, where the person having or entitled to the guardianship of such orphan child or children, is or shall be a papist, shall be disposed of by the high court of chancery to some near relation of such orphan child or children, being a protestant, and conforming himself to the church of Ireland as by law established, to whom the estate cannot descend, in case there shall be any such protestant relation fit to have the education of such child; otherwise to some other protestant conforming himself as aforesaid, who is hereby required to use his utmost care to educate and bring up such child or minor in the protestant religion. . . .

VI. And be it further enacted . . . that every papist, or person professing the popish religion, shall from and after the said twenty-fourth day of March be disabled, and is hereby made incapable, to buy and purchase either in his or in their own name, or in the name of any other person or persons to his or her use, or in trust for him or her, any manors, lands, tenements, or hereditaments, or any rents or profits out of the same, or any leases or terms thereof, other than any term of years not exceeding thirty-one years, whereon a rent not less than two-thirds of the improved yearly value, at the time of the making such leases of the tenements leased, shall be reserved. . . .

VII. And be it further enacted . . . that from and after the first day of February, in this present year of our Lord 1703, no papist or person professing the popish religion, who shall not within six months after he or she shall have become entitled to enter, or to take or have the profits by descent, or by virtue of any devise or gift, or of any remainder already limited, or at any time hereafter to be limited, or by virtue of any trust, of any lands, tenements or hereditaments, whereof any protestant now is, or hereafter shall be seized in fee-simple absolute, or fee-tail, or in such manner that after his death, or the death of him and his wife, the freehold is to come immediately to his son or sons, or issue in tail, if then of the age of eighteen years, or if under within six months after he shall attain that age, until which time from his being so entitled he shall be under the care of such protestant relation or person conforming himself as aforesaid, as shall for that purpose be appointed by the high court of chancery, for his being educated in the protestant religion, become a protestant, and conform himself to the church now established in this kingdom, shall take any benefit by reason of such descent, devise, gift, remainder, or trust, by from thenceforth during the life of such person, or until he or she do become a protestant, and conform as aforesaid, the nearest protestant relation or relations, or other protestant or protestants, and his and their heirs, being and continuing protestants, who shall or would be entitled to the same in case such person professing the popish religion, and not conforming as aforesaid, and all other intermediate popish relations and popish persons were actually dead, and his and their heirs shall have and enjoy the said lands. . . .

X. And further be it enacted . . . that all lands tenements and hereditaments, whereof a papist now is, or hereafter shall be, seized in fee-simple or fee-tail, shall from henceforth, so long as any papist shall be seized of or entitled to the same in fee-simple or fee-tail, be of the nature of gavelkind; and if not sold, aliened, or disposed of by such papist in his life time for good and valuable consideration of money really and *bona fide* paid for such estate, shall from such papist descend to, and be inherited by, all and every the sons of such papist any way inheritable to such estate, share and share alike, and not descend on or come to the eldest of such sons only, being a papist, as heir-at-law; and shall in like manner from such respective sons, being papist, descend to and be inherited by all and every the sons of such sons, share and share alike, and not descend to the eldest of such sons, being a papist, as heir-at-law only; and that for want of issue male of such papist, the same shall descend to all his daughters any way inheritable to such estate in equal proportions; and for want of such issue, among the collateral kindred of such papist, of the kin of his father, any way inheritable to such estate in equal degree; and for want of such kindred, to the collateral kindred of such papist of the kin of his mother, any way inheritable to such estate, and not other-wise; . . .

XI. Provided nevertheless, it shall and may be lawful to and for such papist to charge such his estate with reasonable maintenances and portions for his daughters, to be raised and paid in such manner as he shall direct.

XII. Provided always, that if the eldest son or heir-at-law of such papist shall be a protestant at the time of the decease of such papist, . . . the lands whereof such papist shall be seized, shall descend to such eldest son or heir-at-law according to the rules of the com-mon law of this realm, . . . and if the eldest son or heir-at-law of any such papist, who shall at the time of the decease of such papist, whose heir he is, be of the age of one and twenty years, shall become a protestant and conform himself to the church of Ireland, as by law established, within one year after such decease of such papist, or being then under the age of one and twenty years, shall within one year after he shall attain that age become a protestant, and conform himself as aforesaid, . . . he shall be entitled to, and shall have, and enjoy from thenceforth the whole real estate of such papist. . . .

XV. Provided always, that no person shall take benefit by this act as a protestant within the intent and meaning hereof, that shall not conform to the church of Ireland as by law established, and sub-scribe the declaration, and also take and subscribe the oath of adjuration following, viz. I A.B. do solemnly and sincerely, in the presence of

God, profess, testify and declare, that I do believe, that in the sacrament of the Lord's-Supper, there is not any trans-substantiation of the elements of bread and wine into the body and blood of Christ, at or after the consecration thereof by any person whatsoever, and that the adoration or invocation of the Virgin Mary, or any other saint, and the sacrifice of the mass, as they are now used in the church of Rome, are superstitious and idolatrous. And I do solemnly, in the presence of God, profess, testify, and declare, that I do make this declaration, and every part hereof, in the plain and ordinary sense of the words read unto me, as they are commonly understood by protestants, without any evasion, equivocation or mental reservation whatsoever; and without any dispensation already granted me for this purpose by the pope, or any other authority or person whatsoever, or without any hope of dispensation from any person or authority whatsoever, or without believing that I am, or can be acquitted before God or man, or absolved of this declaration, or any part thereof, although the pope, or any other person or persons, or power whatsoever should dispense with or annul the same, or declare that it was null and void from the beginning.

I A.B. do truly and sincerely acknowledge, profess, testify and declare in my conscience, before God and the world, that our sovereign lady Queen Anne is lawful and rightful queen of this realm, and of all other her majesty's dominions and countries thereunto belonging. And I do solemnly and sincerely declare, that I do believe in my conscience, that the person pretending to be Prince of Wales during the life of the late King James, and since his decease pretending to be, and taking upon himself the style and title of King of England by the name of James III, hath not any right or title whatsoever to the crown of this realm, or any other the dominions thereto belonging, and I do renounce, refuse and abjure any allegiance or obedience to him. And I do swear that I will bear faith and true allegiance to her majesty Queen Anne, and her will defend to the utmost of my power against all traiterous conspiracies and attempts whatsoever, which shall be made against her person, crown, or dignity. And I will do my best endeavour to disclose and make known to her majesty, and her successors, all treasons and traiterous conspiracies, which I shall know to be against her or any of them. And I do faithfully promise to the utmost of my power to support, maintain and defend the limitation and succession of the crown against him the said James, and all other persons whatsoever, as the same is and stands limited by an act, entitled, An act declaring the rights and liberties of the subject, and settling the succession of the crown, to her present majesty, and the heirs of her body being protestants; and as the same by one other act, entitled, An act for the further limitation of the crown, and better securing the rights and liberties of the

329

subject, is and stands limited, after the decease of her majesty, and for default of issue of her majesty, to the Princess Sophia, electress and duchess dowager of Hanover, and the heirs of her body being protestants. And all these things I do plainly and sincerely acknowledge and swear, according to the express words by me spoken, and according to the plain and common sense and understanding of the same words, without any equivocation, mental evasion or secret reservation whatsoever. And I do make this recognition, acknowledgement, abjuration, renunciation and promise, heartily, willingly, and truly, upon the true faith of a Christian. So help me God.

XVII. And be it further enacted . . . that all and every such person and persons, that shall be admitted, entered, placed or taken into any office or offices, civil or military, or that shall receive pay, salary, fee, or wages belonging to or by reason of any office or place of trust, by reason of any patent or grant from her majesty, or that shall have command or place of trust from or under her majesty, or any of her predecessors or successors, or by her or their authority, or by authority derived from her or them, within this realm of Ireland, after the first day of Easter-term aforesaid, shall take the said oaths and repeat the said declaration, and subscribe the said oaths and declaration, in one of the said respective courts in the next term, or at the general quarter-session for that county, barony, or place where he or they shall reside, next after his or their respective admittance or admittances into any such office . . . and all and every such person or persons so to be admitted as aforesaid, shall also receive the sacrament of the Lord's supper according to the usage of the Church of Ireland, within three months after his or their admittance in or receiving their said authority and employments in some public church, upon the Lord's-day commonly called Sunday, immediately after divine service and sermon, and every of the said respective persons, touching whom the said several provisions are herebefore made, in the respective court, where he or she takes the said oaths, shall first deliver a certificate of such his or her receiving the said sacrament as aforesaid, under the hands of the respective minister and churchwardens, and shall then make proof of the truth thereof by two credible witnesses at the least, upon oath, all which shall be required of and put upon record in their respective courts.

XVIII. And be it further enacted, that all and every the person or persons aforesaid, who do or shall refuse or neglect to take the said oath and sacrament, and to deliver such a certificate of his receiving the sacrament, as aforesaid, or to subscribe the said declaration as aforesaid in one of the said courts and places, and at the respective times aforesaid shall be ipso facto adjudged incapable and disabled in law to all intents and purposes whatsoever to have, occupy, or enjoy the said office or offices, . . .

XXIV. And for the preventing papist having it in their power to breed dissention amongst protestants by voting at elections of members of parliament; be it further enacted . . . that from and after the twenty-fourth day of March 1703 no freeholder, burgess, freeman, or inhabitant of this kingdom, being a papist or professing the popish religion, shall at any time hereafter be capable of giving his or their vote for the electing of knights of any shires or counties within this kingdom, or citizens or burgesses to serve in any succeeding parliament, without first repairing to the general quarter sessions of the peace to be holden for the counties, cities, or boroughs wherein such papists do inhabit and dwell, and there voluntarily take the oath of allegiance in the words following, viz. I A.B. do sincerely promise and swear, that I will be faithful and bear true allegiance to her majesty Queen Anne. So help me God, etc.

And also the oath of abjuration aforesaid: . . .

XXVI. And whereas the superstitions of popery are greatly increased and upheld by the pretended sanctity of places, especially of a place called Saint Patrick's purgatory in the county of Donegal and of wells, to which pilgrimages are made by vast numbers at certain seasons, by which not only the peace of the public is greatly disturbed, but the safety of the government also hazarded, by the riotous and unlawful assembling together of many thousands of papists to the said wells and other places, be it further enacted, that all such meetings and assemblies shall be deemed and adjudged riots and unlawful assemblies, and punishable as such. . . .

[Source: Ir. Stat., iv. 12–31. Copied from *Irish Historical Documents, 1172–1922*, ed. Edmund Curtis and R. B. McDowell (London, 1943), pp. 188–194.]

Appendix II — *The Penal Law of 1709 (précis)*

An act for explaining and amending an act intituled, an act to prevent the further growth of popery (8 Anne, c.3)

I. No papist shall be allowed to take any annuity for life.

III. Whenever any child or children of popish parents conform, the parents shall be obliged to distribute their real and personal estate to and among such Protestant children.

XII. All converts in public employment, members of parliament, barristers, attorneys, or officers of any court of law, shall educate their children as Protestants.

XIV. The popish wife of a papist, having power to make a jointure, conforming, shall, if she survive her husband, have such provision, not exceeding the power of her husband, to make a jointure, as the chancellor shall adjudge.

331

XV. The popish wife of a papist, not otherwise provided for, conforming, shall have a proportion of his chattels, notwithstanding any will or voluntary disposition.

XVI. A papist teaching school publicly, or in a private house, or as an usher to a Protestant, shall be deemed and prosecuted as a popish regular convict.

XVIII. Any popish priest who conforms shall receive £30 per annum, the funds to be levied and paid by grand juries.

XX. Rewards for discovering popish clergy and schoolmasters shall be:

(1) for discovering an archbishop, bishop, vicar-general, or other person exercising foreign ecclesiastical jurisdiction, £50;

(2) for discovering each regular clergyman not registered, £20;

(3) for discovering each popish schoolmaster or usher, £10.

XXI. Justices were empowered to summon any papist aged eighteen. If he refused to testify where and when he heard Mass celebrated and who and what persons were present, and likewise touching the residence and abode of any priest or papist schoolmaster, the justices could commit him to jail, without bail, for twelve months, or until he paid £20.

XXV. No priest shall officiate except in the parish for which he was registered by the act of 2 Anne, c. 7.

XXX. This clause provided for the discovery of all trusts in favor of papists, and enabled any Protestant to file a bill in chancery against any person concerned in any sale, lease, mortgage, or encumbrance, in trust for papists, and to compel him to discover the same. It was further provided that all issues tried in any action founded upon this act should be tried by none but known Protestants.

XXXVII. No papist in trade, except in the linen trade, shall take more than two apprentices.

[Source: Henry Parnell, *A History of the Penal Laws Against the Irish Catholics* (Dublin, 1808), pp. 53–57.]

Appendix III — The Catholic Relief Act of 1778 (excerpts)

An act for the relief of his majesty's subjects professing the popish religion
(17 & 18 Geo. III, c.49)

Whereas by an act made in this kingdom in the second year of her late majesty Queen Anne, entitled, *An act to prevent the further growth of popery*, and also by another act made in the eighth year of her said reign for explaining and amending the said act, the Roman catholics of Ireland are made subject to several disabilities and incapacities therein particularly mentioned; and whereas for their uniform peaceful behaviour for a long series of years it appears reasonable and expedient to relax the same, and it must tend not only to the cultivation and improvement of this kingdom, but to the prosperity and strength of all his majesty's dominions, that his subjects of all denominations should enjoy the blessings of our free constitution, and should be bound to each other by mutual interest and mutual affection, therefore be it enacted . . . that from and after the first day of August 1778 it shall and may be lawful to and for any papist, or person professing the popish religion, subject to the proviso hereinafter contained as to the taking and subscribing the oath and declaration therein mentioned, to take, hold, and enjoy any lease or leases for any term or term of years, not exceeding nine hundred and ninety-nine years certain, or for any term of years determinable upon any number of lives, not exceeding five, provided always, that upon every such lease a rent *bona fide* to be paid in money shall be reserved and made payable during such terms with or without the liberty of committing waste, as fully and beneficially to all intents and purposes, as any other his majesty's subjects in this kingdom, and the same to dispose of by will or otherwise as he shall think fit; and all lands tenements, hereditaments, whereof any papist or person professing the popish religion is now seized or shall be seized by virtue of a title legally derived by, from, or under such person or persons, now seized in fee simple or fee tail, whether at law or in equity, shall from and after the time aforesaid be descendable, deviseable, and transferable, as fully, beneficially, and effectually, as if the same were in the seizin of any other of his majesty's subjects in this kingdom.

III. Provided that no papist or person professing the popish religion shall take any benefit from this act, unless he or she shall on or before the first day of January 1779, or some time previous to any such lease made to or in trust for him, if he or she shall be in this kingdom, or within six months after any devise, descent, or limitation shall take effect in possession, if at that time within this kingdom, or if then abroad beyond the seas, or under the age of twenty-one years, or in prison, or of unsound mind, or under coverture, then within six months after his or her return from abroad, or attaining the age of twenty-one years, or discharge from prison, or becoming of sound mind, or after she shall become a *femme sole*, take and subscribe the oath of allegiance and the declaration prescribed by an act passed in this kingdom in the thirteenth and fourteenth years of his present majesty's reign, . . .

['An act to enable his majesty's subjects of whatever persuasion to testify their allegiance to him' permitted catholics to take an oath in which they promised allegiance to the king and his successors and repudiated the opinions that faith need not be kept with heretics, that it was lawful to murder heretics, that sovereigns excommunicated by the pope could be deposed or murdered by their subjects, and 'that the pope of Rome, or any other foreign prince, prelate, state or potentate hath or ought to have any temporal or civil jurisdiction, power, superiority or pre-eminence, directly or indirectly within this realm' (Ir. Stat., X. 589–590).]

V. And be it enacted . . . that no maintenance or portion shall be granted to any child of a popish parent, upon a bill filed against such parent . . . out of the personal property of such papist, except out of such leases which they may hereafter take under the powers granted in this act, . . .

VI. And whereas by an act made in this kingdom in the second year of the reign of her late majesty Queen Anne, entitled, An act to prevent the further growth of popery, it is amongst other things enacted to the effect following; in case the eldest son and heir of a popish parent shall be a protestant, . . . such popish parent shall become and be only tenant for life of all the real estate, whereof such popish parent shall then be seized in fee tail or fee simple, and the reversion in fee shall be vested in such eldest son, being a protestant subject, . . . and whereas it is found in expedient to continue any longer that part of the said recited act, be it enacted . . . that from and after the first day of November 1778 the conformity of the eldest son . . . shall not affect or alter the estate of any popish parent . . . but such popish parent shall remain seized and possessed of the same estate and interest in all and every his or her real estate, as he or she would have been, if such eldest son had not conformed, or the said act of the second year of Queen Anne had not been made.

X. Provided also that no person shall take benefit by this act who having been converted from the popish to the protestant religion shall afterwards relapse to popery, nor any person who being a protestant shall at any time become a papist, or shall educate or suffer to be educated, any of his children under the age of fourteen years in the popish religion.

[Source: Ir. Stat., xi. 298–301. Copied from *Irish Historical Documents, 1172–1922*, ed. Edmund Curtis and R. B. McDowell (London, 1943), pp. 194–196; *English Historical Documents*, Vol. X: 1714–1783, ed. D. B. Horne and Mary Curtis (London, 1957), pp. 705–707.]

Appendix IV — The Catholic Relief Act of 1782 (excerpts)

An act for the further relief of his majesty's subjects of this kingdom
professing the popish religion (21 & 22 Geo. III, c.24)

I. Whereas all such of his majesty's subjects in this kingdom, of whatever persuasion, as have heretofore taken and subscribed, or shall hereafter take and subscribe, the oath of allegiance and declaration prescribed by an act passed in the thirteenth and fourteenth years of his present majesty's reign, entitled, *An act to enable his majesty's subjects of whatever persuasion, to testify their allegiance to him*, ought to be considered as good and loyal subjects to his majesty, his crown and government; and whereas a continuance of several of the laws formerly enacted, and still in force in this kingdom, against persons professing the popish religion, is therefore unnecessary, in respect to those who have taken or shall take the said oath, and is injurious to the real welfare and prosperity of Ireland; therefore be it enacted . . . that from and after the first day of May 1782 it shall and may be lawful to and for any person or persons professing the popish religion, to purchase, or take by grant, limitation, descent, or devise, any lands, tenements, or hereditaments in this kingdom, or any interest therein (except advowsons, and also except any manor or borough, or any part of a manor or borough, the freeholders or inhabitants whereof are entitled to vote for burgesses to represent such borough or manor in parliament) and the same to dispose of as he, she, or they shall think fit, . . .

V. And be it enacted . . . that no popish ecclesiastic, who hath heretofore taken and subscribed, or who shall hereafter take and subscribe, the oath of allegiance and declaration, prescribed by an act passed in the thirteenth and fourteenth years of his present majesty's reign, entitled, *An act to enable his majesty's subjects of whatever persuasion, to testify their allegiance to him*, in the manner and form as hereinafter is particularly specified and set forth and who shall register his christian and surnames, place of abode, age, and parish, if he have a parish, and the time and place of his receiving his first, and every other popish orders, and from whom he received them, with the register of the diocese where his place of abode is (for every which registry the sum of one shilling and no more shall be paid to the register) shall, after the passing of this act, be subject to any of the penalties, incapacities, or disabilities, mentioned in an act made in the ninth year of the reign of the King William the third, entitled, *An act for banishing all popish papists exercising any ecclesiastical jurisdiction, and regulars of the popish clergy out of this kingdom*, or in an act made in the second year of Queen Anne, entitled, *An act for registering the popish clergy*, or in an act made in the second year of Queen Anne, entitled, *An act to prevent the further growth of popery*, or in an act made in the second year of Queen Anne, entitled, *An act to prevent popish priests from coming into this kingdom*, or in an act made in the fourth year of Queen Anne, entitled, *An act to explain and amend an act, entitled, An act for registering popish clergy;* or in an act made in the eighth year of Queen Anne, entitled, *An act for explaining and amending an act, entitled, An act to prevent the further growth of popery.*

335

VI. Provided always, that no benefits in this act contained shall extend, or be construed to extend, to any regular of the popish clergy, who shall not be in this kingdom at the time of passing this act, . . .

VIII. Provided always, that no benefits in this act contained shall extend, or be construed to extend, to any popish ecclesiastic who shall officiate in any church or chapel with a steeple or bell, or at any funeral in any church or church-yard, or who shall exercise any of the rites or ceremonies of the popish religion, or wear the habits of their order, save within their usual places of worship, or in private houses, or who shall use any symbol or mark or title whatsoever, . . .

IX. Provided also, that nothing in this act contained shall be construed to extend to any person or persons who shall be perverted from the protestant to the popish religion, but that all the pains penalties and disabilities, which now subsist, according to the laws now in being, shall remain in full force against such . . .

X. Provided also, that no benefits in this act contained shall be construed to extend to any popish ecclesiastic, who shall procure, incite, or persuade any protestant to become a papist; . . .

XII. And be it enacted . . . that so much of an act passed in the seventh year of King William III, entitled, An act for the better securing the government by disarming papists, as subjects any papist, who shall after the twentieth day of January 1695 have or keep in his possession, or in the possession of any person to his use or at his disposal, any horse, gelding, or mare, which shall be of the value of five pounds or more, to the penalties therein mentioned; and also so much of an act passed in the eighth year of Queen Anne, entitled, An act for explaining and amending an act, entitled, An act to prevent the further growth of popery, as enables the lord lieutenant or other chief governors of this kingdom, to seize and secure any horse, mare or gelding belonging to any papist or reputed papist, upon any invasion likely to happen, or in case of intestine war broke out, or likely to break out, shall be, and is, and are hereby repealed.

XIII. And be it enacted . . . that so much of an act passed in the ninth year of King George the second, entitled, An act for continuing and amending several statutes now near expiring, as enables the grand jury to present for the reimbursing such persons who have been robbed by privateers in time of war, for such losses as they shall respectively sustain thereby and for applotting and levying the fame on the lands, tenements and hereditaments, goods, and chattels of all the popish inhabitants of the country where such robbery shall be committed, shall be, and is hereby repealed.

XIV. And be it enacted . . . that so much of an act passed in the sixth year of King George the first, entitled, An act for the better regulating the parish watches, and amending the highways in this kingdom, and for preventing the misapplication of public money, as subjects such papist or papists who shall not provide a protestant watchman to watch in their turn, to the penalties therein mentioned shall be, and is hereby repealed.

XVI. Provided also, that no benefit herein contained shall extend or be construed to extend, to any person who hath not heretofore, or who shall not hereafter before the accruing of such benefit to such persons or persons, being of the age of twenty-one years, or who being under the age of twenty-one years, shall not within six months after he or she shall attain the age of twenty-one years, or being of unsound mind, or in prison, or beyond the seas, or under coverture, then within six months, after such disability removed, take, and subscribe the oath of allegiance and declaration prescribed by an act passed in the thirteenth and fourteenth years of his present majesty's reign, entitled, An act to enable his majesty's subjects of whatever persuasion, to testify their allegiance to him, . . .

[Source: Ir. Stat., xii. 237–242. Copied from *Irish Historical Documents, 1172–1922*, ed. Edmund Curtis and R. B. McDowell (London, 1943), pp. 196–198.]

Appendix V — The Catholic Relief Act of 1793 (excerpts)

An act for the relief of his majesty's popish, or Roman catholic
subjects of Ireland (33 Geo. III, c.21)

Whereas various acts of parliament have been passed, imposing on his majesty's subjects professing the popish or Roman catholic religion many restraints and disabilities, to which other subjects of this realm are not liable, and from the peaceful and loyal demeanour of his majesty's popish or Roman catholic subjects, it is fit that such restraints and disabilities shall be discontinued; be it therefore enacted . . . that his majesty's subjects being papists, or persons professing the popish or Roman catholic religion, or married to papists, or persons professing the popish or Roman catholic religion, or educating any of their children in that religion, shall not be liable or subject to any penalties, forfeitures, disabilities, or incapacities, or to any laws for the limitation, charging, or discovering of their estates and property, real or personal, or touching the acquiring of property, or securities affecting property, save such as his majesty's subjects of the protestant religion are liable and subject to; and that such parts of all oaths as are required to be taken by persons in order to qualify themselves for voting at elections for members to serve in parliament, as import to deny that the person taking the same is a papist or married to a papist, or educates his children in the popish religion, shall not hereafter be required to be taken by any voter, but shall be omitted by the person administering the same; and that it shall not be necessary, in order to entitle a papist, or person professing the popish or Roman catholic religion to vote at an election of members to serve in parliament, that he should at, or previous to his voting, take the oaths of allegiance and abjuration, . . .

VI. Provided also, that nothing herein contained, shall extend to authorize any papist, or person professing the popish or Roman catholic religion, to have or keep in his hands or possession any arms . . . or to exempt such person from any forfeiture, or penalty inflicted by any act respecting arms, armour, or ammunition, in the hands or possession of any papist, or respecting papists having or keeping such warlike stores, save and except papists, or persons of the popish or Roman catholic religion seized of a freehold estate of one hundred pounds a year, or possessed of a personal estate of one thousand pounds or upwards, who are hereby authorized to keep arms and ammunition as protestants now by law may; and also have and except papists or Roman catholics, possessing a freehold estate of ten pounds yearly value, and less than one hundred pounds, or a personal estate of three hundred, and less than one thousand pounds, who shall have at the session of the peace in the county in which they reside, taken the oath of allegiance prescribed to be taken by an act passed in the thirteenth and fourteenth years of his present majesty's reign, entitled, *An act to enable his majesty's subjects, of whatever persuasion, to testify their allegiance to him.* . . .

VII. And be it enacted, that it shall and may be lawful for papists, or persons professing the popish or Roman catholic religion, to hold, exercise, and enjoy all civil and military offices, or places of trust or profit under his majesty, his heirs and successors, in this kingdom; and to hold or take degrees or any professorship in, or be masters, or fellows of any college, to be hereafter founded in this kingdom, provided that such college shall be a member of the university of Dublin, and shall not be founded exclusively for the education of papists or persons professing the popish or Roman catholic religion, nor consist exclusively of masters, fellows, or other persons to be named or elected on the foundation of such college, being persons professing the popish or Roman catholic religion, or to hold any office or place of trust, in, and to be a member of any lay-body corporate, except the college of the holy and undivided Trinity of Queen Elizabeth, near Dublin, without taking and subscribing the oaths of allegiance, supremacy, or abjuration, or making or subscribing the declaration required to be taken, made and subscribed, to enable any person to hold and enjoy any of such places, and without receiving the sacrament of the Lord's supper, according to the rites and ceremonies of the church of Ireland, any law, statute, or bye-law of any corporation to the contrary notwithstanding; pro-

338

vided that every such person shall take and subscribe the oath appointed by the said act passed in the thirteenth and fourteenth years of his majesty's reign, entitled, *An act to enable his majesty's subjects of whatever persuasion to testify their allegiance to him*; and also the oath and declaration following, that is to say, I A.B. do hereby declare, that I do profess the Roman catholic religion. I A.B. do swear, that I do abjure, condemn, and detest, as unchristian and impious, the principle that it is lawful to murder, destroy, or any ways injure any person whatsoever, for or under the pretence of being a heretic; and I do declare solemnly before God, that I believe that no act in itself unjust, immoral, or wicked, can ever be justified or excused by or under pretence or colour, that it was done either for the good of the church, or in obedience to any ecclesiastical power whatsoever. I also declare, that it is not an article of the catholic faith, neither am I thereby required to believe or profess that the pope is infallible, or that I am bound to obey any order in its own nature immoral, though the pope or any ecclesiastical power should issue or direct such order, but on the contrary, I hold that it would be sinful in me to pay any respect or obedience thereto. I further declare, that I do not believe that any sin whatsoever, committed by me, can be forgiven at the mere will of any pope, or of any priest, or of any person or persons whatsoever, but that sincere sorrow for past sins, a firm and sincere resolution to avoid future guilt and to atone to God, are previous and indispensible requisites to establish a well-founded expectation of forgiveness, and that any person who receives absolution without these previous requisites, so far from obtaining thereby any remission of his sins, incurs, the additional guilt of violating a sacrament; and I do swear that I will defend to the utmost of my power the settlement and arrangement of property in this country, as established by the laws now in being; I do hereby disclaim, disavow and solemnly abjure any intention to subvert the present church establishment for the purpose of substituting a catholic establishment in its stead; and I do solemnly swear, that I will not exercise any privilege to which I am or may become entitled, to disturb and weaken the protestant religion and protestant government in this kingdom. So help me God!

IX. Provided always, and be it enacted, that nothing herein contained shall extend, or be construed to extend to enable any person to sit or vote in either house of parliament, or to hold, exercise, or enjoy the office of lord lieutenant, lord deputy, or other chief governor of this kingdom, lord high treasurer, chancellor of the exchequer, chief justice of the court of king's bench, or common pleas, lord chief baron of the court of exchequer, judge of the high court of admiralty, master or keeper of the rolls, secretary, vice-treasurer, teller and cashier of the exchequer, or auditor-general, lieutenant or governor, or custos rotulorum of counties, secretary to the lord lieutenant, lord deputy, or other chief governor or governors of this kingdom, member of his majesty's most honourable privy council, prime serjeant, attorney-general, solicitor-general, second and third serjeants-at-law, or king's counsel, masters in chancery, provost, or fellow of the college of the Holy and undivided Trinity of Queen Elizabeth, near Dublin, postmaster-general, master and lieutenant-general of his majesty's ordnance, commander-in-chief of his majesty's forces, generals on the staff, and sheriffs and sub-sheriffs of any county in this kingdom or any office contrary to the rules, orders and directions made and established by the lord lieutenant and council, in pursuance of the act passed in the seventeenth and eighteenth years of the reign of King Charles the Second, entitled, *An act for the explaining of some doubts arising upon an act, entitled, An act for the better execution of his majesty's gracious declaration for the settlement of his kingdom of Ireland,* . . . unless he shall have taken, made, and subscribed the oaths, and declaration, and performed the several requisites which by any law heretofore made, and now of force, are required to enable any person to sit or vote, or to hold, exercise, and enjoy the said offices respectively.

XII. Provided also, and be it enacted, that nothing herein contained, shall be construed to extend to authorize any popish priest, or reputed popish priest, to celebrate marriage between protestant and protestant, or between any person who hath been or professes himself or herself to be a protestant at any time within twelve months before such celebration of marriage, and a papist, unless such protestant and papist shall have been first married by a clergyman of the protestant religion; and that every popish priest, or reputed popish priest, who shall celebrate any marriage between two protestants, or between any such protestant and papist, unless such protestant and papist shall have been first married by a clergyman of the protestant religion, shall forfeit the sum of five hundred pounds to his majesty, upon conviction thereof.

XIII. And whereas it may be expedient, in case his majesty, his heirs and successors, shall be so pleased so to alter the statutes of the college of the Holy and Undivided Trinity near Dublin and of the university of Dublin, as to enable persons professing the Roman catholic religion to enter into, or to take degrees in the said university, to remove any obstacle which now exists by statute law; be it enacted, that from and after the first day of June 1793 it shall not be necessary for any person upon taking any of the degrees usually conferred by the said university, to make subscribe any declaration, or to take any oath, save the oaths of allegiance and abjuration. . . .

XIV. Provided always, that no papist or Roman catholic, or person professing the Roman catholic or popish religion, shall take any benefit by, or under this act, unless he shall have first taken and subscribed the oath and declaration in this act contained and set forth, and also the said oath appointed by the said act passed in the thirteenth and fourteenth years of his majesty's reign, entitled, *An act to enable his majesty's subjects of whatever persuasion to testify their allegiance to him,* in some one of his majesty's four courts in Dublin, or at the general sessions of the peace, or at any adjournment thereof to be holden for the county, city, or borough wherein such papist or Roman catholic, or person professing the Roman catholic or popish religion, doth inhabit or dwell, or before the going judge or judges of assize, . . .

[Source: Ir. Stat., xvi. 685–692. *Irish Historical Documents, 1172–1922,* ed. Edmund Curtis and R. B. McDowell (London, 1943), pp. 198–202.]

Appendix VI — The Penal Laws In Effect After 1793 (summary)

[The act of 1793 concluded further concessions to the Roman Catholics of Ireland until many years later. Accordingly, there now follows a summary of the penal laws still in effect after 1793.]

Education. Catholics could not teach school unless they took the oaths of the 13th and 14th Geo. III, c. 35. They could not take Protestant scholars or be ushers to Protestant schoolmasters, 32d Geo. III, c. 20.

Guardianship. They could not be guardians unless they took the oaths of 13th and 14th Geo. III, c. 35. If ecclesiastics, they could not under any circumstances be guardians. Nor could any Catholic be the guardian of a Protestant child, 30th Geo. III, c. 29.

Marriage. If a Catholic clergyman married a Protestant and a Catholic, the marriage was null and void, and the clergyman was liable to death, 32d Geo. III, c. 21.

Self-defense. No Catholic could keep arms unless he possessed a freehold estate of 10£ per annum or a personal estate of 300£. If so qualified, he had to qualify further by taking the oaths of the 13th and 14th Geo. III, c. 35. He was excused from the further qualification only if he had a freehold estate of 100£ per annum or a personal estate of 1000£, 33d Geo. III, c. 21.

Exercise of religion. The Catholic clergy were required to take the oaths of the 13th and 14th Geo. III, c. 35 and to register their place of abode, age, and parish. No chapel could have a steeple or bell; no funeral could take place in any church or chapel yard; and no rites or ceremonies of the religious orders or the wearing of habits of their orders were permitted except within their several places of worship or in private houses. 21st and 22d Geo. III, c. 24, cl. 6.

Property. The laws of Anne remained in force against all Catholics who did not take the oaths of the 13th and 14th Geo. III, c. 35 and also against all Protestants who may have lapsed or become converts to Roman Catholicism.

Franchise. Catholics were, of course, excluded from parliament. They could not vote at elections for members unless they took the oaths of the 13th and 14th Geo. III, c. 35 and of the 33d Geo. III, c. 21. They could not vote at vestries. They could not be barristers, attorneys, or professors of medicine on Sir Patrick Dunne's foundation without taking the oaths of the 13th and 14th Geo. III, c. 35 and of the 33d Geo. III, c. 21. They were excluded from the long list of offices enumerated in clause 9 of the Relief Act of 1793 as well as from the offices of Governor, Deputy-Governor, and Director of the Bank of Ireland.

Catholic soldiers. Under the terms of the Mutiny Act, such soldiers, if they refused to attend services of the established church when ordered to do so by their commanding officer, would forfeit 2d. for the first offence; for the second they would not only forfeit 12d. but be laid in irons for twelve hours; and for the third refusal would be liable to capital punishment. Furthermore, any Irish Catholic officer or soldier upon landing in Great Britain, Jersey, or Guernsey was immediately liable to the penalty, among others, of forfeiting £300.

[Source: Henry Parnell, *A History of the Penal Laws Against the Irish, From the Treaty of Limerick to the Union* (Dublin, 1808), pp. 173–174 n.]

A Note on Sources and a Selected Bibliography

I. MANUSCRIPT SOURCES

Burke MSS, Sheffield
Burke MSS, Lamport Hall
Fitzwilliam MSS, Sheffield
O'Hara MSS, Annaghmore
Portland MSS, Nottingham
Rockingham MSS, Sheffield

In 1949, through the kindness of the late ninth Earl Fitzwilliam, the principal collection of the papers of Edmund Burke was placed on deposit at the Sheffield Central Library. At the same time, Captain Thomas W. Fitzwilliam, now the tenth Earl Fitzwilliam, graciously placed the next largest collection of Burke manuscripts, which had been kept at Milton near Peterborough, on deposit with the Northamptonshire Record Office where they were placed at Lamport Hall. Both of these collections, through the courtesy of the Earls and their Managers of the Wentworth Wood-house Estates Co., have been available to qualified scholars ever since. In the endnotes which follow, all items which simply bear the date of the correspondence are from the Sheffield collection.

At the same time that the Burke papers in the possession of the ninth Earl Fitzwilliam were deposited at Sheffield, the papers of the second Marquis of Rockingham and the fourth Earl Fitzwilliam were also placed there and made available.

About thirty-five Burke letters are located in the manuscripts of the Duke of Portland in the University of Nottingham Library.

Other Burke manuscripts used in the preparation of this book may be found in the Huntington Library, the Pierpont Morgan Library, the New York Public Library, the British Museum, and the Harvard, Yale, and Princeton Libraries.

Over eighty letters from Burke to his Irish friend, Charles O'Hara of Annaghmore, County Sligo, were published by Professor Ross J. S. Hoffman in 1956. While I was in Sheffield, Professor Thomas W. Cope-land kindly made available to me photostatic copies of the transcripts of the original Burke-O'Hara correspondence made by the late Canon Robert H. Murray. I had previously used Canon Murray's transcripts at the Bodleian Library, Oxford, with Mrs. Murray's permission. This was in 1948, and it is probable that I was thus the second Burke student to see these manuscripts.

In 1955, Professor Copeland and Professor Milton S. Smith edited and published a check list of Burke's correspondence. This exhaustive project constitutes a thorough survey of the complete Burke correspondence, approximately 7000 pieces, still extant. All manuscripts known to survive are listed together with their locations at the time of publication of the check list, their length, date, and condition.

II. BURKE'S PUBLISHED CORRESPONDENCE AND WRITINGS

Adam, Robert Borthwick. *The R. B. Adam Library Relating to Dr. Samuel Johnson and His Era.* 3 vols. Buffalo, N.Y., London, and New York, 1929. There are letters of Burke's in volume I which long escaped notice due perhaps to the fact that this work was privately printed and limited to 500 copies.

The Autobiography of Arthur Young. Ed. M. Bethman-Edwards. London, 1898.

The Correspondence of Edmund Burke. Vol. I, April 1744 — June 1768. Ed. Thomas W. Copeland. Cambridge, Eng., and Chicago, 1958. This is the first volume in the new and definitive edition of Burke's correspondence. Further volumes will appear annually until the work is completed.

The Correspondence of the Right Honourable Edmund Burke: Between the Year 1744, and the Period of His Decease, in 1797. Ed. Charles William, Earl Fitzwilliam, and Lieutenant-General Sir Richard Bourke. 4 vols. London, 1844. Upon Burke's death his papers came into the possession of his literary executors, Dr. French Laurence and Dr. Walker King. Upon King's death in 1827 the papers passed into the hands of the fourth Earl Fitzwilliam and remained the property of the Fitzwilliam family. The fifth Earl was co-editor of the four-volume edition of Burke's correspondence published in 1844. This was a highly selective edition which omitted Burke letters already published. Also neglected were many other pieces of Burke papers held by others than the Fitzwilliams. In addition, the editors saw fit to exercise a strict censorship of their materials.

Correspondence of Edmund Burke & William Windham. Ed. J. P. Gilson. Cambridge, Eng., 1910.

The Epistolary Correspondence of the Right Hon. Edmund Burke and Dr. French Laurence. London, 1827.

Grattan, Henry. *Memoirs of the Life and Times of the Rt. Hon. Henry Grattan.* 5 vols. London. 1849.

Historical Manuscripts Commission. *Eighth Report.* London, 1881.

—— *Ninth Report.* London, 1884.

—— *Twelfth Report, Appendix, Part IX. The Manuscripts of the Duke of Beaufort, K.G., the Earl of Donoughmore, and Others.* London, 1891.

—— *Twelfth Report, Appendix, Part X. The Manuscripts and Correspondence of James, First Earl of Charlemont.* 2 vols. London, 1891.

—— *Thirteenth Report, Appendix, Part III. The Manuscripts of J. B. Fortescue, Esq., Preserved at Dropmore. London, 1892.*

—— *Fourteenth Report, Appendix, Part I. The Manuscripts of His Grace the Duke of Rutland, K.G., Preserved at Belvoir Castle.* London, 1894.

———— *Fourteenth Report, Appendix, Part IV. The Manuscripts of Lord Kenyon.* London, 1894.

———— *Fifteenth Report, Appendix, Part VI. The Manuscripts of the Earl of Carlisle, Preserved at Castle Howard.* London, 1897.

Hoffman, Ross J. S. *Edmund Burke, New York Agent: With His Letters to the New York Assembly and Intimate Correspondence with Charles O'Hara, 1761–1776.* Philadelphia, 1956.

The Journal and Correspondence of William, Lord Auckland. Ed. George Hogge. 4 vols. London, 1862.

The Leadbeater Papers: A Selection from the Manuscripts and Correspondence of Mary Leadbeater. Ed. Mrs. Leadbeater. 2 ed. 2 vols. London, 1862.

New Monthly Magazine, XIV (1825), 380–386, 453–462, 529–533; XVI (1826), 153–161.

A Notebook of Edmund Burke. Ed. H. V. F. Somerset. Cambridge, Eng., 1957.

Original Letters, Principally from Lord Charlemont, Edmund Burke, [and] William Pitt, Earl of Chatham, to the Right Hon. Henry Flood. London, 1820.

Owen, Hugh. *Two Centuries of Ceramic Art in Bristol.* Gloucester, 1873. This curious work contains Burke's correspondence with Richard Champion, the porcelain manufacturer who was his principal supporter in Bristol.

Samuels, Arthur P. I. *The Early Life, Correspondence and Writings of the Rt. Hon. Edmund Burke LL.D.* Cambridge, Eng., 1923.

The Speeches of the Right Honourable Edmund Burke in the House of Commons and in Westminster Hall. 4 vols. London, 1816. A suitable edition of Burke's speeches is needed, since this one is most inadequate.

The Writings and Speeches of Edmund Burke. 12 vols. Boston, Mass., 1901. There is no standard edition of Burke's works. This one is a more satisfactory edition of that of 1865–1867 of which it is a reprint.

III. OTHER PUBLISHED MATERIAL

The Annual Register, 1758–1785.

Barker, Ernest. *Burke and Bristol, a Study of the Relations Between Burke and His Constituency During the Years 1774–1780.* Bristol, 1931.

———— "Burke and His Bristol Constituency," *Essays on Government.* Oxford, 1945.

Barnes, Donald Grove. *George III and William Pitt, 1783–1806.* Stanford, 1939.

Barrington, Sir Jonah. *Personal Sketches of His Own Times.* 1 ed. 3 vols. London, 1827–1832.

Barry, Liam. *Our Legacy from Burke.* Cork, 1952.

Bemis, Samuel F. *The Hussey-Cumberland Mission.* Princeton, 1931.

Bisset, Robert. *The Life of Edmund Burke.* 2 ed. 2 vols. London, 1800.

Bonn, Moritz J. *Die englische Kolinisation in Irland.* Vol. II. Stuttgart, 1906.

Bryant, Donald C. *Edmund Burke and His Literary Friends.* St. Louis, 1939.

"Burke," *Appreciations and Addresses Delivered by Lord Rosebery.* Ed. Charles Geake. London, 1899.

Butler, Charles. *Historical Memoir of the English, Irish, and Scottish Catholics Since the Reformation.* 3 ed. 4 vols. London, 1822.

Butterfield, Herbert. *Man On His Past.* Cambridge, Eng., 1955.

A Citizen. *A Review of Mr. Burke's Conduct As the Representative of Bristol, in Parliament.* London, 1780.

Cobban, Alfred. *Edmund Burke and the Revolt Against the Eighteenth Century.* New York, 1929.

The Collected Essays and Addresses of the Rt. Hon. Augustine Birrell, 1880–1920. Vol. I. London, 1922.

Cone, Carl B. *Edmund Burke and the Nature of Politics: the Age of the American Revolution.* Lexington, Ky., 1957.

Copeland, Thomas W. *Our Eminent Friend Edmund Burke: Six Essays.* New Haven, 1949.

Correspondence Between the Right Honble. William Pitt and Charles Duke of Rutland. Ed. Lord Mahon. Edinburgh, 1890.

The Correspondence of John Beresford. Ed. William Beresford. 2 vols. London, 1854.

The Correspondence of Thomas Percy and Edmund Malone. Ed. Arthur Tillotson. Baton Rouge, La., 1944.

The Croker Papers. Ed. Louis J. Jennings. Vol. I. London, 1884.

Curtis, Edmund. *A History of Ireland.* 2 ed. London, 1936.

de Castro, J. Paul. *The Gordon Riots.* London, 1926.

Diary and Letters of Madame d'Arblay. Ed. Charlotte Barrett. 2 vols. London, 1904–1905.

The Diary of the Right Hon. William Windham. Ed. Mrs. Henry Baring. London, 1866.

Dilke, C. W. *Papers of a Critic.* Vol. II. London, 1875.

English Historical Documents. Vol. X, 1714–1783. Ed. D. B. Horn and Mary Ransome. London, 1957.

"Extracts from Mr. Burke's Table-Talk at Crewe Hall, Written Down by Mrs. Crewe," *Miscellanies of the Philobiblion Society.* Vol. VII. London, 1862–1863.

Falkiner, C. Litton. *Studies in Irish History.* London, 1902.

Froude, J. A. *The English in Ireland in the Eighteenth Century.* 3 vols. New York, 1874.

Gwynn, Denis. *John Keogh.* Dublin, 1930.

Hardy, Francis. *Memoirs of the Political and Private Life of James Caulfield, Earl of Charlemont.* 2 ed. 2 vols. London, 1812.

Harlow, Vincent T. *The Founding of the Second British Empire, 1763–1793.* Vol. I, London, 1952.

Hayden, M. and G. Moonan. *A Short History of the Irish People.* Dublin, 1921.

Hearnshaw, Fossey J. C. "Edmund Burke," *The Social and Political Ideas of Some Representative Thinkers of the Revolutionary Era.* London, 1931.

———— "Burke and Sublimated Common Sense," *Some Great Political Idealists of the Christian Era*. London, 1937.

Hutchinson, John Hely. *The Commercial Restraints of Ireland*. Dublin, 1882.

Ireland, Tom. *Ireland Past and Present*. New York, 1942.

Irish Historical Documents, 1172–1922. Ed. Edmund Curtis and R. B. McDowell. London, 1943.

Johnsonian Miscellanies. Ed. George Birkbeck Hill. Oxford, 1897.

Laski, Harold J. *Political Thought in England from Locke to Bentham*, New York, 1920.

Lecky, William E. H. *A History of England in the Eighteenth Century*. 8 vols. New York, 1887.

———— *A History of Ireland in the Eighteenth Century*. 5 vols. New York, 1893.

The Lectures, Essays, and Letters of the Right Hon. Sir Joseph Napier, Bart. Dublin, 1888.

Lennox, Richmond. *Edmund Burke und sein politisches Arbeitsfeld in den Jahren 1760. bis 1790*. Munich, 1923.

The Letters of David Hume. Ed. J. Y. T. Greig. 2 vols. Oxford, 1932.

Letters of George III. Ed. Bonamy Dobrée. London, 1935.

Letters of Samuel Johnson. Ed. George Birkbeck Hill. 8 vols. Oxford, 1892.

Life of Johnson: Boswell's Life of Johnson. Ed. George Birkbeck Hill. Revised and enlarged by L. F. Powell. 6 vols. Oxford, 1934–1950.

Life and Letters of Sir Gilbert Elliot. Ed. Countess of Minto. 3 vols. London, 1874.

Life of Theobald Wolfe Tone. Ed. William T. W. Tone. 2 vols. Washington, 1826.

MacCunn, John. *The Political Philosophy of Burke*. New York, 1913.

MacKnight, Thomas. *History of the Life and Times of Edmund Burke*. 3 vols. London, 1858–1860.

Magnus, Sir Philip. *Edmund Burke: a Life*. 1 ed. London, 1939.

M'Cormick, Charles. *Memoirs of Edmund Burke*. 2 ed. London, 1798.

McDermott, R. P. *The College Historical Society*. Dublin, 1932.

Memorials and Correspondence of Charles James Fox. Ed. Lord John Russell. 4 vols. London, 1853.

Memoirs of the Marquis of Rockingham and His Contemporaries. Ed. Earl Albemarle. 2 vols. London, 1852.

Morley, John. *Edmund Burke: a Historical Study*. London, 1867.

———— *Burke*. London, 1888.

Newman, Bertram. *Edmund Burke*. London, 1927.

O'Brien, George. *The Economic History of Ireland in the Eighteenth Century*. Dublin and London, 1918.

O'Brien, William. *Edmund Burke As an Irishman*. 2 ed. Dublin, 1926.

O'Connor, Sir James. *History of Ireland, 1798–1924*. Vol. I. New York, n.d.

O'Flanagan, J. R. *Lives of the Lord Chancellors of Ireland*. Vol. II. London, 1870.

Osborn, Annie M. *Rousseau and Burke: a Study of the Idea of Liberty in Eighteenth-Century Political Thought*. London, 1940.

Parkin, Charles. *The Moral Basis of Burke's Political Thought*. Cambridge, Eng., 1956.

Plowden, Francis. *Historical Review of the State of Ireland*. 2 vols. London, 1803.

Prior, James. *Life of the Right Honourable Edmund Burke*. 2 ed. 2 vols. London, 1826. This is the most satisfactory edition.

—— *Life of the Right Honourable Edmund Burke*. 5 ed. London, 1854.

Reynolds, Ernest E. *Edmund Burke, Christian Statesman*. London, 1948.

Robertson, James B. *Lectures on the Life, Writings and Times of Edmund Burke*. London, 1869.

Rogers, Patrick. *The Irish Volunteers and Catholic Emancipation, 1778–1793*. London, 1934.

Romilly, Sir Samuel. *Memoirs*. Vol. I. 2 ed. London, 1840.

[Scully, Denis]. *A Statement of the Penal Laws which Aggrieve the Catholics of Ireland*. 2 ed. Dublin, 1812.

Sherrard, O. A. *Lord Chatham and America*. London, 1958.

Stanhope, Earl. *Life of the Right Honourable William Pitt*. 4 vols. London, 1861–1862.

Stanlis, Peter J. *Edmund Burke and the Natural Law*. Ann Arbor, 1958.

Straus, Ralph. *Robert Dodsley*. London, 1910.

Therry, Sir Roger. *A Letter to the Right Hon. George Canning on the Present State of the Catholic Question*. 2 ed. London, 1827.

Underdown, P. T. "Edmund Burke As a Member of Parliament for Bristol." Unpublished dissertation, University of London, 1954.

Van Schaack, Henry C. *Henry Cruger: The Colleague of Edmund Burke in the British Parliament*. New York, 1859.

Von Sybel, Heinrich. "Edmund Burke and Ireland," *Kleine historische Schriften*. Vol. I. Marburg, 1869.

Weare, G. E. *Edmund Burke's Connection with Bristol, from 1774 to 1780*. Bristol, 1894.

Wecter, Dixon. *Edmund Burke and His Kinsmen: a Study of the Statesman's Financial Integrity and Private Relationships*. Boulder, Colo., 1939.

Wilson, Woodrow. "The Interpreter of English Liberty," *Mere Literature*. Boston, 1896.

The Windham Papers. Ed. Anon. 2 vols. London, 1913.

Wraxall, Sir Nathaniel W. *Posthumous Memoirs of His Own Time*. Philadelphia, 1836.

Wright, Thomas. *A Caricature History of the Georges*. London, 1867.

Notes

All Burke correspondence cited in the following notes, unless otherwise identified, is to be found in the collection of Burke manuscripts at the Sheffield Central Library, England. The citation "O'Hara MSS" refers to the transcripts of the original correspondence between Burke and Charles O'Hara made by the late Canon Robert H. Murray, on deposit in the Bodleian Library, Oxford.

I EARLY DAYS IN ENGLAND AND IRELAND

1. There is still some difference of opinion as to the exact date of his birth. The authorities whom I have chosen to follow in this matter are Arthur P. I. Samuels, *Early Life, Correspondence and Writings of The Rt. Hon. Edmund Burke, LL.D.* (Cambridge, 1923), p. 1, and Dixon Wecter, "Burke's Birthday," *Notes and Queries*, CLXXII, 441. Sir Philip Magnus, *Edmund Burke: A Life* (London, 1939), p. 1, holds out for the once generally accepted date of 1 January 1729.

2. "It is but too well known that I debate with great vehemence and asperity, and with little management either of the opinions or persons of many of my adversaries. They deserve not much quarter, and I give and receive but very little." *The Leadbeater Papers: A Selection from the Manuscripts and Correspondence of Mary Leadbeater*, ed. Mrs. Leadbeater (2 ed., 2 vols., London, 1862), II, 3.

3. *Leadbeater Papers*, II, 102.

4. William O'Brien, *Edmund Burke As An Irishman* (2 ed., Dublin, 1926), pp. 6 f.

5. *Leadbeater Papers*, I, 49–51.

6. James Prior, *Life of the Right Honorable Edmund Burke* (5 ed., London, 1854), p. 41.

7. Samuels, *Early Life of Burke*, pp. 69, 77, 84.

8. *Ibid.*, pp. 128–129.

9. *Ibid.*, pp. 97 f.

10. *Ibid.*, pp. 214, 216. For the history of the Trinity Society of which Burke's group was the ancestor, consult R. P. McDermott, *The College Historical Society* (Dublin, 1932).

11. Magnus, *Burke*, p. 7.

12. Samuels, *Early Life of Burke*, pp. 251 f. As will be demonstrated below, Burke changed his mind on this subject when he became a member of the British House of Commons and never again reverted to the position he had taken in his student days. The reason for this transformation in his thought lies mainly in his Irish nationalism having been replaced by his enlightened imperialism. On the other hand, it is conceivable that his ex-

traordinary loyalty to the Marquis of Rockingham, one of the richest absentees, is the explanation.

13. *Ibid.*, pp. 175–176.

14. *Ibid.*, p. 57.

15. William E. H. Lecky, *A History of England in the Eighteenth Century* (8 vols., New York, 1887), III, 382.

16. E.g., Magnus, *Burke*, p. 6.

17. Samuels, *Early Life of Burke*, p. 136.

18. *Ibid.*, p. 137.

19. E.g., Robert Bisset, *The Life of Edmund Burke* (2 ed., 2 vols., London, 1800), I, 28.

20. E.g., Thomas Macknight, *History of the Life and Times of Edmund Burke* (3 vols., London, 1858–1860), I, 35; Magnus, *Burke*, pp. 7 f.; Alfred Cobban, *Edmund Burke and the Revolt Against the Eighteenth Century* (London, 1929), p. 105; Robert H. Murray, *Edmund Burke: A Biography* (Oxford, 1931), pp. 45–48; Dixon Wecter, "The Missing Years in Edmund Burke's Biography," *PMLA*, LIII (1938), 1102.

21. Charles O'Hara (c. 1715–1776) of Annaghmore, County Sligo, was a member of the Irish House of Commons. He was on intimate terms with the ruling body in Ireland and was deeply interested in English politics. His correspondence with Burke is remarkable because of the confidence he inspired in Burke who expressed himself without reservation in these letters. This correspondence has been published by Ross J. S. Hoffman in the revealing study *Edmund Burke, New York Agent: With his Letters to the New York Assembly and Intimate Correspondence with Charles O'Hara, 1761–1776* (Philadelphia, 1956).

22. O'Hara MSS.

23. For a persuasively written article which maintains that Burke was not a supporter of Lucas, see Gaetano Vincitorio, "Edmund Burke and Charles Lucas," *PMLA*, LXVIII (1953), 1047–1055.

Another factor which adds weight to this position is that Lucas was a rabid anti-Catholic. This would seem to militate strongly against Burke's supporting him. As far as can be determined, no commentator on the Lucas question in Burke's career, including Professor Vincitorio, has taken this important point into consideration.

24. Burke's biographers, almost without exception from the earliest to the most recent, have quoted or printed at length a letter which he purportedly wrote to one Matthew Smith shortly after his arrival in London in 1750. In this letter Burke told his correspondent of his trip from Ireland and of his first impressions of what was to become his adopted land.

In the first published volume of the definitive edition of Burke's correspondence, the editor, Thomas W. Copeland, *The Correspondence of Edmund Burke* (Cambridge and Chicago, 1958), I, 357–359, demonstrates convincingly that Burke could not have written such a letter at that particular time. He shows among other things that even Smith's Christian name had been changed from Michael to Matthew by one of the biographers (Prior), since the problem of identifying Michael Smith was too formidable.

25. Prior, *Burke*, p. 35.

26. Professor Carl B. Cone in his competent biography, *Burke and the*

Nature of Politics (Lexington, Ky., 1957), is firmly convinced that they were actually cousins. On the other hand, the older view that it is doubtful whether a relationship existed is taken by another careful scholar, Sir Ernest Barker in his foreword to H. V. F. Somerset, ed. *A Notebook of Edmund Burke* (Cambridge, 1957), ix.

27. In "An Epistle to Dr. Nugent by E.B.", written in September 1751 (although there is a probability that it was 1752), are the lines:

> 'Tis now two Autumns since he chanc'd to find
> A youth of Body broke, infirm of mind.
> He gave him all that man can ask or give;
> Restor'd his Life, and taught him how to Live.
> But what, and when, and How this Youth shall pay,
> Must be discuss'd upon a Longer day.

Somerset, ed., *Burke Notebook*, p. 38.

28. Magnus, *Burke*, p. 11.

29. A recent critic, Murray N. Rothbard , "A Note on Burke's Vindication of Natural Society," *Journal of the History of Ideas*, XIX (January 1958), 114–118, claims that there is "hardly a trace of irony or satire" in the book and calls it "perhaps the first modern expression of rationalistic and individualistic anarchism." Mr. Rothbard holds that the only way Burke could avoid "politically disastrous" consequences after his authorship had been discovered and he stood on the threshold of his parliamentary career "nine years later" was to brush it off as a satire. Actually, Burke had explained as far back as 1757 in the preface to the second edition of the *Vindication* that his purpose had been to show that "the same engines which were employed for the destruction of religion, might be employed with equal success for the subversion of government." Furthermore, it is to be remembered that Burke's first canvass was in a pocket borough, hardly a place to be concerned over whether the electors took seriously or not something he had published almost nine years ago.

30. Although Mrs. Burke subsequently joined her husband's church and adhered to it for the rest of her life, any doubts as to what her religion was when she married Burke should have been removed by the following incident.

An account of Burke's life which had been written many years previously by his old friend Richard Shackleton found its way into print in the *London Evening Post*, 14–17 April 1770. In it the writer revealed that Mrs. Burke was a Catholic and stated that this was the origin of the erroneous belief that Burke himself was a member of that faith. Burke was greatly upset over the publication of this old letter of Shackleton's and expressed his indignation to the latter in a letter dated 19 April 1770. In it there was no denial of his wife's former religion, simply the complaint that her name had been dragged into the public prints. Samuels, *Early Life of Burke*, p. 404.

31. Some three years later in a letter to Charles O'Hara, 10 July 1761, he wrote: "When you look at the Atlantick ocean do you think of America? In our old fabulous History I think I have read that the Prophet Moses advised the antient Scots to go as far Westward as possible; is this good advice to their posterity?" O'Hara MSS.

32. Richard, Jr., named after Burke's younger brother, and Christopher who died in infancy. There is a possibility that a third son, Edmund, was born in 1760 and also failed to survive. This, however, is a matter of conjecture.

33. This was *The Abridgment of English History*. For a variety of reasons Burke never finished it, stopping at the end of the reign of King John. It was not published until well after Burke's death. Edmund Malone, the Shakespearean scholar, writing in 1811 when publication was imminent, said that it appeared to him "to surpass any production of Hume, Robertson, or Gibbon." Arthur Tillotson, ed., *The Correspondence of Thomas Percy and Edmund Malone* (Baton Rouge, La., 1944), p. 277. Not until recently has this view been shared. Thanks to Professor Herbert Butterfield, *Man on His Past* (Cambridge, 1955), students of Burke have been reminded of their serious neglect of this work. Butterfield notes (pp. 68–69) that Lord Acton was so impressed that he once said that Burke would have been the first among English historians had he continued his historical work. Acton also described the *Abridgment* as Burke's "most remarkable literary production" and quoted Lappenberg's statement that "if Burke had devoted himself continuously to historical pursuits, England might have possessed a history worthy to rank with the masterpieces of the Attic and Tuscan historians."

34. Thomas W. Copeland, "Burke and Dodsley's 'Annual Register,'" *PMLA*, LIV (1939), 223–245 and LVII (1942), 446–468. See also Ralph Straus, *Dodsley* (London, 1910), pp. 256–259, and Donald C. Bryant, *Edmund Burke and His Literary Friends* (St. Louis, 1939), pp. 289–297.

There is an original receipt signed by Burke for payment in full from the Dodsleys for the *Annual Register* of 1761 in the Pierpont Morgan Library, New York. It is for the amount of £50 and is dated "this 30 day of March 1762."

Bertram D. Sarason, "Edmund Burke and the Two *Annual Registers*," *PMLA*, LXVIII (1953), 496–508, challenges the earlier assumption of Copeland that Burke remained the "principal conductor" of the *Register* for over twenty years after the issue of 1765 when he clearly ceased doing the entire volume himself.

35. Burke to Mrs. Elizabeth Montagu, 6 October 1759, Henry E. Huntington Library and Art Gallery, San Marino, California. This letter to Mrs. Montagu reveals that Burke had unsuccessfully sought her aid in securing for himself a vacant consulship at Madrid. He then turned to other sources but was disappointed in his quest.

36. A letter from David Hume to Adam Smith, 28 July 1759, remarked that Burke was then in Ireland. *Letters of David Hume*, ed. J. Y. T. Greig (Oxford, 1932), I, 312. There is, however, no other evidence to support this statement of Hume's.

37. Thomas W. Copeland, "Burke's First Patron," *History Today*, II (1952), 398.

38. Referring to Burke's trip to Ireland in this capacity, a contemporary periodical later commented that no man was better acquainted with conditions in Ireland than Burke. *Universal Magazine*, LVI (March 1775), 133.

39. *Irish Historical Documents, 1172–1922*, ed. Edmund Curtis and R. B.

McDowell (London, 1943), p. 186; *English Historical Documents*. Vol. X. 1714–1783, ed. D. B. Horn and Mary Ransome (London, 1957), p. 683.

40. Among the nearly four hundred patent offices in the establishment of Ireland were the following: Keeper of the Signet, Pursuivant, Master of the Game, Interpreter of the Irish Tongue, Star Chamber with Commissioners, Marshals, Clerks, etc., Courts of Wards and Liveries with Masters, the Court of the Palatines, the Lord Almoner, Transcriptor, and Foreign Apposer, Summonister and Clerk of Estreats, the Trustees of the Linen Manufacture, Commissioners of Wide Streets, Commissioners of Array, Constables of Castles, Muster Master General, Commissioners for Victualling, Provincial Provost Martials, Alnager, Clerk of the Pells, Hearth Money Collectors, Poll Tax Collectors, Cursitors in Chancery, Register of Appeals Spiritual, Clerk of the Pipe, Prothonotary, Philizer or Filacer Clerk of Privy Council, Winetaster, Escheator, Searcher, Packers, Craners, Seneschals, Presidents of the Four Provinces, Governors of Forts, Clerks of the First Fruits, Deputy Master of the Rolls, Examinators, Master of the Revels, Clerk of the Nickells, Exigenter, Clerk of the Outlawries, Clerk of the Essions, Chirographers, Sirographers, etc. John Hely Hutchinson, *The Commercial Restraints of Ireland* (Dublin, 1882), p. xxi, n.

41. Macknight, *Burke*, I, 144.

42. Historical Manuscripts Commission, *Twelfth Report, Appendix, Part X: The Manuscripts and Correspondence of James, First Earl of Charlemont* (London, 1891), I, 19. [Hereafter cited as *Charlemont MSS.*]

43. For detailed examples of the penal laws see Appendixes I & II.

44. *The Writings and Speeches of Edmund Burke* (12 vols., Boston, 1901), VI, 299–360. [Hereafter cited as *Works.*]

45. An explanation for this, it is claimed, was the fact that Burke had inherited some property, Clogher in County Cork, on his brother Garret's death in 1765. The latter had acquired it on a nine hundred and ninety-nine years' lease to protect his mother's family, the Nagles, who, as Catholics, could not then hold land beyond thirty-one years under the penal laws. To avoid the danger of some dishonorable member of the family's turning Protestant in order to claim the land for himself under the penal laws, a dummy Protestant "discoverer" had been put up by prearrangement. He secured the property and immediately turned it over to Garret Burke. Thus, the Protestant Burkes held the property in trust for the Catholic Nagles.

In 1777, a Robert Nagle turned Protestant in order to claim the estate but he was unsuccessful. Burke's refusal to have anything to do with him gave rise to the charge by his enemies that he was guilty of conniving with his brother to defraud Robert Nagle of his just due. C. W. Dilke, *The Papers of a Critic* (London, 1875), II, 364, said that this business, in which he believed Burke guilty, may have prevented his publishing the *Tract*. Magnus, *Burke*, pp. 336 f., could find no evidence to support this view and exonerates Burke fully. The most complete account is in *The Lectures, Essays, and Letters of the Right Hon. Sir Joseph Napier, Bart.* (Dublin, 1888), pp. 50–57.

Burke himself reviewed much of the affair in a letter dated 9th December 1777 addressed to an unknown person. In it he called attention to the fact that the courts had ruled against Robert Nagle. *New Monthly Magazine*, XVI (1826), 153–156.

An epigram designed to damage Burke's character was written in 1777 by one Counsellor Harwood. It may be found in Dilke, *Papers of a Critic*. The lines are:

> Fraternal love inspires good Edmund's breast,
> Of his dear virtue hear this glorious test —
> He writes, declaims in mild Religion's cause
> Yet he's enriched by Fraud and penal laws.
> He 'gainst his conscience beggars a whole race,
> To save a brother's memory from disgrace;
> Rather than blast the generous donor's fame,
> From him he heirs the profit, cheat, and shame;
> Sarcastic truth with calm contempt he braves,
> And from pure virtue shines the first of— knaves.

Burke held the property until about 1790 when he disposed of his interest to Edmund Nagle, the future admiral. The property was supposed to yield some £300 per annum to Burke, but he seldom realized this sum since he had taken upon himself responsibility for the welfare of the tenants, many of whom were his indigent relatives.

Although the *Tract* was not published during Burke's life, it was widely circulated privately, e.g., Lord Kenmare to Burke, 18 February 1780; and Thomas Braughall to Burke, 17 March 1790. The former calls it a "most Elegant Abstract of our Penal Statutes" and admits that "I never had before a Conception of their diversity & Extent." The latter mentions the "eagerness of the First men in this Country to peruse it" and names some of those to whom it had been shown, including Edmund Sexton Pery, Speaker of the Irish Commons.

46. 22 November 1796, *The Epistolary Correspondence of the Right Hon. Edmund Burke and Dr. French Laurence* (London, 1827), p. 79. [Hereafter cited as the *Burke-Laurence Corr.*]

47. Writing to Sir Hercules Langrishe many years later in 1792, Burke justly characterized these laws to have been as efficiently devised for the mistreatment, impoverishment, and ruination of a people as the mind of man could conceive.

48. See Appendixes I and II. Moritz J. Bonn, *Die englische Kolinisation in Irland* (Stuttgart, 1906) II, 169 ff. is excellent. See also [Denys Scully], *A Statement of the Penal Laws which Aggrieve the Catholics of Ireland* (2 ed., Dublin, 1812). A first-rate article on the penal laws is R. E. Burns, "The Irish Penal Code and Some of Its Historians," *The Review of Politics*, XXI (January 1959), 276–299.

49. Curiously enough one of Burke's biographers, the Rev. Robert H. Murray, *Edward Burke*, p. 99, holds that Burke was oblivious of the Huguenots at the time he was stressing the injustices of the penal laws.

50. In 1795, he declared in the words of his friend, Lord Fitzwilliam that the persecution of the Irish Catholics was not that of a religious sect but rather it constituted "tyranny over a people." *The Correspondence of the Right Honourable Edmund Burke: Between the Year 1744 and the Period of His Decease, in 1797.* Edited by Charles William, Earl Fitzwilliam, and

Lt. Gen. Sir Richard Bourke (4 vols., London, 1844) IV, 323. [Hereafter cited as *Corr.*]

51. The author of a study on the role of the natural law in Burke's system of thought is much impressed with this early work of Burke's and holds it to be the most explicit example of Burke's belief in the natural law. See Peter J. Stanlis, *Edmund Burke and the Natural Law* (Ann Arbor, 1958), p. 43.

52. After the French Revolution broke out, Burke had to shift from this lofty argument on behalf of the Catholic cause to one of prudence, justice, and expediency. For an explanation, see p. 20.

53. On this aspect of Burke's life, the following are revealing: Burke to Garret Nagle, 23 August 1771, Pierpont Morgan Library; Burke to Garret Nagle, 6 May 1771, Harvard Theatre Collection MSS, Widener Library, Harvard University; undated letter to an unknown person, Historical Manuscripts Commission, *Ninth Report* (London, 1884), p. 484; another letter to Nagle, Robert Borthwick Adam, *The R. B. Adam Library Relating to Dr. Samuel Johnson and His Era* (3 vols. Buffalo, N.Y., London, and New York, 1929), I, 1 [Hereafter cited as *Adam Library*]; Letters to Arthur Young, *Corr.*, I, 257–265; "Extracts from Mr. Burke's Table-Talk at Crewe Hall. Written down by Mrs. Crewe," *Miscellanies of the Philobiblion Society.* (London, 1862–3), VII, 33 ff. [Hereafter cited as "Burke's Table-Talk"]; Burke MSS, Sheffield, *passim*, and O'Hara MSS, *passim*.

Lord Rosebery observed once that because Burke was a gentleman farmer, he was an unsuccessful one. "Burke," *Appreciations and Addresses Delivered by Lord Rosebery*, ed. Charles Geake (London, 1899), p. 25. Burke's latest biographer shows quite clearly that Burke was really a pretty accomplished farmer. Cone, *Burke and Politics, passim*.

54. See letter to Sir Hercules Langrishe, 3 January 1792, *Works*, IV, 244. See also second letter to Langrishe, 26 May 1795, *ibid.*, VI, 384 wherein he said that they had discussed this legislation almost thirty-five years ago and were then and continued ever since in agreement on every part of the system.

55. *Corr.*, II, 292.

56. Burke's fellow member of Dr. Johnson's Literary Club (founded in 1764), Oliver Goldsmith has the enclosure movement in England and its disastrous results to the poor country people as the theme of his *The Deserted Village*.

For the enclosure movement in Ireland, see Bonn, *Kolinisation*, II, 278.

57. The inequities of the tithe system as it affected the Catholic peasant were numerous. He was taxed for the support of the clergy of an alien faith, a clergy which ministered at the time to less than one-sixth of the entire population, and he was also burdened with the support of his own clergy as well. Added to this double expense was the irritant that a majority of the state clergy were absentees which meant that the money was not spent in the district where it was raised but went largely to England.

Furthermore, the manner in which the tithe was collected was perhaps the worst feature of the system. The clergy became accustomed to appointing proctors to collect tithes for them or to the practice of renting the tithes to a tithe-farmer or tithe-jobber. The tithe-farmer acted as the middleman of the clergy and was noted for his greed and cruelty. Frequently, he was a Catholic, a point which in itself demonstrates the nonsectarian nature of the Whiteboys. No proctor could legally act as a tithe-farmer, but from the standpoint of a peasant this was the only distinction between the two since they were equally rapacious.

Pasture land was exempt from tithes since it was usually the property of the well-to-do, whereas tillage farms were generally in the possession of poor farmers. The tithes on each crop grown were generally exorbitant but the one which bore most heavily on the poor was for potatoes.

The distressing results of such a system were several. In the first place, pasture was encouraged at the expense of tillage; secondly, the addition of the tithe to rent and county charges frequently pauperized the peasants; thirdly, all disputes were settled in the Ecclesiastical Courts, whose findings were so severe that the victims frequently ran away rather than face them and often terminated their flight in emigration; and, finally, the disturbances which so often broke out as a protest against both tithes and enclosure threw the country continually into a state of unrest. See George O'Brien, *The Economic History of Ireland in the Eighteenth Century* (Dublin and London, 1918), ch. xiv.

58. For accounts of this body, see *ibid.*, pp. 81 ff., 150 ff.; M. Hayden and G. Moonan, *A Short History of the Irish People* (Dublin, 1921), pp. 380 f.; and Tom Ireland, *Ireland Past and Present* (New York, 1942), pp. 192 ff.

59. *Charlemont MSS*, I, 20 n.

60. Hunting Whiteboys became fashionable and for many replaced the chase.

61. Burke to O'Hara, [post 10 August 1762], O'Hara MSS.

62. *Works*, II, 418.

63. *Corr.*, I, 39 f.

64. Conveniently overlooked at the time and largely forgotten since then is the fact that the Whiteboys endeavored to regulate payments to the Catholic clergy as well as to protest payments to the Protestants. A letter from the Whiteboys addressed to the peasantry of Munster fixed the rate which should be paid for tithes and then fixed the rates which they felt a priest was entitled to for his services. These were: for a marriage, 5/; a baptism, 1/6; a funeral mass, 1/; all other masses, 1/; and extreme unction, 1/6. "Address to the Nobility and Gentry of the Church of Ireland," (Dublin, 1786), quoted in O'Brien, *Econ. Hist. of Ireland*, p. 151.

65. *Corr.*, I, 45.

66. E.g., *Works*, IV, 224 f., 254; VI, 371; *Corr.*, IV, 273.

67. O'Hara MSS.

68. When the news became belatedly known it was well received by Burke's Catholic well-wishers in Ireland who considered him their sincere friend. Charles O'Conor to Dr. John Curry, 6 December 1763, Historical Manuscripts Commission, *Eighth Report* (London, 1881), p. 479.

69. *Corr.*, I, 46–51.

70. Born of humble parentage as John Hely in 1715, he assumed the name of Hutchinson in 1751 after succeeding to the estate of his wife's uncle. He had entered Trinity as a pensioner, graduating in 1744. He was

called to the bar in 1748, entered parliament in 1759, was appointed Prime-Sergeant in 1762, became Provost of Trinity in 1774 (a post he held for the rest of his life), and in 1777 was made Secretary of State for Ireland and Keeper of the Privy Seal. A noted pluralist he was simultaneously Secretary of State, Provost, Major of Horse, and Searcher, Packer, and Gauger of the Port of Strangford. In 1783 he obtained a peerage for his wife. His appointment as Provost caused quite a controversy since, as a layman, he was considered unsuitable. He was attacked in the newspapers and in cartoons and pamphlets. Especially strong are the censures on him in *Lachrymae Academicae*, *Baratariana*, and *Pranceriana*. The latter derived its title from "Prancer" or "Jack Prance," Hutchinson's nickname. His tenure of office was very stormy but there is evidence that he performed his functions satisfactorily on the whole. A lifelong friend of Catholic emancipation, he died in 1794.

71. James Caulfield, the future Earl of Charlemont, was born in Dublin in 1728. He was the great-grandson of Sir Toby Caulfield, the first Baron Charlemont. Following an eight-year grand tour, he returned to Ireland at the age of twenty-six and was made a member of the Privy Council and appointed Governor of Armagh. In 1763 he was created an Earl by George III. An intimate of Burke, Johnson, Hume, Goldsmith, Reynolds, Hogarth, and others, he was widely known in England. In 1780 he was chosen commander-in-chief of the Irish Volunteers, was chairman of the Dungannon Convention of the Volunteers in 1783, first president of the Royal Irish Academy, which was founded in 1785, and was founder of the Northern Whig Club. Long an opponent of Catholic emancipation, he began to change his mind toward the end of his life, which came in 1799.

72. Born near Kilkenny in 1732, son of the Chief Justice of the King's Bench, Flood studied at Trinity and Oxford. He entered the Irish Commons in 1759, the sixth of the name and family to sit there during the eighteenth century. Within two years he had become the idol of the "patriots" but after long years in opposition came to terms with the administration in 1774 and received a vice-treasureship. Five years later he again went into opposition and advocated free trade. In 1781 he lost his place and his name was removed from the rank of Privy Councillor. He championed Protestant ascendancy in 1782 but left Ireland following a quarrel with Henry Grattan only to return the following year. He took the part of the Volunteers and agitated for a reform bill but still opposed the Catholics. He made another attempt to put through a reform of the Irish parliament in 1784 but again failed. His influence waning, he went to England again in 1787 where he tried to make a new career in the British parliament where he had held a seat since 1785. He attracted little attention there, retiring in 1790. He died in 1791.

73. Burke to John Ridge, 23 April 1763.

74. Born in 1707 he rose in the church through the influence of the Duke of Newcastle until he was made primate in 1747. During the second vice-royalty of the Duke of Dorset, 1751–1755, he was virtually the governor of Ireland and ruled by means of the pension list. Called the "Beauty of Holiness," he was very unpopular. An advocate of the removal of Catholic disabilities, he died in 1764.

75. After having long befriended the Dissenters, Burke changed after the French Revolution began and opposed any further relief for them.

76. While fighting to retain his seat at Bristol in the general elections of 1780, Burke undertook to explain some of these statutes to his constituents. *Works*, II, 391–396. See also "A Letter to a Peer of Ireland [Lord Kenmare] on the Penal Laws," *ibid.*, IV, 219–239, and "A Letter to Sir Hercules Langrishe on the Subject of the Roman Catholics of Ireland, etc.," *ibid.*, IV, 244–306.

II BURKE ENTERS PARLIAMENT

1. Hoffman, *Edmund Burke, New York Agent*, p. 25.

2. Magnus, *Burke*, pp. 22 f.

3. *Corr.*, I, 71.

4. *Ibid.*, I, 78. Burke had once described Hamilton to Charles O'Hara in glowing terms: "Every thing is with him, as you know, manly & honest; he is one of the few men of business, whose honour, I am satisfied is entirely to be relied on, & can neither deceive or betray; . . ." 3 July 1761, O'Hara MSS.

The finality of the dissolution of their friendship and connection is well brought out in a letter of Robert Jephson to Hely Hutchinson, August or September 1765, Historical Manuscripts Commission, *Twelfth Report, Appendix, Part IX. The Manuscripts of the Duke of Beaufort, K.G., the Earl of Donoughmore, and Others* (London, 1891), p. 256. [Hereafter cited as the *Beaufort MSS.*]

For a good recent account of the relations between Burke and Hamilton, see Thomas W. Copeland, "Burke's First Patron," *History Today*, II (1952), 394–399.

5. O'Hara MSS.

6. 4 [July 1765], *loc. cit.*

7. 9 July 1765, *loc. cit.*

8. I am in thorough agreement with this analysis of Cone, *Burke and Politics*, pp. 58 f.

9. Monck Mason to Burke, 28 June [1765], Burke MSS, Lamport Hall.

10. O'Hara MSS. Will's "better thing" was Under-Secretary of State for the Southern Department.

11. 16 July 1765.

12. *Sir Henry Cavendish's Debates of the House of Commons, During the Thirteenth Parliament of Great Britain, Commonly Called the Unreported Parliament*, ed. John Wright (London, 1841), I, 276 n.; Francis Hardy, *Memoirs of the Political and Private Life of James Caulfield, Earl of Charlemont* (2 ed., 2 vols., London, 1812), II, 281.

13. The rumormongers thus gained lasting satisfaction from their unsuccessful efforts to ruin Burke. The suspicion, never verified by subsequent discoveries, has long obtained that Hamilton was behind the attempt. Incidentally, Hamilton, who had tried to keep Burke's services to himself principally by a modest pension of £300, had a life sinecure himself. In 1763, he managed to secure the Irish Chancellorship of the Exchequer at £1800 per annum. He was permitted to refrain from any functions in con-

nection with the office and later sold it to the Irish government in 1784 for a life pension of £2500 per annum.

14. E.g., *The Public Advertiser*, 19 October 1770; *Gentleman's Magazine*, L (December, 1780), 619; *The Daily Universal Register*, 22 January 1785; and *Morning Chronicle*, 11 March 1796. His supposed education at St. Omer tagged him for life with the nicknames of "Neddy St. Omers" and "Jesuit Ned."

The notorious John Wilkes once explained the origin of the St. Omer rumor in this way: "In reply to an argument used by Burke in the House, somebody said it was only fit for a Jesuit to urge. It was clear from his accent, name, and connexions, that he was an Irishman; and Irishman and a papist, in the opinions of some of our honest country gentlemen, were synonomous: St. Omer contained a Jesuit seminary: at this seminary many Irish priests were educated: — ergo, it was a clear case among the wise men of Gotham, that Burke must be a Jesuit, and must have been educated at St. Omer." Prior, *Burke*, p. 39.

15. In a cartoon published 1 December 1797 by S. W. Fores, London, Burke was caricatured as a "Blade in a Jesuit rug." The Sir Robert Peel Collection of Political Caricatures, Broadsides, Portraits, etc., Vol. XII, Pierpont Morgan Library, New York.

16. "Burke's Table-Talk," pp. 52 f.; Prior, *Burke*, p. 39.

17. There can be little doubt that throughout Burke's career his Irish background was a distinct handicap. Yet it can be argued that it was his knowledge of Irish politics and personalities together with his appreciation of Ireland's needs which probably did more than anything else to recommend him to Rockingham. The recent agrarian disturbances in Ireland, described in the previous chapter, made it likely that Irish problems would require attention very shortly in England. Hence the Prime Minister's need of someone close to him qualified to supply information and give advice on these problems seems obvious.

18. Burke to O'Hara, [24] December [1765], O'Hara MSS. Writing on the same day to John Ridge in Ireland, Burke complained of feeling the effects of the drinking combined with exposure to the misty weather. This was the beginning of an ailment which plagued him throughout the entire winter. Hoffman, *Edmund Burke, New York Agent*, p. 326.

Incidentally, at this time one newspaper issued a warning that "popery" should not be encouraged. *The Craftsman; or Say's Weekly Journal*, 21 December 1765.

19. It is not clear to what Burke was alluding. O'Hara, under date of 10 January 1766, plainly told Burke that he was mystified by his complaint and simply did not know to what he referred. Quoted in Hoffman, *Edmund Burke, New York Agent*, p. 328, n. 15.

20. Thomas Leland, then a fellow of Trinity College, Dublin, wrote the Earl of Charlemont that he expected great things of Burke in parliament but was disappointed over reports of Burke's speeches which indicated much jealousy at his expense in the House. *Charlemont MSS*, I, 278. However, the praises of such disparate figures as the elder Pitt and Samuel Johnson show that he had made a great impression.

21. 11 December [1767], O'Hara MSS.

22. 1 March 1766, *loc. cit.*

23. 3 March 1766, *loc. cit.*

24. 11 March [1766], *loc. cit.*

25. [Ante 29 March 1766], *loc. cit.*

26. 8 April 1766, *loc. cit.*

27. The Rev. Nicholas Sheehy (1728–1766), parish priest of Clogheen, Tipperary, was hanged, disembowelled, and quartered on charges of instigating a murder growing out of a Whiteboy rising. The execution, which was a gross miscarriage of justice, took place at Clonmel in Munster.

Among Burke's papers at Sheffield there is a copy of a petition of Edmund Sheehy; the substance of another petition of Edmund Sheehy; and also a copy of his speech declaring his innocence prior to being hanged at Clogheen on 3 May 1766. There are also copies of the speeches of James Farrell who was hanged at the same time and of James Buxton who was executed the previous day. Finally, there is a letter written by Mr. Buxton while he was in jail. In it he claimed that he could have received a pardon had he been willing to implicate a number of Catholic gentlemen, among whom was a relative of Burke's, James Nagle.

28. 8 April 1766, O'Hara MSS.

29. 24 May [1766], *loc. cit.* The reference to septennial parliaments is to the desire in some Irish quarters to limit the duration of the Irish parliament to seven years.

30. These constant references to the severe punishments of the Catholic peasantry appear early in Burke's correspondence. Writing to John Ridge, 23 April 1763, he sarcastically remarked: "I see that you have but one way of relieving the poor in Ireland. They call for bread, and you give them not a stone, but the gallows." It is likely that Burke felt so strongly about this out of the wish to protect his numerous Catholic relatives living in agrarian parts of Ireland which were scenes of occasional risings by secret societies.

31. O'Hara to Burke, 20 March 1766.

32. Burke did not think that Pitt should have accepted a peerage. He ought to have retained "the power of superintendancy, if not of direct management of the H. of Commons, in his own hands, for some time at least." Burke to O'Hara 29 July 1766, O'Hara MSS.

33. *Ibid.*

34. O'Hara MSS.

35. See *Corr.*, I, 308–309, where Burke says that he gave some thought to going with the new government, talked it over with a friend or two, and then dropped the idea. This was in 1771, and either his memory played a trick on him or he had rationalized the whole business so thoroughly that he himself believed that it was he who had made the decision.

This all relates to what happened *prior* to going to Ireland. For what happened upon his return, see below, pp. 38 ff.

36. Cone, *Burke and Politics*, p. 103.

37. *Corr.*, I, 111.

38. Prior, *Burke*, pp. 98 f.

39. *Ibid.*, pp. 6 f.

40. Burke MSS, Sheffield.

41. 17 January 1767.

42. 20 January 1767.

43. *Corr.*, I, 114.

44. 4 October 1766, O'Hara MSS.

45. 21 October 1766, *loc. cit.*

46. [Post 11 November 1766], *loc. cit.* In October the Duke of Grafton suggested Burke to Chatham for the Board of Trade. Chatham said that Burke might be a man of parts and an ingenious speaker but that he held "notions and maxims of trade" which he (Chatham) could never endorse. O. A. Sherrard, *Lord Chatham and America* (London, 1958), p. 235. Nevertheless, Chatham was willing a few weeks later to offer him a place, but Burke evinced interest in a better one than Chatham would offer.

47. [29] November [1766], O'Hara MSS.

48. 23 December [1766], *loc. cit.*

49. Burke to O'Hara, 27 October 1767, *loc. cit.*

50. Burke to O'Hara, 27 November 1767, *loc. cit.*

51. Burke to O'Hara, 20 February [1768], *loc. cit.*

52. An act which made the maximum life of the Irish parliament eight years. The Irish had sought a septennial bill but agreed to the change since their parliament met only every other year in the odd numbered years.

53. Quoted in Vincent T. Harlow, *The Founding of the Second British Empire, 1763–1793* (London, 1952), I, 512. I have drawn heavily on Professor Harlow for this account of British government motives and actions at this time.

54. Burke, incidentally, disapproved of this change.

55. Cone, *Burke and Politics*, pp. 166 f. makes this point.

56. By this act, no parliament could be summoned in Ireland without first securing the consent of the English, and no legislation could be enacted without first forwarding its substance for the consent of the king and the English Privy Council. This act dated from 1494 and took its name from Sir Edward Poynings, Irish Lord Deputy under Henry VIII.

57. The British parliament "had, hath, and of right ought to have full power and authority to make laws and statutes of sufficient force and validity, to bind the kingdom and people of *Ireland*." "Statutes at Large", XIV, pp. 204–205, 6 Geo. I, c.5, quoted in *Eng. Hist. Docs., 1714–1783*, X, 683.

58. Burke to O'Hara, [11 April 1768], O'Hara MSS.

59. Magnus, *Burke*, p. 41, proves this to be the price thus settling a long unsolved question.

60. *Corr.*, I, 153.

61. Burke to O'Hara, 9 June 1768, O'Hara MSS.

62. 1 June 1769, *loc. cit.*

63. 9 June 1768, *loc. cit.*

64. *Works*, I, 271–432.

65. It had actually been written by William Knox but "under the inspiration, and with the help of Grenville." Sherrard, *Chatham and America*, p. 139.

66. *Works*, I, 398.

67. "Permit me to touch on my own affairs, which concern me a great deal. To make out this purchase price, I can raise ten thousand pound upon

Mortgage, but no more. I want towards 14 to compleat the Transaction. God knows how much I want money for other occasions, which press me sorely; . . ." Burke to O'Hara, 12 November 1769, O'Hara MSS.

68. *Works*, I, 435–537.
69. *Ibid.*, p. 470.
70. Burke to O'Hara, 21 May 1770, O'Hara MSS.
71. Will Burke to O'Hara, [ante 20 June 1770], *loc. cit.*
72. *The Daily Advertiser*, 1 February 1770.
73. Burke MSS, Sheffield.
74. *Ibid.*
75. *Parl. Hist.*, XVI (1765–1771), 1069.
76. Magnus, *Burke*, p. 67.
77. For the history of Burke's agency, see Hoffman, *Edmund Burke, New York Agent.*
78. O'Hara MSS.
79. 18 November 1771, *loc. cit.*
80. 30 September 1772, *loc. cit.*
81. Magnus, *Burke*, p. 68.
82. Burke to O'Hara, 30 September 1772, O'Hara MSS.
83. Magnus, *Burke*, p. 72.
84. *Works*, VII, 36–37.
85. It had gone on so long that Burke thought it might be endless: "The India Business, which has subverted the little sense of mankind, has so distracted our party, that the Idea of opposition to the ministry is ridiculous, on that, or anything else. This is the leading object, which gives the Tone & character to the rest. It is to be our Business all this session, all the next, & I suspect for ever." Burke to O'Hara, 26 March 1773, O'Hara MSS.
86. J. E. Tyler, "A Letter from the Marquis of Rockingham to Sir William Mayne on the Proposed Absentee Tax of 1773," *Irish Historical Studies*, VIII, no. 32 (September 1953), 362.
87. See above, p. 6.
88. Burke to Rockingham, 29 September 1773, *Corr.*, I, 440.
89. *Ibid.*, p. 441.
90. Their combined annual Irish rentals amounted to £66,000. Cone, *Burke and Politics*, p. 248.
91. Lecky, *Eng. Hist.*, IV, 437.
92. *Original Letters, Principally from Lord Charlemont, Edmund Burke, [and] William Pitt, Earl of Chatham, to the Right Hon. Henry Flood* (London, 1820), pp. 59 f.
93. Tyler, "A Letter from the Marquis of Rockingham . . . ," p. 365.
94. 16 October 1773.
95. *Works*, VI, 125.
96. *Ibid.*, 126 f. In 1795, over twenty years later, Burke maintained that it was of inestimable advantage that an Irishman possessed all the privileges of a natural-born Englishman simply because the former was a member of the Empire.
97. Here Burke employed one of the very arguments advanced against him during the debate in the Trinity Debating Club over his proposal of an absentee tax.

98. *Works*, VI, 132.
99. Burke MSS, Sheffield.
100. 7 November 1773.
101. 11 November 1773.
102. Burke was sincere in his praise as the letter to O'Hara cited below indicates, but as usual he was blind to the faults of a friend. Rockingham's style was rather involved as a rule and difficult to follow.
103. 16 November 1773.
104. 17 November 1773.
105. A nickname for Shelburne.
106. 19 November 1773, O'Hara MSS.
107. Burke MSS, Sheffield.
108. N.d. November 1773.
109. N.d. December 1773.
110. Burke to O'Hara, 22 December 1773, O'Hara MSS.
111. *Burke-Laurence Corr.*, p. 233.
112. 15 March 1797.
113. Cone, *Burke and Politics*, pp. 250 f., makes this point quite emphatically.

III MEMBER OF PARLIAMENT FOR BRISTOL

1. *Corr.*, I, 465.
2. 1 July 1774.
3. 11 July 1774, *Corr.*, I, 468.
4. *Ibid.*, pp. 469–483.
5. *Ibid.*, p. 490.
6. Burke MSS, Sheffield.
7. *Ibid.*
8. 9 October 1774.
9. *Ibid.*
10. See P. T. Underdown, "Henry Cruger and Edmund Burke: Colleagues and Rivals at the Bristol Election of 1774," *William and Mary Quarterly*, XV (January 1958), 14–34. See also P. T. Underdown, "Edmund Burke as a Member of Parliament for Bristol" (unpublished dissertation, University of London, 1954).
11. A broadside printed that day urged Burke's election on the grounds that there should be "no Tricks. Honesty is the best policy." Bristol Election Broadsides, October 1774, New York Historical Society, N.Y.
12. Bristol Election Broadsides, *loc. cit.*
13. *Ibid.*
14. 25 October 1774. One of these "noble fellows," Thomas Mullett, later informed Burke that his friends in Bristol had spent £10,000 on his election. 14 April 1775.
15. Burke to unknown, 29 October 1774, Burke MSS, Lamport Hall.
16. Burke to Mr. H. Lloyd, 29 October 1774.
17. Votes cast before he withdrew.
18. 2 November 1774, O'Hara MSS.

19. *London Chronicle*, 14–16, 16–18, 18–21 February 1775; *The Daily Advertiser*, 20 February 1775.

20. *Adam Library*, I, 5.

21. *Works*, II, 136, 181. Rockingham wrote him that very day to say that "I never felt a more Complete Satisfaction on hearing any Speech, than I did on hearing yours this day. The Matter & the Manner were equally perfect; & in spite of Envy & Malice & in spite of all Politicks, I will venture to prognosticate that there will be but one opinion, in regard to the wonderful ability of the Performance." Burke MSS, Sheffield.

James Boswell, with whom Burke corresponded, wrote him some three years later to say that he was not in perfect accord with the *Speech on Conciliation* because "I deny the Declaratory Act, and I am a warm Tory in its true Constitutional sense." Boswell to Burke, 3 March 1778.

22. A very long but intensely interesting letter to O'Hara reveals that Burke had knowledge of the commencement of hostilities in America before Lord North's government had received the news [ante 4 June 1775], O'Hara MSS.

23. Burke to O'Hara, 26 July 1775, *loc. cit.*

24. J. Almon, *The Parliamentary Register* (London, 1775), I, 428–430.

25. 26 April 1775, O'Hara MSS.

26. Burke to O'Hara, 26 July 1775, *loc. cit.*

27. 9 May 1775.

28. *Corr.*, II, 73. Burke's private opinion of the Duke's attainments was not very flattering. Burke to Walker King, 15 September 1774, Pierpont Morgan Library, New York.

29. *Corr.*, II, 52.

30. *Ibid.*, p. 51.

31. Will Burke to Champion, 16 November 1775, Burke MSS, Lamport Hall.

32. 7 January [1776], O'Hara MSS.

33. Burke wrote Arthur Young, the celebrated agricultural expert, to this effect in 1776. *The Autobiography of Arthur Young*, ed. M. Bethman-Edwards (London, 1898), p. 67.

34. 4 June 1776, *Charlemont MSS*, I, 334.

35. 8 October 1777.

36. Hardy, *Life of Charlemont*, I, 377.

37. Patrick Rogers, *The Irish Volunteers and Catholic Emancipation, 1778–1793* (London, 1934), p. 41.

38. *The Annual Register*, with which Burke was so intimately connected, noted that England's example in relaxing the laws against Catholics was such an obviously prudent act that it was quickly followed by Ireland's parliament. *Annual Register*, 1780, p. 25.

39. See following chapter. In addition he had only recently digressed during a speech in the House in which he was furthering Ireland's commercial position to deliver a scorching blast against the Irish penal laws which he termed odious, oppressive, and impolitic. *The London Packet*, 6–8 April 1778.

40. J. Paul de Castro, *The Gordon Riots* (London, 1926), pp. 8 f.

41. *Works*, II, 399. Dunning has been called the foremost advocate of the day. De Castro, p. 8.

42. Richmond Lennox, *Edmund Burke und sein politisches Arbeitsfeld in den Jahren 1760 bis 1790* (Munich, 1923) p. 229.

43. *Annual Register*, 1778, p. 189.

44. *Ibid.*, p. 190.

45. A. Paul Levack, "Edmund Burke, His Friends, and the Dawn of Irish Catholic Emancipation," *The Catholic Historical Review*, XXXVII (January 1952), 406.

46. *The London Packet; or, New Lloyd's Evening Post*, 29 May — 1 June 1778.

47. *Corr.*, II, 233.

48. Hayden and Moonan, *Short History of Irish People*, p. 418.

49. *The London Packet*, 29–31 July 1778.

50. 26 June 1778.

51. O'Halloran to Burke, 1 August 1778.

52. *Corr.*, II, 232.

53. *Ibid.*, pp. 233 ff.

54. *Ibid.*, pp. 239 f.

55. *Ibid.*, pp. 226 f.

56. Burke MSS, Lamport Hall.

57. *Corr.*, II, 237 f.

58. Curry to Burke, 6 August 1779, and Anthony Dermott to Burke, 9 August 1779, *ibid.*, pp. 281 f. and 290.

59. *Ibid.*, pp. 291–295.

60. *Ibid.*, p. 296.

61. Burke to Pery, 12 August 1778, quoted in Lecky, *Eng. Hist.*, IV, 518 f.

62. Burke to Nagle, 25 August 1778, *New Monthly Magazine*, XVI (1826), 156 f.

63. Burke to unknown, n.d. August 1778, Pierpont Morgan Library, New York. This is pretty clearly to Luke Gardiner in answer to his letter of 11 August to Burke.

64. *Corr.*, II, 296.

65. *Corr.*, II, 219.

66. Charles O'Hara, Jr. to Burke, n.d. 1775. The American war deprived the Irish linen manufacturers of their chief market. To make matters worse, the British government shortly placed an embargo on the exportation of Irish provisions which lasted for three years. The ostensible reason for this action was to prevent Irish provisions from reaching either the Americans or the French but it was openly charged that the real reason was to benefit a few English contractors.

67. As the former Lord Clare, Nugent's unexpected withdrawal from the Bristol poll in 1774 to accept the safe constituency of St. Mawes had opened the way for Burke's supporters to enter him as a candidate.

68. *Parl. Hist.*, XIX (1777–1778), 1100 ff.

69. *Ibid.*, p. 1103.

70. *The London Packet*, 6–8 April 1778.

71. For his criticism of the penal laws he received from Dr. John Curry

in Dublin "the Thanks of many thousands of Your Countrymen here . . . In Endeavouring to Procure some Mitigation, or Redress, of their Many, & long Continued Grievances." Curry to Burke, 29 April 1778.

72. *The London Packet*, 10–13 April 1778.

73. *Parl. Hist.*, XIX (1777–1778), 1112.

74. Burke to Champion, 11 April 1778, *Corr.*, II, 210 f. He followed this letter up with another three days later in the same vein. *Ibid.*, pp. 211–214.

75. Span to Burke, 13 April 1778.

76. Harford, Cowles, Getley & Co. to Burke, 27 April 1778.

77. *Parl. Hist.*, XIX (1777–1778), 1115.

78. Burke to Miss Palmer, 19 January 1786, Huntington Library, Em HM 22523.

79. *Annual Register*, 1778, p. 183.

80. *Ibid.*

81. At that particular time, conditions in Ireland were universally deplorable. Taxes were high, starvation and unemployment rampant. *The London Packet*, 15–18, 18–20, 20–22 May 1778.

82. "The will of the many, and their interest must very often differ." *Works*, III, 299.

83. *Parl. Hist.*, XIX (1777–1778), 1119 ff.

84. *Ibid.*, p. 1124 Burke claimed that the arguments he had employed "to the utmost" of his strength converted at least twenty members to his views. His efforts characteristically included "those that were not visible." *Works*, VI, 217. Part of his success was due to intimating that refusal to grant these concessions might well result in an Irish revolt. *London Chronicle*, 7–9 May 1778.

85. A letter Burke wrote to Samuel Span on 12 May 1778 noted this surrender of several important points by the Irish engaged in lobbying for the bills with the assertion that the Irish yielded concessions which should have been granted them in justice. *Corr.*, II, 219.

86. *Parl. Hist.*, XIX (1777–1778), 1126 f.

87. *Lloyd's Evening Post*, 18–20 May 1778.

88. Burke to John Noble, 24 April 1778, *Corr.*, II, 216 f.

89. Pery to Burke, 25 May 1778.

90. G. E. Howard to Burke, 14 May 1778.

91. Ponsonby to Burke, 27 May 1778.

92. *Parl. Hist.*, XX (1778–1780), 133.

93. *Ibid.*, pp. 136 ff.

94. *St. James's Chronicle, or, British Evening Post*, 13–16 February 1779.

95. *Works*, VI, 221 f.

96. *Annual Register*, 1779, pp. 125–128.

97. *Works*, VI, 223.

98. *Parl. Hist.*, XX (1778–1780), 136 ff.

99. E.g., *St. James's Chronicle*, 9–11 September 1780. His name was long remembered with fear and bitterness in England. When he died, there was an epitaph to the memory of Paul Jones, "the noted pirate," in *The Times*, 1 August 1792.

100. Just prior to this, landing parties from the "Ranger" raided White-

haven and, on the following night, Dumfries in Scotland. In both cases great fear was produced. *Aris's Birmingham Gazette*, 4 May 1778.

101. Rogers, *The Irish Volunteers*, p. 45.

102. *Dublin Review*, XV (August 1843), 215. Just about this time Burke was speculating to Rockingham about what was going on in Ireland. He felt pretty sure that the old idea of an absentee tax was to be revived and thought that the government backed the idea in the hope that it might keep Ireland quiet with respect to her demands for the improvement of trade. Burke to Rockingham, 17 October 1779.

103. *Annual Register*, 1780, p. 3. Burke had earlier suggested that Ireland do this. Cf. Burke to Richmond, 26 September 1775, *Corr.*, II, 73.

104. *Parl. Hist.*, XX (1778–1780), 1134 ff.

105. *The London Courant, and Westminster Chronicle*, 26 November 1779.

106. *Annual Register*, 1780, p. 23.

107. To Burke the quiet springing up of these armed bodies, serving at their own expense and so well equipped and disciplined as to win widespread admiration was "one of the most extraordinary revolutions recorded in history." *Ibid.*, p. 24. In reality, however, he was deeply disturbed by the rise of the volunteers on several grounds. They were an extralegal body, used the threat of force as a lever, and posed a real threat to the constitutional connection between Britain and Ireland.

108. *Parl. Hist.*, XX (1778–1780), 1203 ff.

109. *Annual Register*, 1780, p. 72.

110. *Ibid.*, p. 78.

111. An exception was Londonderry which voted him its freedom.

112. Burgh had undertaken to defend Burke. *Works*, VI, 209 n. Rockingham was afraid that Burke would get heated and tried diplomatically to get him to refrain from any such exercise. He was too late, however. Rockingham to Burke, 6 January 1780.

113. Naturally, he was quite upset and remained so for sometime. In a letter to a Mr. Tighe, 10 April 1781, in regard to a proposed absentee tax, Burke tartly replied to Tighe's letter: "Mr. Burke, having been long out of Ireland, cannot pretend to any accurate knowledge of the state of that kingdom, and his experience of the ill reception which his humble labours on a former occasion have met with, makes him unwilling, as he is unable to meddle much in any thing which relates to it." *Corr.*, II, 415 f.

114. John Hely Hutchinson, Provost of Trinity College, to whom Burgh had shown Burke's letter, wrote him that "the Statue would have been in no danger of prostration; and if it had fallen, the fragments wou'd not have injur'd Scott's windows if no person was at liberty to assail them who was not better dispos'd to Ireland than yourself." 3 February 1780.

The Scott referred to in this letter, John Scott, who later became Chief Justice of Ireland and who was raised to the peerage as the Earl of Clonmel, himself wrote that if Burke paid a visit to Dublin he would be happy to receive him "in that House the windows of which I shall be content to have broken by the fragments of your Statue provided I can afterward collect & restore them to the original Figure. . . ." 2 November 1780.

115. E.g., North was given the Freedom of Cork in a gold box and

hailed as the "Protector of the Commerce, Assertor of the Liberties, and the Patriot and Friend of Ireland." *Lloyd's Evening Post*, 19–21 July 1780. It is small wonder that Burke was so disgusted.

116. Rockingham was convinced that the reason for Ireland's dissatisfaction with Burke and his friends was the feeling that the latter group had not shown themselves sufficiently enthusiastic over the Volunteers. 6 January 1780.

117. *Works*, VI, 209–233.

118. 7 January 1780, *Corr.*, II, 314.

119. 13 January 1780.

120. 16 January 1780.

121. 27 January 1780. Before filing this letter Burke wrote on the outside of it as follows: "Tom Burgh on the abuse almost universally cast on me in Ireland, having endeavoured to serve that country with incessant trouble & no small risque of my seat in Parlt." A later letter from Burgh, 25 September 1780, contains an apology that Burke's letter had recently found its way into print through no fault of his or of the printer who had made copies to give to Burke's friends in Ireland.

122. "Nathan" to Burke, 27 January 1780.

123. For a good account of the riots in Scotland, see the *Annual Register*, 1780, pp. 25–33.

124. For Burke's strong and undisguised hatred for this organization, see his letters to Patrick Bowie and the Reverend John Erskine, *Corr.*, II, 255–261; 268–274. Both of these gentlemen wrote Burke a good many letters on the subject of Scotland and Catholicism as did the Reverend Dr. George Campbell. On the Catholic side, Dr. George Hay of Edinburgh frequently corresponded with him. Burke MSS, Sheffield.

125. Boswell to Burke, 22 February 1779. In his reply Burke was very vehement toward the Protestant Association, 1 March 1779, Yale University Library.

126. *Parl. Hist.*, XX (1778–1780), 322 ff.

127. A similar event happened the year previous. Burke, attacking the government's lack of alertness, called the House's attention to the fact that "the Pilot Palinarus" was sound asleep at that very moment. *The London Packet*, 6–8 May 1778.

128. *Parl. Hist.*, XX (1778–1780), 327.

129. One newspaper correspondent wrote about this time that "Popery" was fatal to government and that "no Country whatsoever (except a Popish one) ought to tolerate Popery." *St. James's Chronicle*, 6–8 April 1780.

130. "A Philanthropist" from Edinburgh volunteered the information to Burke that the Protestants of Scotland were convinced that Burke was "a staunch Roman." 10 April 1779.

131. *The Daily Universal Register*, 23 June 1785.

132. 18 February 1780.

133. *Lloyd's Evening Post*, 19–22 May 1780.

134. *Parl. Hist.*, XXI (1780–1781), 706.

135. *Ibid.*, p. 669. Contemporary accounts of the riots which ensued may be found in *Gentleman's Magazine*, L (June, July, and August 1780), 265–268, 312–316, and 366–369; *London Magazine*, XLIX (June 1780), 282ff.;

Annual Register, 1780, pp. 254–299; *The London Courant*, 3, 5, 7, 8, 9, 10, 12, 13 June 1780; *St. James's Chronicle*, 1–3, 3–6 June 1780; *Courier de l'Europe*, 6, 9, 13, 23 Juin 1780. See also William Vincent, *A Plain and Succinct Narrative of the Riots and Disturbances in the Cities of London and Westminster and Borough of Southwark* (London, 1780) and [Thomas L. O'Beirne], *Considerations on the late Disturbances by a consistent Whig* (London, 1780).

136. *Parl. Hist.*, XXI (1780–1781), 660.

137. In an undated letter to some unknown persons, Burke writing from the Thatched House Tavern said: "Mr. Burke presents his most respectful & grateful compliments to the Gentlemen, who have shewn their Zeal in favour of the general rights of humanity, in offering to defend his house against those, who in pretended principles of religion have declared war, to the best of their miserable power, on Mankind. But Mr. Burke for the present begs leave with the sincerest thanks to decline this offer so honourable to him. He is clearly of opinion that this mode of defending our houses is the most reputable & the most effectual; but as it is not generally adopted, he does not know whether he would not be accused of singularity & affectation, if he should choose it. He once more returns his sincerest thanks. He has removed his Books & pictures. The rest is at the service of this Body of Zealots." Quoted with the kind permission of Professor and Mrs. Charles K. Warner, Middlebury, Vermont.

138. *Corr.*, II, 350.

139. Prior, *Burke*, p. 188.

140. De Castro, *The Gordon Riots*, p. 65.

141. *Corr.*, II, 353 f. For a somewhat similar account of what happened, except that the great danger to Burke is brought out, see a letter from Mrs. Lloyd Kenyon to an unknown person, 6 June 1780. Historical Manuscripts Commission, *Fourteenth Report, Appendix, Part IV. The Manuscripts of Lord Kenyon* (London, 1894), p. 510.

142. Noble to Burke, 8 June 1780.

143. "The Writer," to Burke, 7 June 1780.

144. *Corr.*, II, 350.

145. Cf. *Annual Register*, 1780, pp. 194 f.; *Parl. Hist.*; XXIX (1791–1792), 386, 426; *Works*, II, 410 ff.; and *Corr.*, II, 369, 372 ff.

146. *London Chronicle*, 6–8 June 1780.

147. *Parl. Hist.*, XXI (1780–1781), 663.

148. Burke thought at first that it was "pusillanimous and unbecoming" for parliament to take "that flagitious petition, which came from that base gang called 'the protestant association' into our serious consideration." But he changed his mind and was satisfied that it was done since he said that the destruction which would follow a refusal would have been blamed onto the intransigence of parliament. *Corr.*, II, 354.

149. *London Gazette*, 3–6 June 1780.

150. *Parl. Hist.*, XXI (1780–1781), 689.

151. I can find no evidence that such was the case, but the supposition is not far-fetched.

152. 18 June 1780.

153. 19 June 1780.

154. *Parl. Hist.*, XXI (1780–1781), 690.
155. *Corr.*, II, 358 f.
156. Prior, *Burke*, p. 191; Macknight, *Burke*, II, 376; Bisset, *Burke*, II, 73.
157. On this occasion, Burke spoke for three hours, as did Fox also. *Annual Register*, 1780, p. 196.
158. *Parl. Hist.*, XXI (1780–1781), 710.
159. 24 June 1780.
160. 7 July 1780.
161. See Cobban, *Burke and Revolt*, ch. iv.
162. He was given particulars by Charles Butler in two such cases. One involved George Fishbourne, a boy whom Catholics were accused of having stolen from the Charity School near St. Leonard's, Shoreditch, and the other had to do with a Miss Webbe, a Roman Catholic girl whom Catholics were accused of having perverted to their religion. In each case the evidence supplied by Butler showed the Catholics in a satisfactory light. Charles Butler to Burke, 15 July 1780.
163. *Parl. Hist.*, XXI (1780–1781), 718 f.
164. *Works*, II, 412 f.; Bisset, *Burke*, II, 74; Macknight, *Burke*, II, 377 f.
165. Earl Bathurst to Burke, 15 June 1780, reveals that Burke was so determined at that time.
166. Magnus, *Burke*, p. 102.
167. A squib in *The Morning Post and Daily Advertiser*, 15 October 1779, if accurate, and there is no other evidence to substantiate it which I have been able to find anywhere, would make it appear that this was the second time in consecutive years that he narrowly escaped. Supposedly, in early October 1779, Burke and Rockingham had a close call from the hands of an enfuriated mob in the city of Hull. The crowd pursued their carriage for some miles after they had escaped through "a back part of town."

IV SEVERANCE OF THE BRISTOL CONNECTION AND ITS AFTERMATH

1. Cone, *Burke and Politics*, p. 380. See also pp. 381 f. Rumors about Burke's political future were flying about at this time. Among them was one to the effect that Rockingham was to become Lord Lieutenant of Ireland and that Burke was to be his Chief Secretary. Edmond Malone to the Earl of Charlemont, 5 July 1780, *Charlemont MSS*, I, 374.
2. The story of this relationship may be found in G. E. Weare, *Edmund Burke's Connection with Bristol, From 1774 to 1780* (Bristol, 1894); Ernest Barker, *Burke and Bristol, a Study of the Relations Between Burke and His Constituency During the Years 1774–1780* (Bristol, 1931); Ernest Barker, "Burke and His Bristol Constituency," in *Essays on Government* (Oxford, 1945); and Underdown, "Edmund Burke as a Member of Parliament for Bristol."
3. Burke to John Noble, August 1777, Huntington Library, Em HM 22583. Shortly after giving up his canvass at Bristol, which he concluded was hopeless, Burke expressed joy upon hearing of "the hopeful way our Whig Club is in." He relied upon it, he said, "not only for the reformation of Bristol, but, (through the prudent management of our friends) for the

principal means of reforming the adjacent Counties." Burke to Noble, 5 October 1780, Huntington Library, Em HM 22586.

4. 23 August 1775, *Corr.*, II, 56.

5. Burke to John Noble, n.d., Huntington Library, Em HM 22584. Other letters of Burke's to Noble, which are chiefly concerned with the relations of Burke to his constituents and which are to be found in this collection, are Em HM 22582–7.

6. Burke to Joseph Harford, 4 April 1780, *Corr.*, II, 335–345.

7. *Ibid.*, p. 369.

8. *Ibid.*, pp. 372 ff.

9. *The Sunday Gazette, and Weekly Intelligencer*, 27 August 1780.

10. *Works*, II, 367–423.

11. Prior, *Burke*, p. 193. Macknight, *Burke*, II, 386, called it the most outstanding speech ever made on an English hustings, and Sir Samuel Romilly, a contemporary, thought it possibly the greatest piece of oratory in the English language. *Memoirs* (2 ed., London, 1840), I, 213. Other complimentary contemporaries were "Xenophon" and the Bath correspondent, both in *Lloyd's Evening Post*, 15–18 September 1780.

12. He was openly accused of having put Ireland's interests in this matter first and of having acted more as if he were a member for Cork or Dublin than Bristol. *Gentleman's Magazine*, L (1780), 819.

13. He knew that he faced a highly critical audience on this subject. Bristol had nearly emulated London's example in the Gordon Riots. In fact, the Corporation had spent £85 12s. 5d. in "sundry expenses on account of threatened and expected riot." Barker, *Burke and Bristol*, p. 92. Moreover, the rumor that he was a disguised Jesuit educated at St. Omer had been kept in circulation at Bristol ever since 1774. Weare, *Burke's Connection with Bristol*, p. 153.

An actual attempt to start an anti-Catholic riot in Bristol had been checked by a group of leading citizens. *Courier de l'Europe*, 23 Juin 1780.

14. Burke gave the total as fifty thousand but observed with characteristic nationalism that the Catholics consisted chiefly of England's best manufacturers and warned that they might have emigrated to Flanders had they been refused some relief in return for their loyalty and devotion.

15. A Citizen, *A Review of Mr. Burke's Conduct, As the Representative of Bristol in Parliament* . . . ([London], 1780), p. 19.

16. *Gentleman's Magazine*, L (1780), 618; *Lloyd's Evening Post*, 15–18 September 1780; Weare, *Burke's Connection with Bristol*, pp. 147–166.

17. *Lloyd's Evening Post*, 5–8 January 1780.

18. Burke to Mary Palmer, 19 January 1786, Huntington Library, Em HM 22523.

19. *Works*, III, 353.

20. *Corr.*, II, 395. Sheriff Harford was the mover. Barker, *Burke and Bristol*, p. 130.

21. Romilly, *Memoirs*, I, 135; Burke MSS, Sheffield, 1780, *passim*.

22. "Derisor," in *St. James's Chronicle*, 16–19 September 1780.

23. 15 September 1780, *Corr.*, II, 376.

24. Burgoyne to Burke, 17 September 1780.

25. The Marchioness of Rockingham to Burke, 17 September 1780.

Her confusion might also be attributed to the fact that she had also written to Admiral Keppel that same day.

26. The Prince of Dashkov to Burke, 19 September 1780, *Corr.*, II, 376.

27. Burke to Champion, 3 November 1780, *ibid.*

28. It was reported in 1782 that Burke was to stand for the important Westminster constituency, but nothing came of it. Historical Manuscripts, Commission, *Fifteenth Report, Appendix, Part VI. The Manuscripts of the Earl of Carlisle, Preserved at Castle Howard* (London, 1897), p. 610.

29. Burke to Champion, 7 January 1781, *Corr.*, II, 400.

30. Magnus, *Burke*, p. 105. It is the opinion of Magnus that Burke had never forgiven those whom he believed responsible for Will's financial ruin in East Indian stock and thus that Will's personal grievances were a major cause of Burke's interest in India. While he undoubtedly felt quite strongly about Will's misfortune, I hardly think that it was the dominant force in his feelings about India.

31. *Parl. Hist.* XXII (1781–1782), 223–226.

32. 18 February 1780.

33. 17 March 1780.

34. 14 February 1781.

35. 10 March 1781.

36. 15 September 1781, *Corr.*, II, 432.

37. 18 September 1781, *ibid.*, p. 436.

38. *Ibid.*, pp. 437 f. A few years later, the *Annual Register* remarked that the Austrian Emperor was a ruler equipped with "sufficient comprehension to discover that his own interests are, in a less or greater degree, inseparably connected with the security and prosperity of every class and order of his subjects." *Annual Register*, 1784–1785, p. 5.

39. 11 June 1782.

40. 4 February 1782.

41. *Works*, IV, 217–240. Thirteen years later in a letter to the Reverend Dr. Thomas Hussey, his Irish Catholic sacerdotal friend, Burke said that the opinions he expressed were his "fixed sentiments," as he had stated them in his letter to Lord Kenmare, 21 February 1782. This letter to Kenmare had been published, and anyone could see what his views were. Time had strengthened rather than weakened them. They were views which "are not founded upon chimerical abstractions, upon the rights of states, and governments to regulate education, &c. &c., with all that silly prattle of metaphysical politics, which a parrot could go through as well as they who use it and is much more becoming green plumage than black gowns. No! You will see that I have walked in another path. I have endeavoured to build what I there advanced on the knowledge of men, as they are modified by their habitudes and their circumstances, and as they ought to be provided for according to their variable necessities." *Corr.*, IV, 229 f. Cf. *Works*, IV, 303.

42. Prior, *Burke*, p. 210, says that he was so busy at this time that the reply had to be dictated at dinner, while dressing, and even while carrying on conversations.

43. Hutchinson had made a speech in the Irish Commons emphasizing the need of Catholic education in Ireland, especially for clergymen. He

advocated the establishment of schools in the Catholic dioceses at government expense. There Catholics could receive an education at no cost which would prepare them for Dublin University, where a few sizarships would be available together with special advantages for needy students. Hutchinson also proposed that a Catholic divinity professor train them in theology. In matters of secular education, he suggested that there be no distinctions made between Protestants and Catholics. *The Parliamentary Register: or, History of the Proceedings and Debates of the House of Commons of Ireland* (2 ed., 15 vols., Dublin, 1784-1795), I (1781-1782), 309 f. [Hereafter cited as *Irish Parl. Debs.*]

Burke had only a few days before writing this reply to Kenmare received information from Thomas Braughall in Ireland which pointed out the very real difficulties the Catholics of Ireland found in Hutchinson's proposals. Braughall told Burke that the Provost's scheme to open the college to Roman Catholics by "procuring 30 Servitors places . . . does credit to his humanity, but when it is considered that near 2000 Ecclesiastics are scarce adequate to the Duties required from the priests in this Kingdom & that [to] procure a Succession of such it is necessary that upwards of 600 students in Divinity should be constantly supported at Colege, it must be evident to every unprejudiced Reasoner that the R.C. of this Kingdom are unequal to furnish funds for such Education, the many foundations on the Continent which now supply this deficiency could not be transplanted hither. It has been proposed that at a future period all vacant dignities should be filled only with such Ecclesiastics as had received their Education in this Kingdom, which would induce every person who was equal to the expense of Domestic Education to procure it for every Child of his destined for the Church." 9 February 1782.

44. Denis Gwynn, *John Keogh* (Dublin, 1930), *passim*.

45. In his character sketch, "Sir Boyle Roche," in *Studies in Irish History* (London, 1902), pp. 228-240, C. Litton Falkiner says that "Herodotus is not more indisputably the father of history than is Sir Boyle Roche the father of bulls." An example of one of Sir Boyle's famous bulls is the following: "The best way to avoid danger is to meet it plump." Another is his invitation to a peer whom he invited to partake of his hospitality by saying "I hope, my lord, if you ever come within a mile of my house, that you'll stay there all night."

46. Henry Grattan, *Memoirs of the Life and Times of the Rt. Hon. Henry Grattan* (5 vols., London, 1849), III, 116-122.

47. 22 March 1782, *Corr.*, II, 459.

48. 14 March 1782.

49. Poole to Burke, 7 March 1782.

50. The term meant at this time freedom from the restrictions on Irish trade imposed by Britain.

51. Grattan, *Life*, II, 36.

52. *St. James's Chronicle*, 20-22 February 1781.

53. *Parl. Hist.*, XXI (1780-1781), 1292 f.

54. *Ibid.*, pp. 1304 ff. Fox's speech had been a repetition of what Burke had said on the twenty-first. *St. James's Chronicle*, 22-24 February 1781.

55. *Analytical Review*, I (July 1788), 339.

56. Grattan, *Life*, II, 204.

57. *The London Packet*, 27–29 March 1782. On the eve of North's resignation, while he was speaking, a dog appeared from under one of the benches and began to howl loudly. North, who had a good sense of humor, remarked, as the dog was being removed from the House, "As the new member has ended his argument, I beg to be allowed to continue mine." In some of the later caricatures of North, the dog is frequently to be seen.

58. *Memorials and Correspondence of Charles James Fox*, ed. Lord John Russell (4 vols., London, 1853), I, 114. Burke was once called "the Trumpeter of a particular connection." Maurice Morgann to Lord Shelburne, 29 October 1782, photostatic copy in the New York Historical Society from the Shelburne Papers, Misc. MSS, Clements Library, University of Michigan.

59. *The London Packet*, 27–29 March 1782.

60. Magnus, *Burke*, p. 111.

61. See, e.g., H.V.F. Somerset, "New Light on Edmund Burke," *Discovery*, XIII (December 1932), 397; Goldwin Smith, "Burke on Party," *AHR*, XI (October 1905), 41; *The Collected Essays and Addresses of the Rt. Hon. Augustine Birrell, 1880–1920* (London, 1922), I, 171–179; *The Croker Papers*, ed. Louis J. Jennings (London, 1884), I, 289 f. Despite these obstacles it was only two years since George III had privately indicated that he would have no objection to seeing Burke achieve a cabinet post.

62. Burke MSS, Sheffield.

63. *Parl. Hist.*, XXII (1781–1782), 1228.

64. *Ibid.*, pp. 1257 f.

65. *The Times*, 11 December 1794.

66. Grattan, *Life*, II, 216 f.; Hardy, *Life of Charlemont*, II, 13.

67. The Bishop of Killaloe to Burke, 4 April 1782; and Hely Hutchinson to Burke, 6 April 1782.

68. Grattan, *Life*, II, 219; Hardy, *Life of Charlemont*, II, 6.

69. Grattan, *Life*, II, 225.

70. It was said of Eden that the loss of place had suddenly converted him into a patriot. *Memoirs of the Marquis of Rockingham and His Contemporaries*, ed. Earl Albemarle (2 vols., London, 1852), II, 470.

71. *Annual Register*, 1782, p. 178.

72. *Parl. Hist.*, XXII (1781–1782), 1241–46.

73. *Ibid.*, pp. 1247–52.

74. *Ibid.*, p. 1252.

75. There was often a lamentable failure on the part of Hansard to do justice to Burke's speeches, and this might have been such an instance, although I do not think so. For a good article on the subject, see H.V.F. Somerset, "Burke's Eloquence and Hansard's Reports," *English Review*, LII (March 1931), 342–350.

76. Burke and Eden (later Lord Auckland) were never friendly, although they did enter into a correspondence. For some Burke letters not to be found elsewhere in print, see *The Journal and Correspondence of William, Lord Auckland*, ed. George Hogge (4 vols., London, 1862), *passim*.

77. *Parl. Hist.*, XXII (1781–1782), 1257 f.

78. *Ibid.*, pp. 1264 ff.

79. In his college days, Grattan was so named owing to a peculiarity in his gait, and the name clung to him in later life. *The Times*, 11 December 1794.

80. *Irish Parl. Debs.*, I (1781–1782), 339. A good newspaper account may be found in *The Morning Post and Daily Advertiser*, 28 April 1782.

81. Thomas Braughall to Burke, 20 April 1782.

82. *Burke-Laurence Corr.*, p. 88.

83. There is a draft of an unfinished letter to an unknown person in Burke's handwriting among his papers in Sheffield. While the draft is un-dated, it is clear that it was made not long after the Rockingham government took office. In it Burke expressed the opinion that the relative situation be-tween England and Ireland required more than the repeal of the Declaratory Act. The latter by its very definition "is no more than a parcel of words. I am indeed astonished to find that this repeal rather than some clear & solid settlement should be desired." Burke's position here was that a formal com-pact between Great Britain and Ireland was now necessary if important British interests were not to be jeopardized and if the possibility of nume-rous future disputes were to be avoided. He told his unknown correspondent that he knew that "you could not love yr. country as you do & hate & per-secute four fifths of its inhabitants [&] that you are too good a politician to think that any external privileges can make a country great & flourishing."

84. *Rockingham Memoirs*, II, 471. Portland's performance left much to be desired. His dispatches frequently contradicted one another and his actions can best be described as confused. One is here given a preview, as it were, of his conduct in the Fitzwilliam episode, which will be described be-low.

85. *Parl. Hist.*, XXIII (1782–1783), 20–28. For Fox's correspondence on the subject of Irish legislative independence and the attempted delay, see *Fox's Correspondence*, 388–418.

86. *Parl. Hist.*, XXIII (1782–1783), 33 f. It was this speech which has led all those who have previously written on this phase of Burke's career to con-clude erroneously that he favored legislative independence.

87. Harlow, *Founding of Second British Empire*, I, 549 ff.

88. Attention needs to be called again to the highly unrepresentative character of the Irish parliament. The House of Lords consisted of the bishops of the establishment together with the holders of vast estates and a number of important men whose elevation to the peerage was the result of "services rendered" to British government in Ireland. The members of the upper house had great influence in the selection of those of the lower house. There were 300 members of the House of Commons, 220 of whom repre-sented 110 boroughs, all of which were either of the pocket or rotten spe-cies. Indeed many of these boroughs had only a single elector. One hundred individuals returned about two-thirds of the membership of the House and some of these persons controlled more than one seat. 64 of the members were returned by the 32 counties, while 7 cities had 14 members, and the University of Dublin was represented by two.

89. The Bishop of Killaloe to Burke, 2 June 1782.

90. As far as I have been able to discover, no biographer or other com-

mentator on Burke has hitherto noted this revealing letter despite the fact that it was published in 1929.

91. Yet in a letter to Rockingham he enclosed a copy of part of a letter he had just received from Portland in Ireland. See above, note 35.

92. *Adam Library*, I, 6 f.

93. Hardy, *Life of Charlemont*, II, 45 f.; Grattan, *Life*, II, 301.

94. 7 June 1782.

95. *Parl. Hist.*, XXIII (1782–1783), 325. For a reiteration a few years later, see *ibid.*, XXVII (1788–1789), 1149–52.

96. *Charlemont MSS*, I, 427.

97. Hardy, *Life of Charlemont*, II, 219 f.; Grattan, *Life*, III, 430. Due to sympathy shown for France by the original Whig Club in London in later years, Burke resigned from both clubs. *The Times*, 4 March 1793.

98. Burke was in error. The government which did this was, of course, that of his friends headed by the Marquis of Rockingham. When Burke wrote this, his mind had played a trick on him.

99. Burke to Fitzwilliam, 20 November 1796.

100. Cf. note 83.

101. 26 September 1794.

V BURKE'S OPPOSITION TO PITT'S PLAN FOR IRISH FREE TRADE

1. This one bore the caption of "Cincinnatus in Retirement." Pierpont Morgan Library, Peel Collection, Vol. XII.

One of Burke's Irish correspondents, Andrew Buck, wrote him that the death of Rockingham had caused great concern in Ireland which was increased by "the Assertors of Liberty retiring from the exercize of Power." 13 July 1782.

2. Portland to Burke, 1 April 1783.

3. Peel Collection, Vol. XII. The caricaturist, Gillray took pleasure in representing him as a Jesuit.

4. Adam Smith to Burke, 15 April 1783.

5. Hay to Burke, 13 April 1783.

6. Richard Burke, Jr. to Mrs. Burke, July 1783, comments with deep concern on the particularly low state of his father's spirits.

7. Cartoon published March 1783, by H. Humphrey. Peel Collection, Vol. XII.

8. Harlow, *Founding of Second British Empire*, I, 559–562.

9. Magnus, *Burke*, pp. 146 f. 1784 was not a very happy year for Burke but there were a few pleasant incidents. He was elected to Brooks's Club, made a Fellow of the Royal Society of Edinburgh, awarded the freedom of Glasgow, and installed as Lord Rector of Glasgow University. *Ibid.* p. 142. In November he received word of his enthusiastic reelection as rector for one year. Burke MSS, Lamport Hall.

10. Thomas Wright, *A Caricature History of the Georges* (London, 1867), pp. 399–401.

11. Michael Kearney to Richard Burke, Sr. 14 November 1783.

12. *Works*, VII, 104.

13. *The Morning Chronicle, and London Advertiser*, 19 October 1784.

14. *The Daily Universal Register*, 12 January 1785.

15. Grattan, *Life*, III, 239.

16. *The Daily Universal Register*, 5 March 1785.

17. Harlow, *Founding of Second British Empire*, I, 566–568.

18. *Parl. Hist.*, XXIV, (1783–1785), 1382.

19. *Ibid.*, pp. 1405 ff. One of the caricatures of Burke published during the debates on the Irish propositions showed him putting the House to sleep by the windiness of his harangues.

20. *The London Packet*, 24–26 January 1785.

21. *The Daily Universal Register*, 26 January 1785.

22. *Parl. Hist.*, XXIV (1783–1785), 1413.

23. Professor Harlow, *Founding of Second British Empire*, pp. 558–616, has written the best account of this entire episode which I have seen. In it, he has made clear that the commercial and manufacturing interests in Britain did a *volte face* in this matter. Initially, with few exceptions they had taken the position that they had nothing to fear from Irish competition in either domestic or foreign markets. They did, however, ask for "level" competition, i.e., they disliked the policy of the Irish government in aiding their infant industries by bounties. It is Professor Harlow's feeling that historians have been misled into accepting what was skillfully organized political propaganda.

24. *The Daily Universal Register*, 22 February 1785.

25. *Parl. Hist.*, XXV (1785–1786), 311.

26. The hereditary revenue of Ireland amounted at that time to about £652,000. Its component parts were customs, excise taxes, hearth-money, and quit-rents. *The Daily Universal Register*, 25 February 1785.

27. *Ibid.*, 23 February 1785.

28. Peel Collection, Vol. XII.

29. This pamphlet failed to "wipe away the public prejudices." *The Daily Universal Register*, 1 April 1785.

30. *A Reply to the Treasury Pamphlet Entitled, "The Proposed System of Trade with Ireland Explained"* (London, 1785), p. 50.

31. E.g., *The Daily Universal Register*, 26 June, 7 July 1785.

32. There is an excellent collection of these pamphlets in the Baker Library, Harvard Business School, Boston.

33. *Parl. Hist.*, XXV (1785–1786), 366.

34. *Annual Register*, 1786, pp. 18 f.

35. *Ibid.*, pp. 19 ff.

36. *Parl. Hist.*, XXV (1785–1786), 647–51.

37. *The Speeches of the Right Honourable Edmund Burke in the House of Commons and in Westminster Hall* (4 vols., London, 1816), I, 192, 195.

38. *The London Packet*, 26–29 August 1785.

39. *Irish Parl. Debs.*, V (1785), 443.

40. *Ibid.*, pp. 350–58; *Annual Register*, 1786, p. 23; Grattan, *Life*, III, 263 f.; Hardy, *Life of Charlemont*, II, 148.

41. *Correspondence Between the Right Honble. William Pitt and Charles Duke of Rutland*, ed. Lord Mahon (Edinburgh, 1890), p. 116.

42. *The Daily Universal Register*, 9 May 1785.

43. See An Irish Gentleman, *Defence of Opposition, with Respect to Their Conduct on Irish Affairs* (London, 1785), *passim*.

44. Prior, *Burke*, p. 244.
45. Bisset, *Burke*, II, 193 ff.
46. Cone's first volume of *Burke and Politics* ends with 1782. Presumably this episode will be treated in his projected second volume.
47. Macknight, *Burke*, III, 134 ff.
48. Lennox, *Burkes politisches Arbeitsfeld*, pp. 222 ff.
49. That this was so, we have already seen. Cf. note 32. One of Burke's contemporaries, Sir Nathaniel Wraxall, noted Burke's opposition as based on this ground. Sir Nathaniel Wraxall, *Posthumous Memoirs of His Own Time* (Philadelphia, 1836), p. 150.
50. John Morley, *Burke* (London and New York, 1888), pp. 182 f.

VI THE IRISH MISSION OF RICHARD BURKE, JR.

1. Burke to John Hely Hutchinson, 11 November 1786, *Beaufort MSS*, p. 318; see also Historical Manuscripts Commission, *Fourteenth Report, Appendix, Part I. The Manuscripts of His Grace the Duke of Rutland K.G. Preserved at Belvoir Castle* (London, 1894), III, 360; Historical Manuscripts Commission, *Thirteenth Report, Appendix, Part III, The Manuscripts of J. B. Fortescue, Esq., Preserved at Dropmore* (London, 1892), I, 270. [Hereafter cited as *Fortescue MSS.*]
2. Burke to Thomas L. O'Beirne, 29 September 1786.
3. *Leadbeater Papers*, II,138.
4. *Ibid.*, I, 172–174.
5. Lord Earlsfort to Burke, 17 January 1787.
6. Magnus, *Burke*, pp. 179 ff.
7. *Ibid.*, pp. 180 f.
8. *Parl. Hist.*, XXVII (1788–1789), 1149–52.
9. Charlemont to Burke, 24 March 1789, Burke MSS, Sheffield and Lamport Hall. His Lordship asked Burke to lay his "humble and respectful Acknowledgments at the Feet of his royal Highness" whom he described as "the most accomplished, the most endearing, the most gracious, and what is still more, . . . the best of Princes."
10. Wright, *Caricature History of the Georges*, p. 436.
11. *Life and Letters of Sir Gilbert Elliot*, ed. Countess of Minto (3 vols., London, 1874), I, 262. Elliot was very fond of Burke. He once sent him the following amusing birth announcement: "This time I must send you some account of a work of which I am the Author, not the Critic. Lady Elliot has this morning been deliver'd of another boy & they are both as well as possible. I flatter myself that you will not be angry at my troubling you, with this information & that you will not refuse to share my satisfaction in this event —." 1 August 1786, Burke MSS, Lamport Hall.
12. *Elliot's Life and Letters*, I, 262.
13. *Ibid.*, p. 263.
14. Magnus, *Burke*, p. 181.
15. A caricature entitled "Smelling Out A Rat; or, — the atheistical-revolutionist disturbed in his midnight 'calculations.' *Vide* — a troubled conscience" was published by Gillray on 3 December. It shows Burke's elongated beak with a huge pair of spectacles perched on it and a pair of piercing

eyes peering out from behind the glasses. In his left hand he bears a cross and in his right a crown. He is otherwise enveloped in clouds. This apparition has penetrated Dr. Price's study and has surprised him as he sits at his desk surrounded by considerable evidence of sedition against both the church and state. The significance of this lampoon lies in the fact that the *Reflections* had been occasioned by a sermon preached by Price at a dissenting chapel in the Old Jewry before the members of the Revolutionary Society, a body which met annually on 4 November to celebrate the memory of the Glorious Revolution of 1688. A reproduction of this caricature appears in Wright, *Caricature History of the Georges*, opposite p. 452.

16. *Charlemont MSS*, II, 126.

17. For the history of this body, see Thomas Wyse, Jr., *Historical Sketch of the Late Catholic Association of Ireland* (2 vols., London, 1829).

18. He has been called "probably the most distinguished Irish scholar writing in English in the eighteenth century." Giovanni Costigan, "The Tragedy of Charles O'Conor: An Episode in Anglo-Irish Relations," *American Historical Review*, XLIX (October 1943), 33.

19. The address was printed in the *Annual Register*, 1759. To it was appended this comment by Burke: "It must be a great pleasure to all true lovers of his majesty's person and government, to find so much loyalty amongst all the subjects of this kingdom, the Roman Catholics of this city as well as of Corke, having offered large loans in case of necessity, to support our present happy establishment, against all enemies, which is the strongest test of their fidelity." p. 266.

20. John Keogh (1740–1817) "devoted near thirty years of his life for the purpose of breaking the chains of his countrymen." His mansion at Mount Jerome was the headquarters for discussion and organization of the Catholic Association's efforts to achieve Catholic emancipation. Although he himself refrained from becoming involved in the work of the United Irishmen, he was the warm friend and confidant of a great many of them.

21. For Burke's complimentary estimate of his character, see *Corr.*, IV, 389. See also Charles Butler, *Historical Memoir of the English, Irish and Scottish Catholics Since the Reformation* (3 ed., London, 1822), IV, 438–441; and *Irish Magazine and Monthly Asylum for Neglected Biography*, I (March 1808), 110.

22. Burke was in the habit of frequently going in secret to the Spanish Ambassador's chapel to hear Hussey deliver sermons. James B. Robertson, *Lectures on the Life, Writings, and Times of Edmund Burke* (London, 1869), p. 358.

23. For a good example, see Samuel F. Bemis, *The Hussey-Cumberland Mission* (Princeton, 1931). When the priest returned from this mission, it was rumored that he brought back preliminary articles of peace. As a result, there was feverish activity on the London Stock Exchange. *Sarah Farley's Bristol Journal*, 21 October 1780.

24. Denis Gwynn, *Keogh*, pp. 22 f.

25. *Corr.*, III, 150 ff.

26. The new name given to the old Catholic Association, Burke felt success was bound to be their lot and later said: "Let this committee stick together, and sooner or later they cannot fail." *Ibid.*, p. 412.

27. *Ibid.*, pp. 154 f.

28. *Works*, VI, 387.

29. Burke MSS, Sheffield.

30. It was rumored as early as January 1791 that Burke was to be given a peerage and a pension. Sir Joshua Reynolds to Burke, 25 January 1791.

31. Burke MSS, Sheffield.

32. *Corr.*, III, 349.

33. Burke MSS, Sheffield.

34. Burke was later accused of sending his son over to stir up revolution in Ireland while at the same time doing his best to prevent any uprisings in England. See letter of the Shakespearean scholar, Malone, to Lord Charlemont, 3 December 1792, *Charlemont MSS*, II, 204.

35. Richard concluded a letter to his horrified father which was written after the affair: "I have received the congratulations of many on my safety & of many likewise on my conduct." Saturday, [?] March 1784.

36. Burke MSS, Sheffield.

37. *Loc. cit.*

38. *Loc. cit.*

39. 13 October 1791. I have been unable to find the letter of Richard's mentioned by Pitt.

40. *The Times*, 8 November 1791.

41. Burke to Fitzwilliam, 21 November 1791.

42. Burke to Richard, 13 and 15 December 1791. Burke would later change his mind on the relations which he thought should obtain between the Catholics and the Dissenters.

43. *Corr.*, III, 359 f.

44. Grenville to Dundas. Private. Whitehall. 29 October 1791, *Fortescue MSS*, II, 221. For a good illustration of this jealousy, see a letter from Charlemont, who, although not a member of the government, was one of the most powerful figures in Ireland, to Dr. Alexander Haliday, 21 January 1792, *Charlemont MSS*, II, 186.

45. *Fortescue MSS*, II, 191.

46. *Corr.*, III, 365 f.

47. Dundas to Westmorland, 26 December 1791, Home Office 100/33, quoted in Harlow, *Founding of Second British Empire*, p. 634.

48. Dundas to Westmorland, 26 December 1791, Westmorland Papers, Public Record Office, Dublin, quoted by William E. H. Lecky, *A History of Ireland in the Eighteenth Century* (5 vols., New York, 1893), III, 40–41.

49. Burke actually labored under the delusion that his son was superior to him. He once declared publicly: "How extraordinary it is that I and Lord Chatham and Lord Holland, should each have a son so superior to ourselves!" *Letters of Samuel Johnson, LL.D.*, ed. George Birkbeck Hill (8 vols., Oxford, 1892), II, 227 n.

50. *Corr.*, III, 363 f.

51. *Ibid.*, p. 426.

52. 1 January 1792.

53. John Thomas Troy (1739–1823) became Archbishop of Dublin in 1786. A very cautious man, he could usually be counted upon to cooperate with Dublin Castle and was a strong foe of any use of force against the

government by Catholics. He was most instrumental in helping Pitt carry the union between Great Britain and Ireland.

54. Burke MSS, Sheffield.

55. Langrishe was a member of the Irish House of Commons who had long been friendly with Burke. On 10 December 1791, he had written to Burke to ask for his views on the subject of the Roman Catholics of Ireland. As Burke told his son in a letter dated 1 January 1792, he had intended only a long letter in response but "I have got into a long dissertation." This letter will be discussed below.

56. [Ante 8 January 1792].

57. *Corr.*, III, p. 367 ff.

58. 9 January 1792, Burke MSS, Sheffield and Lamport Hall

59. Richard to Hobart, 11 January 1792.

60. 13 January 1792.

61. Burke MSS, Sheffield.

62. *Loc. cit.*

63. Dundas to Richard, 20 January 1792.

64. Burke to Richard, 26 January 1792, *Corr.*, III, 379.

65. *Works*, IV, 243–306.

66. In the light of the king's subsequent opposition in 1795 to Catholic emancipation, Burke's interpretation is illuminating. George III was persuaded by Fitzgibbon, the Irish Chancellor, and others that his oath would be violated if the Catholics were to be allowed to hold seats in the Irish parliament once more.

67. The feeling that the influence of the Papacy was dead, however, was widely circulated during the debates over Catholic Emancipation in the Irish Commons in both 1792 and 1793. See *Irish Parl. Debs.*, XII (1792) and XIII (1793), *passim*.

68. This idea was a dangerous half-truth based on the unfortunate lack of unity within the Catholic ranks. The timidity of the aristocratic Kenmare wing lent strength to this charge but opposed to it was the temerity of the democratic merchant element headed by Keogh. The breach came in 1792, when Lord Kenmare was publicly repudiated by the Catholic Committee for having addressed the Lord Lieutenant to the effect that the Catholics were in "perfect submission" to the existing laws. Kenmare had also professed Catholic opposition to all forms of agitation. The Kenmare address further had disavowed all the proceedings of the Catholic Committee as well as its authority. See *The Times*, 20 December 1791, and *Lloyd's Evening Post*, 30 January–1 February 1792.
Burke had a very low opinion of Kenmare at this time. Letters to his son contained such references as: "What is that unfortunate man Lord Kenmare doing?" *Corr.*, III, 429; "How comes it that the Roches of Limerick did not sign? Are they Kenmared?" *Ibid.*, p. 444; "He is resolved to preserve a perfect consistency in his folly and meanness." *Ibid.*, IV, 26.

69. There was strong feeling against this class in England on the part of the defenders of the status quo. The conservative *Times* said that they were the friends of the French Revolution and the descendants of those who had martyred Charles I. Furthermore, they would decapitate every king in the world so that they could rule despotically. Parliament ought to watch them

closely. They had dispersed "millions of artful books" and established "thousands of Republican Schools" to train the next generation to overthrow the government. 8 November 1792.

70. *Burke MSS*, Sheffield.

71. *Corr.*, III, 429.

72. *Ibid.*, p. 439 f. Although Burke does not seem to think very highly of the letter, a contemporary says that it was "of material importance to the history of the progress of Catholic emancipation." Francis Plowden, *Historical Review of the State of Ireland* (London, 1803), vol. II, pt. II, p. 338 n.

73. Westmorland to Pitt, 1 January 1792, "Private & Secret." Pitt Papers, G.D. 8/331 quoted in Harlow, *Founding of Second British Empire*, pp. 635 f.

74. Westmorland to Dundas, 14 January 1792, Home Office 100/36, quoted in Harlow, p. 637.

75. Burke had furnished Langrishe with "all the letters and publications written on the subject by Catholics and others." Plowden, *Historical Review of Ireland*, vol. II, pt. II, p. 338 n. But it was to no avail.

76. *Corr.*, III, 486 ff. See also *The Report of the Committee Appointed by the Society of the United Irishmen of Dublin to Enquire into, and Report the Popery Laws in Force in that Kingdom* (Dublin printed. London reprinted, 1792).

77. Richard to Burke, [post 19 February 1792].

78. The petition is printed in *Corr.*, III, 427 f.

79. *Corr.*, III, pp. 427 ff.

80. Richard to Burke, [post 19 February 1792].

81. *An Address from the General Committee of Roman Catholics to their Protestant Fellow Subjects, and to the Public in General, etc.* (Dublin printed. London reprinted, 1792). Burke ordered this printing.

82. *Corr.*, III, 440.

83. *Ibid.*, p. 418.

84. Richard to Burke, [post 19 February 1792].

85. *The Times*, 28 February 1792.

86. John King, Undersecretary of State for the Home Department, to Burke, 11 February 1792; Dundas to Burke, 11 February 1792, *Burke MSS*, Lamport Hall.

87. Burke to Richard, 19 February 1792, *Corr.*, III, 414.

88. *Ibid.*, III, 417.

89. Richard to Will Burke, 17 August, 1792.

90. 20 March 1792.

91. *Corr.*, III, 496. Richard admitted that he might have been "a few inches within the body of the House." See Sir Jonah Barrington, *Personal Sketches of His Own Times* (3 ed., London, 1871), I, 188.

92. Richard to Burke, [post 19 February 1792].

VII PARTIAL CATHOLIC EMANCIPATION

1. Richard to John King, [? August 1793].

2. Dundas to Richard, 21 March 1792.

3. 23 March 1792, *Corr.*, III, 451–455.

4. Richard to Burke, April 1792.

5. *Corr.*, III, 456 ff.

6. 17 May 1792.

7. Burke MSS, Sheffield.

8. 16 May 1792.

9. *Life of Theobald Wolfe Tone*, ed. William T. W. Tone (2 vols., Washington, 1826), I, 166

10. 28 May 1792.

11. *Corr.*, III, 455–466.

12. Burke MSS, Sheffield.

13. *Loc. cit.*

14. 26 July 1792.

15. Burke to Richard, 29 July 1792.

16. 1 August 1792

17. *The Times*, 15 September 1792.

18. *Life of Tone*, I, 163. Tone himself was also handsomely treated by the Catholics. When they dissolved their body in 1793, he received £1500. *Lloyd's Evening Post*, 3–6 May 1793.

19. August 1792.

20. *The Times*, 15 September 1792; *Lloyd's Evening Post*, 14–17 September 1792. This report of Richard's arrival in the London press indicates that there was some interest there in his return to Ireland.

21. Richard to Edmund and Jane Burke, 3 September 1792.

22. *Lloyd's Evening Post*, 19–21 September 1792.

23. 9 September 1792, *Corr.*, IV, 17.

24. *The Times*, 17 September 1792.

25. *Corr.*, III, 523.

26. *Ibid.*, IV, 28 f. For another example of this belief of Burke's, on the source of Ireland's wrongs, see *Burke-Laurence Corr.*, p. 103.

27. Robertson, *Lectures on Burke*, p. 336.

28. E.g., Lecky, *Irish Hist.*, III, *passim;* Hayden and Moonan, *Short History of Irish People*, pp. 420–530.

29. See letter to Hussey, 1 January 1796: "Dreadful as it is, but it is now plain that Catholic *defenderism* is the only restraint upon Protestant *ascendency*." *Corr.*, IV, 330; *Edinburgh Review*, XLVI (October 1827), 289.

30. *Corr.*, III, 527.

31. 29 September 1792, *ibid.*, IV, 9–16.

32. See above, Chapter VI, pp. 171–173.

33. Burke MSS, Sheffield. This failure to date his letters more exactly was an annoying habit of Richard's and his father complained of it more than once.

34. For a good discussion of Burke and the British Constitution, see Annie M. Osborn, *Rousseau and Burke; a Study of the Idea of Liberty in Eighteenth-Century Thought* (London, 1940), ch. viii.

35. *Corr.*, IV, 17.

36. Burke to Fitzwilliam, 5 October 1792.

37. 10 October 1792.

38. 14 October 1792.

39. 17 October 1792, *Corr.*, IV, 19–24.

40. 2 November 1792, *ibid.*, pp. 24–29.
41. 6 November 1792, *ibid.*, pp. 30–37.
42. 19 November 1792.
43. He had a brother who was a Brigadier-General in the American forces under George Washington.
44. Richard to Burke, [ante 21 November 1792].
45. 25 November 1792, *Corr.*, IV, 37–42.
46. *The Times*, 10 December 1792.
47. 3 December 1792.
48. See, e.g., J. B. Burgess to Lord Grenville, 16 October 1792, *Fortescue MSS*, II, 323.
49. *The Times*, 23 October 1792.
50. The petition is attached to a pamphlet printed by the General Committee entitled *A Vindication of the Conduct and Principles of the Catholics of Ireland* (London, 1793), pp. 78–85.
51. Upper Ossory to Burke, 19 December 1792, *Corr.*, IV, 58–61.
52. *Lloyd's Evening Post*, 14–17 December 1792.
53. *The Times*, 19 December 1792.
54. E.g., 18 December 1792, *Corr.*, IV, 46–57; "end of 1792," *ibid.*, pp. 61–64; and [December 1792], *ibid.*, pp. 97–111.
55. *Ibid.*, pp. 65–96.
56. Catholics were excluded from the Irish parliament by an English act of 1691 (3 William and Mary, c.2). They were deprived of their right of voting at elections by an Irish act of 1727 (2 George II, c.9).
57. (1) "The Roman Catholics of the kingdom shall enjoy such privileges in the exercise of their religion as are consistent with the laws of Ireland, or as they did in the reign of Charles II.
(2) And all right, title, and interest, — privileges and immunities, — which they were lawfully entitled to in the reign of Charles II."
58. *Lloyd's Evening Post*, 24–26 December 1792.
59. *Ibid.*, 2–4 January 1793; *The Times*, 3 January 1793.
60. *The Times*, 5, 7, 10, 15 January 1793.
61. Quoted in Harlow, *Founding of Second British Empire*, p. 638.
62. *Corr.*, IV, 113–122.
63. This was a widely circulated phobia. For example, *The Times*, 23 October 1792, noted that if Catholics were allowed to sit in the Irish Commons, it would become a "Papist House." This, in turn, would result in the overthrow of the Established Church of Ireland.
64. "I have no idea of a liberty unconnected with honesty and justice. Nor do I believe that any good constitutions of government, or of freedom can find it necessary for their security to doom any part of the people to a permanent slavery." *Works*, II, 416.
65. *Ibid.*, VI, 387–412.
66. A year later he wrote to his friend William Windham that the Ascendancy's corruption, so harmful to Ireland, was now in danger of ruining the entire British Empire. *The Diary of William Windham*, ed. Mrs. Henry Baring (London, 1866), p. 331.
67. Lit., "an honorable name is placed upon a vice."
68. Lit., "slightly altered."

69. Charles Sheridan defined Protestant Ascendancy in the Irish Commons to mean "a Protestant King, to whom only, being a Protestant, they owned allegiance; a Protestant House of Peers, composed of Protestant Lords Spiritual in Protestant succession; of Protestant Lords Temporal with Protestant inheritance; and a Protestant House of Commons elected by Protestant constituents, a Protestant legislature, a Protestant judiciary, a Protestant executive, in all and each of their varieties, degrees, and gradations." *Irish Parl. Debs.*, XII (1792), 134 f.

Sheridan once referred to Richard Burke, Jr. as "the nuncio of the British Minister to the Irish Catholics." *Belfast Northern Star*, 18–22 February 1792.

70. It was an unshaken conviction of Burke's, held from the days of the Whiteboy disturbances, that the motive for all Catholic risings in Ireland had always been economic and not religious.

71. Lecky, *Irish Hist.*, III, 150, says that the Castle, by using its influence instead of opposing the amendment, could have insured its success.

72. Butler, *Memoir of the English Catholics*, IV, 63.

73. *Corr.*, IV, 123.

74. *Ibid.*, p. 128. In a postscript omitted by the editors of Burke's correspondence, Grattan severely castigated the Irish Chancellor, Fitzgibbon, an enemy of the Catholics. Burke MSS, Sheffield.

75. Grattan, *Life*, IV, 112.

76. As might be expected, Richard was quite proud of himself. As he had earlier told his "uncle" Will Burke, "I have, in my Irish expedition, made a kind of essay on the public stage, and upon the whole, I have left a tolerably good impression." *Corr.*, III, 487.

In view of all the conflicting contemporary estimates of Richard together with the division of opinion among later commentators, it is difficult to reach a balanced estimate of him.

For favorable estimates, the following may be consulted: *Diary and Letters of Madame d'Arblay*, ed. Charlotte Barrett (London, 1904–1905), II, 159; *Life of Johnson: Boswell's Life of Johnson*, ed. George Birkbeck Hill, rev. ed. L. F. Powell (Oxford, 1934), IV, 219; Bisset, *Burke*, II, 405; Von Sybel, "Edmund Burke und Irland," I, 482 f.

For the opposite, consult: *Johnsonian Miscellanies*, ed. George Birkbeck Hill (Oxford, 1897), II, 32 n.; *Life of Tone*, I, 165 f., 179; Grattan, *Life*, IV, 93; Lecky, *Irish Hist.*, III, 56; Sir Roger Therry, *A Letter to the Right Hon. George Canning on the Present State of the Catholic Question* (2 ed. London, 1827), p. 61.

78. *The Times*, 30 April 1793.

79. Two years later, when the parliamentary privilege was again denied, it was stated that this group had "a very liberal way of thinking in respect to religion, and pay but little respect to the authority of the POPE." Hence, no harm would come from them. However, "the lower and middling class of people, who make up the greatest part of the inhabitants, are as strongly attached to the absurdities of the Church of Rome, as they were a century past, and would go as great lengths now as they ever did in support of them." This, it was said, was the strongest objection to reopening parliament to the Catholics. *Ibid.*, 16 May 1795.

VIII THE PROJECTED IRISH VICEROYSHIP OF FITZWILLIAM

1. *Correspondence of Edmund Burke & William Windham*, ed. J. P. Gilson (Cambridge, 1910), pp. 64 ff. [Hereafter cited as *Burke-Windham Corr.*] Hippisley (afterwards Sir John), attached to the British embassy at Naples, had commenced negotiations with the Vatican over various matters of common interest. In a previous letter which he had written to Burke, Hippisley told him that the *Reflections* "is as well known at the Vatican as at St. James's" and that it "has become a Roman Classic." 18 September [?] 1793, Burke MSS, Lamport Hall.

2. Fox's organ, the *Morning Chronicle*, later stated (21 March 1795) that in the first three years of the war against France the Irish Catholics had contributed one hundred and twenty thousand men contrasted with some ten thousand members of the Church of Ireland who fought for Britain.

3. The Catholic prelates later justified Burke's praise by their formal pledge of unqualified allegiance to the king. *The Times*, 22 January 1794.

4. A basic reason for Catholic opposition on the whole was dissatisfaction over the small number of Catholic officers. *Ibid.*, 19 June 1793.

5. His son's thoughts, however, were very much on Ireland, especially his late mission for the Catholics. His letters in this connection attempted to make a defense of his conduct in that business. They were long, heated, and rambling, and both Dundas and John King considered one of them "strange." For this correspondence, see, e.g., Richard to John King, [August 1793]; Richard to King, 26 October 1793; and Hobart to Richard, Richard to Dundas and Hobart at this time, which may be found in the Public Record Office, London.

6. [Post 30 December 1793].

7. 15 January 1794.

8. Burke to unknown, 6 June 1794.

9. *Morning Chronicle*, 24 July 1794.

10. As early as 3 and 6 December 1792, *The Times* had devoted editorials to urging this union. It would have taken place earlier but for the death of the Duchess of Portland. *Ibid.*, 3 July 1794.

Fox's organ, the leading opposition paper, was most uncomplimentary and called the new administration a "Hotch Potch" and a "motley cabinet." *Morning Chronicle*, 10, 12, 21 July 1794.

11. *The Times*, 19 July 1794.

12. *Ibid.*, 12 July 1794.

13. F. J. C. Hearnshaw, "Burke and Sublimated Common Sense," *Some Great Political Idealists of the Christian Era* (London, 1937), p. 190.

14. He had served previously in this position in 1782.

15. The vote was 50–21. By prearrangement, Burke then returned thanks to the House for the honor. *Morning Chronicle*, 21 June 1794.

16. 21 June 1794.

17. 24 June 1794.

18. 25 June 1794. In a letter of the same date, Pitt used similar language in notifying Burke of his appointment to the Chiltern Hundreds when he wrote: "You could not easily have imposed on me a task which I should

execute with more regret, nor am I prepared for my defense if I [am] charged (with being accessory to depriving the House of one of its greatest ornaments, and the public of the continuance of services for which it is already so deeply indebted). Allow me at least to take the opportunity of expressing for myself the sentiments of Respect and Gratitude, with which I trust those services will long be recollected by all who feel for the honour and interests of the country." Burke MSS, Lamport Hall.

19. 27 June 1794.

20. See Fitzwilliam to Richard, 8 August 1793; Richard to Fitzwilliam, 11 and 16 August 1793; Fitzwilliam to Richard, 27 August 1793; and Richard to Fitzwilliam, 31 August 1793.

21. Burke to Fitzwilliam, 28 June 1794.

22. *Morning Chronicle*, 8 July 1794.

23. *The Times*, 3, 10, 23 July 1794.

24. Sir Gilbert Elliot, a friend of Burke's, once wrote his wife concerning a man who became Irish Chief Secretary: "Fitzherbert's taste is so good and delicate, and his health so bad and delicate, that I think he cannot possibly survive it. That office requires nerves and bad taste, as Windham proved by flying from it." *Burke-Windham Corr.*, p. 1 n.

25. A very poignant elegy signed W[alker]. K[ing]. appeared in the papers acquainting the public with Burke's great loss. *The Times*, 4 August 1794; *Morning Chronicle*, 4 August 1794.

26. Later, however, his pessimism over the affairs of Ireland caused him to declare to Windham that he had begun to think that God had taken away "what was dearest to me to Himself in a good time." *Windham Diary*, p. 330.

27. *Burke-Laurence Corr.*, p. 31.

28. [Post 4 August 1794].

29. *Works*, V, 208.

30. *Ibid.*, VI, 415–429.

31. *Burke-Laurence Corr.*, p. 253.

32. *Morning Chronicle*, 14 November 1794.

33. *The Times*, 15 August 1794, said that Burke's appointment would be very popular in Ireland. See also *ibid.*, 11 August and 26 September.

34. 15 August 1794, *Corr.*, IV, 227.

35. 17 August 1794, *Burke-Windham Corr.*, p. 119.

36. 17 September 1794, Pierpont Morgan Library.

37. 31 August 1794.

38. 31 August 1794.

39. Burke to Pitt, 31 August 1794, Public Record Office, London.

40. 31 August 1794.

41. 9 September 1794.

42. 14 September 1794.

43. 23 September 1794.

44. 26 September 1794.

45. Had this been accomplished, the misunderstanding which arose to blight Fitzwilliam's tenure of office would have been obviated.

46. 1 October 1794.

47. *Burke-Windham Corr.*, pp. 122 ff.

48. *Ibid.*, p. 128.
49. *Windham Diary*, p. 329.
50. *Loc. cit.*
51. Loughborough, a Scot, was the former Alexander Wedderburn.
52. Burke to Loughborough, [ante 3 October] 1794.
53. This is an apparent reference to Fitzwilliam's wish to get rid of the powerful Irish Chancellor, Fitzgibbon, one of the worst enemies of the Catholics. The matter will be discussed below.
54. 15 October 1794.
55. 16 October 1794, *Burke-Windham Corr.*, pp. 132–138.
56. Fitzwilliam had earlier written Grattan that a change of viceroys was being contemplated, and the news had spread throughout Ireland. Grattan, *Life*, IV, 173.
57. "Not government but a great plunder."
58. 18 October 1794.
59. 20 October 1794, *Burke-Windham Corr.*, pp. 140–141.
60. "Even to the point of destruction."
61. 21 October 1794.
62. 21 October 1794.
63. 7 November 1794.
64. Burke MSS, Sheffield.
65. George Ponsonby (1755–1817) was the third son of the Rt. Hon. John Ponsonby (son of the Earl of Bessborough and of Lady Elizabeth Cavendish, daughter of the Duke of Devonshire). The Ponsonby family, thanks to its great alliances and the natural ability of many of its members, was a great power in Ireland.

George Ponsonby was called to the bar in 1780. Two years later through the influence of his father, a former Speaker of the Irish House who was nicknamed Jack Promise, and the Duke of Portland, he was admitted to the inner bar and given the post of first Counsel to the Commissioners of Revenue. He had entered the Irish parliament in 1776 where he served until its independent existence was terminated. From 1801 until his death, he was a member of the imperial parliament. During the brief viceroyship of Portland in 1782, he was Chancellor of the Exchequer. Because of his strong stand in favor of the Prince of Wales in the Regency crisis in 1789, he was deprived of his office in the revenue board by the Lord Lieutenant, the Marquis of Buckingham. In 1792 he took a conservative position on the Catholic bill, arguing for the need of time to allow recent concessions to take their proper effect and for a fuller system of education before the Catholics should be entrusted with political power. In 1793, however, he strongly favored the Catholic measure of that year. He was slated to become Attorney-General during Fitzwilliam's viceroyalty, but the latter's swift recall killed this prospect of returning to office. He later became Lord Chancellor of Ireland in 1806 under the brief Fox-Grenville coalition. Married to Mary Butler, eldest daughter of the Earl of Lanesborough, he died in London leaving no male issue and one daughter.

William Brabazon Ponsonby (1744–1806) was the eldest son of the Rt. Hon. John Ponsonby and his wife. He entered the Irish Commons in 1764 and served until the union with Great Britain in 1801, whereupon he was elected to the imperial parliament. Married to Louisa, fourth daughter of Viscount Molesworth, he was appointed Joint Postmaster-General of Ireland and made a member of the Irish Privy Council in 1784. Because of his part in the Regency affair, he, like his brother, was deprived of office in 1789 by Buckingham. An original member of the Whig Club, founded in Dublin 1789, he was recommended by Fitzwilliam to be his principal Secretary of State in 1795. After five years in the British House of Commons, he was created Baron Ponsonby of Imokilly in 1806 and elevated to the House of Lords. His death occurred that same year.

66. Lecky, *Irish Hist.*, III, 261. This is also the view of Harlow, *Founding of Second British Empire*, p. 640.

67. [Post 18 November 1794].

68. Fitzwilliam's nephew, Lord Milton, who was his Irish Chief Secretary, wrote Burke from Dublin on 15 December 1794 that should he ever have "some protégé to recommend," he could be certain of Milton's delight in obliging him.

IX FITZWILLIAM'S BRIEF AND TRAGIC TENURE OF OFFICE

1. John Beresford (1738–1805) was the second son of Marcus, Earl of Tyrone, and Lady Catherine, Baroness de La Poer. He graduated from Trinity in 1757 and was called to the bar in 1760 but never practiced. He entered parliament in 1761 as a member for Waterford, a constituency which he represented for the rest of his life, first in the Irish and later in the imperial parliament. In 1768 he was made a Privy Councillor and in 1770 became one of the Commissioners of Revenue. He married Constantia Ligondes of Auvergne, niece of the Countess of Moira who persuaded her to go to Ireland rather than enter the convent as she had planned. Following his wife's death, Beresford remarried in 1774. His second wife was Barbara Montgomery, a celebrated beauty whom Sir Joshua Reynolds depicted with her sisters, Lady Mountjoy and the Marchioness of Townshend, as the "Graces" in his famous painting. This marriage greatly aided Beresford's career. In 1780 he became first Commissioner of Revenue and was responsible for notable improvements in the architecture of government buildings and in the street layout of Dublin.

In 1786 Beresford was made a British Privy Councillor, an indication of the importance attached to him by Pitt. Until John Fitzgibbon superseded him as the leading Irishman in Pitt's estimation, Beresford was virtually entrusted with the management of Irish affairs by the British government. Even after Fitzgibbon's rise, Beresford ran him a close second. Related by marriage the two cooperated harmoniously and together their advice shaped Britain's political policy toward Ireland. The father of seventeen children by his two marriages, Beresford had a brother who was an earl, another an archbishop and a baron; one nephew an archbishop and primate, and another a lieutenant-general. Space precludes listing the posts held by his offspring or the important marriages they made. Suffice to say that among his descendants half a century after his death, there were an archbishop, bishop, colonial governor, knight of the Legion of Honor, Privy Councillor, and several high ranking officers.

2. "There is in Ireland a numerous tribe, well known by the name of the FAMILY, who have been so long in the habit of living in splendour and opulence at the expense of the public, that they at length begin to think of their places as an inheritance." *Morning Chronicle*, 30 March 1795. Beresford proudly admitted that he had been told that he was considered "the King of Ireland." *The Correspondence of John Beresford*, ed. William Beresford (2 vols., London, 1854), II, 51.

3. Fitzwilliam MSS, Sheffield.

4. According to Grattan, "Mr. Beresford's injuries, are a pension of 2000 in addition to a former pension of 1000 with a place in the law of 2000 to one son & various places in the revenue to another & a Bishoprick to his brother of 5000 & [not clear] to the amount of 4000 — the various injuries heaped on Mr. Beresford which animate so justly the english cabinet in their leisure at the present moment are calculated from 12000 to 13000 a year & these include no secret fortune by a clandestine job suspected tho' not proved — the services for which Mr. Beresford has obtained these gifts are the compound of his capacities as commissioner of the treasury, commissioner of revenue, store-keeper, banker that is to say in the person of his son & dealer in the sale of public ground." Grattan to Burke, 11 March 1795.

5. Von Sybel, "Edmund Burke und Irland," I, 489 f.

6. 29 January 1795, *Corr.*, IV, 266–269.

7. 4 February 1795, *ibid.*, p. 270.

8. Fitzwilliam to Portland, 15 January 1795, Fitzwilliam MSS, Sheffield.

9. John Fitzgibbon (1749–1802) was the son of a man originally destined for the Catholic priesthood but who had conformed. The elder Fitzgibbon served many years in the Irish parliament and amassed a fortune of over £ 100,000 from his extensive legal practice. The son, a contemporary in college of Henry Grattan's, graduated from Trinity in 1767, took an M.A. at Oxford in 1770, and was called to the Irish bar in 1772. In 1778 he entered the Irish House as a member for the University of Dublin. Because of the unrestrained severity of the language with which he habitually denounced opponents, he was nicknamed "Fitzpetulant," although in some circles he is remembered as "Black Jack." His father's great wealth enabled him to make advantageous marriages for his daughters, one of whom married a member of the Beresford family who became Archbishop of Tuam and a peer. This connection helped the career of John Fitzgibbon by gaining him the friendship of the powerful John Beresford. In 1783 Fitzgibbon became Attorney-General, then the most influential office open to a lawyer short of the Lord Chancellorship for which only Englishmen were deemed eligible.

In 1786 Fitzgibbon married the eldest daughter of a vehement anti-Catholic known as "Burn-Chapel" Whaley because of his fondness for destroying Catholic houses of worship in the aftermath of peasant uprisings. A brother of his wife was a well-known character Jerusalem Whaley, so-called because of winning a bet that he would play ball against the walls of Jerusalem and return to Dublin in what was then considered an impossibly short time.

As a reward for his unflinching loyalty to Dublin Castle and Pitt in the Regency crisis in 1789, Fitzgibbon achieved a distinction never before conferred upon an Irishman. He was made Lord Chancellor of Ireland. His appointment was well received throughout Ireland, indicating that the widespread hatred he aroused grew more from his subsequent actions. At the same time he was created Baron Fitzgibbon; in 1793 was raised to Viscount; and in 1795 became Earl of Clare. When the union took place in 1801, his peerage was changed to that of the United Kingdom. His bitter anti-Catholicism together with his role in the union stirred up national hatred for him to such an extent that his funeral was marked by some of the most unruly scenes ever witnessed in Ireland, culminating when a dead cat was thrown on his coffin.

There are no biographies of Fitzgibbon whose papers were destroyed in 1802 by orders in his will. See, however, Falkiner, *Studies in Irish Hist.*, pp. 101–154 and J. R. O'Flanagan, *Lives of the Lord Chancellors of Ireland* (London, 1870), II, 156–283. Robert E. Burns has unearthed considerable material for his "The Political Career of John Fitzgibbon: a Study in Anglo-Irish Politics, 1790–1802," a Harvard Ph.D. dissertation presently uncompleted.

10. 29 January 1795, Fitzwilliam MSS, Sheffield.

11. *The Times*, 2 February 1795.

12. 20 January 1795, *Corr.*, IV, 260–266.

13. *Works*, VI, 363–373. It was finished at "Twelve at night." Prior says that Burke's reply was shown by Smith to various people and found its way into Dublin press without the knowledge or consent of either Smith or Burke. Prior, *Burke*, p. 412.

There are two copies of the reply in the British Museum, a fourteen page version in the New York Public Library, and an incomplete draft at Sheffield. The latter reveals Burke in a fit of melancholy. Smith was informed that he was disabled from business owing to the tragic loss of his son and that "the existence I have I do not know that I should call life: & accordingly I am not consulted upon any one measure of Government whatsoever, though, for what reasons I know not you suppose me deeply in the Secret." He had seen Fitzwilliam two or three times before the latter went to Ireland but all he could say was that he knew the viceroy's "perfectly pure intentions" toward Ireland and the mass of its people, whose management would make either for Ireland's strength or weakness. But as to the specific measures contemplated, Burke was "in the most complete ignorance about them, as I am of all measures here more perhaps than any man. I do not even read the newspapers, nor have not for several months. I hear too much, in spite of me, from the few friends that come hither (for I have no house or lodging in Town) of what is going on."

14. See *The Times*, 6 March 1795.

15. A favorite opinion of Burke's. See, e.g., "Burke's Table-Talk," VII, 8.

16. See, e.g., *The Times*, 19, 24 March 1795.

17. 3 February 1795, Fitzwilliam MSS, Sheffield.

18. After his recall, in his published letter to Lord Carlisle, mentioned below, Fitzwilliam said of Beresford that "I decided at once not to cloud the dawn of my administration by leaving, in such power and authority, so much imputed malversation."

19. Earl Stanhope, *Life of the Right Honourable William Pitt* (London, 1861–1862), II, xxiii–xxv.

20. Portland to Fitzwilliam, 8 February 1795, Fitzwilliam MSS, Sheffield.
21. 9 February 1795, *loc. cit.*
22. *Loc. cit.*
23. *Loc. cit.*
24. 12 February 1795, *loc. cit.*
25. *Morning Chronicle*, 2 March 1795.
26. Hussey to Burke, 19 February 1795, *Corr.*, IV, 277–281.
27. Fitzwilliam to Pitt, 12 February 1795, Fitzwilliam MSS, Sheffield.
28. Fitzwilliam to Portland, 12 February 1795, *loc. cit.*
29. 16 February 1795, *loc. cit.*
30. 18 February 1795, *loc. cit.*
31. 20 February 1795, *loc. cit.*
32. Portland to Fitzwilliam, 21 February 1795, *loc. cit.*
33. Pitt to Fitzwilliam, 21 February 1795, *loc. cit.*
34. *Loc. cit.*
35. Fitzwilliam to Portland, 25 February 1795, *loc. cit.*
36. Fitzwilliam to Portland, 28 February 1795, *loc. cit.*
37. He subsequently refused. Fitzwilliam to Grattan, 25 April 1795, *loc. cit.*
38. 10 February 1795.
39. 19 February 1795.
40. Macknight, *Burke*, III, 620.
41. 26 February 1795, *Corr.*, IV, 282 f.
42. 27 February 1795, *ibid.*, pp. 283–285.
43. [Ante 2 March 1795].
44. 4 March 1795.
45. *Burke-Windham Corr.*, p. 156.
46. Fitzwilliam to Burke, 9 March 1795.
47. Hussey to Burke, 3 March 1795, *Corr.*, IV, 288.
48. Speech of Sir Lawrence Parsons, 26 February 1795, *Irish Parl. Debs.*, XV (1795), 133 f.
49. *Morning Chronicle*, 4 March 1795.
50. *The Times*, 7 March 1795.
51. *Morning Chronicle*, 4 March 1795.
52. 5 March 1795, *Corr.*, IV, 289–291.
53. If he saw Portland on this occasion, as seems likely, it was the last time in about a year that they met. Burke told John Noble, 24 February 1796, that it had been eleven months or more since he had last seen Portland. Huntington Library, Em HM 22475.
54. 10 March 1795, *Corr.*, IV, 292.
55. *The Times*, 9, 12, 31 March 1795.
56. Byrne and Keogh to Burke, 19 March 1795, *Corr.*, IV, 306.
57. *Morning Chronicle*, 31 March 1795.
58. 14 March 1795.
59. *Morning Chronicle*, 6 April 1795.
60. *Ibid.*, 9 April 1795.
61. 14 March 1795, *Corr.*, IV, 293.
62. 11 March 1795.
63. Burke's unfortunate language here has been interpreted by one of

his recent biographers as an example of grovelling on his part. See Magnus, *Burke*, p. 110. I would, however, suggest that Burke was merely indulging in the sorrowful and remorseful mood still gripping him since his son's death.

64. 14 March 1795.

65. Fitzwilliam to Burke, 21 March 1795, Fitzwilliam MSS, Sheffield.

66. 20 March 1795, *loc. cit.*

67. Fitzwilliam to Burke, 3 April 1795, *loc. cit.*

68. Burke to Fitzwilliam, [12 April 1795], *loc. cit.*

69. See above, pp. 250–253.

70. Burke MSS, Sheffield.

71. Grattan, *Life*, IV, 210.

72. George III to Pitt, 29 April 1795, Pitt MSS, 104, quoted in Donald Grove Barnes, *George III and William Pitt, 1783–1806* (Stanford, 1939), p. 352.

73. Burke to Fitzwilliam, 10 May 1795.

74. 15 May 1795.

75. Among Fitzwilliam's papers at Sheffield, there is a statement in his own handwriting of his declaration in the House of Lords on 19 March 1799. He admitted that "I had never receiv'd orders to bring forward the Catholick Emancipation." But, he said, at the time he had "enter'd the most solemn protest against resisting on the part of Government, that Question; should it be brought forward from any other quarter, & I made the most distinct, unequivocal declarations, that in that case, it should receive my full & decided support. With these declarations so made, I was permitted to assume the Government." See *Parl. Hist.*, XXXIV (1799), 672.

Lord Grenville, in March 1795, drew up a memorandum putting forth the government's side which differs from Fitzwilliam's interpretation as just given. Grenville says that the matter of Catholic emancipation was considered in a meeting held in December 1794 at which Pitt, Portland, Fitzwilliam, Spencer, Windham, and he, Grenville, were present. Grenville claims that "no decided sentiment as to the line which it might ultimately be right to adopt upon it was expressed by any person present. The result of the discussion was an unanimous opinion that Lord Fitz-William should inform himself in Ireland as to the state and disposition of the country in this respect, and should transmit that information, with his opinion, to the King's servants here; that he should, as much as possible, endeavour to prevent the agitation of the question during the present session; and that, in all events, he should do nothing in it which might commit the King's Government here or in Ireland without fresh instructions from hence. With this subject the conversation finished. At the close of it, Lord Fitz-William, who had brought to the meeting a memorandum of matters to be talked of, was repeatedly asked whether there were any other points to be discussed, or any new measures to be proposed. The answer was that he knew of none." *Fortescue MSS*, III, 38.

76. The whole affair is dramatically related in the Burke MSS, Sheffield. The following are pertinent: Lord John Cavendish to Burke, [28 June 1795]; Portland to Burke, 28 June; Burke to Fitzwilliam, [28 June]; Fitzwilliam to Burke, [30 June]; Burke to Fitzwilliam, 5 July; and Fitzwilliam to Burke,

[post 5 July]. Beresford's interpretation may be found in *The Correspondence of John Beresford*, II, 111–120.

77. E.g., *Burke-Windham Corr.*, p. 154; *Carlisle MSS*, pp. 712, 722; Magnus, *Burke*, p. 281; Falkiner, *Studies in Irish Hist.*, p. 129; and Lord Rosebery, *Pitt* (London, 1895), pp. 174–185.

78. The delay on the part of Portland in replying to Fitzwilliam's clear intention of purpose is a matter which demands careful analysis. For a long time perhaps the most thorough study of the matter was that of Lecky who took the position that Portland's failure to answer Fitzwilliam until it was too late completely justified the latter in pursuing the course of action which he did. In other words, not having heard from the cabinet, Fitzwilliam naturally assumed that his position met at least tacit approval.

The Lecky interpretation was first seriously challenged in a scholarly way by Professor J. Holland Rose, *Pitt and Napoleon: Letters and Essays* (London, 1912), p. 31, who says: "Unfortunately owing to stress of weather a long delay occurred in the despatch of the mails for England, namely, from the 10th to the 23rd January, a fact which fully explains the 'astounding neglect of duty' of the Pitt ministry against which Lecky declaims (*Eng. Hist.*, VII, 70)." Rose bases his discovery of the weather conditions on a letter from Beresford to Auckland, 19 January, which is in the Pitt MSS, 325.

It now remains for us to attempt a judgment on which interpretation is the more convincing. In the first place, it is true that the weather was bad although this cannot be established officially since the Meteorological Office's records of meteorological observations at sea go back only to 1854. However, a file of the newspaper, *The Oracle*, in possession of the National Maritime Museum in Greenwich contains the shipping news of the time. Remember that as early as the 8th, Fitzwilliam informed Portland that emancipation seemed a sure thing, and that Portland had acknowledged receipt of this letter in his reply of the 13th, which made no reference to this observation by Fitzwilliam. Then, on the 15th, Fitzwilliam flatly stated that, since emancipation was certain, he would not oppose it unless he received unmistakable instructions to the contrary. If the weather was good, it took from three to four days at that time for a letter from Dublin to reach London or vice versa. Thus, with favorable weather, Fitzwilliam's letter would have reached London by the 18th or 19th.

In *The Oracle's* reports of the Irish mails, we find that since 18 January was a Sunday there was no paper printed but that from the 19th no mails from Dublin arrived in London until the 27th when two came in followed by nine more on the 28th. Thus, the earliest day under the circumstances on which Portland could have received Fitzwilliam's letter of the 15th was the 27th. Recalling that ordinarily it would have been in his hands on Monday, the 19th, the weather thus delayed it a matter of only eight days.

Investigation of the Home Office files pretty well establishes 27 January as the day on which Portland received Fitzwilliam's letter since a despatch from John King, the Home Office Undersecretary, to Lord Milton, Fitzwilliam's Chief Secretary, says that on 27 January he received the latter's letters "dated 12th 14th 15th & 17th inst." It would seem logical that Fitzwilliam's of the 15th to Portland was in the same mail, although the Home Office files unfortunately do not contain a record of it. The only acknowledgments by Portland of receipt of Fitzwilliam's despatches for this period are dated 19 January for a letter of the 7th and 27 January for one of the 22nd.

In the light of the foregoing, I cannot see how Lecky's position has been seriously challenged by the later interpretation of Professor Rose and therefore it is my feeling that Fitzwilliam was justified in concluding that the British government had no objections to Catholic emancipation since it was the wish of the Irish parliament.

79. *Second Letter from Earl Fitzwilliam . . . to the Earl of Carlisle* (2 ed., reprinted, London, 1795), p. 24.

80. *Irish Parl. Debs.*, XV (1795), 175.

81. *Ibid.*, p. 192.

82. 21 March 1795.

83. Grattan to Burke, 11 March 1795.

84. *The Letters of King George III*, ed. Bonamy Dobrée (London, 1935), pp. 234 f.; Stanhope, *Life of Pitt*, II, xxiv.

85. Barnes, *George III and Pitt*, p. 345.

86. Hardy, *Life of Charlemont*, II, 347 f. The Society of United Irishmen was founded at Belfast in October 1791. At first, it aimed simply at a political union of Catholics and Dissenters, but the real goal emerged as a desire to emulate the French and establish an Irish republic freed from connection with Britain.

87. *Morning Chronicle*, 25 April 1795.

88. This was also the expressed opinion of Charles Fox. See *Fox's Correspondence*, III, 100 f.

X THE END OF A "GREAT, JUST, AND HONOURABLE CAUSE," 1795–1797

1. Burke to Malone, 22 May 1795, Pierpont Morgan Library, New York. See also Burke to John Coxe Hippisley, 22 May 1795, Historical Manuscripts Commission, *Ninth Report* (London, 1884), p. 486.

2. Burke to Hussey, 17 March 1795, *Corr.*, IV, 295–306.

3. Grattan, *Life*, IV, 155. For Grattan's views, which coincided with Burke's, see *ibid.*, pp. 155 f.; *Corr.*, IV, 244 f.

4. See note 2.

5. "To command . . . opinion, the first step is to establish a dominion over those who direct it." *Works*, III, 378.

6. In the *Reflections* when speaking of the possibility of elected bishops in the Anglican Church, he said that it would cause "the utter ruin of the clerical character, the most dangerous shock that the state ever received through a misunderstood arrangement of religion." *Ibid.*, p. 429.

7. Burke to Hussey, 28 November 1795, *Corr.*, IV, 328. Although the cornerstone had been laid before this, the plans for the building had not been fully completed.

The maintenance problem proved a thorny one. Speaking on it in the Irish House of Lords on 11 April 1799, Fitzgibbon delivered one of his typical anti-Catholic speeches, saying "that the object of limiting the amount to 25£ a year for each student, was, that they should be from the lowest class of society, and thus the priesthood of Ireland would continue to be taken from the dregs of the people." Quoted in O'Flanagan, *Irish Chancellors*, II, 258.

8. An unusual occurrence was the presentation by Grattan of a Catholic petition protesting against the institution's being exclusively Catholic. *Irish Parl. Debs.*, XV (1795), 201 ff.

9. Troy to Burke, 13 July 1795.

10. Von Sybel, "Burke und Irland," I, 492.

11. For a sympathetic account of the meeting, see *Morning Chronicle*, 15 April 1795.

12. *Authentic Statement of the Proceedings of the Roman Catholics of Dublin, April 9, 1795* (London, [1795]), p. 10.

13. Burke to Hussey, 18 May 1795, *Corr.*, IV, 308–317.

14. There are but two instances of this language in the *Authentic Statement* of the Catholics: (1) mention was made of "that wonderful revolution which has taken place in France"; (2) a speech by a Mr. Lewines stressed "the rights of the People." These are on pp. 5 and 31–37, respectively.

15. The Catholics had actually dissolved the General Committee in 1793. The Francis Street meeting was merely local in scope.

16. *Irish Parl. Debs.*, XV (1795), 208–361.

17. *Works*, VI, 377–384.

18. Just as there were Irish and Jacobin "factions," so, too, there was a dangerous one operating in Indian affairs. Burke to Dundas, 25 March 1787, Princeton University Library, AM 11349.

19. Lit., "oh, the dryness of studies."

20. 21 June 1795.

21. 26 June 1795.

22. 19 July 1795.

23. Burke to Hussey, 18 January 1796, *Corr.*, IV, 329 f.

24. The Defenders was a Catholic organization whose aim was the protection of the members from the tithe-proctors and others. The movement was quite similar to the earlier Whiteboys and was primarily economic, although religion did enter into it. As the name indicates, it was originally for defensive purposes, but the members were apt to forget this on occasion.

25. Burke to Hussey, December 1796, *Corr.*, IV, 379–401.

26. 5 July 1795.

27. [Post 5 July 1795.]

28. 8 August 1795.

29. 12 August 1795.

30. 31 August 1795.

31. Burke to unknown, 5 January 1796.

32. Peel Collection, Vol. XII, The Pierpont Morgan Library.

33. *Morning Chronicle*, 11 March 1796.

34. *Ibid.*, 1, 13, 14 January; 26 February; 7, 10, 19 March 1796.

35. Note in Burke's handwriting, The Pierpont Morgan Library.

36. Magnus, *Burke*, p. 271.

37. Lit., "I press forward against adversity."

38. *Works*, V, 133–169.

39. Back in 1785 there had been bad relations in Armagh between the Protestant Peep-of-Day Boys and the Catholic Defenders which grew out

of a series of burnings of Catholic farms and chapels by the Presbyterian common people of the area. In September 1795, a new clash had taken place at the village of the Diamond in Armagh, and the Catholics had been defeated. A fierce repression was then visited upon them by the victorious Peep-of-Day Boys.

40. 16 January 1796.

41. 18 January 1796, *Corr.*, IV, 329 f.

42. The scarcity of food combined with high prices had led to serious rioting in London in the summer and fall of 1795. On 29 October as the king left to open the session of parliament which had been summoned early due to the crisis, his carriage had to pass over a route which, it is estimated, was crowded with some 200,000 persons. Gradually, shouts of "Give us peace and bread!" "No war!" "No King!" "Down with Him!" "Down with George!" "No Famine!", etc. were raised with increasing vehemence. Opposite the Ordinance Office, a stone or a bullet from an airgun shattered the windowglass of the royal carriage. On his return from the session, the king was treated to a worse display of violence and his carriage was further damaged by the stones of the mob. Near the royal palace the carriage was stopped by a crowd crying bread and peace, and the king was only rescued from possible harm by the intervention of troops.

43. 21 January 1796.

44. *Works*, V, 233–341; 342–383; 384–508.

45. Fitzwilliam said that his pamphlet had many "many converts, and confirmed numbers in your principles." Fitzwilliam to Burke, 10 November 1796, *Corr.*, IV, pp. 356 f.

46. 6 November 1796.

47. 10 November 1796, *Corr.*, IV, 359.

48. 20 November 1796.

49. The threatened invasion of Ireland by the French was actually begun only a month later. An expedition which set sail on 23 December to invade Ireland proved, however, a failure.

50. Arthur O'Connor was a man of considerable ability who came from an excellent family. Along with Thomas Emmet, a lawyer, and Dr. W. J. MacNeven, a Catholic physician, he joined the United Irishmen in the fall of 1796 and soon became one of the leaders. He was later betrayed at Margate while en route to France on 28 February 1798. Along with Emmet and MacNeven, who were captured two weeks later, he was exiled.

51. The first was dated 20 July and merely offered to bring Burke up to date on "the real state of Ireland" since Fitzwilliam's recall. Ireland, too, had its "Robertspiers, the inferior in Talents to their Prototype," and the events in Armagh made it the "la Vendee of Ireland." Keogh was intruding on Burke's time because "I know you are so uncourtly as to be a true Irishman — to Love your Country — may You live long its Ornament & Pride, the defender of Virtue, & of Ireland, & yet See her rise from her persecutions & persecutor's."

The other, dated 16 November, was equally innocuous although briefer. It was a renewed offer to inform Burke firsthand of happenings in Ireland. It was a duty due both Burke and Ireland that he know what was transpiring.

52. Burke to Keogh, 17 November 1796. Burke professed to be "much out of the world." He was obliged to Keogh for his offer to convey news of Ireland to him, "but I really thought you had known that I have no kind of correspondence with that Country, & that for a good While, I had not taken any part whatsoever in its affairs." Furthermore, he had no influence with the government.

In a general way, he admitted that he was "but too well acquainted with the distracted state of Ireland & with the designs of the public Enemy pointed to that Kingdom." Keogh had done him the honor in his July letter to call him a "true Irishman." He himself considered England as "my Country, of long habit, of long obligation, & of establishment, and that my primary duties are here. I cannot conceive how a Man can be a genuine Englishman without being at the same time a true Irishman, tho' fortune should have made his birth on this side of the Water. I think the same Sentiments ought to be reciprocal on the part of Ireland, and if possible with much stronger reason. Ireland cannot be separated one moment from England without loosing [the] source of her present prosperity, & even every hope of her future."

53. 27 November 1796.

54. Fitzgibbon once described the Whig Club in a speech in the Irish Lords as "a porter club, a horde of miscreant traitors professing peace but practicing corruption." Falkiner, *Irish Hist. Studies*, p. 124.

55. Burke to Fitzwilliam, 30 November 1796.

56. Keogh to Burke, 24 November 1796.

57. Laurence agreed to see him but would not go out of his way to do it, "especially suspecting in what hands he is, and knowing his dissatisfaction at your letter." Laurence to Burke, 24 November 1796, *Corr.*, IV, 365.

58. Fitzwilliam to Burke, 5 December 1796, *ibid.*, p. 374.

59. Burke to Fitzwilliam, 7 December 1796. Laurence gave an account of his meeting with Keogh to Fitzwilliam. Much of the information reported by Keogh had already been known by Fitzwilliam except a part "which wounds me to the quick; of which I was apprehensive, & foresaw . . . the lower Orders of Catholicks have lost all confidence, not only in the Government, but in *all publick men*, & in the Gentry of their own persuasion, & even in their own Clergy — Whoever recommends *moderation*, is a false friend, or rather an undoubted enemy They conceive — a mischief, as I s[ai]d before, to have been foreseen, as necessarily arising out of the duplicity of the Govt, but it is a state of mischief, that really drives one to despair . . . that country cannot be saved without the most complete change of *Men* it may produce no effect, but still it is the last, & the *only* chance left. . . ." Fitzwilliam to Burke, 9 December 1796.

60. Fitzwilliam to Burke, 5 December 1796, *Corr.*, IV, 374–377.

61. Burke to Fitzwilliam, 7 December 1796.

62. Burke to Fitzwilliam, [13 December 1796].

63. *Corr.*, IV, 369–373.

64. Burke to Fitzwilliam, 6 December 1796.

65. Fitzwilliam to Burke, [13 December 1796].

66. Fitzwilliam to Burke, 14 December 1796.

67. Burke to Fitzwilliam, 15 December 1796.

68. Henry Lawes Luttrell (1743–1821), second Earl of Carhampton, was both a soldier and a politician. In the latter capacity he served in first the imperial and later the Irish parliament. He began his military career as an ensign at the age of fourteen and enjoyed successive advancements in rank until he stood third in the list of generals at his death in 1821.

At various times he held important military posts in Ireland and in 1795 was given the job of suppressing the Defenders in Connaught. Pursuing a practice of impressing his captives as sailors, he was bitterly criticized. In 1796 he was promoted to the chief command in Ireland and "continued his high-handed policy." (*DNB*, XXXIV, 299).

Lord Camden, the viceroy, wrote Portland on 22 January 1796 that "Carhampton [i.e., Luttrell] did not confine himself to the strict rules of law." (Lecky, *Irish Hist.*, III, 419).

69. Burke to Fitzwilliam, 18 December 1796.

70. Burke to Fitzwilliam, 20 December 1796.

71. Burke to Hussey, undated December 1796, *Corr.*, IV, 379–401.

72. In answering a letter of French Laurence's at this time in which Laurence described Pope Pius VI as a "heroic figure" and expressed the wish that "we had half his spirit," Burke expressed approval. He asserted that, whatever Protestants might think about it, their fate in the face of the common enemy, Bonaparte, was entwined with that of their "great enemy," the pope. The Protestants of the British Isles were cutting their own throats in order to be revenged on "this said old Pope." It was odd that the power which was menacing the world produced in them so little terror while "this poor old bugbear," who frightened nobody and was himself frightened by everybody, was "the great object of terror, of persecution, and of vigorous attack." *Burke-Laurence Corr.*, p. 82.

73. Burke later described the failure of Malmesbury's mission to Windham thus: "The Mongrel has been whipped back to the Kennel yelping and with his tail between his legs." 25 December 1796, *The Windham Papers*, ed. Anon. (2 vols., London, 1913), II, 35.

74. Hussey to Burke, 2 April 1797, *Corr.*, IV, 437–439.

75. 29 December 1796.

76. Burke to Fitzwilliam, 4 [January 1797].

77. November 1796, *Burke-Laurence Corr.*, p. 78.

78. Burke to Laurence, November 1796, *ibid.*, pp. 79–86.

79. [Ante 22 March 1797], *ibid.*, pp. 157–162.

80. [Ante 22 March 1797], *ibid.*, pp. 162–163. A reply from Laurence, 22 March 1797, which was marked "secret," expressed agreement with Burke's views and said that the project had been dropped. *Ibid.*, p. 164.

81. 15 March 1797

82. 30 March 1797, *Corr.*, IV, 431–436.

83. *Auckland Correspondence*, III, 318.

84. Jerningham Collection, Huntington Library.

85. 7 January 1797, *Corr.*, IV, 421.

86. 8 February 1797.

87. There is a copy of the deed in the Pierpont Morgan Library, New York.

88. Burke's original will is preserved in the same place.

89. 26 April 1797.

90. Jane Burke to Mr. Woodford, 8 May 1797, Houghton Library, Harvard University.

91. Burke to Fitzwilliam, 7 May 1797.

92. 15 May 1797.

93. 10 May 1797, *Burke-Windham Corr.*, pp. 245 f.

94. 12 May 1797, *Burke-Laurence Corr.*, pp. 204–218.

95. 21 May 1797, *Corr.*, IV, 448 f.

96. 21 May 1797.

97. This was still his opinion a couple of weeks later. The only thing upon which Pitt was convinced was "a plan of Military coercion." Burke to Fitzwilliam, 4 June 1797.

98. *Works*, VI, 415–429.

99. Burke attributed Hoche's failure at Bantry Bay in December 1796 to "an Arm stronger than ours, and . . . a Wisdom capable of counteracting our Folly." *The Windham Papers*, II, 39.

100. Burke's repeated use of this dilemma to picture the plight of the Catholics might seem overdone, but it was a favorite claim of the anti-Catholics in the Irish parliament. Cf. *Irish Parl. Debs.*, I–XV (1781–1795), *passim*.

101. As must be clear by now, he frequently contradicted himself on this point.

102. Burke to Captain Woodford, 31 May 1797, and Burke to Fitzwilliam, 4 June 1797.

103. Burke to Fitzwilliam, 18 June 1797.

104. He died quite appropriately trying to articulate a blessing. Magnus, *Burke*, p. 296.

A beautiful eulogy written by Walter King, one "who long and intimately knew him," appeared in the newspapers, e.g., *The Times*, 11 July; *London Chronicle*, 8–11 July; *Morning Chronicle*, 10 July; and *Lloyd's Evening Post*, 10–12 July.

105. *Corr.*, IV, 439; *Burke-Laurence Corr.*, pp. 236 f.

XI RETROSPECT

1. *Works*, IV, 230.

2. Burke to Baron Loughborough, [ante 3 October 1794].

3. The late Professor Laski was never noted for his love of conservatives but he had nothing but praise for Burke's devotion to principle. Harold J. Laski, *Political Thought in England from Locke to Bentham* (New York, 1920), p. 225.

4. E.g., *Works*, VI, 337 f.; *ibid.*, III, 240; *Corr.*, II, 437; *ibid.*, IV, 399.

5. *Speeches*, IV, 55.

6. Burke to Windham, 16 October 1794, *Windham Diary*, p. 324. See also *Parl. Hist.*, XXIX (1791–1792), 1381.

7. For a provocative article on this, see Robert M. Hutchins, "The Theory of the State: Edmund Burke," *Review of Politics*, V (April 1943), 139–155.

8. *Corr.*, IV, 3.

9. *Works*, IV, 301.

10. *Corr.*, III, 423.

11. Lennox, *Burkes politisches Arbeitsfeld*, p. 212.

12. *Annual Register*, 1763, pp. 258 f. Writing to Anthony Dermott, 17 August 1779, he said: "My principles make it my first, indeed almost my only earnest wish, to see every part of the empire, and every denomination of men in it, happy and contented, and united on one common bottom of equality and justice." *Corr.*, II, 296.

13. *Charlemont MSS*, I, 149. Froude makes the erroneous claim that Burke's most intimate friends were Catholics and that this was true even more at the end of his life than at the beginning. J. A. Froude, *The English in Ireland in the Eighteenth Century* (New York, 1874), III, 24.

An obscure and short-lived periodical, *The Irish Magazine and Monthly Asylum for Neglected Biography*, I (March 1808), 108, declares also quite erroneously that Burke actually died as a Roman Catholic.

14. *Parl. Hist.*, XXI (1780–81), 710.

15. *Speeches*, IV, 56.

16. Goldsmith in his famous *Retaliation* said of Burke that he was "too fond of the *right* to pursue the *expedient*."

17. John MacCunn, *The Political Philosophy of Burke* (New York, 1913), p. 98.

18. Writing to William Burgh, 9 February 1775, he said that he would give "a full civil protection, in which I include an immunity from all disturbance of their publick religious worship, & a power of teaching in schools, as well as Temples, to Jews Mahometans & even Pagans; especially if they are already possessed of any of these advantages by long & prescriptive usage; which is so sacred in this exercise of Rights, as in any other. Much more am I inclined to tolerate those, whom I look upon as our brethren; I mean all those who possess our common hope; extending to all the reformed and unreformed Churches, both at home & abroad; in none of whom I find any thing capitally amiss, but their mutual hatred of each other. . . . But toleration does not exclude national preference, either as to modes, or opinions; & all the lawful & honest means which may be used for the support of that preference." *Corr.*, II, 18 f.

19. *Works*, III, 351.

20. *Ibid.*, p. 429.

21. *Ibid.*, p. 350.

22. *Ibid.*, pp. 353 f. He applied this sentiment strictly in his own life and did not confine it to others. See Burke to Captain Mercer, 26 February 1790, *Corr.*, III, 141–150.

23. *Works*, III, 356.

24. *Ibid.*, pp. 308 f.

25. E.g., "Burke's Table-Talk," VII, 8.

26. He once flaunted public opinion by introducing two French priests into the House of Commons and by seeking permission of the Speaker to allow them to sit under the Gallery. The abuse he heaped upon him for his refusal was startling. *Lloyd's Evening Post*, 15–17 May 1793.

Burke's cosmopolitanism was well known to his contemporaries. One of his correspondents once remarked that "you, Sir, are from principle a great patron of foreigners." Mr. Litchfield to Burke, 20 December 1787, Burke MSS, Lamport Hall.

27. Lecky, *Irish Hist.*, III, 364.

28. For his great esteem, both for the pope's personal character and his office as well, which, if common knowledge, would have been disastrous for Burke, see H. V. F. Somerset, "Edmund Burke, England, and the Papacy," *Dublin Review*, CCII (January 1938), 138–148.

29. Sir John Coxe Hippisley, "Substance of Additional Observations intended to have been delivered in the House of Commons on May 13 or 14, 1805," pp. 94 f. quoted in Lecky, *Eng. Hist.*, VII, 461.

Burke and Hippisley enjoyed an extensive correspondence on this subject. A number of the letters and documents may be found in the Burke MSS, Lamport Hall.

30. *Corr.*, IV, 284.

31. Robertson, *Lectures on Burke*, p. 360.

32. *Dublin Review*, XXXV (March 1853), 86.

33. Laski, *Political Thought in England*, p. 231.

34. Burke to Fitzwilliam, 7 December 1796.

35. Burke to Laurence, 12 May 1797, *Burke-Laurence Corr.*, pp. 204–218.

36. *Works*, VI, 399.

37. Quoted in Therry, *A Letter to Canning*, p. 42.

38. Laski, *Political Thought in England*, p. 228.

Index